The Boswell Thesis

THE BOSWELL THESIS

Essays on *Christianity, Social Tolerance, and Homosexuality*

Mathew Kuefler

The University of Chicago Press · *Chicago & London*

The University of Chicago Press, Chicago 60637
The University of Chicago Press, Ltd., London
© 2006 by The University of Chicago
All rights reserved. Published 2006
Printed in the United States of America

15 14 13 12 11 10 09 08 07   5 4 3 2

ISBN (cloth): 0-226-45740-0
ISBN (paper): 0-226-45741-9

Library of Congress Cataloging-in-Publication Data

The Boswell thesis : essays on Christianity, social tolerance, and homosexuality / edited
   by Mathew Kuefler.
       p.   cm.
   Includes index.
   ISBN 0-226-45740-0 (cloth : alk. paper) — ISBN 0-226-45741-9 (pbk : alk. paper)
   1. Boswell, John. Christianity, social tolerance, and homosexuality.   2. Homosexuality—Europe—History—To 1500.   3. Homosexuality—Religious
aspects—Christianity—History.   I. Kuefler, Mathew.
   HQ76.3.E85B67   2006
   306.76'6'094—dc22

                                                                    2005009157

⊗ The paper used in this publication meets the minimum requirements of the American
National Standard for Information Sciences—Permanence of Paper for Printed Library
Materials, ANSI Z39.48-1992.

CONTENTS

v

ACKNOWLEDGMENTS

My thanks, along with my admiration, go to all those who contributed to this volume, despite busy and productive scholarly lives. Thanks also to the many who wanted very much to contribute to this volume but who, for various reasons, were unable to do so. Sincerest thanks also to Doug Mitchell, who acted as editor for this volume and for *Christianity, Social Tolerance, and Homosexuality* when it was first published, for his encouragement of this volume, to Richard Allen, who so skillfully edited the work of many hands, and to the others at the University of Chicago Press for their expert assistance. The University of Chicago Press has taken countless professional risks over the years in innovative if controversial publishing, and also deserves thanks. Thanks to Sarah Elkind for her help with this volume and for her friendship, and to Beth Holmberg, too, and as always, to Brian and Joe for their love and support. Thanks also to Susanne Hillmann, the research assistant who located all of the reviews of *CSTH*. I hope that *The Boswell Thesis* is a fitting tribute to a pioneering scholar of the caliber of John Boswell, to whom it is dedicated, and to all pioneers and risk takers.

Thanks to publishers for permission to reprint excerpts from or earlier versions of chapters published previously as follows. Chapter 3, by Carolyn Dinshaw, is based in part on her *Getting Medieval: Sexualities and Communities, Pre- and Postmodern*, copyright © 1999 by Duke University Press. All rights reserved. Chapter 7, by Dale B. Martin, is reprinted with permission from *Biblical Interpretation* 3 (1995): 332–55. Chapter 8, by E. Ann Matter, first appeared in the *Journal of Feminist Studies in Religion* 2 (1986): 81–93. Chapter 10, by Mathew Kuefler, is reprinted from *Gender and Difference in the Middle Ages*, edited by Sharon Farmer and Carol Braun Pasternack (Minneapolis: University of Minnesota Press, 2002).

The photograph of John Boswell reproduced below on page 60 is from *Newsweek*, 29 September 1980, © 1980 Newsweek, Inc. All rights reserved. Reprinted with permission.

CHAPTER 1

The Boswell Thesis

Mathew Kuefler

In 1980, John Boswell published *Christianity, Social Tolerance, and Homosexuality: Gay People in Western Europe from the Beginning of the Christian Era to the Fourteenth Century* (hereafter and throughout this collection *CSTH*). Twenty-five years later, in 2005, it is time to appraise the impact of the book, to consider the strength of some of its arguments, and to reflect on the different directions the study of sexuality in Antiquity and the Middle Ages has taken since its publication. This collection, with essays written by many of the leading scholars in their fields, is just such an attempt. Since 2005 is also the tenth anniversary of John Boswell's death, it seems fitting to reflect more broadly on his career and on the revolutionary ideas that he put forward about the relationship between Christianity and homoeroticism: an opportunity to revisit what I am calling the Boswell Thesis.

Nineteen eighty might not seem that far removed in time from current events. In that year, Ronald Reagan was elected president of the United States, and Saddam Hussein became president of Iraq. Also in that year, the U.S. and other countries boycotted the Olympic Games held in Moscow, in retaliation for the Soviet Union's invasion of Afghanistan. The news information television channel CNN first broadcast in 1980, and the first personal computers were sold.

Within the gay community, though, 1980 seems a long way off. It was arguably the highest early peak of the gay rights move-

1

ment. The Stonewall Riots, largely credited as the birth of the modern gay movement, had taken place eleven years earlier in 1969, and the movement had grown throughout the 1970s. There had been setbacks: Anita Bryant's successful campaign to repeal gay rights legislation, first in Florida and then across America (1977), and the assassination of the openly gay San Francisco supervisor Harvey Milk (1978). Still, the first March on Washington (1979) and the public protests at the release of the film *Cruising* (1980) were clear signs of emergent political strength. But the future was not to be so bright. Nineteen eighty also saw the first deaths from AIDS in American gay men, although identifying the virus that caused it would still be three years away and a cure or even a vaccine has still not yet been found. AIDS diverted the energies of the gay rights movement for the next decade and beyond into public health issues and into protecting the freedoms won rather than into seeking new rights, and it gave opponents of gay rights a renewed drive and a powerful rhetoric still used and claimed.

In 1980, however, the publication of *CSTH* created something of a furor in academic circles and in the popular and gay presses, and it continued to be talked about for many years; indeed, it still is. It is rare that a scholarly book reaches an audience much wider than the group of other specialists in the same field, rarer still that its ideas continue to be debated for decades by those specialists. But such a book was *CSTH*. It still ranked first, for example, on a 2004 list of the "top 100" best and most influential nonfiction books about gay men and lesbians, prepared by scholars and community leaders for *The Advocate*.[1]

It is important to begin by noting the main arguments in *CSTH*. There were four main points that form the narrative for the book: First, that Christianity had come into existence in an atmosphere of Greek and Roman tolerance for same-sex eroticism. Second, that nothing in the Christian scriptures or early tradition required a hostile assessment of homosexuality; rather, that such assessments represented a misreading of scripture. Third, that early medieval Christians showed no real animosity toward same-sex eroticism. Fourth, that it was only in the twelfth and thirteenth centuries that Christian writers formulated a significant hostility toward homosexuality, and then read that hostility back into their scriptures and early tradition.

In addition to these main points, Boswell made a number of ancillary points that were woven throughout *CSTH*. First, that homosexuality was a legitimate field of historical study; indeed, that it was as useful a modern gauge of social tolerance as studies of past attitudes toward women or religious minorities. Second, that sexual terminology had carefully to be taken into consideration, since assumptions about language might obscure as easily as they might clarify historical relationships. Third, that the terms "nature" and "natural" in particular had changed through time and varied considerably in intellectual coherence and usefulness, especially when animal behavior was put into service to understand what was natural for human sexual activity. Fourth, that tolerance of homoeroticism shared an uncomfortable relationship with urbanism: rural, kin-based societies tended to be less tolerant of sexual and other differences than urban ones, yet urbanism was no guarantee of tolerance. Taken together, we might consider these arguments as the Boswell Thesis.

To understand the significance of the Boswell Thesis, it is important to be reminded of the study of the history of homosexuality in Antiquity and the Middle Ages as it was in 1980 when *CSTH* was published. There was little available on the subject. Beginning in the late nineteenth century, a few works had appeared in English, but only a few, including John Addington Symonds's lengthy essay, entitled *A Problem of Greek Ethics* (1873), on pederasty in Antiquity, and Sir Richard Burton's comments on pederasty in traditional societies in section D of a so-called "Terminal Essay" and part of his monumental translation of *The Thousand and One Nights* (1885). Readers of German might also have been aware of various articles of a historical nature submitted to Magnus Hirschfeld's journals, the *Jahrbuch für sexuelle Zwischenstufen* ("Yearbook for Sexually Intermediate Types," published between 1901 and 1933) and the *Zeitschrift für Sexualwissenschaft* ("Journal of Sexology," published between 1908 and 1932). All of these works were difficult to obtain, however, and often circulated only privately.

The first detailed study to appear on the subject of homoeroticism and Christianity was undoubtedly Derrick Sherwin Bailey's *Homosexuality and the Western Christian Tradition,* published in 1955. As Bailey recounts in his introduction, he was an Anglican clergyman who studied the biblical and historical roots to contemporary Christian attitudes toward homosexuality for a 1954 church report, notably entitled *The Problem of Homosexuality.*[2] Boswell relied heavily on Bailey's book, so it is worth considering some of Bailey's influence on Boswell's ideas. Like Boswell, Bailey argued that the Bible had been wrongly interpreted to condemn modern homosexuality. In contrast to Boswell, however, Bailey also argued that such a biblical (mis)interpretation had been set in place already during the earliest Christian centuries, and that from its beginnings Christian writers had uniformly condemned homoeroticism. Bailey also dismissed any discussion of ancient Greek or Roman attitudes toward homoeroticism as unimportant in a Christian historical perspective. Overall, Bailey's ideas seem to have provided Boswell with a springboard for his own arguments.[3]

In the wake of increased awareness of and sympathy for the gay rights movement in the 1970s, there had also been published by 1980 a few general historical works on the history of homosexuality. A true pioneer in this regard was Vern Bullough, who published *Sexual Variance in Society and History* in 1974, and the much briefer *Homosexuality: A History* (additionally subtitled *From Ancient Greece to Gay Liberation*) in 1979.[4] (Only the former book is mentioned in the bibliography to *CSTH*, not surprisingly, given the usual lapse in time between completion of a book manuscript and its appearance in print.) Like Bailey, Bullough argued in both books that Christianity had always been hostile to homosexuality: in *Sexual Variance* he termed it a generally "sex-negative religion." But Bullough felt it important to compare ancient attitudes toward same-sex eroticism, which he considered mostly positive. Again, while Boswell accepted some of this argument in *CSTH*, and doubtless found Bullough's research into the Greek and Roman past useful to his own work, he disputed Bullough's assessment of the Christian contribution to the history of homosexuality.

The reappraisal of longstanding attitudes toward homosexuality was also apparent in other books published on Christianity and homosexuality in the 1970s. Among the earliest of these was John McNeill's *The Church and the Homosexual* (1976). McNeill, a Catholic priest, tried to demonstrate that official Catholic teaching about homosexuality was unfounded and based on faulty interpretations of certain biblical passages, through detailed analyses of the passages considered as most relevant. McNeill's debt to Bailey is obvious, but his influence on Boswell was also considerable.[5]

By a curious coincidence, two other works of great importance in this early history of homosexuality were published shortly before *CSTH*. One was Kenneth Dover's *Greek Homosexuality,* a book that marked the beginning of the serious study of the topic of homosexuality in Greek antiquity, published in 1978. Boswell knew of Dover's research, as Dover did of Boswell's, and the two corresponded about some of their findings.[6] Like *CSTH*, Dover's book also attempted to shift the weight of the scholarly consensus, in his case, about the near universal condemnation of same-sex eroticism in history. On the first page of his study he wrote:

> Greek culture differed from ours in its readiness to recognize the alternation of homosexual and heterosexual preferences in the same individual, its implicit denial that such alternation or coexistence created peculiar problems for the individual or for society, its sympathetic response to the open expression of homosexual desire in words and behavior, and its taste for the uninhibited treatment of homosexual subjects in literature and the visual arts.[7]

Dover knew that his argument would be controversial but seemed willing to defend it, stating quite bluntly in his preface: "I know of no topic in classical studies on which a scholar's normal ability to perceive differences and draw inferences is so easily impaired," a remark that echoes Boswell's thoughts on the same subject.[8]

The second important book, published a year before *CSTH,* was Michael Goodich's *The Unmentionable Vice* (1979). I am unaware of any personal connection between Goodich and Boswell that might be considered as influencing each other's research, but Goodich had previously published on the subject of medieval homosexuality, with two articles published in the *Journal of Homosexuality* in 1976, both of which Boswell must have known, although he cited only one in his bibliography.[9] Goodich held a more negative assessment of the role of Christian teachings in the hostility toward homosexuality:

> The precedents laid down by Augustine and the Church Fathers classified same-sex relations as an illicit form of lust *(luxuria),* contrary to nature, likely to consign its perpetrators to the fires of Hell. All forms of homoerotic relations were indiscriminately labeled as sodomy *(sodomia)* and were regarded in canon law and theology as the most heinous of sins, comparable to homicide.[10]

Still, Goodich also seemed to predict Boswell's soon-to-be-made-public findings:

> Until the eleventh century, occasional voices were heard condemning same-sex relations, but it was not until the Gregorian reform movement that a determined effort was made to impose the canons of Catholic sexual morality on an often indifferent public. The polemical lines were laid down in the eleventh and twelfth centuries. . . . Thereafter, discussions of the sin against nature were monotonously similar. . . . But persecution was still episodic and a willingness to prosecute homosexuals by burning as prescribed by law did not become evident until the fourteenth century.[11]

Independently, it seems, both Dover and Goodich were reaching conclusions on their own research that coincided in broad terms with Boswell's own ideas.

The public response to *CSTH* was immediate and thunderous. One of the earliest reviews of the book appeared in *The New York Times* on 10 August 1980. The reviewer, Paul Robinson (a historian at Stanford University and the author of several works on the history of sexuality, including the history of homosexuality), praised the book in the most glowing of terms:

> John Boswell restores one's faith in scholarship as the union of erudition, analysis and moral vision. I would not hesitate to call his book revolutionary, for it tells of things heretofore unimagined and sets a standard of excellence that one would have thought impossible in the treatment of an issue so large, uncharted and vexed.[12]

The book came quickly to the attention of the larger popular press. Beginning in the late summer of 1980, reviews appeared in the British journal *History Today* as well as the American journals *Newsweek, The New York Review of Books, The Weekly News,* and *The New Republic.* At the same time, *CSTH* was reviewed in several gay periodicals across the U.S., including *Gay Community News* (published out of Boston), *The Advocate* (Los Angeles), *Gay Books Bulletin* and *Christopher Street* (New York), and *Alternate* (San Francisco). And it was in the fall of 1980 that the first review of *CSTH* appeared in a religious journal, *Cross Currents: The Journal of the Association for Religion and Intellectual Life.* In the years that followed, *CSTH* would be reviewed by over fifty journals in a variety of disciplines, mostly history and theology, but also sociology and pastoral counseling, mostly in the U.S. but also in Britain, France, and Italy.

It is difficult to generalize about the reviews of *CSTH.* The most favorable reviews came from the popular press, which was clearly intrigued by and interested in publicizing the most controversial elements of the book. In *The New Republic,* Martin Bauml Duberman (a gay historian who would later found the Center for Lesbian and Gay Studies in New York City) noted: "Boswell's study is indubitably one of the most profound, explosive works of scholarship to appear within recent memory. His book will inaugurate controversies bound to rage for years."[13] Psychologist Tom Smith declared in the *Bloomsbury Review* that the book was "one of those unusual events, a truly important, ground-breaking work."[14] But even here, the praise was not unanimous. In *Commonweal,* Louis Crompton (also a historian of homosexuality) concluded that

> Boswell's book will be an inexhaustible source and an inescapable point of departure for future scholars and apologists. It is a pity that it is, at the same time, vitiated by a determination to construe all its voluminous evidence in the light of an untenable leading idea.[15]

The idea Crompton found so untenable was, indeed, a central tenet of the Boswell Thesis: that neither the Bible nor the early Christian tradition was as hostile to homoeroticism as they were generally thought to be. This accusation would return in many other reviews and be voiced by conservative and radical voices alike.

Professional historical and religious journals provided even more mixed results. Some praised the book; others panned it. Some provided legitimate grounds for criticism; others seemed openly hostile to any reappraisal of Christian attitudes toward homosexuality. Jeremy duQ. Adams (a medieval historian at Southern Methodist University) applauded the book in *Speculum,* the journal of the Medieval Academy of America, as "daring in range and purpose and provocative in method."[16] In *The American Historical Review,* the journal of the American Historical Association, John C. Moore (a medieval historian at Hofstra University) was less enthusiastic: "Only partially compelling are [some of] his arguments" and "Boswell is not entirely successful at keeping his own values from intruding," although he concludes with "let me recommend this book as a splendid piece of scholarship."[17] James Brundage (a medieval historian at the University of Kansas) reviewed the book in *The Catholic Historical Review,* where he wrote that he was unconvinced by Boswell's argument that urbanization led to greater intolerance in the Later Middle Ages, although he admitted that Boswell himself had noted the weaknesses of the hypothesis.[18] Much lengthier and more negative reviews appeared, for example, in *Communio: International Catholic Review* by Glenn Olsen (a medieval historian at the University of Utah), who criticized Boswell's interpretation of Aristotelian and Thomistic natural law philosophy, and in the *Anglican Theological Review* by Robert J. Wright (a professor of Christian history at Oxford), who considered Boswell ill informed about biblical interpretation, including biblical citations in early Christian writers.[19] Yet, *CSTH* was praised again by Lawrence Cunningham (now a distinguished professor of Christian theology at the University of Notre Dame) in *The New Catholic World* and by Patrick Henry (a professor of the Christian religion at Swarthmore College) in *Church History.*[20] It is nearly impossible, therefore, to arrive at any scholarly consensus in the reaction to the Boswell Thesis.

The collective response of gay journals to *CSTH* was equally mixed. Steven Saylor spoke passionately about the book in *The Alternate,* a San Francisco based publication, extending Boswell's own comments on the lack of gay history:

> Gay people, unlike racial or religious minorities, emerge individually and in isolation. If raised in an environment hostile to gays, they may grow up without knowing that others of their kind even exist, and imagine themselves to be freaks. We have no racial or family heritage to guide and reassure us, no favorite uncle to tell us as children what intolerance was like in his day

and how he got by, no oral history of pride and survival passed from the old to the young. We lack the sense "of belonging to the long and hallowed traditions of those who went before." We have no roots. John Boswell has taken a long step toward rectifying that lack. Approaching his subject with the sober objectivity of the historian, he has, intentionally or not, taken the place of that wise uncle. "This is what it was really like," his book says; "these are your deepest roots." [21]

Nonetheless, some of Boswell's harshest critics were his reviewers in the gay press. Most unforgiving were the scholars involved in the Gay Academic Union, a group formed in New York City in 1973. They published the *Gay Books Bulletin,* where a review of *CSTH* by Wayne Dynes (the editor of the journal and a professor of art history at Hunter College) appeared in the fall of 1980, and was thus one of the earliest reviews of the book. Dynes wrote with equal passion:

> Long before the publication of his book, Boswell was saluted by various adherents of the gay Christian denominations as a knight in shining armor who would save them from both the secularist opponents of religion and the fag-baiting fundamentalists by showing through history that "it's OK to be a gay Christian." Whether it is or not remains, in my libertarian, non-Christian view, essentially a matter of personal choice. But Christianity is definitely guilty of the stigmatization and persecution of same-sex relations in our civilization. It has served as a redoubt for bigotry of all sorts, and until those who call themselves Christians are ready humbly to acknowledge this, they are coming to us with dirty hands. [22]

By 1981, Dynes, together with nonacademics Warren Johansson and John Lauritson, had privately published a collection of their essays entitled *Homosexuality, Intolerance, and Christianity: A Critical Examination of John Boswell's Work.* The essays, with such titles as "The Historical Guilt of the Christian Church" and "Christianity and the Politics of Sex," minced no words as they sought to undermine the Boswell Thesis. [23]

Other gay writers had different objections. Walter Kendrick (a professor of modern English literature at Fordham University, writing in *The Village Voice* under the pseudonym Keith Arrowsmith) objected to Boswell's use of the word "gay" to refer to premodern individuals:

> The very concept of "selfhood," of a private individuality unique to each human being . . . simply did not exist until the very end of the period with which

Boswell is concerned. Without self-consciousness, no self-definition; without self-definition, no "gayness"—no "straightness" either for that matter.[24]

Kendrick referred the reader to the work of Michel Foucault and others on these broader questions of medieval identity; but his claim bears the imprint of Colin Morris, who in *The Discovery of the Individual, 1050–1200,* published in 1972, argued the same at length.[25]

Out of this type of response to *CSTH* would come one of the central and most acerbic debates among scholars in the history of homosexuality. It is known as the Essentialist–Social Constructionist debate (although no scholar in the humanities ever described him- or herself as an Essentialist, so the label was something of a straw horse). The debate centered on the existence of a homosexual identity before the end of the nineteenth century, and thus called into question Boswell's determination that one could speak of "gay people" in Antiquity and the Middle Ages, as he put it: "persons who are conscious of erotic inclination toward their own gender as a distinguishing characteristic" (*CSTH,* 44). Chapter 2 of *CSTH* included several lengthy comments that qualified his usage precisely on this point, for example (and the following is taken from a much longer discussion of these questions):

> In the ancient world so few people cared to categorize their contemporaries on the basis of the gender to which they were erotically attracted that no dichotomy to express this distinction was in common use . . . [and] no one thought it useful or important to distinguish on the basis of genders alone, and the categories "homosexual" and "heterosexual" simply did not intrude on the consciousness of most Greeks or . . . Romans. (*CSTH,* 59)

Despite such comments, Boswell was harshly criticized by some for not taking sufficient account of the differences between ancient and medieval forms of sexuality, on the one hand, and modern analogies, on the other. In other words, in applying a modern terminology and the concepts that underlie such terminology to premodern individuals and societies, he was considered as ignoring or even obscuring the differences between these periods, and thus, as being an Essentialist.

The controversy stemmed especially from two scholarly works published shortly before *CSTH.* The first was by a distinguished professor at the Collège de France, Michel Foucault, and entitled *La volunté du savoir* ("The Will to Knowledge"), the first volume in his *Histoire de la Sexualité* ("History of Sexuality"); it was published in French in 1976 and first translated into English in 1978, after which it reached a much broader American audience. Foucault admired *CSTH*, and his assessment of it was excerpted in the paperback edition of the book published in 1981: "A truly groundbreaking work. Boswell reveals unexplored phenomena with an unfailing erudition."[26] But Foucault's own comments in print were seen as contradicting Boswell's thesis overall: "as defined by the . . . [medieval] canonical codes, sodomy was a category of forbidden acts," and "their perpetrator was nothing more than the juridical subject of them," while, in contrast, only "the nineteenth-century homosexual became a personage."[27] Foucault pointed to the publication of one account as seminal:

> We must not forget that the psychological, psychiatric, medical category of homosexuality was constituted from the moment it was characterized—Westphal's famous article of 1870 on "contrary sexual sensations" can stand as its date of birth—less by a type of sexual relations than by a certain quality of sexual sensibility. . . . The sodomite had been a temporary aberration; the homosexual was now a species.[28]

Foucault had made more than a few errors: the article had in fact been published in German in 1869, and only translated into French in 1870. Moreover, while Carl Friedrich Otto Westphal had indeed used the term "contrary sexual feeling" *(conträre Sexualempfindung)* to describe same-sex desire, others had already coined new terms to describe similar attractions: Karl Heinrich Ulrichs had used the term "uranian" *(Urning)* as early as 1864, and Károly Mária Kertbeny (a.k.a. Karl Maria Benkert) had already used the word "homosexuality" *(Homosexualität)* in 1868. Nonetheless, Foucault's position was clear: the notion of sexual orientation was a modern invention, dating from the late nineteenth century.

More pointed on this subject was an 1979 article by Robert Padgug (an unaffiliated classicist), published in the *Radical History Review,* who argued the same point on economic rather than psychological grounds, suggesting that only in modern capitalist societies was sexual activity separated sufficiently from other aspects of human life—labor, marriage and family regulations, religion, and so on—for sexual identities to come into existence or even for the notion of "sexuality" to make sense as a category of analysis.[29] Padgug reviewed *CSTH* for the Canadian gay journal, *The Body Politic,* in a generally positive light, but mentioned this criticism:

> Boswell constantly assumes that human sexuality is, at root, essentially fixed and that the modern tendency to divide humanity into homosexuals and het-

erosexuals is valid for earlier periods as well. . . . Thus, for him, homosexual acts are performed by "gay people" and one can legitimately speak of "gay subcultures" differing from our own only in detail. But many of us would see as anachronistic the very concept of "homosexuals" and "heterosexuals" . . . and its application to historical study is a real stumbling block to understanding homosexual behavior before, at the earliest, the seventeenth century. Boswell's implicit assumption certainly may turn out to be the correct approach, but needs to be demonstrated rather than left unexplored.[30]

Scholars after Padgug would be less generous in giving Boswell the benefit of the doubt.

Among Boswell's most unsympathetic critics was David Halperin (earlier a professor of literature at the Massachusetts Institute of Technology and now a professor of English at the University of Michigan). In a series of articles published and revised throughout the 1980s, Halperin repeatedly criticized Boswell on this point. In an article pointedly entitled "Sex Before Sexuality: Pederasty, Politics, and Power in Classical Athens," published in 1989, for example, he wrote that it was no coincidence that there is no ancient Greek or Latin term equivalent to "homosexual," just as we have no word "pectoriphage" to identify someone who prefers or eats only chicken: it is simply a meaningless distinction, because the ancients did not think in terms of sexuality, just as we do not think in terms of "dieticity." (He later admitted in print that we do have diet-related concepts, such as "anorectic," to categorize individuals based on their eating patterns, but maintained his point without the exact parallel.)[31] In *One Hundred Years of Homosexuality*, Halperin had this to say about Boswell:

> The dangers of taking our sexual categories for granted are well illustrated by the work of Boswell who, arguing correctly that many societies have contained individuals capable of deriving sexual pleasure from contact with members of their own sex, claims on that basis that homosexuality is universal. To be sure, even Boswell does not regard homosexuality as a *thing*, an item in a cultural inventory whose presence or absence can be simply and positively checked off; he contents himself with the more modest claim that homosexuality takes different forms in different contexts, changing in character according to its cultural environment. But redescribing same-sex sexual contact as homosexuality is not as innocent as it may appear: indeed, it effectively obliterates the many different ways of organizing sexual contacts and articulating sexual roles that are indigenous to human societies.[32]

Halperin's point could not have been that it was impossible to comprehend or properly analyze the history of premodern homoeroticism, since he published several essays on the subject. His objection, and the objections of most other detractors, seems largely to have been Boswell's insistence on drawing attention to the similarities rather than the differences between premodern and modern sexual identities, and in using modern analogies of sexual behavior to elucidate premodern realities, notwithstanding the modern analogy of dieticity that Halperin himself used.

Boswell seems to have been much more concerned about the other attack made against him: that he was too sympathetic to Christianity and its historical tolerance of homosexuality. He defended himself in an address he gave to the Gay Christian Movement in London in 1982, published privately as *Rediscovering Gay History: Archetypes of Gay Love in Christian History*. In his address, he noted the attacks in the gay press, but responded:

> Gay people in the United States, finding themselves beset on all sides with hostility and injustice, often find it easier to believe that *somebody* causes this than to face the fact that the causes are large and complex and probably cannot be easily identified or removed. A great many gay people in the United States want to believe that Christianity is the enemy and that if they could get rid of Christianity everything would be much better.[33]

He called it scapegoating in reverse. (In that same address, Boswell also mentioned for the first time the ceremony of same-sex union on which he would publish twelve years later.)

On the issue of anachronism, Boswell at first remained silent. Perhaps he felt that he had sufficiently defended his point of view in *CSTH* itself. There, in fact, he notes that "one must be extremely cautious about projecting onto historical data ideas about gay people inferred from modern samples," and gives as his example the conflation of effeminacy and male homosexuality, which varies from culture to culture and from era to era (*CSTH*, 24). He continues by suggesting that "one must avoid transposing across temporal boundaries ideas about gay relationships which are highly culture-related" (25), here giving the example of changing definitions of marriage. In a lengthy footnote, he rejects the significance of a lack of sexual terminology in premodern societies: "English appears to have no real equivalent for the French term 'fiancé,' but this is certainly no indication that the idea of heterosexual engagement was unknown . . . prior to its adoption." He also rejects the idea that age-differentiated or gender-differentiated patterns of same-sex eroticism (that is, pederastic or cross-dressing customs) are not "real homosexuality," saying that "one must immediately wonder whether heterosexual relations between men and girls are any less heterosexual for the difference in age," and adds, seeming to allude to his usage as a modern heuristic device, that "the whole point of the homosexual/heterosexual distinction, it would seem, is to subsume all varieties of erotic interest into categories of gender relations" (28). He concludes this discussion with a wish "that the difficulties of avoiding anachronistic projections . . . will be outweighed by the advantages" (30–31).

Eventually, however, the reaction among gay scholars roused Boswell to defend his position and take his own stand on the Essentialist–Social Constructionist debate in an article published in *Salmagundi* in 1983, entitled "Revolutions, Universals, and Sexual Categories."[34] In it, he suggested that the controversy was simply the latest form of a debate, long known to philosophers, between "nominalists" and "realists," those who believe that categories are arbitrary divisions and those who believe that they represent something real. He seemed to place himself firmly on one side of the argument, saying: "if the categories 'homosexual/heterosexual' and 'gay/straight' are the inventions of particular societies rather than real aspects of the human psyche, there is no gay history."[35] He also seemed to want to move beyond the debate, preferring to think that there are three main ways in which sexual categories have been viewed by individuals and societies: Type A, in which all human beings are seen as "capable of erotic and sexual interaction with either gender," Type B, in which there are believed to be "two or more sexual categories, to which all human beings belong," often along lines of sexual object choice but also into categories of preferred sexual roles, and Type C, in which "one type of sexual response [is considered] normal (or 'natural' or 'moral' or all three) and all other variants abnormal ('unnatural,' 'immoral')."[36] He went on to argue that in some societies, for example, in ancient Greece, there is evidence for individuals holding each of these three perspectives.

Pro or *contra* Boswell, the history of homosexuality continued, indeed, has grown exponentially in the last twenty-five years. For the most part, though, the debates that began with *CSTH* as part of the Boswell Thesis continued as the dominant lines of inquiry. That is not to say that scholars did not uncover new findings or garner new insights. It is rather to say that in the ongoing work of scholars, Boswell's presence continued to be felt. (For the sake of brevity in the section that follows, and since the literature on related subjects has become so vast, I have had to confine myself mostly to book-length studies, together with a few especially influential articles, and even among those to works devoted predominantly to homoeroticism, to those specializing in the same eras of Antiquity and the Middle Ages, and likewise among those to works set within a historical rather than literary context: that is, seeking to understand the past rather than a text or texts or an author or authors.)

Classicists, for example, have continued to debate the distinctions between ancient Greek and Roman forms of homoeroticism, on the one hand, and modern forms, on the other. Most have fallen on the side of the fence that argues for difference. In the same year that Boswell published *CSTH*, and so not a response to his work, French scholar Felix Buffière published *Eros adolescent: La pédérastie dans la Grèce antique* ("Adolescent Eros: Pederasty in Ancient Greece") describing the sexual initiation of adolescent boys as a sexual system wholly different from modern forms of homosexuality, and saying that while the ancient Athenians praised the former, they severely condemned the latter.[37] A decade later, the collection of essays edited by David Halperin and others and entitled *Before Sexuality* (1990) made the same point succinctly in its title, and hammered home the "otherness" of ancient sexuality in a broad range of essays using philosophical, medical, visual, and literary sources. The collection included an essay by John J. Winkler, entitled "Laying Down the Law: The Oversight of Men's Sexual Behavior in Classical Athens," that was repeated in a collection of his essays published in the same year (and the year of his death), entitled *The Constraints of Desire* (1990), and in which, like Buffière, he argued for Athenian disapproval of sexual activity between men apart from those sanctioned by the institution of pederasty, including sexual activity between two adult males.[38] Eva Cantarella's *Secondo natura: La bisessualità nel mondo antico* (1988, translated into English as *Bisexuality in the Ancient World*, 1992), was more or less alone in the field, describing the relations as "homosexuality" throughout her book, despite its title, although she noted briefly that the ancient Greeks and Romans "experienced relationships between men very differently from the way in which they are experienced (with exceptions, obviously) by people who opt for a homosexual existence today."[39]

Even if most classicists disputed the Boswell Thesis on the similarities between same-sex eroticism in ancient Athens and modern America, most shared the idea also contained in *CSTH* that it was part and parcel of ancient Athenian society and socially sanctioned. In contrast, Michel Foucault, who published the second volume of his history of sexuality, entitled *L'usage du plaisir* in 1984 (and translated into English as *The Use of Pleasure* in 1985), disagreed, arguing for extreme discomfort among ancient Athenian writers about the meaning and virtue of pederasty, in large part because it brought two males—and two males of roughly equivalent status at that, regardless of age differences—together in sexual behavior that generally carried with it strongly gendered implications of dominance and subordination. In studies comparing pederasty to other forms of sexual activity from the Greek historical record, both David Cohen in *Law, Sexuality, and Society* (1991) and Bruce Thornton in *Eros* (1997) laid out an even stronger position on cultural discomfort with pederasty in ancient Athens.[40]

Classicists interested in the history of homoeroticism have also sought to move beyond the Boswell Thesis, in part by trying to understand homoerotic relations as part of a larger whole. Here Paul Ludwig's recent *Eros and Polis* (2002) is notable for integrating the history of ancient Athenian sexuality into its political context as "the birthplace of democracy." Others have extended their studies into archaic Greece, to see the origins of its sexual customs. Included in this project have been Claude Calame, with *L'Eros dans la Grèce antique* in 1996 (translated into English as *The Poetics of Eros in Ancient Greece* in 1999), William Percy, with *Pederasty and Pedagogy in Archaic Greece* (1996), and Daniel Garrison, with *Sexual Culture in Ancient Greece* (2000).[41]

While most of the work of classicists interested in ancient homoeroticism has been focused on ancient Athens, a smaller number have illuminated the particulars of Roman sexuality. Here, two articles inspired by the Boswell Thesis have touched off a debate still ongoing. The first was a brief but significant 1982 article, entitled "Roman Attitudes to Greek Love," and written by Ramsey MacMullen, a colleague of Boswell at Yale.[42] It can only be considered a rebuttal to *CSTH*, especially if one looks at the footnotes to the article. In the article, MacMullen argued that there was no native Roman institution of pederasty, that it was practiced by only a small elite of Hellenophiles, and that it was condemned by most other Romans. Against this opinion, Amy Richlin's *The Garden of Priapus* (published in 1983, so not a direct response to MacMullen's article; Richlin is also a contributor to this collection), argued that Roman sexual traditions included male homoeroticism on a widespread and popular level. Craig Williams published in 1999 a book, entitled *Roman Homosexuality,* that seems finally to have shelved MacMullen on this point, demonstrating at length both the native Roman traditions of homoeroticism and, as in classical Athens, its coherence within larger notions of Roman masculinity.[43]

The second and much lengthier article on the Roman era stemming from the Boswell Thesis was Amy Richlin's "Not Before Homosexuality: The Materiality of the *Cinaedus* and the Roman Law Against Love Between Men," published in 1993. Its title communicates its perspective: refuting the Social Constructionist viewpoint that there were no equivalents to modern homosexuality in Antiquity.[44] In it, Richlin argued that the Romans did have notions of sexual categories, and that one of them—the *cinaedus,* a derogatory Latin term with a Greek equivalent *(kinaidos)* meaning an adult male who enjoys being penetrated sexually—constituted a real sexual minority not un-like modern homosexuals, and that individuals identified as such were subject to popular hostility, which she called "homophobia." Others, following after Richlin, have continued to examine the ways in which prejudice against some forms of sexuality formed part of ancient Roman society, including Catharine Edwards in *The Politics of Immorality in Ancient Rome* (1993, whose work thus appeared independently of Richlin's article). The collection published in 1997 as *Roman Sexualities,* edited by Judith Hallett and Marilyn Skinner, demon-strates how these and other ideas about homoeroticism in ancient Rome are still debated.[45]

Most of the work done by classicists on sexuality in ancient Greece and Rome has centered on men's experience, as Boswell had in *CSTH.* Indeed, while Boswell included some discussion of female homoeroticism in *CSTH,* he tended to assume that male patterns of sexuality could be used to understand female ones. He was taken to task on this point by Jane Vanderbosch, his reviewer in *Signs:*

> As Gerda Lerner has pointed out, "Women's history challenges the androcen-tric assumptions of traditional history and assumes that the role of women in historical events—or the absence of women from them—must be properly illuminated and discussed in each and every case." . . . Boswell not only failed to consider sources that might have shed light on the lesbian experience, he also failed to prove that what he did do . . . is not seriously flawed by what he failed to do.[46]

In the same year that *CSTH* was published, Adrienne Rich published her seminal article, "Compulsory Heterosexuality and Lesbian Existence," that expressed the view that since women were seldom in control of their sex-ual lives in Antiquity or the Middle Ages, female homoeroticism had to be understood on its own terms, and that researching only sexual relationships between women might be missing opportunities to think about other sorts of women's emotional connections to other women. (Boswell had speculated about the fuzzy lines between male friendship and sexual relationships in *CSTH,* but he did not pursue that insight into women's sexuality.)[47]

Since 1980, however, classicists have been exploring connections such as these in approaching the history of lesbianism. Judith Hallett's "Female Homoeroticism and the Denial of Roman Reality in Latin Literature" in 1989 was an important milestone in the study of Roman female homoeroticism.[48] Studies of Sappho—among these, Page DuBois's *Sappho is Burning* (1995) and Jane McIntosh Snyder's *Lesbian Desire in the Lyrics of Sappho* (1997) are important—have also tried to shed light on a tantalizingly shadowy area of Greek female homoeroticism. Bernadette Brooten's *Love Between Women,* published in 1996, examines a range of types of evidence that provide glimpses into ancient women's sexuality, as does the recent collection of essays published by Nancy Sorkin Rabinowitz and Lisa Auanger, *Among Women* (2002).[49]

Brooten's *Love Between Women* is an exploration not only of ancient Greek and Roman notions of woman-to-woman sexuality but also of early Christian ones. Like Boswell, she found it useful to examine early Christian attitudes toward homoeroticism after placing them within their ancient social contexts. Brooten's work comes as one of the latest in a long series of scholarly discussions of the place of and attitudes toward homoeroticism in the Bible and in the early Christian centuries. And while the Boswell Thesis argued that most hostility found in the Jewish and Christian scriptures had been read into them, scholars after him have deliberated this point over and over again without achieving anything close to a consensus. The books and articles devoted to this question are too numerous even to summarize here (interested readers can find all but the most recent included in a lengthy annotated bibliography in Brooten's book).

For this reason, I will content myself with a brief discussion of the work done on early Christian interpretations of biblical texts, rather than on biblical studies *per se.* Shortly after the release of *CSTH,* and in response to it, William Petersen published "On the Study of Homosexuality in Patristic Sources," one of the few examinations of this topic.[50] Many of the classicists working in the field have final chapters that deal with early Christianity and Roman or Greek culture, but virtually none of the specialists in the history of sexuality and early Christianity have written on the subject of same-sex eroticism. Brooten is an exception. I should also mention my own book, *The Manly Eunuch* (2001), which includes some information on the subject.[51] Clearly, this is an area with much potential for future scholars.

The Boswell Thesis also argued that the Early Middle Ages was not as hostile to homoeroticism as the Later Middle Ages or since. Vern Bullough's "The Sin Against Nature and Homosexuality" in 1982 made the case for a continued hostility to homoeroticism throughout the Middle Ages, against the Boswell Thesis and in keeping with his own earlier studies of the subject.[52] R. I. Moore, who studied the medieval persecution of heretics and Jews, found it useful to compare the persecution of homosexuals in his 1987 book, *The Formation of a Persecuting Society: Power and Deviance in Western Europe, 950–1250,* and relied heavily on Boswell's findings.[53] My own work in this area, an article published in 2003, entitled "Male Friendship and the Suspicion of Sodomy in Twelfth-Century France" and reprinted in this collection, agrees with *CSTH* that a major shift occurred between the Early and the Later Middle Ages, but offers an alternative set of explanations for it.[54]

The most thorough analysis of the topic of homoeroticism in the Middle Ages since *CSTH* to date has been Mark Jordan's *The Invention of Sodomy in Christian Theology* (1997; Jordan is also one of the contributors to this volume). In some ways, it roughly coincides with Boswell's argument that later medieval hostility was of a different sort than early medieval: in Jordan's case, it was in the eleventh century that "sodomy" was invented "as the name and the category."[55] Nonetheless, Jordan distances himself from Boswell's familiarizing approach in *CSTH,* seeing it as more valuable intellectually not to emphasize similarities, given the difficulties in making our modern understandings of terms or categories correspond to medieval realities. Jordan is also a theologian—albeit a historically minded one—and he is not all that interested in situating the works of medieval thinkers within a social context. Most of the studies on medieval homosexuality have been of the same sort, usually done by literary scholars, showing ample homoerotic impulses in texts but leaving aside the question of social and historical application.[56] Carolyn Dinshaw's *Getting Medieval* (1999; Dinshaw is also a contributor to this volume) is an exception, integrating literary and historical approaches, but her period—the fifteenth century—falls outside of that studied by Boswell in *CSTH.*[57]

Female homoeroticism in the Middle Ages has been less well studied, in part because of the paucity of sources, but there are important articles that have appeared in print, most following Rich's suggestion that sexual relationships between women need to be studied within a broader context of social relationships, and most replying in some way to the Boswell Thesis. In the same year that *CSTH* appeared, an article by Louis Crompton, "The Myth of Lesbian Impunity: Capital Laws from 1270–1791," suggested that hostility toward female homoeroticism in the Later Middle Ages was as strong as that toward male.[58] One of the earliest articles to appear in response to *CSTH* was Ann Matter's "My Sister, My Spouse: Woman-Identified Women in Medieval Christianity" in 1986 (and reprinted in this collection).[59] In that same year, Judith Brown's *Immodest Acts: The Life of a Lesbian Nun in Renaissance Italy* contained a useful preliminary chapter on medieval attitudes toward lesbianism.[60] Jacqueline Murray (another contributor to this collection) published in 1996 "Twice Marginal and Twice Invisible: Lesbians in the Middle Ages," which drew upon and extended Boswell's insights in discussing the sources for lesbian history.[61] More recently, Judith Bennett's " 'Lesbian-Like' and the Social History of Lesbianisms" (2001) tries to speculate about the lives of women who might today be considered lesbian, but for whom we have so little evidence, and Ulrike Wiethaus's "Female Homoerotic Discourse and Religion in Medieval Germanic Culture" (2003) explores the possibility of sublimated lesbian desire in women's spirituality.[62]

Curiously, while scholarship on male homoeroticism in Antiquity and the Middle Ages often remained absorbed in the Essentialist–Social Constructionist controversy, and defined more and more narrowly what was possible to study under the rubric of homosexuality, scholarship on female homoeroticism, even if it did not ignore the issues at stake in the debate, opened the field up to broader questions of social interaction and desire, and subsumed them all within the framework of a "lesbian continuum" (a phrase from Rich's article) even without evidence of sexual (meaning genital) activity. It is only recently that the scholarship on male homoeroticism has been willing to explore these broader questions.

The recent turn in scholarship on male homoeroticism has been due in large part to the impact of queer theory on the study of history. If the Essentialist–Social Constructionist debate narrowed the field of study by insisting that only the close historical equivalents to modern homosexuality could be studied as such, queer theorists threw open the doors to research into any sort of transgressions from the sexual norms of the past, including homoeroticism. Eve Kosofsky Sedgwick led the way with her *The Epistemology of the Closet* (1990), which, if it was an exploration of what she called "homosocial" relations in modern English literature, asked a number of broader questions about the assumptions of the Essentialist–Social Constructionist debate: whether the search for the "birth of homosexuality" as we know it presumed that we did in fact know what "it" was, even though we have no firm answers to the origins or nature of sexual orientation, and whether assumptions about the "differentness" of premodern sexualities (what she called "allo-identification") can be as misguiding as assumptions about the "sameness" of them ("auto-identification").[63]

Queer theory has reopened most of the cans of worms sealed and set aside during the last twenty-five years of scholarship, and while it is still too early to tell its full impact on scholarship, it will undoubtedly be substantial. Already new scholarly approaches to homoeroticism in Antiquity and the Middle Ages are appearing in print, with titles that flaunt the queerness of their perspectives (an "ironic" sense of history is one of the attributes of queer theory): Dinshaw's *Getting Medieval,* mentioned above, Simon Goldhill's *Foucault's Virginity: Ancient Erotic Fiction and the History of Sexuality* (1995), Stephen Moore's *God's Beauty Parlor: And Other Queer Spaces in and Around the Bible* (2001), or Virginia Burrus's *The Sex Lives of Saints: An Erotics of Ancient Hagiography* (2004), just to name a few that rework the ground broken by *CSTH*.[64] In all of these works, homoerotic desires mix happily with heteroerotic, sadomasochistic, and even ascetic impulses.

◆ ◆ ◆

The essays collected in this volume, divided into three sections—"Impact," "Debates," and "Innovations"—represent some of the profound effects that *CSTH* has had on scholarship of the last twenty-five years. The first four essays assess the direct impact of the book in different areas. Ralph Hexter begins with an essay that is part personal reminiscence of Boswell (it was to Hexter that *CSTH* was dedicated) and part recollection of the times in which *CSTH* was written. Carolyn Dinshaw continues with an assessment of the popular impact of the book from correspondence and early news reports, and uses this information to remind us how much the search for the past is an attempt to understand ourselves. Bernard Schlager examines the considerable and ongoing impact of *CSTH* within Christian communities and in their determinations about official responses to the gay movement and in moral reflections on the relationship between Christianity and homosexuality. Mark Jordan ends this section by reflecting on the dual role of Boswell as a Christian and a historian and the impact of both on the reception of his ideas.

The next five essays, in the section entitled "Debates," reflect some of the academic debates raised by the Boswell Thesis and *CSTH*. Amy Richlin begins with a detailed analysis of a series of letters that Boswell mentioned in *CSTH*, letters between the Roman Emperor Marcus Aurelius and his former tutor. Richlin demonstrates that while ignored by most classicists, the letters in fact represent what Boswell suspected they did: a real love between the two men. Richlin's essay reminds us how much the impact of *CSTH* lay in Boswell's analysis of long buried or long ignored texts, texts whose meanings are still being debated. In the second of these essays, Dale Martin reprints his discussion from *Biblical Interpretation* of two recent scholarly readings of a biblical passage long considered to condemn homosexuality, showing how modern assumptions about sexuality shape these scholars' points of view. Boswell was among the first to suggest an alternative explanation for this passage—even including an appendix in *CSTH* dedicated to the subject— and Martin's article shows how debates about the historical meaning of this passage still continue unabated. Ann Matter next reprints her well known article from *The Journal of Feminist Studies in Religion,* an extension of *CSTH* on medieval female homoeroticism, showing both evidence for affective and sexual relationships between women in the Middle Ages. Among other things, Matter challenges us to think about same-sex relations between women in different ways than same-sex relations between men have been approached.

The fourth essay in this part, by Bruce O'Brien, provides a history of one of the many disputes touched off by *CSTH,* in this case the meaning to Saint Anselm's writings that Boswell considered part of the "gay subculture" of the Middle Ages. Boswell's willingness to identify medievals as "gay" provoked many scholarly rebuttals, as O'Brien demonstrates. The fifth essay is my own, reprinted from *Gender and Difference in the Middle Ages,* and suggests alternative explanations for the rise of intolerance that Boswell had attributed to twelfth-century urbanization, while still grounding that change in social and political relations of the period. As a group, these essays show the continuing presence of *CSTH* in scholarly debates about homosexuality and history.

The last six essays, in the section called "Innovations," provide some examples of new directions the field has taken since the publication of *CSTH.* The first of these, by Mark Masterson, shows how homosexual desire is explicitly avoided and yet implicitly present in the writings of the early Christian ascetics. His essay is a case in point of the impact of queer theory on the history of homosexuality, which reflects on silences as well as testimonies from the past and on differences ignored as well as marked, and according to which celibacy is among the queerest of sexual identities. Jeffrey Bowman reexamines the tenth-century Christian writer Raguel's *Life of Saint Pelagius,* also brought to scholarly attention by Boswell, but tries to contextualize the *Life* within the broader social and sexual climate of medieval Spain, even while problematizing the sources available for uncovering such a history. Bowman's essay echoes Boswell's early and enduring interest in Spain as a unique and fascinating medieval region, where three religious cultures with distinct traditions about homoeroticism interacted.

The next two essays show how the impact of gender studies has influenced the history of men's sexuality. The one, by Jacqueline Murray, treats of medieval anxiety around the sexed male body, as evidenced in the innumerable references to the fear of castration. The other, by Ruth Mazo Karras, compares the accusations of sodomy among the Knights Templar to their absence among the Teutonic Knights. Both view the history of male sexuality within the broader context of the history of masculinity, and demonstrate the manifold connections between gender and sexual identity, in the first case, through a group conceptualized as less than masculine, and in the second case, a group thought of as more than masculine.

The final two essays demonstrate the lasting influence of *CSTH* in reappraising the relationship between Christianity, gender identity, and eroticism. The one, by Penelope Johnson, describes the sexually ambiguous visions of a thirteenth-century Italian mystic, Gerardesca of Pisa. The other, by Catherine Mooney, explores gendered and erotic ambiguity in early writings by and about Saint Francis of Assisi. The intertwining of issues of gender, sexuality, and spirituality in these and other essays demonstrate the impressive range of innovations in the field, as do their sophisticated investigations into individuals, groups, and texts for traces of gender nonconformity and homoerotic desire. They also reflect an intellectual debt to the Boswell Thesis in continuing the assertion that in medieval Christianity, things may not be as they seem.

✦ ✦ ✦

Fourteen years after the publication of *CSTH,* Boswell surprised the academic community once again with the publication of his second most famous book, *Same-Sex Unions in Premodern Europe* (1994, published simultaneously in Britain as *The Marriage of Likeness*).[65] It was in many ways an extension of the Boswell Thesis as put forth in *CSTH,* since its main argument was that not only did early Christians and the peoples of the Early Middle Ages maintain the tolerance that typified earlier Greek and Roman societies, but they also created church ceremonies to mark the emotional commitments between same-sex couples. Boswell's evidence was drawn mostly from eastern Europe, which distinguished the book from the western European emphasis in *CSTH.* Unlike *CSTH,* Boswell did not press the use of the term "gay people," as he had to so much opposition earlier, but used "homosexual" and "heterosexual" in ways that made them seem still useful categories to him. Still, his introductory chapter included the following remarks:

> The apparently urgent, morally paramount distinction suggested by this question—between all heterosexual acts and relationships and all homosexual acts and relationships—was largely unknown to the societies in which the unions first took place, making the question anachronistic and to some extent unanswerable (if not beside the point), and even where the difference was noticed and commented on, it was much less important to premodern Europeans than many other moral and practical distinctions regarding human couplings.[66]

Like *CSTH,* moreover, the book drew widely varying scholarly reviews, but caught even more the attention of the popular press, including a Doonesbury cartoon strip that briefly discussed the book before its release. Often the reviewers admitted the close relationship between the two books. Mark Jordan, for example, referred to it as "another chapter, the last, in Boswell's great romance of the gay couple in the Christian West."[67]

Already by the release of *Same-Sex Unions,* Boswell was too ill to grant interviews. He died about six months later, on 24 December 1994, of AIDS-related causes. A friend and former graduate student, George Chauncey (now a professor of history at the University of Chicago), eulogized Boswell in the *Guardian* newspaper:

> John Boswell . . . intervened as few scholars have in the great moral debates of his day. . . . It is his second book [*CSTH*] . . . for which he will be best remembered, in part because its publication marked a turning point in the development of lesbian and gay studies. It appeared at a time, only 15 years ago, when a pervasive climate of fear kept most American academics from publishing on gay topics. Many friends and colleagues warned him that publishing the book before he received tenure would sabotage his career. He had the courage to do so anyway.[68]

Many reviewers of *Same-Sex Unions* also noted his passing with sincere regret. Daniel Mendelsohn wrote the following in his lengthy reflections on the book in *Arion,* reflections that might serve as well for *CSTH* and for the whole of Boswell's career:

> Who knows how classical scholarship might have evolved if Oscar Wilde had gone to grad school? . . . When Wilde went up to Oxford, it was on a classics scholarship. . . . Yet when he was asked what he proposed to do after leaving, the otherwise aporetic undergraduate ("God knows," was his immediate response) was emphatic about at least one thing. "I won't be a dried-up Oxford don, anyhow," the twenty-four-year-old replied. "I'll be a poet, a writer, a dramatist. Somehow or other I'll be famous, and if not famous, I'll be notorious." . . . I couldn't help thinking of Wilde as I read and re-read a recent book by another precociously gifted *philologue* who, like Wilde, came to chafe at the dried-up donnish bit, and who as a result sought an audience outside of the academy's walls. . . . Like much of Wilde's *oeuvre,* this work seeks to present a devastating indictment of social and especially religious hypocrisy on the subject of human sexuality. It is a nice further coincidence that its late author was, like Wilde, charming, personable, erudite, and above all an extraordinarily gifted linguist. . . . And like Wilde, he was a homosexual who suffered both personally and, according to some, professionally for it. The book I am talking about is John Boswell's *Same-Sex Unions in Premodern Europe.* In it, the author claims to have unearthed a medieval ecclesiastical ceremony known as the *adelphopoiesis* which, he argues, was in fact a Christian

liturgy to be performed at (primarily male) homosexual marriages. As much today as a hundred years ago, that is the kind of claim that makes you very notorious indeed.[69]

I think Boswell would have been pleased with this comparison.

The release of *CSTH* had, of course, already brought much public attention and even notoriety to Boswell. In 1980, he was thirty-three years old and an untenured assistant professor in the history department at Yale University, where he had taught since 1975. He had been born in 1947 in Boston, Massachusetts, and had traveled and lived in several parts of the globe as a child, including Turkey and Panama, since his father was attached to the U.S. military. He had attended the College of William and Mary and had received his Ph.D. at Harvard University in 1975. *CSTH* was the second of the four books Boswell was to publish. The first, revised from his doctoral dissertation, was *The Royal Treasure: Muslim Communities Under the Crown of Aragon in the Fourteenth Century,* published in 1977 by Yale University Press.[70] Boswell's career, already of great promise, was propelled forward by the success of *CSTH,* which was named one of *The New York Times Book Review*'s ten best books of 1980, and which won the American Book Award for History in 1981. He was promoted to full professor in 1982, and published his third book, *The Kindness of Strangers: The Abandonment of Children in Western Europe from Late Antiquity to the Renaissance* (also by the University of Chicago Press) in 1988. He was named to an endowed professorship (A. Whitney Griswold Professor of History) in 1990, and chaired the Yale history department from 1990 to 1992.

John Boswell once told me that he wished to be remembered as a historian of the sort that Henri Pirenne was. He certainly admired Pirenne, and quoted him at the beginning of the introduction to *CSTH:*

> All those whose lives are spent searching for truth are well aware that the glimpses they catch of it are necessarily fleeting, glittering for an instant only to make way for new and more dazzling insights. The scholar's work, in marked contrast to that of the artist, is inevitably provisional. He knows this and rejoices in it, for the rapid obsolescence of his books is the very proof of the progress of scholarship. (*CSTH,* 3)

Yet Pirenne, who died in 1935, is still well known among medievalists, a scholar who claimed through a series of books to have demonstrated that the Roman Empire did not fall in the fifth century, where universal consensus had placed it, but in the late seventh century with the rise of the Arab and

Carolingian Empires. Boswell admitted that even if no one agreed completely or even mostly with Pirenne's argument—and there have certainly been rebuttals and reappraisals of it in the seventy-odd years since its inception—all scholars after Pirenne were obliged to take a professional stand in support of or opposition to him. His work could not be ignored.[71] The Pirenne Thesis, as it has become known, was a lasting contribution to our knowledge and a challenge to our preconceptions about the Middle Ages. So, too, it would seem, is the Boswell Thesis.

· *Appendix: Reviews of CSTH*

Adams, Jeremy duQ. *Speculum* 56, no. 2 (April 1981): 350–55.

Arrowsmith, Keith. "Toujours gai? Pas du tout!" *Village Voice,* 11 March 1981, 44–45.

Bonds, William. *Journal of Homosexuality* 7, no. 1 (Fall 1981): 94–102.

Boughton, Lynne C. "Biblical Texts and Homosexuality: A Response to John Boswell." *The Irish Theological Quarterly* 58, no. 2 (1992): 141–53.

Bronski, Michael. "Gay History: Setting the Record Straight." *Gay Community News* 8, no. 17 (November 1980): 1–2, 6.

Bruland, E. B. *TSF Bulletin* 7, no. 1 (September-October 1983): 33–34.

Brundage, James A. *The Catholic Historical Review* 68, no. 1 (January 1982): 62–64.

Christensen, E. *English Historical Review* 96 (October 1981): 854–57.

Crompton, Louis. "The Roots of Condemnation." *Commonweal,* 5 June 1981, 338–40.

Cunningham, Lawrence S. *New Catholic World* 225 (January 1982): 44–45.

Duberman, Martin Bauml. *The New Republic* 918 (October 1980): 32–35.

Dynes, Wayne. *Gay Books Bulletin* 4 (Fall 1980): 2–4.

Goodrich, Philip. *Epiphany: A Journal of Faith and Insight* 8 (Winter 1988): 80–83.

Grant, Robert M. "Out of Obscurity." *The Christian Century* 98 (21 January 1981): 60–61.

Guindon, A. *Église et Théologie* [Ottawa] 15 (May 1984): 241–43.

Haeberle, Erwin J. *Journal of Sex Research* 17 (1981): 184–87.

Hamilton, Wallace. "A Different Mirror." *Christopher Street,* September 1980, 50–55.

Harvey, John. *Linacre Quarterly* 50, no. 3 (August 1981): 265–75.

Hauerwas, Stanley. *Saint Luke's Journal of Theology* 28 (June 1985): 228–32.

Henry, Patrick. *Church History* 51 (December 1981): 448–49.

Jewett, P. K. *The Reformed Journal* 33, no. 1 (January 1983): 14–17.

Lemay, Helen R. "Homosexuality in the Middle Ages." *Cross Currents* 30 (Fall 1980): 352–60.

Leroi, Alan. "La chambre des hommes: Le second age d'or de l'homosexualité au moyen-age." *Gai Pied Hebdo* 166 (26 April 1985): 22–24.

Lineham, Peter. *The Times Literary Supplement* [London], 23 January 1981, 73.

Martinelli, Elio. "Cristianesmo e omosessualità." *Paideia* 37 (1982): 31–40.

Matter, E. Ann. *Journal of Interdisciplinary History* 13 (1982): 115–17.

McCollum, Adele B. *Journal of Ecumenical Studies* 20 (Fall 1983): 665.

Mendham, P. M. *Saint Mark's Review* 106 (June 1981): 57–58.

Mills, Jonathan. "Boswell on Homosexuality." *The Reformed Journal* 33, no. 5 (May 1983): 9–10.

Mills, Jonathan. "John Boswell's Corruption of the Greeks." *Crux: A Quarterly Journal of Christian Thought and Opinion* 18, no. 4 (December 1982): 21–27.

Modras, Ronald. *Currents in Theology and Mission* 10 (February 1983): 50.

Monteagudo, Jesse. "New Book Clarifies Homosexuality in the Bible." *The Weekly News* [Miami], 1 October 1980, 3.

Moore, John C. *American Historical Review* 86 (April 1981): 381 82.

Moore, R. I. *History* [London] 66, no. 217 (June 1981): 281–83.

Neuhaus, Richard John. *First Things: A Monthly Journal of Religion and Public Life* (1994): 56–59.

Olson, Glenn W. "The Gay Middle Ages: A Response to Professor Boswell." *Communio: International Catholic Review* 8. no. 2 (Summer 1981): 119–38.

Pagdug, Robert. *The Body Politic* [Toronto] 70 (February 1981): 29.

Patricca, Nicholas. *American Journal of Sociology* 88 (1983): 1333–36.

Robinson, Paul. "Gay Was Beautiful." *The New York Times,* 10 August 1980.

Saylor, Steven W. "What Boswell Uncovered: Digging for Roots in Frozen Ground." *The Alternate,* November 1980, 61–63.

Sheehan, Michael M. "Christianity and Homosexuality." *Journal of Ecclesiastical History* 33 (1982): 438–46.

Shelp, Earl E. *Theology Today* 38 (April 1981–January 1982): 256–58.

Smith, Tom L. "Medieval Limits to Social Tolerance." *Bloomsbury Review* 1, no. 2 (January-February 1981): 5, 20.

Strouse, Jean. "Homosexuality Since Rome." *Newsweek,* 29 September 1980, 79–82.

Thomas, Keith. "Rescuing Homosexual History." *New York Review of Books* 27 (4 December 1980): 26–29.

Touchet, F. H. *The Journal of Pastoral Counseling* 17 (Spring-Summer 1982): 84–85.

Towler, Robert. *Sociological Analysis* 42 (1981): 187–88.

Vanderbosch, Jane. "Comment on John Boswell's *Christianity, Social Tolerance, and Homosexuality.*" *Signs* 7 (Spring 1982): 722–24.

Weeks, Jeffrey. "In Days of Yore When Knights Were Gay." *History Today* 30, no. 7 (9 July 1980): 49.

Williams, Bruce A. "Homosexuality and Christianity: A Review Discussion." *The Thomist* 46, no. 4 (October 1982): 609–25.

Wright, David F. "Early Christian Attitudes to Homosexuality." *Studia Patristica* 18, no. 3 (1989): 329–33.

Wright, J. Robert. "Boswell on Homosexuality: A Case Undemonstrated." *Anglican Theological Review* 66 (1984): 79–94.

Notes

1. *The Advocate,* 22 June 2004, 172.

2. Derrick Sherwin Bailey, *Homosexuality and the Western Christian Tradition* (London: Longmans, Green and Co., 1955), vii.

3. Similar remarks might be made about the relationship between *CSTH* and Herman van de Spijker's *Die gleichgeschlechtliche Zuneigung: Homotropie, Homosexualität, Homoerotik, Homophilie und die Katholische Moraltheologie* (Freiburg: Walter-Verlag Olten, 1968), which was a general work but which included lengthy historical discussions in its larger analysis of homosexuality and society, discussions that also seem to owe much to Bailey's work.

4. Vern Bullough, *Sexual Variance in Society and History* (Chicago: University of Chicago Press, 1976); and idem, *Homosexuality: A History: From Ancient Greece to Gay Liberation* (New York: New American Library, 1979).

5. John McNeill, *The Church and the Homosexual* (Kansas City: Sheed, Andrews and McMeel, 1976). Boswell and McNeill doubtless knew each other, since both were involved in Dignity, the organization for gay and lesbian Catholics, in the 1970s and 1980s.

6. Boswell did refer to two of Dover's earlier works in his bibliography. Ralph Hexter recalls communications between the two, and sometimes participated in those communications.

7. Kenneth J. Dover, *Greek Homosexuality* (Cambridge, Mass.: Harvard University Press, 1978), 1.

8. Dover, *Greek Homosexuality,* vii; cf. Boswell, *CSTH,* 17–22.

9. Michael Goodich, "Sodomy in Medieval Secular Law," *Journal of Homosexuality* 1 (Spring 1976): 295–302; and idem, "Sodomy in Ecclesiastical Law and Theory," *Journal of Homosexuality* 1 (Summer 1976): 427–34. These articles formed the basis for two of the chapters of his book, *The Unmentionable Vice: Homosexuality in the Later Medieval Period* (Santa Barbara, Calif.: Ross-Erikson, 1979).

10. Goodich, *The Unmentionable Vice,* ix.

11. Goodich, *The Unmentionable Vice,* xv.

12. Paul Robinson, "Gay Was Beautiful," *The New York Times,* 10 August 1980.

13. Martin Bauml Duberman, review in *The New Republic,* 18 October 1980, 32.

14. Tom L. Smith, "Medieval Limits to Social Tolerance," *Bloomsbury Review* 1, no. 2 (January-February 1981): 5.

15. Louis Crompton, "The Roots of Condemnation," *Commonweal,* 5 June 1981, 340.

16. Jeremy duQ. Adams, review in *Speculum* 56, no. 2 (April 1981): 350.

17. John C. Moore, review in *The American Historical Review* 86, no. 2 (April 1981): 381–82.

18. James Brundage, review in *The Catholic Historical Review* 68, no. 1 (January 1982): 62–64; see n. 8.

19. Glenn Olsen, "The Gay Middle Ages: A Response to Professor Boswell," *Communio: International Catholic Review* (Summer 1981): 119–38; and J. Robert Wright, "Boswell on Homosexuality: A Case Undemonstrated," *Anglican Theological Review* 66 (1984): 79–94.

20. Lawrence Cunningham, review in *New Catholic World* 225 (January 1982): 44–45; and Patrick Henry, review in *Church History* 51 (December 1981): 448–49.

21. Steven Saylor, "What Boswell Uncovered: Digging for Roots in Frozen Ground," *The Alternate,* November 1980, 61.

22. Wayne Dynes, review in *Gay Books Bulletin* 4 (Fall 1980): 4.

23. Now available online at http://www.galha.org/ptt/lib/hic/.

24. Keith Arrowsmith (Walter Kendrick), "Toujours gai? Pas du tout!" *The Village Voice,* 11 March 1981, 45.

25. Colin Morris, *The Discovery of the Individual, 1050–1200* (London: Society for Promoting Christian Knowledge, 1972). This idea has since been challenged, it should be noted, by more recent scholars; see, for example, Caroline Walker Bynum, "Did the Twelfth Century Discover the Individual?" in *Jesus as Mother: Studies in the Spirituality of the High Middle Ages* (Berkeley: University of California Press, 1982).

26. Boswell, *CSTH,* back cover to paperback edition.

27. Michel Foucault, *History of Sexuality,* vol. 1, *An Introduction,* trans. Robert Hurley (New York: Vintage Books, 1978), 43.

28. Foucault, *Introduction,* trans. Hurley, 43.

29. Robert Padgug, "Sexual Matters: Rethinking Sexuality in History," *Radical History Review* 20 (1979): 3–12; reprinted in *Hidden from History: Reclaiming the Gay and Lesbian Past,* ed. Martin Duberman et al. (New York: NAL Books/New American Library, 1989), 54–64.

30. Padgug, "Casting Light on the Dark Ages," *The Body Politic* 70 (February 1981): 29.

31. David Halperin, "Sex Before Sexuality: Pederasty, Power, and Politics in Classical Athens," in *Hidden from History: Reclaiming the Gay and Lesbian Past,* ed. Martin Duberman et al., 37–53. An earlier version of the article was published as "One Hundred Years of Homosexuality," in *The Metis of the Greeks,* ed. Milad Doueihi, a special issue of *Diacritics* 16 (1986): 34–45; and a later version was published as "One Hundred Years of Homosexuality," in *One Hundred Years of Homosexuality and Other Essays on Greek Love* (New York: Routledge, 1990), 15–40. It is in this later version (pp. 27–28) that Halperin admits that there are human categories of dieticity.

32. Halperin, *One Hundred Years,* 46.

33. John Boswell, *Rediscovering Gay History: Archetypes of Gay Love in Christian History,* The Fifth Michael Harding Memorial Address (London: Gay Christian Movement, 1982), 9.

34. John Boswell, "Revolutions, Universals, and Sexual Categories," *Salmagundi* 58 (1982–83): 89–113; reprinted in *Hidden from History: Reclaiming the Gay and Lesbian Past,* ed. Martin Duberman et al., 17–36.

35. Boswell, "Revolutions," 20.

36. Boswell, "Revolutions," 23.

37. Felix Buffière, *Eros adolescent: La pédérastie dans la Grèce antique* (Paris: Les Belles Lettres, 1980). See also Gundel Koch-Harnack's *Knabenliebe und Tiergeschenke: Ihre Bedeutung im päderastischen Erziehungssystem Athens* (Berlin: Mann, 1983), which further clarifies an aspect of classical pederasty, namely, symbolic gift-giving, and Bernard Sergent's *L'homosexualité dans la mythologie grecque* (Paris: Payot, 1984, English trans. 1986), which describes myths that reinforced pederastic actions and values.

38. *Before Sexuality: The Construction of Erotic Experience in the Ancient Greek World,* ed. David Halperin, John Winkler, and Froma Zeitlin (Princeton, N.J.: Princeton University Press, 1990); John Winkler, *The Constraints of Desire: The Anthropology of Sex and Gender in Ancient Greece* (New York: Routledge, 1990).

39. Eva Cantarella, *Bisexuality in the Ancient World,* trans. Cormac Ó Cuilleanáin (New Haven: Yale University Press, 1992), vii.

40. Michel Foucault, *The History of Sexuality,* vol. 2, *The Use of Pleasure,* trans. Robert Hurley (New York: Vintage Books, 1988); David J. Cohen, *Law, Sexuality, and Society: The Enforcement of Morals in Classical Athens* (Cambridge: Cambridge University Press, 1991); Bruce S. Thornton, *Eros: The Myth of Ancient Greek Sexuality* (Boulder, Colo.: Westview, 1997).

41. Paul Ludwig, *Eros and Polis: Desire and Community in Greek Political Theory* (Cambridge: Cambridge University Press, 2002); Claude Calame, *The Poetics of Eros in Ancient Greece,* trans. Janet Lloyd (Princeton, N.J.: Princeton University Press, 1999); William Armstrong Percy III, *Pederasty and Pedagogy in Archaic Greece* (Urbana: University of Illinois Press, 1996); Daniel Garrison, *Sexual Culture in Ancient Greece* (Norman: University of Oklahoma Press, 2000).

42. Ramsey MacMullen, "Roman Attitudes to Greek Love," *Historia* 31 (1982): 484–502.

43. Amy Richlin, *The Garden of Priapus: Sexuality and Aggression in Roman Humor* (New Haven: Yale University Press, 1983; revised ed. 1992); Craig A. Williams, *Roman Homosexuality: Ideologies of Masculinity in Classical Antiquity* (Oxford: Oxford University Press, 1999).

44. Amy Richlin, "Not Before Homosexuality: The Materiality of the *Cinaedus* and the Roman Law Against Love Between Men," *Journal of the History of Sexuality* 3 (1993): 523–73.

45. Catharine Edwards, *The Politics of Immorality in Ancient Rome* (Cambridge: Cambridge University Press, 1993); *Roman Sexualities,* ed. Judith Hallett and Marilyn Skinner (Princeton, N.J.: Princeton University Press, 1997).

46. Jane Vanderbosch, review in *Signs* 7 (1982): 723–24.

47. Boswell, *CSTH,* 46–48.

48. Judith Hallett, "Female Homoeroticism and the Denial of Roman Reality in Latin Literature," *Yale Journal of Criticism* 3 (1989): 209–27.

49. Page DuBois, *Sappho is Burning* (Chicago: University of Chicago Press, 1995); Jane McIntosh Snyder, *Lesbian Desire in the Lyrics of Sappho* (New York: Columbia University Press, 1997); Bernadette Brooten, *Love Between Women: Early Christian Responses to Female Homoeroticism* (Chicago: University of Chicago Press, 1996); *Among Women: From the Homosocial to the Homoerotic in the Ancient World,* ed. Nancy Sorkin Rabinowitz and Lisa Auanger (Austin: University of Texas Press, 2002).

50. William Petersen, "On the Study of Homosexuality in Patristic Sources," *Studia Patristica* 20 (1989): 283–88. See also his "Can *arsenokoitai* be Translated by Homosexuals?" *Vigiliae Christianae* 40 (1986): 187–91, which also refers to patristic sources.

51. Mathew Kuefler, *The Manly Eunuch: Masculinity, Gender Ambiguity, and Christian Ideology in Late Antiquity* (Chicago: University of Chicago Press, 2001), esp. chap. 6.

52. Vern Bullough, "The Sin Against Nature and Homosexuality," in *Sexual Practices and the Medieval Church,* ed. Vern Bullough and James Brundage (Buffalo, N.Y.: Prometheus Books, 1982), 55–71.

53. Robert I. Moore, *The Formation of a Persecuting Society: Power and Deviance in Western Europe, 950–1250* (Oxford: Blackwell, 1987).

54. Mathew Kuefler, "Male Friendship and the Suspicion of Sodomy in Twelfth-Century France," in *Gender and Difference in the Middle Ages,* ed. Sharon Farmer and

Carol Braun Pasternack (Minneapolis: University of Minnesota Press, 2003), 145–81; reprinted in this collection.

55. Mark Jordan, *The Invention of Sodomy in Christian Theology* (Chicago: University of Chicago Press, 1997), 1.

56. See, for example, Elizabeth Keiser, *Courtly Desire and Medieval Homophobia: The Legitimation of Sexual Pleasure in Cleanness and Its Contexts* (New Haven: Yale University Press, 1997), or Richard Zeikowitz, *Homoeroticism and Chivalry: Discourses of Male Desire in the Fourteenth Century* (New York: Palgrave Macmillan, 2003). There have also been collections of essays on medieval homoeroticism, also dominated by literary scholars: *Constructing Medieval Sexuality,* ed. Karma Lochrie et al. (Minneapolis: University of Minnesota Press, 1997), or *Queering the Middle Ages,* ed. Glenn Burger and Steven Kruger (Minneapolis: University of Minnesota Press, 2001).

57. Carolyn Dinshaw, *Getting Medieval: Sexualities and Communities, Pre- and Postmodern* (Durham, N.C.: Duke University Press, 1999).

58. Louis Crompton, "The Myth of Lesbian Impunity: Capital Laws from 1270–1791," *Journal of Homosexuality* 6 (1980–81): 11–25.

59. E. Ann Matter, "My Sister, My Spouse: Woman-Identified Women in Medieval Christianity," *Journal of Feminist Studies in Religion* 2 (1986): 81–93. See also her "Discourses of Desire: Sexuality and Christian Women's Visionary Narratives," *Journal of Homosexuality* 18 (1989–90): 119–31.

60. Judith Brown, *Immodest Acts: The Life of a Lesbian Nun in Renaissance Italy* (New York: Oxford University Press, 1986). The first chapter was reprinted as "Lesbian Sexuality in Medieval and Early Modern Europe," in *Hidden from History: Reclaiming the Gay and Lesbian Past,* ed. Martin Duberman et al., 67–75.

61. Jacqueline Murray, "Twice Marginal and Twice Invisible: Lesbians in the Middle Ages," in *A Handbook of Medieval Sexuality,* ed. Vern Bullough and James Brundage (New York: Garland, 1996), 191–222.

62. Judith Bennett, " 'Lesbian-Like' and the Social History of Lesbianisms," *Journal of the History of Sexuality* 9 (2000): 1–24; Ulrike Wiethaus, "Female Homoerotic Discourse and Religion in Medieval Germanic Culture," in *Gender and Difference in the Middle Ages,* ed. Sharon Farmer and Carol Braun Pasternack (Minneapolis: University of Minnesota Press, 2003), 288–321.

63. Eve Kosofsky Sedgwick, *The Epistemology of the Closet* (Berkeley and Los Angeles: University of California Press, 1990); the introductory essay of the same name as the book is the most relevant in this regard.

64. Simon Goldhill, *Foucault's Virginity: Ancient Erotic Fiction and the History of Sexuality* (Cambridge: Cambridge University Press, 1995); Stephen Moore, *God's Beauty Parlor: And Other Queer Spaces in and around the Bible* (Stanford: Stanford University Press, 2001); Virginia Burrus, *The Sex Lives of Saints: An Erotics of Ancient Hagiography* (Philadelphia: University of Pennsylvania Press, 2004).

65. John Boswell, *Same-Sex Unions in Premodern Europe* (New York: Villard, 1994).

66. Boswell, *Same-Sex Unions,* xxv.

67. Mark Jordan, "A Romance of the Gay Couple," *GLQ* 3 (1996): 308.

68. George Chauncey, *The Guardian,* 5 April 1995.

69. Daniel Mendelsohn, "The Man Behind the Curtain," *Arion*, 3d series (1995–96), 241, 243–44.

70. Now also available online in its entirety at http://libro.uca.edu/boswell/rt.htm.

71. See Henri Pirenne, *Mahomet et Charlemagne* (Paris: Presses Universitaires de France, 1970; orig. publ. 1937, translated into English in 1939 as *Mohammed and Charlemagne*), although the Pirenne Thesis had been already developed in part in earlier articles; see appraisals in *The Pirenne Thesis: Analysis, Criticism, and Revision,* ed. Alfred Havighurst (Boston: Heath, 1958); or *Mohammed, Charlemagne and the Origins of Europe: Archeology and the Pirenne Thesis,* ed. Richard Hodges and David Whitehouse (London: Duckworth, 1983); see also a biography of Pirenne by Bryce Dale Lyon, *Henri Pirenne: A Biographical and Intellectual Study* (Ghent: E. Story-Scientia, 1974).

PART I

Impact

CHAPTER 2

John Boswell's Gay Science: Prolegomenon to a Re-Reading

Ralph Hexter

It is, in some ways, awkward for me to present myself as offering a fresh perspective on the subject of the present volume, *CSTH*. To state the obvious, my name appears on the dedication page, which will be forever humbling, and I am acknowledged generously in the preface to the book, as I am for assistance of various sorts in the prefaces to all John Boswell's volumes. John and I were close associates and best of friends for over twenty years, briefly at Harvard, then for a much longer period at Yale (for which reason I will refer to "John" as the subject of personal recollection, "Boswell" as the public author and academic). Though he was never formally my instructor or advisor, he was of course my most important teacher. In that regard, the fact that we were in different disciplines counted less than the overlap of areas of academic interest and scholarly expertise. There is no question but that I learned more about scholarship serving as his unofficial, volunteer assistant for three book projects than I did in all my graduate coursework combined. And when his final book, *Same-Sex Unions in Premodern Europe*[1] (henceforth, *SSU*) was published in what was to be the year of his death, when he could no longer respond effectively to some of the published criticism, I took up my pen on his behalf.[2] Given this history, no claim to "objectivity" on my part is likely to be credited, and I have to recognize that my opinions will be branded as "partisan" as a matter of course.

To be sure, among the contributors to this volume are not a

few of Boswell's former students, who have established their scholarly careers in one or more of the areas in which he offered them training. Their careers and their own achievements give their assessments of *CSTH* twenty-five years later appropriate authority and legitimacy. My case is somewhat different. None was, as I, directly involved in the production of *CSTH*. But if that inevitably implicates me in the project, there is something I can offer in compensation: a perspective from a unique vantage point.

I was first introduced to the project that ultimately became *CSTH* a good six years before its publication. Already in the first half of the 1970s John regularly spoke, usually to gay-oriented Christian groups, on the biblical "proscriptions against homosexuality" (as they were thought to be). The concept of writing a larger historical study on the scale of *CSTH* developed at the same time that John was writing his dissertation, completed in 1975 and published two years later as *The Royal Treasure: Muslim Communities under the Crown of Aragon in the Fourteenth Century.*[3] To be more specific, the scope and shape of *CSTH* must have begun to take form in 1973–74, to judge from my memories of discussions we had during long walks along the Charles River in that year. My involvement in *CSTH* continued until its publication, even as my own studies took me to Europe for several extended periods. These travels permitted me to do some archival work for the project. More importantly, I was party to, and more often directly involved in, virtually every version of the manuscript, reading, querying, and hectoring.[4]

If I rehearse all the above at some length, it is merely to establish the background to my current contribution. What I can offer, then, whether it be read as "objective" or "partisan," is a perspective as close as can today be achieved of the world in which *CSTH* took shape, and a view of why it took shape the way it did. I offer no universal history of the 1970s, but a sense of why it might be that John chose to begin the book's lengthy subtitle with the phrase "gay people," to foreground one of his most controversial decisions, then as now. But the perspective I seek to offer now is not merely rooted in a decade, for John Boswell, though of that time, is hardly a standard representative of it. He was a uniquely talented historian, an individual of breathtaking intelligence and immense learning—not to mention wit and wisdom—who in *CSTH* wrote a book of such originality and importance that even its severest critics justly regarded it as epoch-making. To place *CSTH* in its intellectual-historical context and understand the criticisms leveled against it, one has also to consider the particular convictions and interests of its author. I will invoke the particulars of both the times and the man as I reflect on some of the ways in which, it seems to me, *CSTH* has often been misread and "Boswell" misunderstood and misrepresented.

It goes without saying that the scope of this essay does not permit either exhaustive or systematic treatment of all responses to or all aspects of the book's argumentation. Limitations of space above all also do not permit me to cite all the materials that could be mustered either from reviews or from John's own papers.[5] I have included my own perspectives and opinions to a considerable extent, because this is the first time I have published my views on *CSTH* from what may be a "privileged" perspective on its author's intellectual design. When I write "privileged," I mean it in all its senses: to have been where I was was a "privilege," but privilege has its disadvantages. I can disown no part of it and will, therefore, present my case without further apologies on that account. I hope, though, that my "apologetics" may point the way towards the more thorough and systematic analysis my use of that quaint term from the history of doctrinal debate suggests, for as I will have occasion to observe, many of those who criticize *CSTH* or dismiss "Boswell"— when they are not simply retailing opinions at second or third hand—have overlooked Boswell's explanations of the terminology that he is using and the rigor and systematicity of his own thinking.[6]

I

Gore Vidal, in his essay "Pink Triangle and Yellow Star," wrote: "Despite John Boswell's attempts to give legitimacy to the word 'gay,' it is still a ridiculous word to use as a common identification for Frederick the Great, Franklin Pangborn and Eleanor Roosevelt."[7] But in the very first paragraph of this important essay, he credits *CSTH* with breaking what then seemed like a taboo in the United States against mainstream newspapers and journals reviewing books dealing with matters (and people) gay.[8] Such testimony from 1981, and from such an acute critic not only of writers and writings themselves but of the public arena, may help set us back in the world of 1980, and remind us how much the world has changed since then, in part thanks to *CSTH* itself.

The decision to use the word "gay" in a scholarly book in 1980 was a bold one, stirring up controversy and, in some quarters, ridicule. There was, to be sure, a liberatory dimension to its use. The manuscript was complete and sent to press within a decade of Stonewall. John himself was involved, during his years as a graduate student at Harvard (1969–75) in various student-oriented gay organizations, including the Student Homophile[9] League (SHL) and a group of Harvard gay graduate students.[10] The term "gay" was also employed by the Gay Academic Union, a group of largely New York City-based scholars, some inside, some outside the academy, but that was also a bold and decidedly antiestablishment gesture. (On the GAU's response to *CSTH,* see section IV, below.) It need hardly be added that there was at this time no institutionalized "Gay," "Lesbian and Gay," or "LGBT Studies" on university campuses. Many years intervened between the founding of these early organizations and the establishment and legitimacy of academic programs.

Even if no one blinks at "gay" as a term in common use today, contrary to what many of us in the 1970s expected, "gay" itself has not won wide acceptance in academic discourse—the "g" in LGBT hardly counts—and certainly not as applying as broadly as Boswell and others meant it to apply in 1980. "Gay" has entirely lost the "liberationist" overtones it once had. Indeed, for many, "gay" now not merely connotes but virtually denotes privileged white urban homosexual men of North America and Northern Europe. That is a current semantic fact, and it erects a partial barrier to readers accessing *CSTH* today. It is an interesting challenge in historical interpretation to weigh Boswell's usage of "gay" in the subtitle and then throughout *CSTH*, for one must approach a study that is twenty-five years old perhaps with more interpretive tact and sensitivity than a study that is one-hundred-and-twenty-five years old, precisely because one might be tempted to assume terms meant then what they do today.[11] All this before one even gets to the widely discussed problem of applying a term like "gay," which now seems even more "'70s" than it did even in the 1970s, to earlier cultures—on which, more below.

What did Boswell mean, then, by "gay"? In all his works, Boswell, who was a precociously gifted student of languages preternaturally alive to subtle distinctions and shades of meaning, both in contemporary usage and over time within a culture's history, took extraordinary pains to explain why he used the words he did. Despite what many critics of his last book assumed, he used the phrase "same-sex unions," in the title and elsewhere, precisely because it was *not* the exact equivalent of "same-sex marriages." In *CSTH*, the entire second chapter, entitled "Definitions," is devoted to terminology.[12] Despite his clear exposition there, many readers seem to misunderstand what Boswell means by "gay"; they possibly assume that, because "homosexuality" appears in the book's title and "gay" in the subtitle, the words are synonyms in Boswell's idiolect. This is a serious error:[13]

> In this study, therefore, "homosexual"—used only as an adjective—occurs either in its original sense of "all of one sex" (as in "a homosexual marriage") or elliptically to mean "of predominantly homosexual erotic interest" ("a homosexual person"). "Homosexuality" refers to the general phenomenon of same-sex eroticism and is therefore the broadest of the categories employed; it comprises all sexual phenomena between persons of the same gender, whether the result of conscious preference, subliminal desire, or circum-

stantial exigency. "Gay," in contrast, refers to persons who are conscious of erotic inclination toward their own gender as a distinguishing characteristic or, loosely, to things associated with such people, as "gay poetry." "Gay sexuality" refers only to eroticism associated with a conscious preference. This book is primarily concerned with gay people and their sexuality, but it must necessarily deal at length with other forms of homosexuality, because it is often impossible to make clear distinctions in such matters and because many societies have failed to recognize any distinctions at all. (*CSTH*, 44)

Within the terminological framework Boswell here lays out, it is possible, in earlier times as now, to engage in "homosexual sexual acts" but in no sense be "gay"; it is equally possible for an individual whom Boswell would consider "gay" never to engage in sexual acts with a person of his or her own gender. Space does not permit me to elucidate—in most cases simply by citing the precise if often subtly formulated language of *CSTH*—the extraordinarily careful and nuanced way Boswell negotiates a host of related complexities, for example, the question of "love" when it is contrasted, as it tends to be in certain contexts, with "friendship."[14] But his basic analytic, based on a distinction between "homosexual" and "gay," has the sovereign advantage of permitting him to deal with the fact that acts and sentiments are arrayed along two different axes frequently not in alignment, and for a host of different reasons that vary from culture to culture, with class and gender, and among individuals.

It may, of course, have been a miscalculation on Boswell's part to have expected to be able to give so semantically volatile and emotion-provoking a term so precise a sense, but then let that be the criticism. Serious students of the historiography of the field should at least recognize what Boswell meant when he wrote "gay."

II

Boswell needed some such term, for in *CSTH* he set himself the task not just of dealing with "homosexuals," "homosexuality," and laws and attitudes concerning the two—though he does that, too, for a sizable portion of European history—but also of giving voice to a further dimension, a personal dimension, and it is for that something else that he deploys "gay." Ten or fifteen years later, another scholar might have considered whether he or she might have wanted to use the term "queer," though I'm virtually certain John would not have. For one thing, by using "gay," Boswell was not seeking to highlight outsider status or any necessarily minoritarian consciousness; indeed, according to his narrative, for certain cultures at certain periods, being "conscious of erotic inclination" towards a member of one's own sex was neither exceptional nor a matter for shame or condemnation—nor was it necessarily exclusive. Now one might well argue that understood so capaciously, "gay" is not a very helpful category. Such an argument would be a great advance over those which are based, as I have said, on a misprision of the sense the word bears in *CSTH*. Nor would there be a simple answer; there are few if any categories that are optimally shaped and sized, and debates about the utility of any category for historical analysis belong to the serious work of all historical scholars.

To those who argue, further, that Boswell's "gay" is an omnium-gatherum calculated to permit the creation of a "gay people" who have a "history," the dialogue that would ensue would need to be even longer. It is certainly the case that Boswell juxtaposes the history of gay people with the histories of other European minorities, most frequently the Jews; specifically, intolerance of both groups increased in virulence almost simultaneously in the second half of the Middle Ages.[15] While no one doubts that the history of the Jews has a coherence of a different sort from whatever problematic coherence a history of "gay people" might have, for all sorts of reasons (temporal, geographical, definitional), it is worth pointing out that there is no little "construction" involved in the narration of the history of even so well (and self-) identified a group.[16] So-called racial minorities might provide another analogy, especially now that race itself has been unmasked as a purely historical category, without a clear scientific basis.[17]

It is highly risky to be dashing across such contentious, potentially even explosive terrain without having the space to make all the necessary details of one's argumentation explicit. Let it merely be observed that Boswell was fully aware of this, and of the fact that persons he might classify as "gay" who lived in one time and place, whether fifth-century Athens or first-century Rome, eleventh- or twelfth-century France, or twentieth-century North America, might not recognize one another as having much of significance in common. Indeed, they would almost certainly be struck more by the many things that were utterly different about each other's lives compared to which a shared "erotic inclination" towards members of the same sex would pale. That does not, however, mean that "gay" lacks value as a heuristic tool of investigation. For what Boswell the historian in fact does—and I would argue that this is what any historian who is not engaged in institutional apologetics or an ideological enterprise should do—is reconstruct, to the best of his ability, the system of values and meanings within which, at that time and place, being "conscious of [an] erotic inclination toward" a member of one's own sex, in other words, being "gay" according to Boswell's definition, has whatever meaning it does at that particular cultural moment. Performing the reconstruction multiple times sharpens the historian's analytic tools and adds relief and contours to our image of a given society's perspectives and value system; likewise, contrasting comparable reconstructions between cultures, or between different moments in the same culture's history, adds contrast to the images and begins to let a temporal dimensionality emerge.

Now if we are to begin to debate whether this is "history," we will have to go back to Herodotus and Thucydides. (On a related issue of historical causation, see section III, below.) But this is not the major accusation leveled against Boswell. What charge could be more serious than that a historian has applied anachronistic categories to his material, projecting backwards from his own very personal present on to the past? Again, limitations of space make it impossible to discuss the controversy *in extenso*. The bibliography is generally widely known,[18] including Boswell's own published comments,[19] and others in this volume address it directly or indirectly. Here it may be appropriate merely to point out a few passages from *CSTH* that are illuminating in this regard.

In the above-cited definition, to which I have repeatedly recurred, Boswell wrote of people "conscious of erotic inclination toward their own gender as a distinguishing characteristic" and " '[g]ay sexuality' refer[ring] to eroticism associated with a conscious preference." For this and other such formulations, Boswell has been called "ahistorical," branded an "essentialist,"[20] and demonized as the archenemy of "constructionism." Before we descend even a little way into the hell of this dispute, please observe that in the passages picked out here Boswell in no way specifies the psychological form this "conscious preference" takes or took. He does not use the word "identity." Indeed, the extraordinarily supple way he phrases his explanation, namely, that " '[g]ay' . . . persons . . . are conscious of erotic inclination toward their own gender as a distinguishing characteristic," leaves completely open the question of how significant a characteristic that is among the many dimensions of any given individual's life, both in our and, more importantly, in his or her own view.

This variability has at least two dimensions, both of which Boswell took into account. To start at the individual level even within one and the same culture, the erotic register can be of greater interest to some individuals than to others. (As a matter of fact, John was not only aware of this phenomenon; he was perennially fascinated by it.) At the level of culture, clearly the degree to which "sexuality"[21] was a distinguishing characteristic varied. It would be wearisome to catalogue all the points in *CSTH* where this perspective is either explicit or implicit. Just to cite statements from two consecutive pages, consider: "It is apparent that the majority of residents of the ancient world were

unconscious of any such categories [as 'homosexual' and 'heterosexual']"
(58); "In the ancient world so few people cared to categorize their contemporaries on the basis of the gender to which they were erotically attracted
that no dichotomy to express this distinction was in common use. . . . [T]he
categories 'homosexual' and 'heterosexual' simply did not intrude on the
consciousness of most Greeks or—as will be seen—Romans" (59). For a more
general statement of this relativistic—and dare one say "constructionist"—
view, note this sentence: "Majorities, in other words, create minorities, in one
very real sense, by deciding to categorize them" (59). This part of the equation,
then, is something that Boswell has, throughout *CSTH,* in the crosshairs of
his analytic: "Why some societies make invidious distinctions on the basis of
race, religious belief, sexual preference, or other personal idiosyncrasies while
others do not is a complex matter still awaiting elucidation. The following
study is intended to make a small contribution in that direction" (59).

This is not all that Halperin, say, demanded of the new history of sexuality
in 1989 (see n. 18). While Boswell does, I would submit, "include as an essential
part of [his] enterprise the task of demonstrating the historicity, conditions
of emergence, modes of construction, and ideological contingencies of the
very categories" that correspond to our category "sexuality" in a variety of
temporal and geographical "sociosexual" systems from ancient Greece to
late medieval Europe, he does not, by Halperin's standards, devote sufficient
attention to an analysis "of the very categories of analysis that undergird
their own [i.e., the histories' own] practice."[22] Boswell, as I have noted, was
writing for a pre-LGBT audience, and, writing *CSTH* through the second half
of the 1970s, was not in dialogue with what before long became its dominant
discourse.[23] Nor was he writing for an inner circle of fellow disciplinarians,
for, again, if that discipline is taken to be LGBT Studies, the discipline was
some years off and at best just then being called into being. Rather, he was
writing more broadly for historians—of Europe, of minorities and "tolerance"
(also hardly then a discipline; see the next section, below); of Christianity (on
which see section IV); certainly for lesbians and gay people; but also for a
general, interested audience.[24] There was, I suspect he felt, already more
methodological reflection in the book than most of these readers wanted.
What there was, he certainly wanted to cast in a terminology that would
not require any special training or imply a separation of disciplines. This is,
perhaps, ultimately a question of intellectual temperament, but it was—at the
risk of repetition—a question of the years in which the study was formulated.
Indeed, it occurs to me that the parting of the ways that seems to have
characterized the reception of *CSTH* by what soon emerged as the leadership
of LGBT Studies strictly speaking might be attributed to the need of that

then incipient discipline to mark its territories with a specialized discourse. I want to emphasize that I in no way dispute the right of any field to evolve its own specialized discourse; the forceful theoretical work and the historical research that has emerged has profited from the conceptual scholasticism and even from terminological wrangling.[25] I am merely suggesting, twenty to twenty-five years after the events, that when the history of LGBT Studies is written at some future date, students of the period consider the sociology of disciplines in general when they approach the strange case of the reception of *CSTH*.

In an uncannily prescient prediction of the following ten or fifteen years of dispute, Boswell wrote, "If the difficulties of historical research about intolerance of gay people could be resolved by simply avoiding anachronistic projections of modern myths and stereotypes, the task would be far simpler than it is. Unfortunately, an equally distorting and even more seductive danger for the historian is posed by the tendency to exaggerate the differences between homosexuality in previous societies and modern ones" (*CSTH*, 27–28).

III

"Tolerance" is that element of *CSTH*'s title that is, I think, most frequently overlooked. It is often forgotten that Boswell actually begins his study by setting himself the question of investigating the issues of tolerance and intolerance in the Middle Ages. "This study is offered as a contribution to better understanding of both the social history of Europe in the Middle Ages and intolerance as a historical force, in the form of an investigation of their interaction in a single case" (4). It would, I guess, be easy to suppose that this was merely a rhetorical ploy; that Boswell is merely seeking to frame, even disguise, his real interest in "the history of gay people" within and beneath a more "respectable" intellectual enterprise. If so, it would not be the first or last time others presumed they knew better than Boswell what he was really up to.

One makes such presumptions as a reader of Boswell at one's peril, or at least as one who seeks to get from his work all the information and intellectual nourishment to be derived from it. Boswell is at pains to point out, in the footnote attached to the sentence I just quoted, that his prior work addressed the complex contours of "tolerance" and "intolerance"[26] via his study of "Muslim communities in Christian Spain in the later Middle Ages" (*CSTH*, 4 n. 3, with reference to *The Royal Treasure*). I can assure readers that from my knowledge of what moved John personally, and motivated him as a scholar, this profession of purpose is entirely sincere. Racism in all its forms, and particularly anti-Semitism, were so abhorrent to him that he found them well-nigh incomprehensible, a mystery of human history he invested, with all sincerity and seriousness, years seeking to grasp, of course understanding that ultimately intolerance and hatred probably do not admit of explanation.[27]

When it came to the particular issue of homosexuality, the Boswell "thesis"—at the broadest and crudest level; I paraphrase grossly—was that the utter tolerance (indeed, virtual indifference) of the ancient world[28] was replaced by much less tolerant late antique attitudes (Christian, yes, but not only for that reason), and that a relatively tolerant period in the High Middle Ages, in spots virtually an efflorescence of "gay culture," was succeeded by and possibly even provoked fierce and virulent intolerance. As a historian, Boswell was not content merely to describe these periods and justify his (more subtly phrased) characterizations of the specific degrees of tolerance and intolerance (being precise about the limits of tolerance, and of what, specifically). He felt that, ideally, he should offer some explanations as to the causes of these changes. As so often in the course of this essay, I must plead lack of space. Let me offer only the briefest of signposts, very much in the spirit of my own subtitle, "Prolegomenon to a Re-Reading."

I reserve for the final section discussion of those who cannot conceive of institutionalized Christianity as ever having been (and, probably, of being) "tolerant" of homosexuality in any sense. Here I address those who simply don't "agree with Boswell's thesis that the early-medieval Church was tolerant of homosexuality." I am using as the mouthpiece for this view Vern Bullough, who continues, "It was not, but it was not until after the Gregorian reforms that the papal hierarchy was able effectively to move against those who strayed from the Church doctrine."[29] Let me take first the first statement, then the second.

"Tolerance" is another of those difficult terms about which some readers have not reflected with sufficient penetration. One will certainly be misled (and blame Boswell) if one understands it as implying blanket approval. Toleration is certainly not the same as approval. Indeed, one generally uses the verb "to tolerate" to describe an attitude to something of which one (or someone) most distinctly does not approve—for if it were an entirely satisfactory and praiseworthy thing, tolerance would not be called for. Nor does it even imply an intent to be tolerant, for one's tolerance may well be a resigned, even grudging one. (Still less are we dealing with a principled ideal of tolerance of difference or "inclusiveness.") What Boswell was referring to is a kind of practical tolerance, whatever its causes, and certainly a relative tolerance, for Boswell has the historical sense to try to evaluate attitudes to sodomitical acts in every medieval century in the context of official views and practical tolerance (or intolerance) of other delicts. It is in this context that his claim of early medieval "tolerance" must be understood.

There is no question, as Boswell certainly appreciated, that the means of enforcement at the disposal of authority, secular or ecclesiastical, have a great bearing on what that authority's effective tolerance of any given delict or complex of delicts was. Early medieval tolerance was attributable—in this he would agree with Bullough as cited above, though he would likely have added "to some degree" and other shadings—to the absence of techniques of surveillance and enforcement. This constituted one of the most basic lessons learned by any of his students who took one of his numerous seminars on medieval law. However, while "the strengthening and consolidation of civil and ecclesiastical power and administrative machinery" (*CSTH*, 270) might well have been a necessary precondition for increased and increasingly effective suppression and punishment, that alone does not provide a sufficient explanation. A much more complex and plausible analysis is to be found in the work of R. I. Moore, whose valuable survey *The Formation of a Persecuting Society: Power and Deviance in Western Europe, 950–1250*,[30] helpfully complements and expands on Boswell's earlier work. Moore refers quite approvingly to Boswell's work on homosexuals (91–94), but does not use sexuality as one of the major parameters of his study, which he instead focuses on heretics (including, ultimately, "witches"), Jews, and lepers. Though Moore had been working in the field for a number of years (and his own earlier work was certainly known to Boswell), it is hard not to think that Boswell's attempt to explain the rise of intolerance in *CSTH* did not contribute somewhat more to Moore's argument at a higher level. Certainly, the idea of an "open" Middle Ages followed by a "closing" one is older by at least a generation, even if one of Moore's most significant contributions is to shift the demarcating "line" (if you will) earlier.[31] Moore's own thesis for the roots of this change is a subtle and important one. To simplify, as I necessarily must, it has to do with the rise of a "single regime" of "emerging nation states . . . and the nascent papal monarchy" as well as "households of lay and ecclesiastical nobles," all of which increasingly "replace[d] . . . payment in service and kind by payment in cash and of oral process by written instrument." The role of the "literate clerks" was key: "It is among these clerks that we will see most clearly how the emergence of the state represented a new stage in the division of labour, a specialization or professionalization of government—and among them, the agents as well as the theorists of persecution, that we will find its origin and *raison d'être*" (136).

Though the emphases are somewhat differently placed, it is interesting to read what Boswell wrote apropos of this same change:

[A]nother factor discussed previously almost certainly played a large role in the narrowing of social tolerance during the period: the rise of absolute government. Perhaps the single most prominent aspect of the period from the later twelfth to the fourteenth century was a sedulous quest for intellectual and institutional uniformity and corporatism throughout Europe. This trend not only resulted in the strengthening and consolidation of civil and ecclesiastical power and administrative machinery but left its mark on less concrete monuments of European culture as well. Theology was fitted into systematic formulas and collected in comprehensive compendia—summas—of such formulas. The inquisition arose to eliminate theological loose ends and divergences of opinion. Secular knowledge was gathered into . . . encyclopedias. . . . Secular and ecclesiastical concerns were melded in the interests of uniformity. . . .

Probably nothing so exemplifies the later medieval fascination with order and uniformity as the astronomical increase in the amount of legislation of all sorts enacted from the thirteenth century on. (*CSTH*, 270)

R. I. Moore, as noted, instructively sees the start of this process earlier than Boswell, and elaborates a fuller theory of the new "regime," as he calls it, focusing more than Boswell, whose scope in *CSTH* is much broader, on the institutional, even prosopographical dimensions of the transformation. While historians specializing in the period, and in these phenomena in particular, would no doubt offer many qualifications and caveats, general readers will find in Moore, I believe, a confirmation and elucidation more than a correction of Boswell's thesis about the shift from a relatively more open to a distinctly more closed and repressive medieval society.[32]

IV

I referred in the preceding section to those critics who object to Boswell's thesis about the (relative) tolerance of the Christian church to same sex affection in its early (pre-late medieval) phase primarily, or so it would seem, as an article of faith. Many who, not without reason, regard the church, by which is generally understood the Roman Catholic church, as a purveyor and promoter of antigay doctrine and even hatred over the long haul cannot brook the idea that within the history of that religious institution, there has been variation in doctrine, discipline, or both, or anything to which one could apply the term "toleration." Then there are those within the institution who, for very different reasons, do not wish to acknowledge any variation in doctrine or discipline; they, too, have strong personal and institutional reasons to reject any suggestion of a period when Christianity might have been either intentionally or unintentionally lax on the matter of homosexuality.

In the context of this essay, I can neither adequately treat this subtopic within the larger field of *CSTH* "reception studies" nor even offer full documentation of the scholars and other authors who are marshaled *contra* Boswell with either the one or the other *parti pris*. The first group, who despise Boswell as an apologist (and perhaps even as a Christian, in fact a teenage convert to Catholicism from his family's Episcopalianism), are well represented by the authors of *Homosexuality, Intolerance, and Christianity: A Critical Examination of John Boswell's Work*.[33] The three authors evidence considerable learning and no less animus. The conclusion of the third and final section deserves quotation to give a flavor of the whole:

> It is regrettable that one must be harsh on a work with such considerable merit, but willful dishonesty in a scholar must not be condoned. . . . We should invite John Boswell to join gay liberation wholeheartedly; he has skills and knowledge that we need. To join us, Boswell must first extricate himself from the impossible position he's in: attempting to reconcile Christianity and homosexuality. It would be an act of maturity for Boswell to graduate from Christianity to secular humanism. Edward Gibbon has set an illustrious example. . . . There's nothing to fear. The Church no longer has Fire and Faggot at her disposal to condemn apostates to the avenging flames. Comrade lovers of the future will have no need for religion; they will have exchanged the illusory happiness of religion for the happiness of the real world.[34]

A very different response is reflected in the "review discussion" of *CSTH* by Bruce A. Williams, O.P.[35] that its author—like the GAU—sent in preprint form to Boswell himself. Williams builds on any number of reviews, especially in Christian journals but also the GAU's publication, that had in less than two years blasted now this, now that argument in *CSTH*. For Williams as for many other critics from within the institutionalized church, Boswell lacks theological finesse, which goes without saying if by theology is meant harmonizing discordant doctrine and smoothing other inconsistencies rather than historico-critical analysis:

> As these reflections suggest, the satisfactory assessment of homosexuality in church and society will require an adequately nuanced insight into biblical and other theological sources along with an appreciation of historical and other empirical data. Although Boswell is careful at times to moderate his claims, this reviewer's impression is that he has succumbed to the temptation

of trying to prove too much through historical and literary analysis without sufficient theological expertise.

Williams then continues with a sentence that, in its double negatives, gives new meaning to apophatic theology:

> His book should not persuade anyone that a consistent Christian tradition of moral opposition to homosexual practice is either non-existent or vacuous.

He concludes, though, with an abrupt shift of direction. After having dismissed many of Boswell's specific interpretations of biblical passages, Augustine, and Aquinas, Williams nonetheless wants to claim for the church, on the basis of *CSTH*, the very exoneration of the church for which the GAU and their comrades vilify Boswell:

> But a judicious reading should lead responsible people to the realization that this tradition, taken as a whole, does not provide the warrant commonly attributed to it for the homophobic hostilities which persist in Christian and secular society.

The rhetoric has, over the intervening years, certainly cooled, but Boswell's attention to biblical texts, patristic writings, and the theological tradition altogether has won him few fans in either curia or academic senate. He is, of course, patron saint to many thousands, even millions of believing Christians (and not a few adherents of other religions, as the correspondence he received over the years indicates) who have been helped, directly or indirectly, by *CSTH* to reconcile their religious convictions and religious affiliation, on the one hand, with their own sexuality (or that of family members and friends), on the other. The various denominations are as divided in their reception of *CSTH* (and, naturally, *SSU*) as they are on such issues as the ordination of gay priests or solemnization of same-sex unions, even marriages.[36] And while there is, of course, an active scholarly discipline of church history, the degree to which Boswell treated doctrine and even offered interpretations of biblical passages marks *CSTH* as something unusual in the academy, even for a medievalist.

Ultimately, Boswell was unusual in this regard, and there is no question in my mind that he considered it possible, indeed, imperative to be as intellectually active and engaged as a person of faith, in his case a Christian, as it was to be so engaged as a practicing scholar. There was, as far as I could observe, no split between his dedication to truth as a historian and as a moral person and believer. He was probably as iconoclastic a Catholic as he was original and independent as a scholar. It is possible for the "zeal of the convert" to coexist with a critical stance, and if, as has been said, all Americans are Protestant, he came by his Protestantism naturally; no skeptic in matters of faith, he was not the only Catholic who was sympathetic to the spirit of Vatican II, and he was never an apologist for the Roman curia of "J2P2" (as he called him, with apologies to a sweet little drone in *Star Wars*). One can only imagine what Boswell would have to say of the trajectory of the church in the decade since his own death. I have no doubt he would be appalled, perhaps most of all by the most recent assault on Catholics' freedom of conscience. But he always had the long view. Medieval kings were excommunicated from time to time.

Since *CSTH*, outstanding and important work has been done on medieval attitudes to homosexuality. I think first and foremost of the fine books of another of the contributors to this volume, Mark Jordan, in particular *The Invention of Sodomy in Christian Theology*.[37] As for Boswell's interpretations of biblical passages, from (what are for Christians) the Old and New Testaments, some have been received more favorably than others. The work of Saul Olyan on the relevant passages in the Hebrew Bible are elucidations from a professional Semitic philologist, which Boswell, for all his competence in Biblical Hebrew (and Arabic), never claimed to be. With refinements they confirm the general direction of Boswell's interpretations, if not every detail.[38]

The subsequently published material on the New Testament passages is vast. I would highlight only one very recent study (which gives reference to other scholarship): Gareth Moore, O.P., *A Question of Truth: Christianity and Homosexuality*.[39] Moore offers (86–105) a much more convincing reading of Romans 1:26–27 than I have seen before, though, oddly, he arrives at a point not so very dissimilar to Boswell's overall interpretation of this passage (*CSTH*, 107–109) albeit by different and in my view improved means. Moore makes very spare reference to Boswell throughout this carefully and, I think, brilliantly argued book, but, if I might indulge in pure speculation, I suspect that this is in part a canny rhetorical strategy, for, writing as a Dominican, he must be very careful not to cite prominently so hated an authority. Indeed, he writes from a position within the church and argues that, if the church hopes to sustain its current position on homosexuality, it must test its views against difficult counterarguments and really "smarten up" its logic.

I feel there is a deep intellectual affinity between the design of *CSTH* and Moore's recent book (which, again alas, was only published posthumously). I cannot, naturally, presume to speak for an absent John, nor do I have any claims to "channeling" him, but I feel that this is a book he would have appreciated. Like Boswell, Moore confronts "truth" and "tradition." Boswell is engaged more in historical research and narrative, while Moore engages much more overtly and frequently in philosophical analysis.[40] Both deploy what one might, for lack of a better term, call "negative dialectic." Both examine, and ultimately undermine (beneath quite different textual surfaces), the church's claims, and both, again via very different means, establish the possibility—whether or not a past possibility, then certainly a future one—of a church that might be not only "tolerant" but even welcoming to gay people, even gay people who perform homosexual acts.

These are astonishing, even radical ideas. Great scholarship, like great art, has the power to astound the imagination and sustain a revolution. Sometimes that revolution consists of wiping clean the slate of prior "common wisdom," even of suggesting the very possibility of a fresh and radically other perspective. I recall the words from the opening section of the "Preface" to *CSTH*: "What will strike some readers as a partisan point of view is chiefly the absence of the negative attitudes on this subject ubiquitous in the modern West; after a long, loud noise, a sudden silence may seem deafening" (xvi). To those about to read *CSTH*, whether indeed for a second or "nth" time, or in fact for a first time—for even for the latter, it will be a virtual "re-reading," since it will occur against the backdrop of misreadings of the book so long in wide circulation—I recommend that they be prepared to attend to that silence, which, recall, "may" only "seem deafening." It is not.

· **Notes**

1. John Boswell, *Same-Sex Unions in Premodern Europe* (New York: Villard, 1994).

2. "Same-Sex Unions in Premodern Europe: A Response," *The New Republic,* 3 October 1994. Both Brent Shaw's review and my response are reprinted in Andrew Sullivan, ed., *Same-Sex Marriage: Pro and Con. A Reader* (New York: Vintage Books, 1997), 7–21.

3. John Boswell, *The Royal Treasure: Muslim Communities under the Crown of Aragon in the Fourteenth Century* (New Haven and London: Yale University Press, 1977).

4. And typing. To remind those who may have forgotten, and to inform those who are too young to have memory of the years before the advent of the personal computer on the scholar's desk, editing in those days was a much more visible process and occurred on paper, the "correcting" feature of our IBM Selectrics notwithstanding. This paper economy also has value for the archive, and even my travels in retrospect now prove helpful, for there exists correspondence to remind me vividly of the precise issues on our minds at the time.

5. An extraordinarily helpful resource is the "John Boswell Page" on the website "People With a History: An Online Guide to Lesbian, Gay, Bisexual and Trans* History"

maintained by Paul Halsall at http://www.fordham.edu/halsall/pwh/index-bos.html. One of the subsections comprises a listing of a great number of reviews of Boswell's works. Pending their deposit in a public archive, I hold John Boswell's papers as his literary executor.

6. I have marshaled my points in four sections. Only after the essay was well on the way to completion did it occur to me that in a way I was writing an explication, in reverse order, of the main terms of the title of *CSTH*. For those who wish to think of it that way, it falls out thus: I. "Gay People in Western Europe from the Beginning of the Christian Era to the Fourteenth Century"; II. Homosexuality; III. Social Tolerance; and IV. Christianity. Primarily for reasons of space, the four sections are unequal in weight and length, the final two virtually sketches only. While no topic could be treated exhaustively in a single article, the last two by rights deserve much fuller treatment.

7. This essay was first published in *The Nation* (14 October 1981) and was in large measure a response to Midge Decter's infamous (in some circles at least) "The Boys on the Beach" that she had published in *Commentary* (September 1980). Vidal's essay became the cornerstone of a collected volume, *Pink Triangle and Yellow Star: And Other Essays (1976–1982)* (New York, 1982), from which I cite. He clearly found instructive the parallels Boswell drew between the history of prejudice against Jews and homosexuals; he sharpens the point and aims it at Decter, whose essay he described as "outdo[ing] its implicit model, The Protocols of the Elders of Zion."

8. "[U]nfortunately, scholarly studies having to do with fags do not get reviewed in the United States (this was before the breakthrough of Yale's John Boswell, whose ferociously learned *Christianity, Social Tolerance and Homosexuality* obliged even the 'homophobic' *New York Times* to review it intelligently)."

9. Talk about a dated term! John himself never tired of relating the confusion of the secretary (to use another term from the '70s) at Harvard's Phillips Brooks House (where this group and later the Gay Students' Association held meetings) of "homophile" and "hemophiliac." This was of course long before there would be a dark undertone to such a linkage.

10. The undergraduate group formed, with advice from John among others, in 1972–73. It is a historical fact that at the time it was still imaginable that "gay" could refer to both men and women; HGSA (Harvard Gay Students' Association) became HR—"R" for "Radcliffe"—almost immediately, but HRGLSA only after 1974 or 1975. On Boswell's own "inclusive" usage in his 1980 study, see *CSTH*, 45.

11. In reality, every usage, if understood precisely as its author meant it, is by definition dated; it's just that some terms manage not to appear dated. So, for example, "homosexuality" and "heterosexuality" (as Boswell himself pointed out, *CSTH*, 42–43) were once coinages that were regarded as very strange; they have over a century of use grown familiar and now seem "natural" to many. Other examples of even larger concepts whose capacity for natural seeming allow generation after generation (and even culture after culture) to imagine that they are involved in the same institutions might be "family" and "marriage," topics Boswell approached in turn in the two books that follow upon *CSTH*, *The Kindness of Strangers: The Abandonment of Children in Western Europe from Late Antiquity to the Renaissance* (New York: Pantheon Books, 1988) and *SSU*. The process (if that is the right

word) itself, which he referred to as "intellectual slippage," was to form the basis of the second book John planned to write after *SSU*. (The intervening study, which he had only just begun to work on as a book, though he had worked on the materials continually since his graduate years, was to have been on the three religions of medieval Spain: Islam, Judaism, and Christianity.)

12. A further appendix is devoted to terminology in biblical languages and their modern translations ("Appendix I. Lexicography and Saint Paul," 335–53).

13. To name but one among a legion of misreaders, Stephen O. Murray, *Homosexualities* (Chicago: University of Chicago Press, 2000), 1. It is indeed easier to dismiss or ignore a study if one misrepresents or, more charitably, misunderstands it. See, also, *CSTH*, 5, n. 5. There are times, certainly, when one must be very much on one's guard to keep the distinction in mind; e.g., *CSTH*, 55, par. 2.

In further support of my contention, I cite a letter of John Boswell to Nicole Evrard of Éditions Gallimard dated 18 August 1983, offering his commentary on aspects of the draft French translation of *CSTH* submitted for his inspection. In this letter he insists that both "gay" and "homosexuel" in French be only used as adjectives. "In the English both words are used only as adjectives—for reasons carefully explained on p[p]. 41–44—and a careful distinction is made between them throughout the work. The translation constantly uses both "homosexuel" and "gay" as nouns, and appears to use them more or less interchangeably. This not only undermines aspects of the book's subtlety, but directly contradicts the statements [in the chapter "Definitions"]." All John's wishes could not be accommodated: note the title of the published book, *Christianisme, tolérance sociale et homosexualité: Les homosexuels en Europe occidentale des débuts de l'ère chrétienne au XIVᵉ siècle* (Paris: Éditions Gallimard, 1985).

14. I do not mean to imply that Boswell gets everything perfectly right or offers the last word on all subjects; he would be the last to expect this. (Indeed, Boswell himself offered his theses with great modesty and looked to subsequent historians to supersede and surpass him; cf. *CSTH*, 3 [the opening citation from Pirenne], 38–39, and 334.) A superbly nuanced recent study of friendship is to be found in Alan Bray, *The Friend* (Chicago and London: University of Chicago Press, 2003), published, alas, posthumously. I strongly suspect that John, whatever disagreements he might have had with individual details and interpretations, would have admired this book greatly.

15. On the issue of (in)tolerance, see section III, below. For Boswell's own remarks on the comparison, see in particular *CSTH*, 15–16, and for the simultaneity, esp. 271–84. This comparison has striking modern overtones; note, for example, the title of the Vidal essay (and collection of essays) cited in note 7, or the citation from Moritz Goldstein's "Deutsch-jüdischer Parnass" selected by Boswell as the third of the three epigraphs to the entire volume. See also John Eastburn Boswell, "Jews, Bicycle Riders, and Gay People: The Determination of Social Consensus and Its Impact on Minorities," *Yale Journal of Law & the Humanities* 1 (1989): 205–28. As an example of much more recent thinking, on more recent history, see Daniel Boyarin, Daniel Itzkovitz, and Ann Pellegrini, eds., *Queer Theory and the Jewish Question* (New York: Columbia University Press, 2003).

16. I am thinking of such narrative choices as: how to treat Jews in diaspora (where the term, however traditional, already sets up a clear value scale); how to treat periods of

Jewish assimilation in, or tolerance by, other cultures; how to treat the history of "sects" and "heresies" within Judaism. On the last, see the recent book by Daniel Boyarin, *Border Lines: The Partition of Judaeo-Christianity* (Philadelphia: University of Pennsylvania Press, 2004).

17. I do not mean to suggest that there are not genetic differences that are observable, for example, in laboratory studies, along a variety of parameters, between populations, but only that the racial groupings referred to in common parlance, or, say, on the U.S. census form, are there as historical and social artifacts. One could also observe the fact that racial systems vary across time and place. Boswell briefly contrasts the three groups: "drawing inferences about homosexuality from observations of gay people in modern Western nations cannot be expected to yield generalizations more accurate or objective than inferences made about Jews in Nazi Germany or blacks in the antebellum South" (*CSTH*, 23). For another analogy with racial systems and terminology, see 59.

18. While by no means alone in representing "social constructionism," David Halperin provides, in his own contributions and his reflections on and critiques of others' work, immensely helpful access to this "school" (if I might) and its evolution over the past decades, from *One Hundred Years of Homosexuality and Other Essays on Greek Love* (New York: Routledge, 1990) to *How To Do the History of Homosexuality* (Chicago: University of Chicago Press, 2002). A particularly valuable formulation of the argument about history is his "Is There a History of Sexuality," *History and Theory* 28 (1989): 257–74, reprinted in Henry Abelove, Michèle Aina Barale, and David M. Halperin, eds., *The Lesbian and Gay Studies Reader* (New York: Routledge, 1993), 416–31 (from which I cite).

The Lesbian and Gay Studies Reader has helpful "Suggestions for Further Reading" (through c. 1991) on 653–66. Given the scale of this essay, I can do no more than point readers in the direction of such lists and other scholars' notes, obviously for more recent work, and especially for the many studies that continue to emerge refining our understanding of the "sociosexual system[s]" (to echo Halperin, "Is There a History of Sexuality," 424) that obtained in different times and places. To name but two of the latter, Michael Rocke, *Forbidden Friendships: Homosexuality and Male Culture in Renaissance Florence* (New York and Oxford: Oxford University Press, 1996) and Craig A. Williams, *Roman Homosexuality: Ideologies of Masculinity in Classical Antiquity* (New York and Oxford: Oxford University Press, 1999).

19. "Revolutions, Universals and Sexual Categories," in "Homosexuality: Sacrilege, Vision, Politics," a special, double issue of *Salmagundi* 58–59 (1982–83): 89–113; also anthologized in Martin Bauml Duberman, Martha Vicinus, and George Chauncey Jr, eds., *Hidden from History: Reclaiming the Gay & Lesbian Past* (New York, 1989), 17–36.

20. This has, of course, to do with the "status" of the categories themselves, which Boswell himself aptly explicated in the vocabulary of medieval debate between "realism" and "nominalism" (see preceding note). Those who, like Vern Bullough ("Sex in History: A Redux," in Jacqueline Murray and Konrad Eisenbichler, eds., *Desire and Discipline: Sex and Sexuality in the Premodern West* [Toronto and Buffalo: University of Toronto Press, 1996], 3–22, here 10), confuse "essentialism" in the social-constructionist debate with a particular position on the etiology of "homosexuality" itself in the "nature/nurture" debate (e.g., homosexuality is genetic or hormonal) have entirely missed the point.

21. Not that this is a term that Boswell makes much use of, but it seems to have become the canonical term to describe organizing categories on the basis of the relative genders of parties involved pair-wise in sexual activity, in reality or fantasy. Boswell more often uses no term or writes, for example, "sexual preference" (e.g., *CSTH*, 59).

22. David Halperin, "Is There a History of Sexuality," 426.

23. I refer readers to Carolyn Dinshaw's contribution in this volume on specifics of the history of Boswell's acquaintance with Michel Foucault, who hailed the appearance of *CSTH* and whose subsequent work on volumes 2 and 3 of his *History of Sexuality* was significantly impacted by *CSTH*.

24. From about 1978 on, John actually had a specific "ideal reader" in mind for his books: a highly intelligent student of Western culture and successful New York businessman, as it happened, a Yale alumnus and Jewish (the latter not, I think, an accident), living in suburban Connecticut, who happened to be the father of a very good friend (and fellow graduate student) of mine and, then, after I effected the introduction, of John's.

25. Even less do I want it to be thought that behind this is any kind of veiled critique of "esoteric" or "difficult language." I have defended the language of theory, which (to a general audience) can seem obscure and even rebarbative, quite publicly.

26. By the way, I think few if any have questioned whether one could possibly study the history of such obviously nonexistent entities.

27. I cannot, thus, emphasize enough the significance of the Goldstein citation on the page of epigraphs at the front of *CSTH*, especially its concluding words: "intolerance itself will remain finally irrefutable." Certainly his own experience as a young man early on aware of sexual difference contributed to his sensitivity to the issue, but it would be wrong not also to take into account the portion of his school years spent in Virginia (and over a longer period in contact with his father's family which hailed from deeper in the South); the fact that by marriage he had Native American relatives; that he spent time as a child overseas in both Panama and Turkey (his father was with the military). This brief and anecdotal excursion into the biographical only underscores my sense that Boswell ought someday to be the subject of a serious biography.

28. It is, of course, essential to a grasp of the entire project that one understand that Boswell focuses on tolerance of (or indifference to, to use the language employed above) "homosexuality" *stricto sensu*, and that negative attitudes to, for example, citizen males being subordinated in sexually submissive roles is about something else. See, for example, *CSTH*, chap. 3, "Rome: The Foundation," virtually *passim*.

29. Bullough, "Sex in History," (as above, n. 20), 18–19, referring also to a review published much closer to the arrival of *CSTH*.

30. R. I. Moore, *The Formation of a Persecuting Society: Power and Deviance in Western Europe, 950–1250* (Oxford: Blackwell, 1987).

31. Boswell cites the open/closing distinction from Friedrich Heer, *The Medieval World: Europe, 1100–1350*, trans. Janet Sondheimer (New York, 1962): "which advances the idea that the twelfth century was an 'open' one and the thirteenth the beginning of a period of 'closing'" (269 with n. 10). Boswell's own temporal demarcation in general coincides with

Heer's; Moore establishes that the roots of persecution go back well into the eleventh century.

32. I have not in this section addressed the portion of Boswell's historical explanation that is based in an urban/rural distinction. It was an all too convenient target for critics. Again, in the prolegomenal spirit of this essay, I would suggest readers examine carefully pp. 31–39, where this hypothesis is advanced in its fullest form, and observe the extraordinary caution and tentativeness, even diffidence, with which it is presented, starting with "some idea of the types of factors which *could* be responsible for it [sc. intolerance of homosexuality]," "advanced with many reservations," and "most useful for understanding some of the changes in public tolerance treated in parts II and III. . . . It is by no means a sufficient or comprehensive explanation even for these changes and is wholly irrelevant to (if not contradicted by) the social changes characterized in part IV. Both are intended chiefly as suggestions for areas of further inquiry and investigation where there is at present almost no analytical apparatus"—all of which I cite from two adjacent paragraphs on p. 31. I recommend in particular also p. 37, paragraph two. If others have found this hypothesis wanting and unconvincing, as the above indicates, Boswell would hardly be surprised. To my knowledge, we still lack a universally agreed upon explanation for the social revolution of the late antique, though the works of Peter Brown (to cite but one name among many) are certainly helping us advance towards such a goal.

33. This was published as Gai Saber Monograph no. 1 by The Scholarship Committee of the Gay Academic Union, New York City, in 1981. It comprises the following contributions: Warren Johansson, "*Ex parte themis:* The Historical Guilt of the Christian Church" (1–7); Wayne Dynes, "Christianity and the Politics of Sex" (8–15); and John Lauritsen, "*Culpa ecclesiae:* Boswell's Dilemma" (16–21).

34. John Lauritsen, "*Culpa ecclesiae:* Boswell's Dilemma," 20. Lauritsen sent a copy of the publication to Boswell and in a cover note (dated 10 January 1981) not only stated the interest of the Scholarship Committee in "any reply you might wish to make to our three contributions" but invited him to "address or attend meetings of the Scholarship Committee, which are usually held on the second Sunday afternoon of each month during the academic year."

35. Bruce A. Williams, "Homosexuality and Christianity: A Review Discussion," *The Thomist* 46, no. 4 (October 1982): 609–25. I cite from the preprint among Boswell's papers.

36. It would be interesting to survey the reception by individuals and faith communities in the other countries in which *CSTH* was published, but I do not have insight into this apart from having seen in the mid 1990s signs posted in the Biblioteca Apostolica in Vatican City—a very unusual other country—announcing meetings to discuss ways of countering the then recently published *SSU*.

37. Mark Jordan, *The Invention of Sodomy in Christian Theology* (Chicago: University of Chicago Press, 1997).

38. E.g., Saul Olyan, "'And with a male you shall not lie the lying down of a woman': On the Meaning and Significance of Leviticus 18:22 and 20:13," *Journal of the History of Sexuality* 5 (1994): 179–206, reprinted in Gary David Comstock and Susan E. Henking, eds.,

Que(e)rying Religion: A Critical Anthology (New York: Continuum, 1997), 398–414. I have heard more recent papers of Professor Olyan that are just now appearing in press.

39. Gareth Moore, O.P., *A Question of Truth: Christianity and Homosexuality* (London and New York: Continuum, 2003).

40. I think of several moments in his text, for example, his lengthy, even pedantic explication of the concept of "intensionality" in definitions (49–59).

CHAPTER 3

Touching on the Past

Carolyn Dinshaw

"Tell me, Daddy. What is the use of history?" Marc Bloch began his book, *The Historian's Craft*, with this question put to him
by his son.[1] The book was begun in 1941, and as he wrote, it
seemed that the very purpose of historical understanding itself
was collapsing. (The book was never finished; Bloch was shot by
the Nazis in 1944.) Yet a basic structure still holds in the book's
initial interrogatory moment: the relationship of father to son,
along with the expectation that that familial relation should be
the conduit of a sense of historical purpose. A terrifying aspect of
genocide—and the poignancy of these opening lines derives from
this—is the eradication of generations, and thus of history, both
personal and collective, such as gets structured and handed down
by father to son.

But there are other kinds of affiliations, generations that are
not traced via such traditional family relations. What is history
for those of us whose lives are not oriented around generational
reproduction of the traditional family, and what is the use of it?
Whom can we ask? And who will ask *us,* in turn, to explain?
In this essay I shall explore some interrelations of the concepts
of history and community, taking the latter to denote a social
grouping that is not a conventional kinship group. My exploration
will take us back to 1980, an inaugural moment, the year John
Boswell's *CSTH* was published.[2] This book brought the academic
study of the history of homosexuality to widespread attention

and opened considerable—and seemingly interminable—debate, not only about how to do "gay history" but also about this history's relationship to the constitution and political aims of "gay community," that social unit that might in fact be seen in such debates to take the place of the traditional family as presumptive ground, repository, and conduit of historical knowledge and purpose.

John Boswell's own papers, in the care of his literary executor, Ralph Hexter, are a rich resource of information about not only the scholarly but also the popular reception of *CSTH*. I looked in this archive to see how people talked about making use of this history and to understand the relationship between Boswell's approach to this history and his concerns about gay community. In this essay I consider a range of responses to *CSTH*, both by those whose desire was integration into the cultural mainstream and by those who used it as a foundation for a separate gay community. I shall then analyze how Boswell's own concept of community shaped his history, and how that history has underwritten the current national gay agenda; but I shall argue as well that it has resonated perhaps surprisingly with a more radical vision of social organization. Finally I shall consider what brought me to this archive, and what the experience suggests to me about history and community–about bodies touching, even across time.

In *CSTH* John Boswell undertook to tell a different narrative about the Roman Catholic church from the one that had theretofore been told. He wrote a story of relative tolerance among Christians toward homosexuality until about the mid-thirteenth century, providing new translations and interpretations of key scriptural passages to support this radically new scholarly view and developing a discussion of a vibrant, self-consciously gay urban subculture in the twelfth century in Western Europe. Boswell himself was "deeply religious," as Ralph Hexter wrote in his obituary, and his work has indeed proved immensely important not only to scholars ready to enrich the sparse histories of homosexuality but also to gay Christians seeking a place in the institution that other gays blamed for virtually causing "the anti-homosexuality taboo." (That phrase is John Lauritsen's, in an article in the *Gay Atheist League of America Review*.)[3] The book was immediately scrutinized and vigorously opposed in a collection of essays published by the Gay Academic Union entitled *Homosexuality, Intolerance, and Christianity: A Critical Examination of John Boswell's Work;* Lauritsen there indicts Boswell for trying "to whitewash the crimes of the Christian Church."[4] There was immediate gay resistance to the project of recuperating Christianity.

But the desire for a place within the institution dominated the popular reception of *CSTH*, which was enormously positive. The book was an instant mainstream success upon its publication in July 1980, achieving a level of attention in the United States that was staggering—literally so to the book's publisher, the University of Chicago Press, which was immediately overwhelmed and could not keep the book available. To read the Press's correspondence with the author is to witness a growing sense of excitement in the relatively quiet world of academic publishing. The hardcover volume went into five printings in less than a year—even at its steep price, which took it out of the range of many. In September *Newsweek* ran a review and article on the author (with a photo of the young professor, which proved crucial: he is pictured in his office, with *three* buttons of his shirt undone) (fig. 1), and responses to this widely circulated coverage swelled a virtual flood of mail: Boswell claimed to have gotten between three and five hundred letters a week ("fan mail," he called it) at the beginning of this media moment.[5] This may have been an exaggeration; the current archive of letters contains far fewer than that, but he may not have kept all of them; at any rate, I acknowledge that I am working with a body of letters that was retained (perhaps selected) by the author, and so its representativity is certainly not guaranteed. That having been said, the letters do seem to have come from all over: Estonia, Ecuador, Belgium, Montana. They came from mostly male, but some female, correspondents. Within a year the book had won a major prize and high profile recognition. It was eventually translated into French (a process Foucault facilitated), Italian, Spanish, and Japanese.

Boswell's name became a gay household word, as *The Advocate* put it in 1981. But with its emphasis on "social tolerance" the book penetrated various mainstream institutions in the United States as well. The correspondence files are peppered with requests for interviews and articles in mainstream print media (while an energetic fan tried to get Boswell on talk shows with Phil Donahue and the like); a sympathetic reporter wrote, "[Y]our book is such a public act and America adores turning authors into media events."[6] The times were indeed right for this book to be perceived not only as a scholarly venture but also as "a public act." True, an atmosphere of intolerance sat heavily on gays and lesbians: letters to Boswell mention Anita Bryant, Jerry Falwell, Reaganism, and "Moral Majorities" on the national scene as well as persecutions in schools on the local level. But at the same time there was considerable optimism, post-Stonewall and pre-AIDS: the letters witness an expanding gay public discourse and institutional presence in the United States. Letters from gay clergy (Catholic and Protestant) poured forth. One gay clergyman in the mental health professions, for example, wrote that he had gotten a copy of *CSTH* placed in the permanent library of a federal mental hospital.[7] A Christian counselor in the Army wrote to say that he was shaken by the hypothesis

Figure 1. John Boswell, 1980.

of the book and needed clarification, since "in the military I have to counsel young people with all kinds of problems."[8] The staff member of a medical center's Institute of Religion attested to the power of the book: "Your work will assist me in setting my moral analyses within a better historical context."[9] A Houston lawyer wrote to say that the book "has given me some insights that may come into play from time to time when working with juries."[10] Professor Boswell was called upon almost immediately after the book's publication to give depositions in a sodomy case and in military discharge cases. Colorado's Amendment Two came along near the end of his career; in his deposition for the winning side, he mentions that two authoritative translations of the New Testament "have recognized my arguments regarding the proper translation" of key passages.[11] These mainstream institutions (hospitals, the military, law courts, organized religions) were being touched from within by the book; reformation—the "social tolerance" of the book's title—is indeed what was sought by these various correspondents.

The appeal of the book from this institutional point of view was not its argument that there was a distinct gay subculture in the High Middle Ages but that gayness was accepted in dominant ancient and medieval institutions that are still authoritative today. The book's historical analysis legitimated gayness for readers now. In fact, the very existence of the book appears to have conferred legitimacy: a large number of people wrote before they had even read it (they had only seen the *Newsweek* review); a chunky university press history book—read or unread—whose author taught at Yale was enough in their view to strengthen gay claims to cultural legitimacy. (The footnotes alone became something of a "fetish," as one correspondent put it, standing in for or at least signifying such legitimacy.)[12] In the eyes of many letter writers, the assertion of a history—*some* kind of history—seemed fundamental to the mainstream acceptance of gay people now in the United States.

Just how that history would secure acceptance was a further question. Boswell was in fact contacted by two television production companies in 1982 about turning *CSTH* into a TV miniseries—basing a PBS documentary on the book (and on further, modern materials)—and his discussions about the development of such a series reveal something about the function of history in a medium of cultural legitimation such as the Public Broadcasting System. The starting assumption behind development of such a series went something like this: if we gays can be proven to have a legitimate past, if some of the people we take as our gay forefathers were in fact leaders of their societies and profound contributors to Western culture, then we have every right to be part of the culture of the present. "Our story is the story of Western civilization," Boswell stated in a conversation with one of the producers. He went on:

> It is better not to think of gay people as either artistic or military or this or that . . . but to see that at the same time Aristotle is writing . . . there are gay generals and artists and people in other fields and that homosexuality, rather than being some strange thing, was the predominant influence on the leaders of Athenian society.[13]

The series, in Boswell's mind, would show an integrated, holistic approach to gay lives past, not separating out homosexuality from other parts of Western culture but demonstrating the ways in which gays have participated in, have indeed shaped that culture. And thus a TV series, showing the "sweep" (as he put it) of the gay cultural presence, would not only transmit foundational cultural values to people in the United States now but would defamiliarize and thus extend our notion of the mainstream. The fall PBS season in 1981 broadcast various programs transmitting Western cultural values (*Live from the Met, Masterpiece Theater,* Shakespeare plays), programs that were deemed appropriate context for the development of such a series on homosexuality in history.

But there were other programs on PBS in that fall 1981 season, documentaries whose very titles suggest not an integrative approach expanding the mainstream but an objectifying gaze on an abjected other: *Whales That Wouldn't Die* was one such documentary, as was *The Human Face of China.* The conversation between John Boswell and the producer in fact falls apart around the question of the relationship of past to present. Boswell proposed a six-part series that would move from the Greeks to the present, with the rise and times of Christianity at its center (as one would expect from his work); the producer liked the chronological divisions but favored more air time on the modern period. The historical continuum can get to be "terribly dull," he warned, and people wouldn't be able to relate to it. "History" in his view remains something other—whale, Chinese, outer space (another favorite topic of PBS documentaries). It can be studied, but it remains a dull matter; it is cultural ballast and therefore necessary to the assertion of gay community, yet is not living, not part of us now. The producer may here be revealing only that he hasn't thought very deeply about this, but his position, however unreflective, expresses a common assumption about the simultaneous necessity and irrelevance of history. (For abundant examples of this assumption, consider congressional discussions in the mid-1990s of how history should be taught in schools, discussions prompted by the completion of the NEH-funded National History Standards for teaching high school U.S. and world history.)[14]

Both Boswell and the producer use history as a foundation for gays' assertion of a place in culture now, but while Boswell delineates how it might change the notion of what that culture is, the producer presumes only that history will reinforce the present. There was no doubt a variety of reasons that this TV project didn't go forward, but I suspect that this difference may have been one of them; it pointed to limitations of the standard PBS-style documentary and the way it sought to guarantee legitimacy in an already established cultural field. Boswell's history sought "tolerance"—an expansion of the mainstream, not a revolution—but it was nonetheless going to require pushing beyond the reinforcement of present cultural categories, which is all the documentary producer could envision. As it turned out, even this reformation would not be televised.

The homosexualization of the mainstream such as Boswell proposed to broadcast was not the only concern of people who wrote fan mail to him. The letters also reveal the intense, personally enabling effects of *CSTH,* suggesting the importance of a gay community whose values include not only art and war and philosophy but also gay *sex.* Letters came from people who felt deeply isolated—one, indeed, writes from a sex-offender program because of his involvement with a boy.[15] Married men, some over fifty years of age, wrote narratives of long-hidden desires or of encounters in foreign countries (Spain before the Civil War, for example, or Lebanon); some of these letters, nominally concerning the book, provided the occasions of brief, private, supportive contact with another gay man, creating a tiny and temporary community of two.[16] Other letters were the medium of acting out fantasies or newfound sexual boldness: several *Newsweek* readers were entranced by Boswell's picture and thus driven to write. "Do you have a boyfriend?" inquired one. "If so, do you see any immediate possibility of dumping him?" Wrote another: "I see from the . . . photo that you are also very hot. Most academics aren't."[17] A cartoon from *Christopher Street* made a related point about the way this gay history book fostered a separate gay culture: it featured two guys at a bar, one saying to the other: "How about coming back to my place for a little Christianity, Social Tolerance, and Homosexuality?" Occasionally there was the self-projection characteristic of fandom: "I'm . . . also 33," beamed one man; "I, too, have studied many languages," reflected another, while another remarked hopefully, "You will doubtlessly [have] noted by now a certain similarity in our names."[18] If fairly bald identification with Boswell might be seen to animate such phrases, another correspondent, a young woman studying medieval history and literature, is less forthright, musing, "The reason I am writing to you is mysterious even to myself." Her letter, which attempts to explain her interest in the book (she had read the *Newsweek* review), nervously repeats this protest of incomprehension—"I don't know why I am bothering you with this letter"—and further offers, "Perhaps a partial explanation stems from the fact that I am . . . taking a class in medieval literature." The letter is bursting with the unspoken; the mystery, in this context, seems very possibly to be the mystery of being gay, and the letter an extremely indirect coming out.[19] In yet another deeply felt response based this time on a close engagement with the book's argument, a philosophy professor reflects on the book's effect on him of creating something like a gay community across time:

> Whereas I have often felt intellectual "friendships" across the centuries—historical thinkers with whom I have felt such strong affinities that I feel I know them and that we speak for one another, I had never felt—until I read your book—that I had *gay* friends across the centuries.

For this reader, history becomes a source—directly, itself—of gay community, a community of affinities, of friends, even perhaps (given this letter's impassioned tone) of lovers.[20]

This reader was not only impassioned but astute. Gay history and gay community are indeed tightly linked in Boswell's work. And this is where the issue of Boswell's apparent "essentialism" comes in. I want to turn now to consider how Boswell's concept of "the gay community" is related to his approach to history and how it shaped his findings. The subtitle *Gay People in Western Europe from the Beginning of the Christian Era to the Fourteenth Century* is important, for Boswell suggested in a 1982 essay that the very possibility of "gay community" now might in fact depend on whether or not we can say there were indeed "gay people" back then. In an argument that reframed the essentialism/social constructionism debate on homosexuality in the terms of the realist/nominalist philosophical debate on universals in the High Middle Ages, Boswell hypothesized in this article that the existence of a "real" phenomenon of homosexuality may be necessary to ground and justify homosexual community. He thus implies that if historically speaking one cannot say that there were people who "really" were "gay" or "homosexual" back then, the very concept of gay community now may be incoherent or unfounded:

> Whether or not there are "homosexual" and "heterosexual" persons, as opposed to persons called "homosexual" or "heterosexual" by society, is obviously a matter of substantial import to the gay community, since it brings into question the nature and even the existence of such a community. . . . If the categories "homosexual/ heterosexual" and "gay/straight" are the inventions of particular societies rather than real aspects of the human psyche, there is no gay history.[21]

So a "real" category of homosexuality or gayness (the two mean the same thing here, I believe) is needed for both gay history and gay community.

To Boswell, a gay history is a history of gay persons throughout temporal and cultural locations—people whom we would now call "gay," whether or not they called themselves that. His choice of the term was controversial—to his manuscript editor at the University of Chicago Press; to historians reviewing the book; even to sympathetic readers who wrote fan letters to him.[22] Simon Watney, in a review, noted that its "over-simplifying" was inconsistent with Boswell's own findings of historical variation.[23] But Boswell never swerved from his commitment to the term in premodern contexts. In a letter to his editor at Gallimard about the French translation of *CSTH* in

1984 he stated unequivocally, "[A]lthough it is not ideal, the word 'gay' is the only available term, in any language, for what I wish to convey."[24] Gay history, based on this "real" category of homosexual, may in fact be a necessity for gay community, for it may serve not just as a community resource but as proof of the community's conceptual justification, proof of its capacity to cohere at all. A current Internet website, "An Online Guide to Lesbian, Gay, Bisexual, and Trans* History," maintained by Paul Halsall, is tellingly—polemically—entitled "People with a History": it enters vigorously into this field of contestation over gay history and community.[25] For Boswell, who is featured prominently in this online resource, being a people—a community—without a history is not just a phobic threat or horror but might be simply impossible.

Boswell maintained that referring to a continuous phenomenon such as same-sex eroticism is not clearly "an 'essentialist' position." "Even if societies formulate or create 'sexualities' that are highly particular in some ways," he wrote, "it might happen that different societies would construct similar ones, as they often construct political or class structures similar enough to be subsumed under the same rubric (democracy, oligarchy, proletariat, aristocracy, etc.—all of which are both particular and general)."[26] There is merit to this position, and one of the important challenges to historians stressing the rupture between past and present is to acknowledge and account for such similarities. But Boswell does seem to associate same-sex eroticism with something essential in humans,[27] and the troublesome potential distortions in the phrase "gay people" when used in premodern contexts are not avoided merely by explicit statements about the analytical primacy of historical evidence, which seem to have been Boswell's mode of dismissing the problems.

As I view Boswell's work, a specific gay essence grounds both community and history, and that essence looks very post-Stonewall. The gay relationships in Boswell's gay history resemble those of urban gay males in the United States (like that implied by the two guys, both about the same age, in the *Christopher Street* cartoon): scholars have commented on the problematic lack of differentiation in *CSTH* between "institutionalized pederasty" and "what we nowadays call homosexuality," and made a similar criticism of *Same-Sex Unions*—a book published fourteen years later whose historical approach was effectively the same.[28] Turning to *Same-Sex Unions* for a moment: addressing the relation between premodern and current conventions of marriage, Boswell writes in the epilogue to *Same-Sex Unions* that the answer to the pressing question of "whether the Christian ceremony of same-sex union functioned in the past as a 'gay marriage ceremony'" is clearly yes, adding immediately that "the nature and purposes of every sort of marriage have varied widely over time."[29] But the premodern ceremony he is interested in is, as he presents it, gay marriage in the image of male gay marriages in the West today, between loving adult men; he elides consideration of the age dissonance in some of the documents he analyzes, as Randolph Trumbach contends, and with "the title of the book and the gender-neutral style of presentation," Bernadette J. Brooten points out, "Boswell masked the overwhelmingly masculine character of his material."[30] And earlier, in *CSTH,* as E. Ann Matter argued in 1982, Boswell oversimplified "the history of lesbian love" when he did not address "the differences that must have existed between the experiences of medieval lesbians and homosexual men."[31] (Thus we might read the comment of that young woman correspondent in her fan letter much more harshly than she appeared to mean it: "The reason I am writing to you is mysterious even to myself," because the place of the female in Boswell's work is hard to locate.) Despite his admirable desire that "gay" be understood as a broad category allowing for much historical and cultural variation, then, Boswell's actual historical work was constrained by an essentialism and a relatively narrow conceptualization of gay relationships (the dominant form of urban gay male relations in the United States in the 1970s and 1980s) from which that essence was derived.

This narrowness has had its consequences. True, the book was (in the words of the Gay Academic Union collection, *Homosexuality, Intolerance, and Christianity*) "a starting point for further scholarly investigation," which has proceeded apace.[32] The book opened up a whole field, lesbian/gay history; some works of lesbian/gay history had existed earlier, as Trumbach points out (by Jonathan Ned Katz, Jeffrey Weeks, and Trumbach himself), but the field was not well known or even really established.[33] In the late 1990s the book was still selling about 2,000 copies a year in the United States, and not only had proved enabling to individuals but also had helped move oppressive institutions toward reform: as Trumbach notes, it did not "have much of an impact on either the moral theologians or the church hierarchy,"[34] but, as I have suggested, it infiltrated churches, the military, courts, and schools on a more fundamental level—on the ground level. At the same time, it must be said that the book's popular reputation has lent legitimacy to a national gay agenda that, as Michael Warner argues, has abandoned the goals of a more radical gay activism to focus on reforming institutions such as marriage.[35] Boswell himself noted that "realism," with its transhistoricist tendency, has been viewed by nominalists "as conservative, if not reactionary, in its implicit recognition of the value and/or immutability of the status quo"—even as "nominalism," related to constructivism, has been viewed by realists as "an obscurantist radical ideology designed more to undercut and subvert human values than to clarify them."[36] Certainly we should resist the implication that a particular politics inheres in each of these approaches to history and hold, rather, that each can be deployed in particular political causes. But one might suggest that the fact that Larry Kramer cited Boswell as an authority on homosexuality in his *Reports from the Holocaust,* Kramer's controversial 1989 rallying cry to gay men to cultivate "stable, responsible, mutually gratifying relationships" (which do not, therefore, differ much from heterosexual marriages in their ideal form), does indicate the usefulness of Boswell's approach to an argument that takes homosexuality as a transhistorical constant and would impose a single model on relationships, gay or non-gay.[37]

But I want to complicate this somewhat predictable assessment by turning to yet another sharp and appreciative reader of Boswell: Michel Foucault, whose "fan letter" about *CSTH* was among the letters Boswell preserved. Addressed to Douglas Mitchell, Boswell's editor at the University of Chicago Press, and eventually smoothed out into a blurb on the book's jacket, Foucault's brief letter was written in rough English:

> I receive John Boswell's work with thankfullness. I found through these proofs a very interesting matter: "un vrai travail de pionnier" as we say over here. It makes appear unexplored phenomenons and this because of an erudition which seems infaillible.[38]

Foucault wrote that in late 1979—well beyond publishing volume 1 of the *History of Sexuality* and as he was working on early Christianity: his course at the Collège de France for 1979–80 was "devoted to the procedures of soul-seeking and confession in early Christianity," according to the résumé.[39] In analyzing Christianity he found he needed to shift his assumptions and reconceptualize the entire project of his *History,* as he says in the beginning of volume 2.[40] In an interview in 1982, Foucault in fact stated that he took *CSTH* as a "guide" for his work on the Greeks: in *CSTH* Boswell had drawn a distinction between "homosexual" persons ("of predominantly homosexual erotic interest" regardless of conscious preference) and "gay" persons ("who are conscious of erotic inclination toward their own gender as a distinguishing characteristic"), and it was precisely that sense of self-consciousness that had such a powerful influence on Foucault.[41] He understood that such self-consciousness would imply a historically contingent sexual category, as he put it in another interview a "cultural phenomenon that changes in time while maintaining itself in its general formulation: a relation between individuals of the same sex that entails a mode of life in which the consciousness of being singular among others is present."[42]

Later, however, in 1988 Boswell stated that he had shifted his position, eliminating that consciousness of same-sex inclination as a distinguishing characteristic of gayness and retaining same-sex eroticism only—and thus, it seems to me, increasing the problematic essentializing and anachronizing hazards of the term "gay."[43] But it is important, in these days in which there has been some movement beyond the polemical binaries of transhistorical identification or blanket alteritism in the historiography of homosexuality,[44] to attend to what Foucault got out of Boswell's *CSTH*. We need to reckon with the influence Boswell's work exerted on the direction of Foucault's late work: "Boswell's book has provided me with a guide for what to look for in the meaning people attached to their sexual behavior." A long statement by Foucault highlights what he sees as the methodological advance of the book:

> [Boswell's] introduction of the concept of "gay" (in the way he defines it) provides us both with a useful instrument of research and at the same time a better comprehension of how people actually conceive of themselves and their sexual behavior. . . . Sexual behavior is not, as is too often assumed, a superimposition of, on the one hand, desires which derive from natural instincts, and, on the other, of permissive or restrictive laws which tell us what we should or shouldn't do. Sexual behavior is more than that. It is also the consciousness one has of what one is doing, what one makes of the experience, and the value one attaches to it.[45]

You can hear the Foucault of *The Use of Pleasure*—volume 2 of the *History of Sexuality*—in these lines even as he describes *CSTH*. He is not concerned with the elisions in Boswell's work (which do bother me, and which have importantly been taken up by others, as I have intimated) but with that notion of self-consciousness. And as Didier Eribon has observed, Foucault shifted emphasis in his final works—from the end of the 1970s to his death in 1984— toward not only this concept of self-fashioning but also, and especially, the concept of *collective* self-fashioning, particularly as he found it in the context of gay communities in the U.S.[46] That is, Foucault was interested in self-fashioning outside the bounds of identity but nonetheless in a collectivity—in what could be called "queer community" today. A reckoning with the traces of Boswell in Foucault will expand our understanding of each historian as well as of the various possible social and political uses of their work. It will extend and complicate the relations that we trace as we hand down a history of scholarship on sex in premodern times. In tracing those relations, scholars are not only doing history but are also, as I'll suggest, constructing a community across time.

What brought me to the Boswell archive in the first place? What was I seeking, sifting through boxes and boxes of John Boswell's papers? Did I know, or was it "mysterious even to myself"? Certainly, I was drawn by memories of the times documented in those files, the late 1970s and early 1980s in the U.S.: that period was the crucible of lesbian/gay studies. Some of the religious concerns, too, were ones that I had grappled with, having been raised in a Christian household. But along with some sense of identification with the professor, there was some strong *dis*identification as well: I'm a dyke, after all, happily distanced now from religious institutions, and interested in developing an antifoundational historiography. What was I *doing* there?

What did I see, picking up that 1980 *Newsweek* photograph of the man I never met? It was neither a sexual lure (as it was for others) nor a mirror for me. But another book published in 1980—this one in France—helps me think about this experience. In *Camera Lucida,* Roland Barthes writes, "The photograph is literally an emanation of the referent. From a real body, which was there, proceed radiations which ultimately touch me, who am here." A photograph, he maintains, can convey a core knowledge (a *noeme*)—the certainty that *that has been:*

> [T]he *noeme* "That-has-been" was possible only on the day when a scientific circumstance (the discovery that silver halogens were sensitive to light) made it possible to recover and print directly the luminous rays emitted by a variously lighted object. . . . [T]he thing of the past . . . has really touched the surface which in its turn my gaze will touch.[47]

Barthes reads the photograph as a proof of a "somehow experiential order": it is not inductive but rather is "the proof-according-to-St.-Thomas-seeking-to-touch-the-resurrected-Christ."[48] Barthes's deep desire physically to cross or span temporal divides, a desire that itself crosses into mourning for a lost body, drives this last work published in his own lifetime. In the photographic archive of his own family, he sought something of a resurrection, and he insists that the certainty, the experience of proof, cannot be conveyed by the shifty linguistic signifier, empty and wayward, that he had earlier in his career described and tracked with such gusto.

In the Boswell archive I was not driven by such a desire for proof, a desire to reconstitute a body. But the concept of a touch across time, in Barthes's other works, does not necessarily involve a recomposition or resurrection, or even require the rejection of the signifier; it can be the happy result of a corporeal dispersion, a fragmentation of the author's life seen as a jubilant semiotic dissemination. Barthes wrote earlier in *Sade, Fourier, Loyola:*

[W]ere I a writer, and dead, how I would love it if my life, through the pains of some friendly and detached biographer, were to reduce itself to a few details, a few preferences, a few inflections, let us say: to "biographemes" whose distinction and mobility might go beyond any fate and come to touch, like Epicurean atoms, some future body, destined to the same dispersion.[49]

A desire for some kind of contact with the past, for a touch across time, across death, turns out to have been a constant preoccupation, variously formulated, in the long and varied career of Barthes—whose first book was *Michelet,* on that singularly somatic historian who himself (according to Barthes) manages to "touch" bodies across time, and whose last book was *Camera Lucida.*

This emphasis on the tactile, and away from the mirror or the essence, helps explain what I was doing in the archive. I was working out an answer to the question with which I began this essay: "What is the use of history?" Barthes certainly doesn't provide a historical method; neither does Foucault submit to historical analysis the "vibration" he feels from documents, as he recalls in a 1977 article.[50] But just to imagine bodies extending across boundaries of space and time, as both Barthes and Foucault do (explicitly or implicitly here), is to imagine bodies that undo conventional or ordinary historical conceptions. To imagine such bodies making contact is to put a new spin on the notion of contingent history: think of the etymology of "contingent," from the Latin *to touch.*

Such deep imagining is crucial for thinking sex and sexuality differently. It suggests a use of history for unraveling assumptions about the ways bodies exist in place and time, assumptions about how they are produced and constrained. And it may help us to conceptualize communities that extend beyond bodies in the here and now. This is similar to the insight of the philosophy professor reading Boswell, but without his implication of personal identification with the historical figures (he claimed that he and they speak for one another).

I am imagining a community across time constituted by partial connections—since, as Donna Haraway puts it, "the knowing self is partial in all its guises, never finished, whole, simply there and original; it is always constructed and stitched together imperfectly, and *therefore* able to join with another."[51] My discussion of John Boswell here just gestures in this direction: I have sought not only to analyze the various uses to which his book has been put, and to extend our understanding of the discursive field and political ramifications of the study of sex in history, but I have sought also to open the question, via that photograph, of how we can make contact, how we can make partial connections with bodies and lives, and in so doing, how we can make history.

- **Notes**

A version of this essay was presented as a lecture at The Queer Middle Ages conference in New York, November 1998. Materials from this lecture were subsequently used in the Introduction to my *Getting Medieval: Sexualities and Communities, Pre- and Postmodern* (Durham, N.C.: Duke University Press, 1999), 22–34 *et passim.* I am grateful to Duke University Press for permitting reuse of these materials here. I am grateful as well to Ralph Hexter for permission to quote from the Boswell archive and for his guidance through the papers. The papers in the archive have not been catalogued; I wish to protect the privacy of the correspondents, so I use only dates to identify individual letters.

1. Marc Bloch, *The Historian's Craft,* trans. Peter Putnam (New York: Knopf, 1953).

2. John Boswell, *Christianity, Social Tolerance, and Homosexuality: Gay People in Western Europe from the Beginning of the Christian Era to the Fourteenth Century* (Chicago: University of Chicago Press, 1980).

3. Ralph Hexter, "John Boswell, 1945–1994," *Radical History Review* 62 (1995): 259–61, at 260. On Judeo-Christianity as the cause of "the anti-homosexuality taboo," see John Lauritsen, "Religious Roots of the Taboo on Homosexuality," in four parts, in *GALA* [Gay Atheist League of America] *Review* 1, nos. 2–5 (1978).

4. See the essays by Warren Johansson, Wayne Dynes, and Lauritsen that comprise *Homosexuality, Intolerance, and Christianity: A Critical Examination of John Boswell's Work* (New York: Scholarship Committee, Gay Academic Union, 1981), esp. Lauritsen's: "*Culpa ecclesiae:* Boswell's Dilemma," at 20.

5. Jean Strouse, "Homosexuality since Rome," *Newsweek,* 29 September 1980, 79–81; "Eros, Ethos, and Going to College: An Interview with John Boswell," *Yale Daily News Magazine,* December 1983, 6–9, at 9.

6. Letter, 15 September 1980.

7. Letter, 6 May 1983.

8. Letter, no date.

9. Letter, 3 July 1980.

10. Letter, 19 January 1984.

11. The two new translations are *The New International Version* and *The New Jerusalem Bible;* the passages are 1 Corinthians 6:9 and 1 Timothy 1:10. See Boswell's statement, 8 October 1993, for the plaintiffs in Colorado's District Court; the anti-anti-discrimination amendment was eventually struck down by the United States Supreme Court in 1996.

12. Letter, 6 January 1981.

13. Transcript, 19 August 1982, n.p.

14. See my *Getting Medieval: Sexualities and Communities, Pre- and Postmodern* (Durham, N.C.: Duke University Press, 1999), esp. 178–79, for discussion of these standards.

15. Letter, no date. "Books like yours," the correspondent writes, "will help educate the public."

16. See, e.g., letter, 16 September 1981.

17. Letters, 28 September 1980; no date.

18. *Christopher Street*, January 1981, 5; and letters, 24 September 1980; 28 September 1980; 15 November 1980.

19. Letter, 1 October 1980.

20. Letter, 9 June 1983.

21. John Boswell, "Revolutions, Universals, and Sexual Categories," originally published in 1982. Rpt. with postscript in *Hidden from History: Reclaiming the Gay and Lesbian Past,* ed. Martin Duberman, Martha Vicinus, and George Chauncey Jr (New York: Meridian, 1990), 17–36, at 20.

22. E.g., letters, 22 December 1978; 18 December 1980.

23. "No Such Word as Gay?" *Gay News*, 4–17 September 1980.

24. Letter from John Boswell to Louis Evrard, 10 July 1984: the French were balking at the non-Frenchness and apparent militance of the word "gay."

25. http://www.fordham.edu/halsall/pwh/, accessed 29 June 2004.

26. Boswell, "Revolutions," 35.

27. See "Gay History," Boswell's review of David F. Greenberg's *The Construction of Homosexuality* in *Atlantic,* February 1989, 74–78, esp. 74–75.

28. On *CSTH*, see letter, 5 January 1981, and David M. Halperin's work in his *One Hundred Years of Homosexuality and Other Essays on Greek Love* (New York: Routledge, 1990); on Boswell, *Same-Sex Unions in Premodern Europe* (New York: Villard Books, 1994), see Mark D. Jordan's review of *Same-Sex Unions,* "A Romance of the Gay Couple," *GLQ: A Journal of Lesbian and Gay Studies* 3 (1996): 301–10; and Randolph Trumbach, review of *Same-Sex Unions* in *Journal of Homosexuality* 30, no. 2 (1995): 111–17.

29. Boswell, *Same-Sex Unions,* 280–81.

30. Randolph Trumbach, review of *Same-Sex Unions;* Bernadette J. Brooten, *Love between Women: Early Christian Responses to Female Homoeroticism* (Chicago: University of Chicago Press, 1996), 12; see her discussion of the gender problems in Boswell's work, 10–13.

31. E. Ann Matter, review of *CSTH, Journal of Interdisciplinary History* 13 (1982): 115–17, at 117.

32. "Introduction," *Homosexuality, Intolerance, and Christianity,* n.p.

33. Noted by Trumbach in his review of *Same-Sex Unions,* at 112.

34. Trumbach, review of *Same-Sex Unions,* at 112.

35. Michael Warner, *The Trouble with Normal: Sex, Politics, and the Ethics of Queer Life* (New York: Free Press, 1999).

36. "Revolutions, Universals, and Sexual Categories," 19–20.

37. Larry Kramer, "Report from the Holocaust," *Reports from the Holocaust: The Making of an AIDS Activist* (New York: St. Martin's, 1989), esp. 240–42, 273.

38. Letter to Douglas Mitchell, 19 November 1979.

39. Didier Eribon, *Michel Foucault,* trans. Betsy Wing (Cambridge, Mass.: Harvard University Press, 1991), 317.

40. *The History of Sexuality,* vol. 2: *The Use of Pleasure,* trans. Robert Hurley (New York: Pantheon, 1985), 3–13.

41. Michel Foucault, "Sexual Choice, Sexual Act," interview with James O'Higgins, trans. James O'Higgins, *Salmagundi* 58–59 (Fall-Winter 1982), reprinted in *Foucault Live: Collected Interviews, 1961–1984,* ed. Sylvère Lotringer (New York: Semiotext[e], 1996), 322–34, at 323; *CSTH,* 44.

42. Michel Foucault, "Histoire et homosexualité," interview with J. P. Joecker, M. Ouerd, and A. Sanzio, *Masques* 13 (Spring 1982): 15–25, at 22; reprinted in *Dits et écrits, 1954–1988,* ed. Daniel Defert and François Ewald, 4 vols. (Paris: Gallimard, 1994), 4:286–95, at 292; trans. as "History and Homosexuality" by John Johnston in *Foucault Live,* 363–70, at 366–67.

43. 1988 postscript to his 1982 article, "Revolutions, Universals, and Sexual Categories," 34–36.

44. See, for example, David M. Halperin, "How to Do the History of Male Homosexuality," in his recent volume, *How to Do the History of Homosexuality* (Chicago: University of Chicago Press, 2002), 104–37. In another essay in this collection, "Forgetting Foucault," Halperin reopens the question of the "construction of sexual identities before the emergence of sexual orientations," rereading Foucault's *History of Sexuality,* volume 1; he maintains that this reevaluation does not, however, represent a "posthumous rapprochement with John Boswell" (43).

45. "Sexual Choice, Sexual Act," 323, 322.

46. Didier Eribon, "S'acharner à être gay," *Ex Aequo,* no. 5 (1997).

47. Roland Barthes, *Camera Lucida: Reflections on Photography,* trans. Richard Howard (New York: Hill and Wang, 1981), 80–81.

48. *Camera Lucida,* 79–80.

49. Roland Barthes, *Sade, Fourier, Loyola,* trans. Richard Miller (New York: Hill and Wang, 1976), 9.

50. Michel Foucault, "La Vie des hommes infâmes," reprinted in *Dits et écrits,* 3:237–53, at 238; trans. as "The Life of Infamous Men," by Paul Foss and Meaghan Morris, in *Michel Foucault: Power, Truth, Strategy,* ed. Meaghan Morris and Paul Patton (Sydney: Feral Publications, 1979), 76–91, at 77.

51. Donna J. Haraway, "Situated Knowledges: The Science Question in Feminism and the Privilege of Partial Perspective," in *Simians, Cyborgs, and Women: The Reinvention of Nature* (New York: Routledge, 1991), 193 (emphasis in original).

CHAPTER 4

Reading *CSTH* as a Call to Action: Boswell and Gay-Affirming Movements in American Christianity

Bernard Schlager

> Thank you for your scholarship, your power of expression and the time
> you have placed in this study. The Episcopal Church has been struggling
> to make decisions in the area of human sexuality for years now.[1]

> [T]hough I don't need to recount how widely your book on Chris-
> tian tolerance and homosexuality has been received, still it has pene-
> trated into some rather staid old institutions. . . . I was happy to discover
> that your volume was required reading for a [seminary] course entitled
> "Disputed moral issues." Considering the conservative atmosphere this
> place used to cultivate, the enlightenment now cannot be far away.[2]

To read the dozens of surviving personal letters that congratulate
the author of *CSTH* on his seminal study is to be introduced
to a truly broad array of individuals who were deeply moved
by the book and its thesis that Christianity had not always been
(nor need remain) antagonistic in its attitudes toward homosexual behavior.[3] The first quotation above is taken from a letter
written by prominent bishop in the American Episcopal church
who was struggling with how to help his denomination update
and communicate its teachings on human sexuality; the second
comes from a letter to Boswell from a Roman Catholic priest
who delighted in the use of *CSTH* in a moral theology class at a
Midwestern Catholic seminary. Both of these letters, written to
Boswell within three years of the publication of *CSTH* in 1980,

reflect the widespread approbation this book received from many Christians who, to quote Michel Foucault, considered this book to be a "truly groundbreaking work."[4]

While the influence of *CSTH* has been profound in scholarly debates about biblical references to homosexual behavior, in historical studies on the phenomenon of medieval intolerance, and in gay studies in general, its influence on American Christians (both gay and non-gay) who have called for greater acceptance of gay people within their churches has been equally profound. *CSTH* has been read (and, indeed, continues to be read) by many gay Christians in particular as the most authoritative scholarly treatment of homosexuality and Christianity ever written.[5] Not only did this work help to spark serious and ongoing dialogue in the 1980s among gay Christians about the origins of antihomosexual sentiment within Christianity, but it has also been valued by this audience for its claim that Christianity is not an inherently antigay religion. In fact, *CSTH* has been pointed to by many progressive Christians as providing solid historical evidence that there were moments in Christian history when same-sex love and gay sexual expression were not viewed as particularly heinous sins by either church authorities or theologians. Boswell's claims, for example, that the early Christian church did not penalize homosexual behavior and that vibrant gay subcultures flourished in the medieval West have been used as important evidence that gay Christians of previous eras were allowed to express their affectional preferences without fear of ecclesiastical censure.

In the preface to *CSTH* Boswell writes that "the province of the historian [is] not to praise or blame but merely to record and explain. This book is not intended as support or criticism of any particular contemporary points of view—scientific or moral—regarding homosexuality" (*CSTH*, xv). Despite his insistence that this book offered an objective and morally neutral history of homosexuality and Christianity, *CSTH* has not been read dispassionately by the many who have found in the work historical arguments applicable to contemporary challenges. In fact, many Christians active in gay-affirming movements in American Christian denominations during the 1980s and 1990s read *CSTH* as a text that could be effectively employed in the struggle to change contemporary Christian attitudes regarding homosexuality and gay persons—indeed, it was seen as a potent weapon to employ in battles with those church authorities, theologians, and rank-and-file Christians within every denomination who staunchly resisted efforts to embrace sexually active gay individuals as full-fledged members of their churches.

In a published 1982 lecture delivered to the Gay Christian Movement in Great Britain Boswell stated the following: "I often think of myself as a weapons-maker: that is, I'm trying to produce the knowledge that people can then use in social struggles."[6] While *CSTH* was certainly considered by many gay Christians as an arsenal containing weapons for use in contemporary battles over homosexuality and Christianity, Boswell does not discuss in this work the application of historical models to current day situations nor does he offer any "call to action" for bringing about change within the church. At the time *CSTH* was published, however, Boswell did have clearly formed ideas on how the history of gay people in Western Christianity "from the beginning of the Christian Era to the fourteenth century" (to quote the subtitle of *CSTH*) might be used to reform current Christian attitudes regarding homosexuality, as can be seen in two public lectures he delivered to gay Christian audiences in 1979 and 1980. Before exploring those lectures, I would first like to consider the reception accorded *CSTH* by gay Christian readers.

When *CSTH* was published in 1980, the gay advocacy movement within American Christianity was already over a decade old and growing. Dignity USA (an advocacy group of gay Roman Catholics) and the Protestant Universal Fellowship of Metropolitan Community Churches (a denomination founded by and ministering to homosexual Christians) had been founded in the late 1960s; the Episcopal gay advocacy group Integrity and Evangelicals Concerned, a network of gay and lesbian evangelical Christians and their supporters, were founded in the mid-1970s. In addition, well-received theological and pastoral books calling for a change in Christian attitudes toward homosexuality had been appearing in increasing numbers.[7] Those American religious groups with the most liberal traditions regarding social issues, such as the United Church of Christ and the Unitarian Universalist Association, had issued official statements of support for the full inclusion of homosexuals within their ranks, and both of these groups had established national organizations for gay concerns.[8] By 1980, therefore, a growing audience of socially active gay Christians was eager to read the history of tolerance for gay people in church history that *CSTH* offered. That such a work had been written by an Ivy League professor and published by a major academic press promised that its scholarship was solid and, therefore, that its portrayal of the past might offer historical precedence for modern-day churches to embrace pro-gay theologies and ecclesiastical policies that were genuinely inclusive of homosexual persons.

In specific, there were three ideas outlined in *CSTH* that were taken up by gay Christians and their allies in the 1980s and 1990s to effect positive change for gay people within their respective denominations: (1) that biblical passages long understood to refer to homosexuality needed to be carefully reevaluated and, in most cases, reinterpreted; (2) that one could speak legitimately of gay individuals and gay subcultures within Western Christian history; and (3) that Christianity was not inherently intolerant of homosexuality. Building upon these three ideas, Boswell developed (in the 1979 and 1980 lectures alluded to above) two additional ideas which he believed would bring about such change: (4) that Christian officials have in the past revised theological positions on important moral issues that were thought by many to be immutable; and (5) that the rich history of gay people in the Western church offered gay Christians today a powerful tool to use in their struggles to make Christianity more accepting of homosexuality.

With regard to what contemporary gay Christians and others have often termed the "clobber texts" of the Bible, that is, those seven passages from the Old and New Testaments which have been most frequently cited as clear condemnations of homosexual behavior, *CSTH* offered interpretations that questioned the applicability of these texts to homosexuality and gay people.[9] Boswell's exegesis was not necessarily original in the case of each text discussed in *CSTH*, of course, but his succinct summary of the Jewish and Christian scriptures provided a coherent analysis of biblical texts that many gay Christians and their allies found to be authoritative and highly useful in debates with those who argued that the biblical stance on homosexuality was unquestionably negative.

For example, Boswell argued that two of the passages often cited as clear biblical prohibitions against homosexual activity (the story of Sodom in Genesis 19 and St. Paul's reference to homosexual behavior in Romans 1:26–27) have long been misinterpreted by Christians. The "sin of Sodom" was understood by early Christian theologians not as a reference to homosexual behavior but rather to the sin of inhospitality, and, according to Boswell, St. Paul was not speaking about homosexual persons in his Letter to the Romans; instead, what the saint condemned were "homosexual acts committed by apparently heterosexual persons" (*CSTH*, 109). Likewise, Boswell claimed that Leviticus 18:22 and 20:13, which he argued were the only Old Testament passages that referred unambiguously to homosexual acts, were not read by early Christian authorities to prohibit homosexual behavior among church members (*CSTH*, 104). Rather, since members of the early church had decided that Jewish law was not applicable to the followers of Jesus, "the Levitical regulations," Boswell writes, "had no hold on Christians and are manifestly irrelevant to explaining Christian hostility to gay sexuality" (*CSTH*, 105).

The biblical exegesis of *CSTH* exerted an important influence on the early gay-affirming movement within American Christianity through the writings of gay Christian intellectuals and through the work of gay Christian advocacy groups that began to lobby for changes in church policies regarding homosexuality. In the words of gay theologian Robert Goss,

> Boswell's work initiated serious scholarly discussion of the social context of the biblical texts of terror. . . . What Boswell [and others] precipitated was an apologetic battle for the interpretative control of the biblical text. . . . Perhaps their most important contribution was that they initiated a "biblical Stonewall" rebellion against heterosexist interpretative communities and strengthened the emerging gay/lesbian denominational groups and churches as interpretative communities.[10]

An example of the influence of Boswell's scriptural interpretations can be found in the pioneering work of gay Jesuit theologian and gay-rights activist John J. McNeill, who issued an early call for the rethinking of Roman Catholic positions on homosexuality in his book *The Church and the Homosexual*. McNeill describes the impact of Boswell's scriptural interpretation on his own thinking in these words:

> It was while reading [Boswell's] brilliant scholarly reflections, subsequently published in *Christianity, Social Tolerance, and Homosexuality*, . . . dealing with the loci in the epistles of Saint Paul supposedly concerned with homosexuality, that I first became aware that the traditional scriptural basis for the condemnation of homosexual acts as contrary to the revealed will of God was open to serious question.[11]

In contrast to the often highly critical evaluations of Boswell's biblical exegesis within scholarly circles, members of gay Christian advocacy groups during the 1980s welcomed the scriptural analyses of *CSTH* with enthusiastic approval.[12] For example, an early review of *CSTH* in *Review*, a periodical published by Evangelicals Concerned, described Boswell's book as "the most important of all Christian books on homosexuality" and summarized his interpretation of biblical texts as authoritative.[13] In similar fashion, the Brethren/Mennonite Council for Gay Concerns reported in their newsletter that Boswell had demonstrated that St. Paul's epistles did not, in fact, universally condemn homosexuality,[14] and a 1985 task force appointed by the gay advocacy group Lutherans Concerned/North America (made up of members of the Evangelical Lutheran Church in America [ELCA]) highlighted Boswell as an authority on the interpretation of Pauline scriptural passages regarding homosexuality. Less than a decade after the appearance of this report, Richard

John Neuhaus (a conservative Lutheran pastor who converted to Roman Catholicism in 1990 and became a priest in 1991) lamented the incorporation of Boswell's interpretations of New Testament references to homosexuality in a draft statement on human sexuality issued by an official commission of the ELCA.[15]

Boswell's contention that it was possible to write about gay individuals and gay subcultures in ancient and medieval Christian history was another aspect of *CSTH* that caught the attention of many gay Christians as well as a wide range of scholars from various fields in the 1980s.[16] This notion that gay people had a retrievable history within Christianity that extended back to the early centuries of the church, coupled with the argument advanced in *CSTH* that there was "no general prejudice against gay people among early Christians" (*CSTH*, 135), offered gay Christians not only a sense of a connection with the past but also held out the hope that present-day church leadership might once again adopt an attitude of tolerance with regard to gay people. As ethicist Kathy Rudy summarizes in her book *Sex and the Church: Gender, Homosexuality, and the Transformation of Christian Ethics*: "In his highly influential *CSTH*, Boswell argues that gay people have a recoverable, positive history and a direct lineage with gays who lived in the early Christian church."[17] Donald Messer, in an article tracing the development of theologies of homosexuality, lauds Boswell as well for uncovering "voices and documents from church history demonstrating the possibilities of tolerance or acceptance of gay and lesbian persons and practices," while a 1982 book review of *CSTH* in the prestigious *Journal of Pastoral Counseling* stated that "what has surprised many [about this book] is the proof (beyond measure and doubt) that early Christianity did not condemn homosexuality but looked rather at the quality of love."[18] Finally, the editor of *The Gay Christian*, a theological journal sponsored by the Metropolitan Community Church, wholeheartedly agreed with Boswell's depiction of a tolerant early Christianity and praised *CSTH* because it had provided

> persuasive evidence that the earliest church had nothing to say about homosexuality per se; that none of the most prominent or influential Christian writers considered homosexual attraction "unnatural"; [and] that none of these writers sought to marshal teachings of Jesus or his early followers as objections to physical expression of homosexual feelings.[19]

Particularly noted by many scholars, gay Christians, and their advocates was the claim put forth in *CSTH* that, prior to the dramatic rise in hostility against gay people and other minority groups such as Jews and heretics in the twelfth century, gay people were not the targets of opprobrium by church authorities or theologians. In a personal appearance before a Presbyterian task force on homosexuality in the early 1980s Boswell impressed this audience with his "command of languages, history, biblical interpretation, the church, and theology." His theories on the medieval tolerance of homosexuality, however, had a particular impact on the task force as one observer reported: "We were surprised to learn that homosexuality had been more or less tolerated by Christian society during several periods of history from the early to the medieval church."[20] A southern California gay periodical reported effusively on a public lecture delivered by Boswell in 1983 to an audience at the West Hollywood Presbyterian Church under the headline "Highly Acclaimed Professor Addresses L.A. Gays." Claiming that Boswell had "received a welcome somewhat similar to those usually reserved for teenage heartthrobs," the article's author reported (inaccurately) that Boswell had proved that "Christianity quite comfortably accepted homosexuality" until the eleventh century.[21]

The references in *CSTH* to twelfth-century clerical elites who penned gay poetry (218ff.) and the book's treatment of the Cistercian St. Aelred of Rievaulx (1109–66) as a gay monk whose "erotic attraction to men was a dominant force in his life" (222) revealed a medieval Christian world that appeared to have been remarkably enlightened. In particular, descriptions of a vibrant gay European subculture existing from the mid-eleventh to mid-twelfth centuries (243ff.) amazed many readers of *CSTH*. This idea of a medieval century of conspicuous tolerance which spawned a creative cultural renaissance gave rise to the hope among some theologians that visible and vibrant gay subcultures need not be seen as antagonistic to Christianity. Matthew Fox, a popular author on Christian spirituality and well-known founder of the Center for Creation Spirituality in Oakland, California, directly linked the medieval church's tolerance of homosexuality with a period of "creative rejuvenation" within society at large:

> Boswell's study [has] demonstrated that the most fertile of all Christian periods in the West occurred during the 100-year period from 1050 to 1150 when homosexuality was allowed its space and time and place in society and Church alike. Tolerance becomes the key to creativity not because it is a pious virtue to practice but because its presence indicates a willingness by all citizens of society or Church to *let be*. By letting homosexuals be homosexual, the heterosexual is freed from homophobia and can channel her or his energies into creativity at the same time that the oppressed homosexual is freed to let himself or herself contribute what she/he can to culture's growth and development.[22]

Talk of better days (in both past and future tenses) for gay Christians seemed genuinely possible because of Boswell's argument in *CSTH* that Christianity was not the source of antigay prejudice in history.[23] According to this theory it was not the writings of important individual patristic or medieval theologians that led to the rise of societal intolerance for gay people in the later medieval period; rather, the expansion of absolutist governments interested in regulating more thoroughly the personal lives of their citizens, the development of xenophobic attitudes during and after the crusading period, and a growing hatred of homosexuality and gay people among commoners were the significant factors in the rise of intolerance for gay people. In the above-mentioned 1985 report on homosexuality issued by Lutherans Concerned/North America, Boswell was cited once again as authoritative and his thesis on late medieval intolerance referenced in a call for a reversal of current antigay biases within the church:

> As John Boswell has shown in his definitive study of homosexuality and Christianity, there have been major periods in the history of the church, prior to the twelfth century, when there was considerable acceptance of same-gender love in the Christian community. The contemporary church is the heir of a heterosexual bias which gained ascendancy in the general rise of social intolerance in the thirteenth century. This bias became articulated in late medieval traditions of "natural law," and later, in the Reformation concepts of the "orders of creation." This bias is echoed in all the current Lutheran statements on human sexuality.[24]

In an address delivered to the gay Episcopal group Integrity in August 1980 Boswell spoke at length about past changes to long-held moral positions in Christian history that might serve as a model for the revision of current ecclesiastical policies on homosexuality. In addition, he charged gay Christians in this address to bring about a sea change in church attitudes toward human love and sexuality in general and homosexuality in particular by reviving a historic Christian ethic of love based on what he termed "transcendent love."[25] These two ideas were offered by Boswell to gay Christians in 1980 as the most effective means for changing attitudes toward homosexuality in their churches. Whereas Boswell had claimed in *CSTH* that the book had not been written to advance a specific point of view regarding homosexuality, in this lecture he offered an action plan of sorts by calling for gay Christians to draw upon Christian history to bring about this change.

Boswell detailed several instances from church history in which ecclesiastical officials had altered well-established and seemingly unalterable positions on important moral matters. Using examples such as incest, slavery, and the lending of money at interest, Boswell argued that, in each of these cases, centuries-old church policies had been changed significantly even though it had long seemed impossible that such change could ever take place.[26] In the case of the medieval church's position on incest: complex rules developed over time by church authorities meant that, for many people, it proved extremely difficult to know if one were marrying within the prohibited degrees of relationship (given the poor state of record-keeping in many communities). On the other hand, in places where adequate records were available, the incest laws of the church might well mean that a legitimate marriage would be difficult, if not literally impossible, to arrange given the many types of people (such as far distant cousins) who were considered to be related to each other either by blood or by affinity. As Boswell states, these incest laws "seemed to most Christians of the day to be part of the basic moral code of the Christian religion. It seemed in fact as unchallengeable as sanctions against homosexuality seem to many Christians today. (After all, didn't the Bible forbid incest?)"[27] And yet, church authorities *did* change the longstanding definitions of incest. At the Fourth Lateran Council in 1215 the bishops in attendance drew up a new definition of what constituted incest and, according to Boswell, "admitted two fundamental things which many Christians today would not realize had already been admitted [by church authorities]: sexual laws not specifically uttered by Christ—e.g., those in incest—are 'human statutes'; and these statutes not only can but should change as human circumstances change."[28] In the case of slavery church leaders drew upon basic and long-standing Christian values on the dignity of human persons and the ideals of brotherly love to justify a change in church policy, which had long permitted the holding of humans in bondage; in the case of lending money at interest, fifteenth-century church leaders, realizing that past theological prohibitions on the taking of any amount of interest were interfering greatly with current economic prosperity, greatly revised the church's position on moneylending. As Boswell writes, "the church ingeniously eliminated the whole issue as a matter of moral controversy by simply declaring that all the prohibitions of past centuries applied only to the taking of *excessive* interest, not to the taking of interest itself. That was not true, but it suited the needs of the age perfectly."[29]

Having reminded his audience of the solid historical precedence for profound change on moral issues with Christian tradition, Boswell argued next that current official church policies on homosexuality could, and indeed should, be changed and that such change would be most effectively accomplished through a return to a "transcendent approach" to love and sexuality.

As opposed to a "biological approach" to love and sexuality (which sanctions only sexual activity between husband and wife that is open to the possibility of conception), Boswell contended that the transcendent model constitutes a more authentically Christian approach since the models of love that are most highly prized in the New Testament are not limited to biological considerations such as blood relationship or the production of children. The love which Jesus promoted in the Gospels, for instance, was not a love limited to biological relationships, and the love idealized by Christian monasticism in its views of the religious community as a Christian family was not based on biological relationship but rather on mutual faith and communal love. To quote Boswell: "Voluntary, unconstrained love, fraternal and romantic, was in fact a hallmark of early Christianity, as exemplified not only by pagan admiration for Christian love ('see how these Christians love one another') but by the great popularity among Christians of stories like that of Perpetua and Felicity."[30] These two views of love in Christian history matter significantly for gay people, Boswell concluded, because the biological approach usually condemned homosexual relationships, while the "transcendent [approach] often favored gay affections as exemplifying precisely the sort of voluntary, supra-natural love Christians ought to feel, without biological or legal constraints."[31] Boswell concludes his 1980 Integrity address by calling upon his audience to work toward the reestablishment of a Christian sexual ethic that emphasizes the importance of loving relationships based upon the distinctly Christian ideal of transcendent love because it is this approach to love that will permit the church to sanction same-sex love.

According to Boswell, gay Christians have a particular responsibility to work for the recovery of this transcendent love tradition not only "because theologians and bishops . . . are often the last elements of the church to catch on to advances in moral sensibility,"[32] but because, more significantly, gay persons have a unique contribution to make based on their long history of suffering within the church. This contribution is one in which the suffering of gay people throughout history can effect change in the hearts and minds of others through the distinctly Christian process of redemption. Boswell writes:

> The very special suffering of gay people, the sensitivity and compassion bred of loneliness and isolation, of feeling totally alone, the only one; the strength of character and capacity for fidelity born of the agonizing effort to remain faithful to the church, the parents, the traditions, the friends, the community which persecute and oppress—all of the special courage and understanding and insight afforded gay people by their singular experience in human history—can be redeemed—that is, turned from a sad thing into a glorious

one—by their incorporation into the body of Christ, and through it to the whole human family.[33]

As a historian of Christianity who was himself a committed Christian, John Boswell firmly believed that contemporary negative Christian attitudes toward homosexuality could be changed by appealing to the church's own historical record of tolerance for gay people. In *CSTH* Boswell wrote that he saw the placement of "signposts" for future studies of homosexuality and Christianity as a main and lasting contribution of this book. For many gay Christian readers interested in making their churches more open and accepting of gay people, *CSTH* has indeed contained signposts to guide *present-day* action in this regard. Furthermore, to paraphrase Boswell in a speech quoted above, it has also offered historical weapons for use in the struggle to convince ecclesiastical leaders to embrace more positive attitudes toward gay people. The weaponry of *CSTH* included the contestation of traditional interpretations of biblical passages, the open discussion of gay Christian history, and the insistence that Christianity is not an inherently antigay religion. In his 1980 speech before gay Episcopalians Boswell supplemented this list by describing precisely how he thought gay Christians might effectively use the knowledge of Christian history and their own suffering throughout history in the ongoing struggle to make the church more tolerant of homosexuality and genuinely accepting of gay people.

A true optimist, Boswell believed that Christian attitudes regarding homosexuality could indeed be changed because history showed many instances of a more open stance toward gay people and their sexuality on the part of the church. It was this history, in fact, which Boswell had helped uncover in *CSTH*. Church leaders, however, needed to be taught this history in order to be convinced that their current attitudes are unjust and simply wrong. As Boswell stated in a convention address to fellow gay Catholics in 1979:

> It is possible to change ecclesiastical attitudes toward gay people and their sexuality because the objections to homosexuality are not biblical, they are not consistent, they are not part of Jesus' teaching; and they are not even fundamentally Christian. It is possible because Christianity was indifferent, if not accepting, of gay people and their feelings for a longer period of time than it had been hostile to them. . . . I believe the church's attitude can and must be changed. It has been different in the past and it can be again. . . . I don't think we can afford to be cowardly. We have an abundance of ecclesiastical precedent to encourage the church to adopt a more positive attitude. We must use it.[34]

• *Notes*

1. Letter from an Episcopal bishop to John Boswell (dated 10 July 1981) in a collection of Boswell's papers which include research notes, lecture outlines, personal correspondence, and other materials currently under the care of Professor Ralph Hexter, literary executor of Boswell's estate (hereafter Boswell Papers). The name of the correspondent has been omitted to preserve his anonymity.

2. Letter from a Roman Catholic priest to John Boswell (dated 3 June 1982) in Boswell Papers. The name of the correspondent has been omitted to preserve his anonymity.

3. John Boswell, *Christianity, Social Tolerance and Homosexuality* (Chicago and London: University of Chicago Press, 1980).

4. *CSTH,* back jacket cover.

5. I use the term "gay" in this chapter to refer to both gay men and lesbian women.

6. John Boswell, *Rediscovering Gay History: Archetypes of Gay Love in Christian History.* The Fifth Michael Harding Memorial Address (London: Gay Christian Movement, 1982), 5.

7. Both Dignity USA and The Universal Fellowship of Metropolitan Community Churches were founded in 1968. Integrity was established in 1974, and Evangelicals Concerned was begun in 1975. It should be noted that even today most gay Christian advocacy groups are not officially recognized by the leadership of their respective denominations.

For a brief outline of the American gay Christian movement, see Chris Glaser, "The Love That Dare Not Pray Its Name: The Gay and Lesbian Movement in America's Churches," in *Homosexuality in the Church: Both Sides of the Debate,* ed. Jeffrey S. Siker (Louisville: Westminster John Knox Press, 1994), 153–57. For a brief bibliography of important early theological and pastoral works on the need for more positive Christian attitudes toward homosexuality, consult "Christianity and Homosexuality: An Annotated Bibliography," www.ualberta.ca/ cbidwell/eses/eses-bib.htm.

8. In 1975 the General Synod of the United Church of Christ expressed its support for gays, lesbians, and bisexuals in positions of professional church leadership; in 1977 the General Synod issued a statement which deplored the use of the Bible to generate hatred and deplored the violation of civil rights of gay and bisexual persons. The General Assembly of the Unitarian Universalist Association passed a resolution in 1970 calling for an end to discrimination against homosexuals and bisexuals; in 1973 the General Assembly created a UUA Office of Gay Affairs.

9. Boswell discusses the following "clobber texts" in *CSTH:* Genesis 19; Judges 19:22ff; Leviticus 18:22 and 20:13; 1 Corinthians 6:9; 1 Timothy 1:10; and Romans 1:26–27.

10. Robert Goss, *Queering Christ: Beyond Jesus Acted Up* (Cleveland: Pilgrim Press, 2002), 206–7.

11. John J. McNeill, *The Church and the Homosexual,* rev. ed. (Boston: Beacon Press, 1988), 15–16. Similarly, Letha Scanzoni and Virginia Ramey Mollenkott referred to the importance of Boswell's exegesis in correcting longstanding misinterpretations of biblical texts with regard to homosexuality in their best-selling book *Is the Homosexual My Neighbor? A Positive Christian Response,* rev. ed. (New York: HarperCollins, 1994), 63 and 76. On Boswell's interpretation of Pauline passages see, for example, William Countryman, *Dirt,*

Greed and Sex: Sexual Ethics in the New Testament and Their Interpretation for Today
(Philadelphia: Fortress Press, 1988), 112–13, 118–20, and 128–29.

12. For comprehensive lists of scholarly and popular reviews of *CSTH*, which include
references to scholarly reviews of Boswell's biblical exegesis in *CSTH*, see the Appendix to
chapter 1 above; "Bibliography of Reviews of *Christianity, Social Tolerance, and
Homosexuality*," on the "The Pink Triangle Trust Library" website:
www.galha.org/ptt/lib/hic/bibliography.html; and "Reviews of Boswell's Books" on the
"People With A History" website: http://www.fordham.edu/halsall/pwh/index-bos.html.

13. *Review,* 5, no. 1 (Fall 1980): 1.

14. *Dialogue* 6, no. 2 (Summer 1983): 1–2.

15. Richard John Neuhaus, "In The Case of John Boswell," *First Things* 41 (March 1994):
56.

16. On Boswell's views on the essentialist/constructionist debate among historians of
homosexuality, see his "Concepts, Experience, and Sexuality," in *Que(e)rying Religion: A
Critical Anthology,* ed. Gary David Comstock and Susan E. Henking (New York: Continuum,
1994), 116–29.

17. Kathy Rudy, *Sex and the Church: Gender, Homosexuality, and the Transformation of
Christian Ethics* (Boston: Beacon Press, 1997), 87.

18. Donald E. Messer, "Weaving a Theology of Homosexuality," in *Caught in the
Crossfire: Helping Christians Debate Homosexuality,* ed. Sally B. Geis and Donald E. Messer
(Nashville: Abingdon Press, 1994), 174. Francis H. Touchet, Ph.D., *Journal of Pastoral
Counseling* 17, no. 1 (Spring-Summer 1982): 84–85.

19. "Boswell: A New Standard of Excellence," in *The Gay Christian,* 1980–81: 22.

20. Chris Glaser, *Uncommon Calling: A Gay Man's Struggle to Serve the Church* (San
Francisco: Harper and Row, 1988), 160.

21. Mike Varady, "Highly Acclaimed Professor Addresses L.A. Gays," *Frontiers* (16–23
Nov. 1983): 13.

22. Matthew Fox, "The Spiritual Journey of the Homosexual . . . And Just About
Everybody Else," in *A Challenge to Love: Gay and Lesbian Catholics in the Church,* ed. Robert
Nugent (New York: Crossroad, 1983), 201, 195–96.

23. For criticism of Boswell's thesis that the Christian church was not the cause of
societal intolerance of gay people in Western history, see Warren Johansson, Wayne R.
Dynes, and John Lauritsen, *Homosexuality, Intolerance, and Christianity: A Critical
Examination of John Boswell's Work* (New York: Gay Academic Union, 1981).

24. *A Call for Dialogue: Gay and Lesbian Christians and the Ministry of the Church* (Chicago:
Lutherans Concerned/North America, 1985), 5.

25. John Eastburn Boswell, "A Crucial Juncture: An Address to the 1980 Integrity
Convention," *Integrity Forum* 6, no. 6 (Michaelmas 1980): 1–6.

26. Boswell, "A Crucial Juncture," 1–3.

27. Boswell, "A Crucial Juncture," 2.

28. Boswell, "A Crucial Juncture," 2–3.

29. Boswell, "A Crucial Juncture," 3.

30. Boswell, "A Crucial Juncture," 4.

31. Boswell, "A Crucial Juncture," 4.

32. Boswell, "A Crucial Juncture," 6.

33. Boswell, "A Crucial Juncture," 6.

34. Boswell, "The Church and the Homosexual: An Historical Perspective. Excerpts from the Keynote Address to the Fourth Biennial Dignity International Convention, 1979," on "People With A History" website: www.fordham.edu/halsall/pwh/1979/boswell.html.

CHAPTER 5

"Both as a Christian and as a Historian":
On Boswell's Ministry

Mark D. Jordan

Well before the publication of *CSTH,* John Boswell's scholarship had become a ministry. During August 1976, Boswell spoke in Washington to the General Conference of the Metropolitan Community Churches. He "presented an overview of the relationship of gay people and the Christian church and [he] will soon publish an as-yet-untitled book on this subject."[1] In 1979, he addressed the fourth biennial meeting of Dignity, the most visible organization of queer Catholics. A version of the talk is still posted on the web.[2] By the time *CSTH* appeared, Boswell's popularity with church groups was a cause of complaint among some of his critics.[3] After the book's stunning success, his authority as a religious speaker greatly increased. He began almost immediately to treat the topic of Christian rites for same-sex unions. His 1982 lecture to the Gay Christian Movement (as it was then called) summarized his narrative of Christian intolerance but also forecast his results on the blessing of homoerotic romance. It appeared as a pamphlet.[4] Yet another lecture, and perhaps the best known, was sponsored by the Episcopal group Integrity at the denomination's General Convention in 1988. A minimally produced videotape of that luncheon talk circulated widely.[5] These are only samples of Boswell's engagement with Christian groups or leaders. The archives of his correspondence suggest the fuller span.[6]

In these ministerial texts, Boswell speaks "both as a Christian and as a historian," to quote a phrase from the 1988 lecture. He performs during most of each recorded talk the role of the scholarly expert. He is the witty interpreter of arcane knowledge, the exegete of "boring" manuscripts in "difficult" languages, the indefatigable detective of hidden facts. Another voice appears to frame the talks. When opening and closing, emphasizing or punctuating, Boswell regularly shifts into the role of the Christian teacher leading other Christians. He applies authoritative scholarly results to theological and pastoral issues. He judges and exhorts: "I don't think we can afford to be cowardly. We have an abundance of ecclesiastical precedent to encourage the church to adopt a more positive attitude [toward gay people]. We must use it."[7] These are minister's words.

The ministry is obvious, but its relation to the scholarship is not. Both voices in these marginal, even fugitive texts are witty and fluent, but beyond that they little resemble each other. The first is erudite and professedly dispassionate. The second is passionate and persuasive. Boswell's ministerial presence, even through decaying videotape, seduces after the manner of religious reformers. He is a charismatic, an *erotic* preacher. But the preaching lacks context. There is no defined congregation, no ritual placement, and no approved motive. The ministry, however affecting, does not figure alongside other churchly discourses.

A minister's words without ministerial role—that is the rhetorical puzzle and the real interest of Boswell's talks to church groups. I have no interest in taxing Boswell with the slips or exaggerations that come naturally while extemporizing. I accept as candid Boswell's expression of regret over the decision to speak publicly about same-sex unions while research was still in progress.[8] But I am interested by his description of the motive that pushed him to speak prematurely: "at the time I felt an obligation to share information about the discovery." The obligation appears rhetorically—and I speak only of Boswell's rhetoric, not of his faith or psychological life—as the urgency of a Christian scholar to say what might be both personally consoling and useful to institutional reform. He was moved to his ministry, he suggests, by the chance to offer history to church renewal. Yet the terms in which Boswell makes the offer do not correspond to the church discourses around him.

Boswell's writings have provoked repetitive "secular" controversies over historical method. He was often figured as leader—or poster boy—of "essentialist" gay historians and attacked or defended accordingly. Boswell cared enough about these historiographical debates or his own representation in them to contribute several pieces, both essays and interviews.[9] His religious views have also elicited opposite judgments: he has been adored by queer Christians and quizzed rather aggressively about his Christianity.[10] Sometimes the controversies over method have been linked to the quarrels over his religion, as in the complaint that Boswell's religious motivation led him to commit irremediable historical fallacies or mistakes of interpretation. The complaint misses a more interesting problem: How did Boswell's scholarly project stand in relation to the theology of the church in which he so stubbornly claimed membership? Does the most famous book on Christianity and homosexuality have a coherent theology? Does that matter to its ministerial power?

"The Province of the Historian"

In his books, Boswell writes guardedly about Christian believing. He places his claims under the rubric of history, not of theology or simple faith. The most striking difference between the books and the remarks to church groups is not in qualification or precision. It is true, of course, that the claims in the published version of *Same-Sex Unions* are much more restricted than claims presented earlier to church groups. But the more striking difference is the absence in the books of the voice of the believer. Both of the books on homosexuality take pains to place themselves in "the province of the historian."

In *CSTH*, that province is characterized by its neutrality: "It is . . . the province of the historian not to praise or blame but merely to record and explain. This book is not intended as support or criticism of any particular contemporary points of view—scientific or moral—regarding homosexuality."[11] The historian is no advocate, only a registrar and analyst. Any implications for current Christianity are apparently left for others to draw out. The early book is presented as a contribution to the social history of intolerance—rather than of religion and sexuality, say.[12] Its aim is to show that Christianity cannot be named as the historical cause of intolerance against "gay people." In that sense, it proposes to negate something about Christianity rather than to affirm something of it. Boswell aims to show how little influence Christian theology or Christian belief had on persecution of same-sex acts or dispositions.

In *Same-Sex Unions,* the "province of the historian" is characterized by ethical restraint: "It is not the province of the historian to direct the actions of future human beings, but only to reflect accurately on those of the past" (*SSU*, 281–82). The later book is classed as a contribution to the history of European marriage: "whatever significance the ceremony might (or might not) have for persons living at this juncture of history, its greatest importance lies, along with all the other forms of same-sex union known in premodern Europe, in its role in European history" (*SSU*, 281). Note well: in European history, not in the unfolding life of Christian churches. Here again an element of church life is reassigned, at the decisive moment, to another narrative: the drama of "European history," in which the ceremony had a "role." Boswell ends by claiming to have shown how a Christian rite is subsumed in another history, in a story that is not the liturgy's own.

Many readers have not been persuaded by Boswell's claims only to record and explain, only to reflect accurately. Questions have been raised about his particular interpretations and about his rather old fashioned ideal of the historian as placid mirror. It is worth remembering that Boswell's books and historiographical explanations show him a methodological positivist on many more topics than just sexual orientation. He is faulted for asserting some historical continuity in "gayness" or homoerotic orientation that is evident to common sense. It would be more illuminating to note that he defers to common sense when confronted with a whole range of historiographical questions. From Boswell's books, you would not know that he wrote during decades of divisive debate over the writing of history—especially in regard to discourses of oppression or sexual regulation. To state the obvious: *CSTH* appeared four years after Foucault's *History of Sexuality,* vol. 1, five years after *Discipline and Punish,* and eleven years after the *Archeology of Knowledge.* (Remember that Foucault supplied the only blurb on the back cover of the original edition of *CSTH.*) The same point could be made in terms of the emergence of feminist history or of disputes over the historiography of the Middle Ages.

Before fundamental debates over historiography, Boswell's books keep silent. After repeated readings, the silence remains ambiguous. A reader can imagine Boswell-the-author smiling with common-sense incredulity at the needless complications of theory. After all, history is a matter of discovering and verifying evidence, on its own terms and just so far as it goes. Or one can picture the author as a dogmatic positivist who refuses to waste time on the insoluble. Or one can fantasize "Boswell" as a brilliant antiquarian, an omnivorous philologist, not particularly comfortable with speculative perplexities. (In many ways, *SSU* is an extended telling of what it took to produce the critical edition of a short liturgical text.) A reader can project into the books' silence over historical theory either disdain or discomfort, but they would be equally projections. Boswell's authorial voice presents itself as wishing to practice "the normal skills of the historian" without commenting on the fact that the norms are under siege.

So it seems during most of the reading. At other moments, in other passages, there are hints that the "province of the historian" is for Boswell an elegant façade, a Baroque stage set. The symmetrical face of the normal historian suddenly seems an ironic mask. A reader can begin to suspect irony especially around religious motives. In *CSTH,* for example, the claim that intolerance against "gay people" cannot be explained by appeal to religious teaching requires a curious form of spiritual discernment: "careful analysis can almost always differentiate between conscientious application of religious ethics and the use of religious precepts as justification for personal animosity or prejudice" (*CSTH*, 7). Boswell proposes the test of consistency: If a person insists on religious rules in one area but flouts them in others, the motive in the first case cannot be considered religious. Of course, everything hangs by the word "conscientious" and the (Christianized) notion of religious intention that it implies.[13] To define a religion only in terms of consistent and "conscientious" ethical practice—or, for that matter, the philological reconstruction of the original meaning of canonical texts—is to espouse a specific theology of religious practice. The theology is not exclusively Christian, but for readers inhabiting the remnants of Christendom it is recognizably so. It is the Spirit of intention rather than the Letter of historical practice. It is the purity of the Lord's teaching rather than the sin of church reception. Is this passage from *CSTH*, then, a sort of wink at the Christian reader? Does Boswell deploy the normal historian as a Kierkegaardian pseudonym—without the dialectic?

The reader finds more disconcerting passages in the later book. For *SSU*, the final characterization of the "province of the historian" is preceded by a church story and followed by the surprising invocation of a church author. To a strategic objection from "a well-known prelate," Boswell says that he replied, "I had not composed the same-sex unions ceremony that seems to parallel heterosexual marriage, but only discovered it, and felt it my duty as a historian to share it" (*SSU*, 281). The duty of the historian trumps the prelate's implicit claim on Boswell's Christian prudence. But a few lines later, in support of his characterization of the historian's work, Boswell quotes not von Ranke or Febvre, not Stubbs or Stone, but C. S. Lewis, an author now chiefly identified with Christian apologetics. Another wink? Boswell puts on the mask of the historian to deflect the prelate, but lets the mask slip for the faithful reader.

The winks in the books can be deciphered by turning to the less guarded lectures before church groups. The informal lectures appear to enact rhetorical purposes to which the books can only allude. The lectures regularly suppose that securing certain facts of church history will assist theology or church life in the present. The claim is put bluntly in the peroration to the 1979 talk that I began to quote above: "We have an abundance of ecclesiastical precedent to encourage the church to adopt a more positive attitude. We must use it. . . . These statements came from the Christian community, from Christian faith. That community can and must be reminded of its former beliefs, its former acceptance. And we must do the reminding." Recovered church history provides a precedent to move the church (that is, some churches) away from intolerance. For those within the church, ecclesiastical precedent has not only legal force but the sharp tug of memory. "We must do the reminding." We must remind, because the memories are somehow already ours. The sound of exhortation is clear, but the "we" is not. Given that the audience is a convention of Dignity, "we" must be something like queer Catholics (or their supporters) who are now instructed in (reminded of?) a suppressed piece of church history. But "we" must also be those for whom "ecclesiastical precedent" has the force of binding memory: we have a relation to church history that makes its facts imperative. Indeed, we claim that history as our history—despite questions of historical continuity. Its facts are our facts. As Boswell says a few lines earlier, "It is possible to change ecclesiastical attitudes toward gay people and their sexuality because the objections to homosexuality are not biblical, they are not consistent, they are not part of Jesus' teaching; and they are not even fundamentally Christian." The norm of Christianity is not so much consistency as the binding fact of Jesus' teaching recorded in the Christian Bible. Queer Catholics are bound not only to remind, but to remember.

Boswell lays out this logic more fully in the 1988 talk sponsored by Integrity. Nine years have passed and the topic has become more specific, but the rhetorical frame is the same. The logic appears first in regard to the liturgy: "For Roman Catholics, it's going to be very interesting when I publish this material, because Catholics recognize what is called the *lex orandi,* the law of the prayers of the church. The prayers of the church are thought to embody truth in the same way as the *magisterium* [or teaching authority] of the church." A little later, he repeats the point more jocularly: "Suppose the present pontiff of the Roman Catholic church wanted to say, 'Well, yes, there clearly can be a marriage between two persons of the same sex'—I mean, what's he going to say, there are hundreds of these [manuscript copies] in the Vatican. . . ." The assumption seems to be that liturgical precedents bind the papal *magisterium* in some unequivocal fashion. Further on in the lecture, Boswell appeals to vaguer notions: "After all, in your communion [Anglican] as in mine [Roman Catholic] one of the things we value is the weight of tradition. We don't want to be crushed by it, but we enjoy the strength of having a great tradition behind us." Yet Boswell represents tradition straightforwardly as binding precedent. In the 1988 question period, he is asked when the church suppressed the rite of same-sex unions. He narrates a broad increase in social disapproval of homosexuality, but then adds that the rite "has never been officially suppressed by Rome"—as if the absence of a specific decree to the contrary had left the precedent intact.

In 1988, Boswell imagined a dialogue in which his discovery of historical manuscripts would compel the pope to concede that there could be Christian marriages between two men and two women. We have in fact some specimens of Vatican reaction to *SSU*. Shortly after the book was published, the Catholic News Service reported derogatory remarks about it by the Jesuit Robert Taft, eminent scholar of Orthodox liturgy and longtime consultant to Vatican offices. Taft is quoted as saying that Boswell's book is "just plain bull[shit]." "What's correct [in the book] is not new, and what's new is not correct. . . . There is nothing in the texts of the rituals themselves that would allow this kind of interpretation."[14] A few years later, the Vatican newspaper, *L'Osservatore Romano,* ran an officially encouraged series of articles on homosexuality, with separate essays on scriptural teaching, historical evidence, and contemporary claims for same-sex unions.[15] Boswell is never mentioned by name, but a number of his claims are rejected, more or less directly.[16] The essay on Christian friendship makes no mention of ambiguous rites, but ends by expressing "perplexity at some literary and cinematic attempts to raise the suspicion of homosexuality with regard to the great figures of Christian antiquity and the fundamental experiences that have resulted from the Gospel message."[17] Even if Boswell's reading of Byzantine liturgy had been unassailable (and it is not), anyone familiar with Vatican responses to rebellious claims could have predicted that official or quasi-official responses would be denials, either by thunder or by condescending silence.

Boswell's imaginary dialogue with the pope looks like another instance of willed naïveté. It is not true, for example, that the undisputed existence of a rite binds present teaching or worship. In the prevailing Roman Catholic theology, the meaning of rites—like the meaning of the scriptures—is determined by church authority, not historical scholarship. Doctrinal or liturgical history is precisely not the "province of the historian." What gets counted as part of the history of Christian "tradition" is itself a matter for official determination. A doctrine or practice can be judged heretical or marginal. A widespread belief or ritual can be set aside as a deviation, while a single passage or custom can be emphasized beyond its historical prominence as a forerunner of later "developments." The point has been driven home in recent years precisely on liturgical topics. In November 2000, the Congregation for the Doctrine of the Faith issued an "Instruction," that is, an itemized condemnation, of elements in the liturgical historiography of Reinhard Messner.[18] It notes the difficulty of comparing Messner's scholarship, which employs modern historical terminology, with the classical formulae of the "tradition," but then it proceeds to condemn the notion that historical scholarship may discover contradictions between liturgical history and perennial doctrine (thesis 9).

More emphatically, the Congregation asserts that "liturgical rites recognized by the Church are . . . normative expressions of the faith, in which there is made manifest the apostolic tradition of the Church" (thesis 8). The meaning of apostolic tradition is settled by the successor of the chief apostle. So much for any disconcerting discoveries in liturgical history.

Boswell must have known that the role of historical evidence in theology has been a neuralgic point for Catholic thought during the whole of the modern period, but especially since the middle of the nineteenth century. To stake a historical claim is not the end of a conversation about Catholic tradition. It is barely the beginning—and a stigmatized beginning, at that.

"Critical Methods"

Papal condemnations of independent historical scholarship could be traced back to the Reformation and beyond, but the most remarkable series begins around the middle of the nineteenth century. The condemnations reached their administrative apex in the rejection of "Modernism" and the establishment of a bureaucracy of surveillance to insure its extinction. The encyclical *Pascendi dominici gregis* issued by Pius X in 1907 presents a composite portrait of the Modernist as an intellectual type or species committed to three principles: Agnosticism, Immanentism, and Evolutionism. The three principles combine in various inferences, including a "historico-critical" method that distinguishes sharply between science and history on one side and faith on the other.[19] The historical method of the Modernists, as described by the encyclical, is not historical method simply. The Modernists are represented as philosophical dogmatists first and historical critics only second. Still the encyclical implies that much neutral scholarship of religious history is in fact beholden to agnostic philosophy whether it knows it or not.

The sense of the encyclical was specified through a list of Modernist errors prepared, with papal approval, by the forerunner of the Congregation for the Doctrine of the Faith: the Office of the Roman and Universal Inquisition. A number of the errors it reproves refer to claims on behalf of historical scholarship.[20] So the policing of Modernism became in fact a policing of historical method—especially in sensitive areas, such as biblical studies, dogmatic theology, canon law, and liturgy. The mechanisms of surveillance were condensed in an oath that was required of priests, religious, and seminary teachers, among others. The oath includes these clauses:

> I also reject the error of those who say that the faith held by the Church can contradict history, and that Catholic dogmas, in the sense in which they are

now understood, are irreconcilable with a more realistic view of the origins of the Christian religion. I also condemn and reject the opinion of those who say that a well-educated Christian assumes a dual personality—that of a believer and at the same time of a historian, as if it were permissible for a historian to hold things that contradict the faith of the believer. . . . Furthermore, I reject the opinion of those who hold that a professor lecturing or writing on a historico-theological subject . . . should then interpret the writings of each of the Fathers solely by scientific principles, excluding all sacred authority, and with the same liberty of judgment that is common in the investigation of all ordinary historical documents.[21]

It is as if the Modernist oath were written precisely to condemn Boswell's double voice.

To say that Boswell's method much resembles Modernism hardly shames him. It places him in distinguished theological company. Some of the last century's most admired Catholic theology consists of efforts to retrieve what was legitimate in the projects condemned as Modernism. The efforts can be traced in many fields: the growth of Catholic biblical scholarship animated by modern methods; the liturgical movement's efforts to purify worship by restoring older rites, chants, and artistic styles; even the historical wing of neo-Thomism, which wanted less to refute relativism with slogans snipped from Thomas than to read him well in historical context.

Some of the theologians most associated with these historical projects were aware of their connections to Modernism. The French Dominican Yves Congar wrote in private documents about the need to retrieve Modernism's legitimate requests.[22] One of them is "to apply critical methods to the Christian fact, which presents itself as a historical fact."[23] "The great intellectual problem that is put to the Church in modern times is to open itself to the double discovery and the double request that characterize these modern times, and these are: (1) the formulation of the point of view of the subject, of the power of creation and relation that there is in the subject; (2) the point of view of development, of history."[24] The great intellectual problem of the modern Church is, in other words, to rethink the anti-Modernist campaign.

The best-known historical efforts in doctrine were dubbed "the new theology." One of its tenets was set forth by a manifesto in these terms: "[The Fathers of the Church] are not only true witnesses to a state of things in the past; they are also the most actual nourishment for men of today, because we find in them precisely a certain number of categories that are those of contemporary thought and that were lost by Scholastic thought."[25] If the slogan of papally sponsored neo-Thomism had been to increase and complete the old by means of the new (*vetera novis augere et perficere*), the slogan of the "new theology" would have to be: the old is transfigured in the new. To quote another manifesto: "One never turns back through the flow of time. Our faith is not old, it is not a thing of the past: it is eternal, and always new."[26]

The "new theology," together with its predecessors and fellow travelers, was hardly welcomed with open arms. If its proponents recognized among themselves a certain relation to Modernism, so too did its opponents. In France alone, reaction to the rehabilitation of critical history contributed to purges at a renowned house of studies in 1942, within the French Jesuits during 1950, and across the French Dominicans by 1954. Because so many theologians affiliated with the new theology later played crucial roles at the second Vatican Council in the early 1960s, many felt that the program as a whole had been vindicated. In retrospect, the Council itself appears increasingly as only a slight interruption of longer patterns in the centralization of church control. There are still purges, and it often seems that they are likely to get worse. The condemnation of Messner in 2000 echoes in uncanny ways charges against the "new" theologians in the 1940s and 1950s.

Recalling these scattered events and bits of text, I hardly mean to tell a satisfying story about the progress or regress of Catholic thought. I am trying to suggest only how much the question of history has been at the center of quarrels over method in Catholic theology. To recall those quarrels raises new questions about Boswell's historical project. If some of his passages sound astonishingly like representations of Modernism, the explanation cannot be that Boswell is beholden to the revision of Modernism in the new theology or related projects. Boswell is precisely not a new theologian. He does not evince an interest in contemporary "Continental" philosophy. He is not evidently engaged in contesting the certainties of Scholastic manuals. Most of all, he is not committed to the sense that the contemporary church is curiously anticipated or evoked by the patristic or medieval. In *SSU* and more forcefully in the 1988 lecture for Integrity, Boswell explicitly rejects the notion that the union ceremony provides a model for contemporary Christians. Speaking to Dignity, Boswell does suggest a certain resonance between the old rite and contemporary concerns: "from my own point of view, both as a Christian and as a historian, the gay marriage ceremony [in the manuscripts] is actually much closer to modern sensibilities about what marriage is." But the remark is made just in order to argue that the old rite offers "one of the richest ways I can think of for looking at [the] theological implications" of heterosexual marriage.[27]

On what terms can history be rich for theological reflection? If not the terms of neo-Thomism or of the new theology, what exactly? The clearest answer I know in Boswell's ministry to religious groups comes from the 1982 lecture in London. Boswell begins the lecture with the gesture of autobiographical disclosure: "Part of the reason that I'm a scholar . . . is that knowledge is one of the best weapons one has to fight the forces of evil. . . . I often think of myself as a weapons-maker: that is, I'm trying to produce the knowledge that people can then use in social struggles."[28] The example he gives of a weapon is *CSTH,* and the evil it is supposed to fight is . . . what exactly? Boswell provides more autobiography. It suggests that the evil is social intolerance rather than Christian principle. When the intolerance claims to be Christian, it shows itself ignorant of church history. Yet if, underneath it all, the intolerance is social and not Christian, knowing more about church history will not correct it. Removing a misconceived reason for a disposition need not affect the disposition itself. A bigot once convinced of a historical mistake may then embrace bigotry more candidly. If *CSTH* is a weapon against an evil based on ignorance, the evil must not be social intolerance, but mistaking for Christian something that is not. That sort of mistake becomes an evil only for Christian faith. It may be an intellectual fault to make a historical mistake about a religion, but the mistake can be called "evil" only if being right or wrong about that religion is a matter of great moral significance. Mistaking what is not Christian for what is Christian in history is a matter of great moral significance principally in the eyes of Christians. *CSTH* serves as a weapon against evil for Christians who need to distinguish the social from the evangelical. It is a sword of truth that cuts away counterfeit Christianities.

Of course, that is not what Boswell says at the opening of the 1988 lecture. In his first sentences, he describes himself as forging the weapons of knowledge "that people can then use in *social* struggles." A few paragraphs later, he insists, "I am not commenting in my book or here as a theologian on the most accurate way of understanding those [scriptural] passages now."[29] But what Boswell says and what he does are not always the same—even in a single lecture. A few minutes later, he is discussing the perceived tensions between being "gay" and being Christian. He calls for a Christian ethic of homosexuality and insists that it is not to be found in "the Christian tradition on heterosexual relations."[30] He has rendered a decisive theological judgement. In the peroration, he calls on the audience to "labour to correct [the] misprision" that "gay people" have no place in romantic love and that "they are not part of the tradition of Christian ethics."[31] To say that same-sex desire has been and should be "part of the tradition of Christian ethics" is another theological claim. To read the Byzantine rite as an expression of gay love is a liturgical one. Each carries great moral significance for Christians in traditional and liturgical communions. Each has only a limited value in "social struggles" outside the churches. The claims and others like them can be used to remove the scrim of Christian justification from injustice—but, according to Boswell, the injustice has never really been Christian at any time. It is not clear, then, what effect removing Christian pretexts will have on the causes or effects of injustice. As an armorer, Boswell may be of some preparatory help to secular social movements, but he is most needed by Christians. His weapons cut best against false doctrine. His exhortations call for a new theology.

The call brings forward the persistent difficulty: Boswell's rhetorical position does not fit within the discourses Catholic theology, whether papal or reformist. He gives no account of the relation of historical discovery to the development of doctrine or present church authority. He denies that he has theological motives, but then his main argument depends on a theological distinction between true Christianity and its social deformations. He insists that the recovered union rite is not a ritual or ethical prescription for the present, but then he offers it as a starting point for a new ethics—and eventually translates it in language suitable for use at a high-church altar.

I have tried on various readings to get through such contradictions. The one that has appealed to me most over the years is the one I hinted at earlier: Boswell must be using the mask of the social historian to prepare for a theological program. As he says in the London lecture, Boswell knows full well that the manners of elite scholarship discourage any fervent avowal of Christianity. If he is to be taken seriously as a social historian, he must be coy about his Catholicism. As a gay Catholic, he wants to minister to those who suffer from what they consider Christian condemnation of sexual difference. But that ministry will require his having prestige as a social historian. So he writes books of social history in which Christian faith or theological implications appear rarely and mainly as hints. The appeal to social movements is sincere and yet coded, because the movement of most interest to the books is the movement within Christianity. On this reading, "John Boswell," the author of books, is a Kierkegaardian pseudonym for "John Boswell," minister to disenfranchised Christians. The first, the politely secular social historian, is a cunningly limited figure who must give way for careful readers to the latter, the Catholic advocate.

The problem with this reading is just the second pseudonym, the minister behind the mask. When Kierkegaard lays aside his pseudonyms (if he ever really does), the Christian faith he writes out is more ironic and dialectical than what has preceded it. In Boswell, by contrast, the faith behind the mask of social history appears to possess the (alleged) simplicity of a social fact. It is as fixed as a discovered manuscript. In this way, Boswell's texts exhibit a not unfamiliar partition between highly formed expert knowledge and an uncomplicated, curiously private faith. The same split can often be detected in modern Catholic philosophy: an extraordinary technical elaboration is thrown up around the earnest profession of formulae learned in childhood or adolescence. The problem comes when the author tries to deliver the expert results to wider church conversations. It may be possible to keep internal peace between expertise about Christianity or its history and a protected naïveté about theology. The peace breaks down as soon as the duality is offered up to theological conversation. Those in authority are likely to find the expertise insufficiently submissive, while theologians not in authority are likely to find it not entirely pertinent. Facts about Christianity, however unexpected or exciting, do not by themselves always signify for theological conversation.

The nested hypotheses are not a psycho-biography. They are my attempts as a reader to make sense of tensions in Boswell's texts. They may not resemble in the slightest his conscious intentions while writing (so far as conscious authorial intentions are decisive for readers). Certainly the reception of Boswell's books implies something like these hypotheses. The books operate powerfully on many Christian readers as if social history were the handmaid, not of theology, but of a settled and private faith.

"A New Savior"

I do not need archival files to prove the effectiveness of John Boswell's ministry to queer Christians. I can testify of my own knowledge. As someone who often speaks to Christian groups about homosexuality, as someone who gets typed as one of Boswell's vicars since his death, I will swear to his persistent presence among middle-aged and older Christians who are also gay (and I use that word as distinguished from lesbian). In the mid-1990s, *SSU* spawned a sub-genre of religious art that included medallions and holy cards of Sts. Serge and Bacchus. I wondered how long it would be before there would be icons of "St. John Boswell" in the delightful and deeply pious series that already offers "St. Harvey Milk."

I write those words without cynicism. Boswell as a figure—if not quite as an author—has offered consolation to many thousands tormented by conflicts between faith and desire. The consolation was not a new theology or pastoral practice or ritual (however much Boswell might have thought that the recovered rite for couples would be adapted). The consolation came from knowing that an eminent professor proved that "the church didn't always persecute us" and that "the church used to let us get married." The two facts are not so much readings of Boswell as tenets affixed to Boswell's authority, to Boswell as icon. Faith in these facts continues to be widespread. It has been promoted not so much by Boswell's books themselves as by news accounts, religious newsletters, websites, and other popularizations. The faith is mostly unshakable. In my experience, church groups are not eager for news about critiques of Boswell.

The power of these two facts over many lives begs for explanations. No single one could cover the range of cases, of course, and any combination of explanations would be at best a rough indication of the forces at play. Still a reader puzzled by Boswell's method or form of argument cannot keep from asking why it proved so persuasive. It is not enough to say that Boswell became a celebrity and that celebrity is its own justification, in churches or academia as on daytime television. Boswell's persisting celebrity in Catholic circles is tied specifically to a faith in two facts. The question remains: Why has faith in historical discoveries about church history proved so consoling?

The search for answers leads off in many directions. You can look to some peculiarities of American Catholicism, which has tended historically to neglect theological nuance in favor of simple propositions, quick obedience, and ethnic solidarity. For such Catholicism, solid facts count even (or especially) in the absence of theological context. It would be even better to have the solid facts delivered by an expert to whom one could assent. Having a professor from Yale explain church history—it's almost like having a Jesuit teach you moral theology. Or you can wonder about the way in which all American Christianity conforms in the end to the model of low-church Protestantism. In a country that figures Christianity as picking up your Bible to verify verses when the preacher expounds them, an argument that invites direct verification in church texts is potent indeed. It is as if Boswell delivered the unexpurgated scriptures into your hands: "Here, check it out for yourself." Of course, almost no one does check it out. *CSTH* and, to a lesser extent, *SSU* are talismans more than books. People own them much more often than they read them, because mere possession is enough to allow one to benefit from the results.

Other explanations could be sought in the longstanding tension between religious and antireligious queer politics. With considerable hyperbole, and not a little vitriol, John Lauritsen wrote in 1981: "It is not surprising that Professor Boswell has been enthusiastically hailed by the gay Christians to whom he appears as a new Savior who will rescue them not only from queer-hating religionists, but from gay liberation secularists as well."[32] What is true in this sentence is that Boswell's fame appeared for the moment to vindicate queer Christians by making Christianity central in queer history as a positive force. After all, Lauritsen is not the only one to speak contemptuously of gays and lesbians who try to remain Christians. The place of Christians in queer liberation has been a divisive topic since at least the 1960s. Boswell showed not only that you could be queer and Christian, but that queer Christians mattered for the movement.

Another line of thinking would turn from American religion to American uses of history. Carolyn Dinshaw has shown how the general reception of *CSTH* fits with expectations about how history can confer cultural legitimacy in the American present.[33] Her analysis applies as well, I think, to many of Boswell's Catholic readers. Many of them believe that Boswell's history has conferred legitimacy on them. Underneath the foreign languages and exotic locales, history shows that there have been Catholics just like us long ago and far away. I have tried to show already that this kind of historical reasoning has little to do with Catholic theological method, but it may have a lot to do with what Nietzsche calls "monumental history": it is history that reassures hearers about the stability and grandeur of their identities.[34] Boswell's scholarship is Catholic in the sense that it claims continuity with the Latin-speaking churches, but not in the sense that it adheres to distinctively Catholic methods of critical historical theology. Its method is thoroughly monumental.

I suspect that the most interesting explanations of Boswell's importance for queer Catholics, if not for other Christians, will be found in the logic of church secrecy. Both of Boswell's "gay" books and all of his published lectures to church groups fall into the genre of startling revelations. They disclose secrets from the past that are enforced in the present. The two truths ascribed to Boswell capture the disclosures. "The church didn't always persecute us, even though we have always been told otherwise." "The church used to let us get married, even though everyone denies it." These secrets about same-sex desire resonate with the whole range of Catholic secrets about sex: sex as a confessional secret, sex as a disavowed act, sex as a hidden crime. Church secrets have clustered most thickly around same-sex desire.

It is tempting to call this "the closet," but the metaphor regularly misleads by suggesting that the secrets are spatial or visual. They are above all auditory: they are rhetorical devices and effects. In his ministerial talks, Boswell's revelation of church secrets is accompanied by a plea that his hearers should be allowed to keep secrets. To use the spatial metaphors: he "outs" segments of church history in order to "closet" queer sex in the present. Boswell ends his imagined conversation with the pope by arguing that the sexual activity between members of a same-sex couple should be a confessional matter. "If the Holy Father wanted to say, 'You know, you should talk to your confessor about whether to have sex or not and we think it's not a good thing, but we will recognize you as a couple, and it's not really the public's business whether you have sex or not'—all right."[35] In the earlier talk for the Gay Christian Movement, he tries to restore ambiguity around same-sex copulations by de-eroticizing romance. "The final [Christian] ideal I'd like to mention is what we call romantic love. I should point out here that in calling it 'romantic' rather than 'erotic' or 'sexual' I am begging the question of whether it entails a physical component or not."[36] Sex is set aside partly in deference to gaps in historical evidence and partly because it is not "a crucial issue." The telling of same-sex secrets from church history authorizes the keeping of secrets in the churches' present.

The cut here between public (church) approval and private (Christian) sex calls back to mind the cut between social facts and true Christianity. Christians who claimed they were persecuting homosexuals for religious reasons were in fact motivated by social forces. Real faith was elsewhere. Christian couples can be blessed without its being the "public's business" what will happen afterwards. Sex is elsewhere. Do real faith and sex occupy the same protected space in Boswell's authorships? It would be tempting to think so, but something like the opposite is actually the result. Faith and sex end up in opposite corners. The analogy is in the cut, not the resulting topography. What the reader recognizes in both the historical defense of Christianity and the plea for private sex is the retorsional logic of the cut that severs something important from its public manifestations. Repressed parts of church history are used as precedent to argue that other parts of church history are not in fact churchly, are not truly Christian. Forgotten Christian liturgies for blessing couples now stigmatized on account of their sex are used to argue that those couples need not now disclose their sex to the church. Erased facts are made public so that other facts—of faith, of sex—may be kept appropriately private. Real Christianity is not the publicly authorized Christianity. The reality of sex need not be publicly discussed—especially when the church blesses. And yet faith is not sex.

The logic of the cut in Boswell harmonizes faith with sex by reserving both from public representation. I suspect that this logic is one of the reasons for the deep appeal of Boswell's work to so many gay Christians, especially Catholics. In many queer Catholic circles, one encounters men who want to worship in communities that approve their sexuality without considering its theological implications or moral consequences. They want the wound of official condemnation to be healed, but they also want a recognizably Roman liturgy celebrated by a "real" priest. I refuse to mock their desire for healing, but I notice that they do not want to be healed from the deepest cut, the one that encapsulates sex and faith to protect both—not least, from each other. Boswell is understood to say that it is just fine to be gay and Christian, but you must know what you mean by each and you must not let either be deformed by history. Certainly gayness will not be constructed by Catholicism—nor, *a fortiori*, Catholicism by gayness.

Whether I am right about the appeal of the cut in Boswell's two voices, the segregation of faith and sex from each other in his authorship limits his present usefulness for any constructive theology of sexuality. Christian queer theologies do deplore (with Foucault) the sovereignty of discourses about sex, but they do so on their way to disrupting settled notions about sexual orientation, categories for the analysis of acts, sources of sacraments or liturgies, and central creedal formulae. The task of most queer theologies is precisely to overcome Boswell's logic of the cut, so that faith and church practice, in all their mutations, cannot but confront sex, in all its ephemeral varieties. Christianity and queerness reconstruct each other.

Randolph Trumbach once noted perceptively that *CSTH* never did "have much of an impact on either the moral theologians or the church hierarchy." He then predicted that the fate of *SSU* would be different: its evidence is "of such importance that it will require every serious moral theologian and bishop to listen carefully."[37] I can only take the prediction as a gesture of respect for Boswell's unremitting labors. Boswell held with superb tenacity to historical evidence that has long been manipulated by hostile institutions. He insisted on ideals of historical honesty that vanish early in most church debates. So I am happy to join in the gesture of respect. But Trumbach's prediction must be a utopian vision of another Catholic church—a church that might have been. Under the present Catholic regime, the idea of bishops embracing Boswell is charming—and fantastical. Or else the prediction is really an ameliorating memory, an alternate past. Certainly Boswell's most devoted readers are aging. Like so many epochal ministries, his teaching depended on a celebrated presence, on media buzz, on word-of-mouth transmission. Boswell himself was lost to the plague. The media move weekly to new topics about sex and religion. Gay groups falter when it comes time to transmit culture across generational lines. Dignity today is something much less hopeful than Dignity in 1982.

Of course, church time is hardly linear. Scriptures, doctrines, and rites are endlessly repeated. Every year, students appear in my office asking about golden periods of church tolerance or rediscovered medieval rites for gay weddings. In a space it has cut out for itself, the ministry continues—as a retreating secret.

· *Notes*

1. Herm Mank, in the second of two reports under the title "General Conference '76," *Christian Circle* [MCC San Francisco] 2, no. 8 (September 1976): 11.

2. See John Boswell, "The Church and the Homosexual: An Historical Perspective, 1979."

3. John Lauritsen, *"Culpa ecclesiae:* Boswell's Dilemma," in *Homosexuality, Intolerance and Christianity: A Critical Examination of John Boswell's Work,* Gai Saber Monograph 1 (2d enlarged ed., New York: The Scholarship Committee, Gay Academic Union / New York City, 1985), 16–22, at 16. This edition reprints the pages of the first edition from 1981 and then appends a bibliography of reviews (23–34). The original edition was based on papers Warren Johansson, Wayne Dynes, and Lauritsen presented at a forum held on 14 September 1980. A further revision was published on the web in September 2003 at http://www.galha.org/ptt/lib/hic/.

4. John Boswell, *Rediscovering Gay History: Archetypes of Gay Love in Christian History,* Michael Harding Memorial Address 5 (London: Gay Christian Movement, 1982).

5. *1500 Years of Blessing Gay and Lesbian Relationships: It's Nothing New to the Church,* videocassette, produced by James Przeslowski, 1988. The title of the tape is not the same as the title assigned to the talk by the organizers—which Boswell disclaims in the lecture itself. This tape may also be one of the unauthorized tapes about which Boswell complains at *Same-Sex Unions in Premodern Europe* (New York: Villard Books, 1994), x: "several were videotaped and sold or distributed without my authorization."

6. See Carolyn Dinshaw, *Getting Medieval: Sexualities and Communities, Pre- and Postmodern* (Durham and London: Duke University Press, 1999), especially 24–28, and the essay by Bernard Schlager in this volume.

7. Boswell, "The Church and the Homosexual," paragraph 19.

8. Boswell, *Same-Sex Unions,* x.

9. John Boswell, "Revolutions, Universals, Categories," *Salmagundi* 58–59 (Fall 1982–Winter 1983): 89–113, rpt. Martin Bauml Duberman, Martha Vicinus, and George Chauncey, eds., *Hidden From History* (New York: New American Library, 1989), 17–36, with notes below; idem, "Concepts, Experience, and Sexuality," *Differences* 2 (1990): 67–87; Lawrence Mass, "Sexual Categories, Sexual Universals: An Interview with John Boswell," *Christopher Street* 151 (1990): 23–40.

10. For an example of quizzing, see the interview by Richard Hall, "Historian John Boswell on Gay Tolerance and the Christian Tradition," *The Advocate,* 28 May 1981, 20–23, 26–27.

11. John Boswell, *Christianity, Social Tolerance and Homosexuality: Gay People in Western Europe from the Beginning of the Christian Era to the Fourteenth Century* (Chicago: University of Chicago Press, 1980), xv.

12. Boswell, *CSTH,* 4: "This study is offered as a contribution to better understanding of both the social history of Europe in the Middle Ages and intolerance as a historical force, in the form of an investigation of their interaction in a single case."

13. The word occurs in the same context in the 1982 lecture: "I began to conclude that modern hostility towards homosexuality was probably not the result of a conscientious programme of Christian morality" (*Rediscovering Gay History*, 6).

14. Jerry Filteau, "Comic Strip Draws Attention to Gay Advocacy History Book," *Catholic News Service*, 10 June 1994. Those who know Robert Taft will appreciate that the "colorful" language is typical. It implies no special animus against Boswell.

15. The series was entitled "Antropologia cristiana e omosessualità" and it appeared in *L'Osservatore Romano* irregularly from 1 March to 23 April 1997. The weekly English edition of the *Osservatore* ran a translation under the series title "Christian Anthropology and Homoseuxality" from the issue of 11–12 March to that of 18 June 1997.

16. The clearest reference comes in Romano Penna, "Homosexuality and the New Testament," *L'Osservatore Romano* [weekly English ed.], 2 April 1997, 6–7. Penna argues, for example, that *arsenokoitai* in 1 Tim. 1:9–10 cannot possibly be interpreted "in the restricted sense of only male prostitution, or more specifically, of pederasty, *as some would like*" (6, emphasis added). Again, with regard to Romans 1:18–32, "*some authors* have tried to minimize the radical importance of this condemnation, claiming that Paul is thinking . . . of homosexuality that is contrary to the proper nature of heterosexuals" (6, emphasis added). Compare Boswell, *CSTH*, 344–45 and 109, respectively.

17. Vittorino Grossi, "Sexuality and Friendship in Early Christianity," *L'Osservatore Romano* [weekly English ed.], 9 April 1997, 10–11, at 11.

18. Congregation for the Doctrine of the Faith, "Notification on Certain Publications of Prof. Dr. Reinhard Messner" (30 November 2000), as in *Acta Apostolicae Sedis* 93 (2001): 385–403.

19. See, for example, Pius XI, *Pascendi dominici gregis* (On the Errors of the Modernists, 8 September 1907), para. 18 and 30, though many other passages would make the point just as clearly.

20. Holy Roman and Universal Inquisition, *Lamentabili sane exitu* (Syllabus Condemning the Errors of the Modernists, 3 July 1907).

21. Pius X, *Oath against Modernism* (1 September 1910).

22. Yves Congar, *Journal d'un théologien (1946–1956)*, ed. Étienne Fouilloux with Dominique Congar, André Duval, and Bernard Montagnes (Paris: Cerf, 2001), 59–60 (from "Mon témoignage") and 70 (Roman travel journal).

23. Congar, *Journal*, 59.

24. Congar, *Journal*, 70.

25. Jean Daniélou, "Les orientations présentes de la pensée religieuse," *Études* (April 1946): 5–21, at 10. This particular manifesto set off a round of replies and counter-replies. For an account in English, see Aidan Nichols, "Thomism and the *Nouvelle Théologie*," *The Thomist* 64 (2000): 1–19.

26. Henri de Lubac, *Le Mystère du surnaturel* (rpt. Paris: Aubier, 1965), 39.

27. Boswell, *1500 Years*.

28. Boswell, *Rediscovering Gay History*, 5.

29. Boswell, *Rediscovering Gay History*, 6.

30. Boswell, *Rediscovering Gay History*, 12.

31. Boswell, *Rediscovering Gay History,* 21.

32. Lauritsen, *"Culpa ecclesiae,"* 16.

33. Dinshaw, *Getting Medieval,* 26–27.

34. See Friedrich Nietzsche, "Vom Nutzen und Nachteil der Historie für das Leben," *Unzeitgemässe Betrachtungen* 2, in his *Werke* 3.1, ed. Giorgio Colli and Mazzino Montinari (Berlin and New York: W. de Gruyter, 1972), especially 254. Compare Nietzsche, "History in the Service and Disservice of Life," trans. Gary Brown, in *Unmodern Observations,* ed. William Arrowsmith (New Haven: Yale University Press, 1990), 95.

35. Boswell, *1500 Years.*

36. Boswell, *Rediscovering Gay History,* 16.

37. For both quotations, Randolph Trumbach, review of *Same-Sex Unions, Journal of Homosexuality* 30, no. 2 (1995): 111–17, at 112.

PART II

Debates

CHAPTER 6

Fronto + Marcus: Love, Friendship, Letters

Amy Richlin

In 1815, Angelo Mai discovered in the Ambrosian Library at Milan a palimpsest containing one of the long-lost treasures of Roman history: the letters of Marcus Cornelius Fronto, reputed to have been the greatest Roman orator after Cicero. But Mai's find disappointed its nineteenth-century readers, who had hoped for a political drama like that played out in Cicero's letters. That the collection included passionate love letters between Fronto and the future emperor Marcus Aurelius was politely ignored, or concealed, and the letters are today very little known. For almost two hundred years they have lain hidden in plain sight.

John Boswell was one of the few people who have had eyes to see them.[1] In a brief reference in *CSTH*, he gives the letters as an instance of "passionate or 'erotic' friendship between males" (*CSTH*, 134 n. 40). Boswell's status as an outsider to classics enabled him to notice what specialists could not, as his goal of writing gay history prompted him to look for what they would not. Fronto is treated within classics as a rhetorician and a dull one; the only Fronto letters occasionally listed among required graduate readings deal with rhetoric. Moreover, in casting his net as widely as he did in *CSTH* Boswell was also bucking the trend in the history of sexuality as it has been produced since the nineteenth century. A tradition going back at least to John Addington Symonds focuses on "Greek love" almost to the exclusion of the Romans;[2] unlike Foucault, whose followers have largely been Hellenists, Boswell

111

did not get pulled into this orbit. *CSTH* is exemplary in the breadth of its review of primary materials and in the independence of its perspective.

The letters of M. Cornelius Fronto and his circle, as edited by C. R. Haines in 1919–20, take up two Loeb volumes.[3] Most of the letters were written between Fronto and the young man who gradually turned into the emperor Marcus Aurelius. Fronto came from North Africa; he says in one letter that he comes of indigenous stock, though he may not mean this literally. He was certainly wealthy and had an upper-class upbringing and education; in *Fronto and Antonine Rome* Edward Champlin lays out the evidence on the eminence of Fronto's family.[4] But, eminent or not, Fronto came from the hinterlands and made it big as an orator and politician in Rome—so much so that he was chosen to instruct the young prince in rhetoric, and, while doing so, attained the glory of a suffect consulship.

It is important to keep in mind the relative ages of Fronto and Marcus as their lives intersected. The letters span the years from Fronto's first appointment as Marcus's tutor, in 139 CE, to the end of Fronto's life, probably in 167.[5] Champlin makes a convincing case for locating Fronto's birth around 95, and Marcus was born in 121, so that when the letters begin, Fronto is forty-four and Marcus is eighteen. The many letters that can be dated to the years 139–45 are pervasively amatory.

In 145, at the age of twenty-four, Marcus got married, in an arranged marriage to his cousin Faustina. They began having children right away; they would eventually have twelve, six of whom lived to adulthood. Shortly after the birth of his first child, in 146, Marcus announces to Fronto that he can no longer in good conscience spend time studying rhetoric, due to his serious involvement in philosophy, especially ethics, and there's a sad little letter from Fronto about this. From here on, a lot of the letters are about ill health, with lists of symptoms. The amatory letters, common before the marriage, now disappear. There's a brief flaring up of ardor (from Fronto) when he mistakenly thinks that Marcus has been at death's door. After this, there is only one major amatory letter, again from Fronto, and it's interspersed with a lot of I-know-how-busy-you-are-I-just-don't-want-to-be-a-burden. The usual outline of Fronto's relationship with Marcus holds that Fronto was cast aside like an old shoe when Marcus got tired of rhetoric. I would submit that it may have been the case that rhetoric was cast aside like an old shoe when Marcus got tired of Fronto.

My first project here must be just to lay out the letters I claim to be amatory, since I know this claim will be greeted with skepticism. How could it possibly be that this aspect of the letters has attracted so little comment, if it is really there? Most people who have given this any thought at all will come to the letters expecting to find at most a sentimental friendship, possibly some sort of allusion to pederastic romance in literature, and most likely the conventions of a decade given to flowery style. Scholarship on friendship in the eighteenth and nineteenth centuries has readied scholars to read letters as showing deep emotion without implying any genital sexuality.[6] Even Boswell hedged his claim; he mentions the letters in a footnote to a section on sentimental friendship in late antiquity, but adds his opinion: "to any modern reader these would seem to be passionate love letters" (*CSTH*, 134 n. 40). These texts are so unfamiliar, and so rich and full of surprises, that I think the first step must be to get them out into public view. Their importance reaches beyond classics to precisely the audience Boswell wished to reach: people for whom gay history matters. There seems to be a widespread misconception in popular culture that love between males is Greek, the Romans generally being capable only of crude lust; these letters might go some way toward modifying that view.[7] And even for scholars working on the history of ancient sexuality, it is widely held that first-person statements of love by the junior partner in a pederastic relationship are almost nonexistent; I said so once myself.[8] In that context, these letters are a sensational addition to the corpus of ancient erotic literature.

Reading the *Phaedrus*

The most dazzling of the letters comes from early on in the correspondence and seems to have served explicitly as a move of seduction: this is the *erōtikos logos* written by Fronto for Marcus. Although there are signs of romance in one seemingly earlier letter, Fronto's bravura performance here opens the floodgates.[9]

As an introductory gambit, Fronto evidently sent Marcus three pieces written in Greek, ostensibly examples of a standard rhetorical exercise in which the orator riffs on themes set by famous speeches. The first was a version of the speech of Lysias recounted in Plato's *Phaedrus,* known today by the name Plato gave it in that dialogue: *erōtikos logos,* "the speech about love." The second was a version of Socrates' improvement on that speech in the dialogue, and the third, which is the only one extant, was Fronto's own effort. The brilliance of this move is hard to overstate. Addressing a young man famous for his delight in philosophy, the eminent rhetorician, assigned to teach this young man rhetoric, chose to engage him with a Platonic dialogue that is, in a way, about rhetoric. What could be more blameless, more appropriate, than a discussion of Plato's *Phaedrus?* Indeed the part of it about rhetoric is relatively dull.

The first part of Plato's dialogue, however, is not dull at all, and it is from this section that the purported speech of Lysias comes. This speech is an argument that beautiful young men (*kaloi*) should bestow their sexual favors on men who claim not to love them rather than on men who claim to love them (*erastai*), and within the dialogue it is several things at once: the written words that say this argument; a gift given by Lysias to Phaedrus as a means of seduction; and a book-roll carried by Phaedrus under his clothing, which Socrates manages to make him bring out and read. The setting of the dialogue is flirtatious: Socrates meets Phaedrus going for a walk outside the city walls, and they wander off down by the Ilissus. Their surroundings suggest myths to them: the rape of Orithyia by winged Boreas (*Phaedrus* 229b), and, less explicitly, the rape of Perimele by the river Achelous (230b).

During this initial conversation, rhetoric and sexuality are repeatedly con-flated (e.g., 236d–e, where rhetoric is what brings the boy and his admirer together, the equivalent of wrestling). And the speech of Socrates that so memorably completes the first half of the dialogue is amazingly sexy: the soul like a charioteer with two horses, of which the bad (*akolastos*) horse keeps wanting to go have sex with beautiful boys, more and more explicitly (250e–252b; 253c; 254a–e; 255b–c; 255d–256a; 256b–d); the boys' beauty causes feathers to grow on the soul's wings, feathers that itch and tickle, grow, and threaten to burst out of their sockets, in cascades of erectile and ejaculatory imagery. The dialogue / speech is implicitly itself a form of flirtation, since the interlocutor / addressee, Phaedrus, is himself one of the *kaloi* who play such an important role in the first part of the dialogue; the analogy between Socrates and Phaedrus and the gazing soul and the gazed-at boy is under-lined by the frequent statements that Phaedrus is *kalos*. Occasionally there are role-switches in the dialogue, and Socrates says that Lysias is Phaedrus's *paidika* (236b) or that Phaedrus is the *erastēs* of Lysias (257b; rather than being his *erōmenos,* "beloved"), or Phaedrus threatens to force Socrates to do his bidding (236d), saying that they are alone in a lonely place (*en erēmiai*) and that he is stronger and younger than Socrates.

This idea of role reversal is one key to what Fronto is doing here. One of the main things boys were taught in the ancient rhetorical schools was to play roles.[10] They had to make speeches, *suasoriae,* while taking on vari-ous personae: Agamemnon, Alexander the Great, Cicero. The *erōtikos logos* attributed to Lysias by Socrates in Plato's *Phaedrus* is a typically Plato-ish role-playing game: people are still arguing over who wrote it.[11] Is it really by Lysias, and just quoted by Plato? Is it a parody? Or something in between, not really by Lysias but written by Plato in Lysias's style, like a Roman *suasoria?* Words, as Plato says later in the dialogue, are so enigmatic. Plato, in a way, produces three versions of an *erōtikos logos* in the *Phaedrus;* so Fronto sends three to Marcus. As in tap dancing, or (more pertinently) as in many kinds of traditional Roman performance, an antiphonal response is expected: "now it's your turn."[12] Much as in letter-writing.[13]

This extremely elaborate frame, or mask, allows Fronto to say the most startling things to his young charge. Of course he is in a way pretending to be Lysias addressing Phaedrus, but by means of this fiction he directly addresses Marcus, and in fact at the beginning of the letter the "dear boy" (*phile pai*) has to be Marcus, and the speaker is explicitly Fronto, calling himself "this foreign man," simultaneously inside and outside the frame.

After this metatextual preamble, the letter makes the following points: if the boy wants to know how the speaker can want the same thing lovers want, it is because he can see the boy's beauty as well as they can; the speaker, a non-lover, can benefit the boy more than a lover can; the boy has bewitched another man by means of charms; everybody is talking about how this man is the boy's lover, and this is disgraceful; non-lovers have more credibility in praising the beauty of boys; what the lover has written about the boy is disgraceful and arises from bestial lust, in which the boy should not participate—sex should take place in privacy (*erēmia*); the flower that loved the sun gets no benefit from this love; we can see this flower if we take a walk outside the city, down by the Ilissus.

And here is a selection from what is evidently Marcus's reply:

> Go ahead, as much as you like, threaten me, accuse me, with whole clumps of arguments: but you will never put off your *erastēs*—I mean me. Nor will I announce that I love Fronto any less, or will I love him less, because you by such varied and vehement and elegant expressions have proved that those who love less are more to be helped out and lavishly endowed. No, by God, I am dying so for love of you, nor am I scared off by this dogma of yours, and if you will be more quick and ready for others, who don't love you, I still will love you while I live and breathe. . . . For I love you, and I think that this at last ought to be granted to true lovers, that they take more pleasure in the victories of their *erōmenoi*. We have won, then, we have won, I say. . . . (2) And indeed I will swear this with every confidence: If that Phaedrus guy of yours ever really existed, if he was ever away from Socrates, Socrates didn't burn more with desire for Phaedrus than I've burned during these days—did I say days? I mean months—for the sight of you? Your letter fixed it so a person wouldn't have to be Dion [Plato's big fan and patron] to love you so much, if he isn't immediately seized with love of you. Goodbye, my biggest thing under heaven, my glory. It's enough for me to have had such a teacher.[14]

It is conventional to refer, if at all, to Fronto's *erōtikos logos* as a literary exercise that he has composed for the edification of his new student. Van den Hout, for example, says *ad loc.*, "When in 138 Pius decided to appoint Fronto as a mentor and teacher to Marcus, . . . the forty-five-year-old Fronto had to present himself to his eighteen-year-old pupil. As . . . a pedagogue [he did so] here in his Erotikos, be it in jest. As in Plato's *Phaedrus* . . . not Eros is the point at issue but education, the education of a future emperor." And further: "This trivial work should not be taken seriously, contrary to [Christopher] Wordsworth [1807–85], . . . who thinks that Fronto here tries to deter Marcus from unchaste love and that Marcus mended his ways thanks to Fronto's Erotikos (see *Medit.* 1.16–17)."[15] The reference here is to a passage in his *Meditations* where Marcus, late in life, says that Antoninus Pius taught him to give up sex with boys (*to pausai ta peri tous erōtas tōn meirakiōn*, 1.16.2), and (separately) that the gods taught him to "save his youthful flower and not play the man too early" (*to tēn hōran diasōsai kai to mē pro hōras andrōsthēnai*, 1.17.2). The confusion of 1.16.2 and 1.17.2 I pass over for now, along with the question of what Marcus was talking about in his *Meditations;* the main thing is that I do not see how Fronto's *erōtikos logos* can be described either as primarily about education, trivial, or as an attempt to deter Marcus from unchaste love. Nor does its effect seem to have been deterrent.

Among the thousands of things that could be said about Fronto's letter, these: that this frame enables him to call Marcus beautiful (repeated many times); and to talk about Marcus carrying on with another man, sometimes in graphic terms; and to joke about keeping Marcus's name "inviolate" (i.e. "everyone says you're a slut, but I'd never repeat that"); and to talk about his own desire for Marcus; and to warn Marcus of the need for secrecy and the value of coded speech; and to end with an elegantly Platonic proposition: let's go down by the Ilissus (i.e. let's be like Socrates and Phaedrus, or, let's read the *Phaedrus*, or, let's go where there's *erēmia*—cf. *Phaedrus* 236d). He gets to say all these things, and it's educational.

And Marcus gets to reply in kind. Moreover, he switches the roles around, so that he now becomes the *erastēs* and Fronto the *erōmenos;* he becomes Socrates, and Fronto becomes Phaedrus. And by saying "if that Phaedrus guy of yours ever really existed," Marcus reminds his reader of the lively literary discussion about the reality of the interlocutors in Plato's dialogues; Diogenes Laertius includes Phaedrus among those rumored to have been Plato's *erōmenoi* (*Plato* 3.29, 31).[16]

This interchange of letters sets up a rule for a game that Fronto and Marcus begin to play: the interchange of letters, of books, is like sex. There's a wonderful moment in the *Phaedrus,* when Phaedrus is about to tell Socrates what Lysias said from memory, and Socrates says (228d), "First show me, my love, what you've got in your left hand under your cloak. For I'm guessing that you have the discourse itself [*ton logon auton*]." In other words, are you just glad to see me, or is that a scroll in your pocket? The joke, common in antiquity, in which a book-roll is likened to a phallus, suggests perhaps that in the *Phaedrus* the connection is not metaphorical but metonymic.[17] In other words, the *Phaedrus* does not seem to be about sex when really it is about rhetoric; it is both about sex and about rhetoric. The long time that is spent by Socrates and Phaedrus in flirting at the beginning of the dialogue suggests that this kind of speech be taken seriously, as being a kind of saying without telling, a speech that both is and is not what it seems to be; much as the speech Lysias gives to Phaedrus claims that Lysias is not Phaedrus's *erastēs,* while both the gist of the speech and the gift of the speech itself are cast as a ploy to seduce Phaedrus (and Socrates says as much at *Phaedrus* 237b). This seems to be underscored by the elaborate argument made at the end of the *Phaedrus* that the written word is inferior to the spoken word; if that is so, why does Socrates want to see what Phaedrus has under his cloak? It is *ton logon auton,* but maybe it is not the scroll.

The language or conceit of the *erōtikos logos* well exemplifies the episte-mology of the closet in its adroit exploitation of plausible deniability.[18] As in the structure of jokes,[19] which armors the speaker against a hearer who would take the joke-content seriously, the use of the intertext allows Fronto to get away with a lot here, in fact even more than he puts on paper. That is, just as a person might tell a dirty joke, and then, if someone takes offense, he can say "Hey! It's just a joke!" because it's marked as a "joke" by its structure; so Fronto can say whatever he wants to, if he dresses it up as a Platonic dialogue. And by bringing up the dialogue, he can remind his reader of what it says that he is omitting. This structure permeates the letters, and may in part account for the silence about their amatory content.

The Love of Words

The sharing of literature comes up at the end of another long letter from Marcus to Fronto, of which the main purpose is to thank Fronto for having gone to visit a certain Julianus at Marcus's request:

> (1) . . . Why would I conceal from you what I can't conceal anyway? Even the very fact that you wrote me such a long letter, when I was going to be there tomorrow—that was really by far what I liked most of all: because of this I thought I was the happiest person in the world, because by this you showed

me so greatly and so sweetly how much you think of me and what trust you have in my friendship. What should I add, unless "I love you as you deserve"? But why do I say "as you deserve"? Indeed I wish I were allowed to love you as you deserve! And that's why I'm often angry with you when you're away, and I get so mad, because you won't let me love you as I want to [*facis ne te ut volo amare possim*], that is you won't let my spirit follow the love of you up to its highest peak [*ad summum columen*]. (2) . . . [A]nybody who doesn't love you surely neither understands you in his mind nor sees you with his eyes; for I say nothing about his ears, for everybody's ears bow down before your whisper like bound captives. To me this day seems longer than a day in spring and the coming night will seem wider than a winter night. For not only do I want more than anything to say hi to my Fronto, I especially want to put my arms around the writer of these recent letters. (3) . . . For when I love [*diligam*] you so overpoweringly [*vehementissime*] as my friend, then I ought to remember that as much love as I owe my friend, that's how much reverence I should give my teacher. Good-bye, my Fronto, my dearest and sweetest above all things. (4) The *Sota* of Ennius that you sent back to me seems to be on purer paper and a more delightful book-roll and in gayer letters than it was before. . . . Goodbye, ever my sweetest soul.[20]

These are only scraps of a much longer letter, but I adduce them here for several points of interest. First, a great portion of this letter is simply about Marcus's and Fronto's feelings for each other, and examples of this kind of thing could be multiplied many times over. Second, although almost nowhere in the extant letters are there any physical details except about kissing, it is arguable that the end of section 1 concerns a physical side of their relationship. Third, in section 2 Marcus for once gives some faint details about what it is that he finds so irresistible in Fronto, and it might for once be suggested, since Fronto has impressed few people since 1815 and may not come off so well here, that like many famous orators Fronto was a man of great charisma. Fourth, here as elsewhere, the letters repeatedly use the well-worn tropes of Latin love poetry, full of sleepless nights and burning (forms of *flagro* are common). Fifth, as in section 3, it is arguable that this whole thing is simply a form of sentimental friendship; here Marcus talks about Fronto as his *amicus*.[21] And, finally, in section 4, almost as a postscript, we see the two friends sharing a book. Not just any book, though.

Marcus has sent Fronto the *Sota* of Ennius, and Fronto has sent it back (*remissus a te*). "Sota" is a nickname, a short form, for "Sotades," and Sotades was the eponymous creator of Sotadic verse; Martial, in one of the poems in which he sarcastically defends himself as a refined poet, differentiates himself from *Sotaden cinaedum*, "Sotades the fag" (2.82.2). And, sure enough, several of the fragments of Ennius's *Sota* seem to be about things cinaedic, especially fragment 1 (*ibant malaci viere Veneriam corollam*, "The fags were coming to bind the garland of love"; with fragments 4, 5, 6, possibly a party scene).[22] So when Marcus says that his scroll of Ennius's *Sota* looks better to him now that Fronto has read it, he is talking about something different from his homework—which was usually something like making up *sententiae* in the style of Sallust.[23]

The greatest bond between Fronto and Marcus was their shared passion for words, which shows up at every level: routinely, in countless literary allusions, quotations, homework assignments; climactically, in Fronto's major speeches and Marcus's appreciation of them; fetishistically, in aspects of the (letter-)writing process; in closeup, in a repeated emphasis on handwriting. In Latin as in English, the same word (*littera*/letter) means both an epistle and a letter of the alphabet. Flying in the face of Plato's dictum on the opacity of writing, Fronto and Marcus make love out of the written word.

Routinely: The experience of being critiqued sends Marcus into ecstasies. In a later letter (143?—Marcus now twenty-two), Marcus exclaims, "Oh lucky me, to seem worthy both to be praised and to be chastised by my Marcus Cornelius, greatest of orators, best of men," and such sentiments are often repeated.[24] He here quotes the Greek proverb "love is blind," which he endearingly attributes to Thucydides; of course it is possible that a copyist along the way is the source of this error, but it is entirely typical of Marcus to mess up quotations, and it must have constituted part of his youthful charm. The relationship between Marcus and Fronto was, structurally, oxymoronic, placing the emperor's son, the future emperor, into a subordinate position, and this structure informs a lot of the top/bottom games Fronto and Marcus play together. In this letter, Marcus makes himself out to be clay in Fronto's hands; so grateful is he to be praised, not because he deserves it but because Fronto loves him, that "I, if you want me to, will be something." How touching; but Marcus already is something, and hardly needs Fronto's help. At some level they both must know that this is pretend, and remember Nero competing in the games.

Climactically: When Marcus reads Fronto's great speech in praise of Antoninus Pius, he explodes in praise, not all of it strictly literary:

(1) . . . Oh what a lucky person I am to have been given to this teacher. . . .
(2) . . . And so goodbye, you ornament of Roman eloquence, glory of friends, big thing [*mega pragma*], you most delightful man, greatest consul, sweetest teacher. (3) From now on you'd better watch out and not tell so many lies

about me, especially in the Senate. The way you wrote that speech is awesome [*horribiliter*]! I wish I could kiss your head at every heading of it! You have totally put them all to scorn! Now that I've read that speech I know I'm wasting my time studying, working, straining my muscles. Be well always, sweetest teacher.[25]

The element of hero-worship is of special interest here because of the one-sidedness of ancient *testimonia* of pederasty. Pederastic love poetry conventionally portrays the boy as haughty and powerful (as long as his beauty lasts), and the lover as helpless before him, though the context presupposed by these texts is one in which an adult citizen with money purchases the services of a boy slave/prostitute (i.e. normally the fiction is working in reverse of how it works for Fronto and Marcus). Invective portrays young citizen men as sleeping their way to the top, using their beauty to gain political influence or access to skills. Cicero says all the young men are crazy about his speeches, and, even if we want to take this with a grain of salt, fandom is well attested in the rhetorical writers. It is useful to see that Marcus, at least at this point in his life, really adores Fronto's rhetorical powers.

Fetishistically: At one point he gets so carried away that, having been sent some passages from a speech of Fronto's on provincial wills to be declaimed to Antoninus Pius, he writes Fronto to tell him how glorious the experience was, copying into his letter with his own hand several long excerpts. This letter elicits from Fronto a long response, flattering the royal family but also full of amatory bits:

(1) . . . I thought I had long since been loved enough, but for you even as much as you love me it's still not enough; so that no sea is as deep as your love for me. So much so that I could really complain, why don't you love me as much as ever you can, since by loving me more every day you prove that the love you gave me before wasn't the most possible. (2) Do you think that my consulship brought me as much joy as the proofs of your utmost love, so many of them in one place? . . . (3) And I am that much luckier than Hercules and Achilles, because their arms and weapons were borne by Patricoles and Philoctetes, men much inferior to them in manhood; but my little mediocre speech, not to say ignoble, was lit up by Caesar, most learned and eloquent of all. . . . It's true indeed, as our friend Laberius says, that, to make someone fall in love, "sweet ways are what drive you wild, kind deeds are witchcraft." And nobody could ever have struck such a flame into a lover by potion or love-charm as you, by what you did, have made me dazed and love-struck by your burning love. For every letter on the page, that's how many consulships,

that's how many laurels, triumphs, victory robes I think I achieved. . . . (4) [Marcus's copying out the speech in his own hand makes Fronto luckier than any of a list of famous writers served by famous editors.] Why, even someone who scorns the oration will lust after [*concupiscet*] the letters [in which it is written].[26]

This is one of the best-known of Fronto's little-known letters, not because of what Fronto says he feels for Marcus but because of the debatable information Fronto includes (section 4) about ancient editions of great writers.[27] I would guess that at this point the list of paired names Fronto reels off is only the means to an end, and is parallel to the analogy he draws in section 3 between himself and Marcus, Hercules and Philoctetes, Achilles and Patroclus, whom he calls by the telling archaic form of his name, which falsely analyzed would mean "Father-worshiper." This set of what David Halperin called "heroes and their pals" provides the model for the longer list in section 4,[28] and they are all there mainly to reinforce the relationship between Fronto and Marcus. (One of the earliest literary discussions of the erotic relation between Achilles and Patroclus of course is spoken by Phaedrus, in the *Symposium,* who argues that Patroclus was in fact the *erastēs*.)[29] One is instructively reminded of a letter in which Cicero embarrassingly suggests that he could be Laelius to Pompey's Scipio (*Fam.* 5.7): gruesome to read, we know Cicero is making a fool of himself, but Fronto is not, we can safely guess that Marcus was thrilled with this letter. Note that tops and bottoms pose a problem for Fronto here, though, as in heroizing the field of letters he winds up equating the future emperor with a set of freed slaves and minor literary figures.

In closeup: As for Marcus's adorable alphabet, it pops up elsewhere as well. At the end of one early letter, Fronto writes: "Goodbye, Caesar, and love me the most, as you do. I truly love to pieces every little letter of every word you write [*etiam literulas tuas*], so I wish you would write me by your own hand whenever you write to me."[30] Doubtless also a safety measure, but mainly something from the loved one's hand.

This brings us back to Phaedrus's book-roll, the *Sota,* and the fetishization of writing itself and the letter exchange process. The question of whether the letters themselves were originally autograph, or mostly so, is an old one, and is opened again by van den Hout.[31] What makes it possible to ask the question at all is that the writers frequently bring it up, and the point is that they do so because the written word is a metonym for the lover's body. And so Fronto says he loves each little letter; when Fronto is ill, he cannot write himself, but has used [another's hand?] "contrary to our usual practice"; Marcus is always writing late at night, or in bed; Marcus says, contrasting

Fronto favorably with flatterers, "So it's no wonder, my teacher, I burn so; no wonder I've appointed one man of mine to watch over me; no wonder I think of one person when the pen comes to my hands."[32] And again Marcus: "I've been writing from 10:30 to this hour and I've read a lot of Cato and I'm writing this to you with the same pen [calamo] and I'm saying hi and I want to know how you're getting on. Oh how long it is that I haven't seen you."[33] The copied speech is sent back to its author. The book-roll of the Sota becomes purior, gratior, festivior, because Fronto has had it and read it and sent it back.

Secrecy

When Fronto tells Marcus he wants him always to write by his own hand, maybe he is also thinking of what will be safest. There are hints, here and there, that he has this in mind, and that the plausible deniability of their correspondence might seem to him to be getting close to the edge of implausible.

To a letter in which Marcus has sent him get-well wishes somewhat warmly expressed, Fronto replies:

> (1) You, Caesar, love this Fronto of yours without limit, so that words scarcely suffice to you, the most eloquent of mortals, to disclose your love and declare your goodwill. What, I ask you, could be more fortunate, what could ever be luckier than me alone, to whom you send such burning letters? Why, you even say you want to run to me, to fly to me, as lovers do [quod est amatorum proprium]. (2) My lady, your mother, often says as a joke that she is jealous of me because I am loved by you so much. What if she were to read this letter of yours in which you even call on the gods and pray for my health? Lucky me, entrusted to the gods by your lips! Do you think that any pain would know how to penetrate my body or mind in the face of such joy? . . . [part of word missing] get better—wow! Now I feel no pain at all, I don't even feel ill: I'm strong, I'm healthy, I'm dancing; wherever you want me, I'll come; wherever you want me, I'll run. Believe me, I was suffused with such happiness that I could hardly write back to you at once. . . . (3) [I haven't done anything to deserve such love] . . . So see to it that, if anyone asks you why you love Fronto, you have something ready to give as a response. [4–7, more on the theme "undeserved love is stronger than deserved love."] (8) So if there is any sensible reason for your love of me, Caesar, please let's take good care that it should be unknown and lie hidden. Let people doubt, talk, argue, guess, quest after the origin of our love just like the sources of the Nile. (9) . . . You, my

lord, jewel of the Roman way, my greatest comfort, I love so much. You'll say "Not more than I love you?" I'm not such an ingrate that I'd dare to say so. Be well, Caesar, and your parents too, and cultivate that intellect.[34]

Amid the flow of *sermo amatorius,* Fronto shows two things: that he is conscious that this is *sermo amatorius* (*quod est amatorum proprium*); and that he is a little worried. Marcus's mother is joking that she is jealous; suppose she read your last letter, how amusing that would be for her! Maybe it would be a good idea if Marcus could think of some reason why he thinks so highly of Fronto, or maybe vagueness would be even better.

Sealed with a Kiss

After Marcus's marriage the fire goes out, at least in Marcus's heart, and Marcus explicitly tells Fronto he is turning from rhetoric to philosophy.[35] There are only two more major amatory letters, both from Fronto. In the first, probably from early in 148, Fronto has been frightened by a letter which he thought meant that Marcus was ill (actually it was Marcus's new baby girl); here are some high points from the long letter he sends Marcus as a result:

> (3) If ever I see you in my dreams, when I am "bound," as the poet says, "in slumber gentle and calm," there's never a time when I'm not putting my arms around you and kissing you fondly [*numquam est quin amplectar et exosculer*]: then, according to the plot of whatever dream it is I either weep abundantly or exult with some sort of happiness and pleasure. . . . (4) You know how in all the banks and stands and storefronts and shops and arcades and entryways and windows, everywhere and every moment, images of you are displayed to the public—they're badly painted, sure, and most of them are shaped and carved under the inspiration of a thick, no a mud-caked Muse; but when your image, no matter how unlike you, catches my eye on my way, this never happens without jolting from my mouth the gape and dream of a kiss [*ut non ex ore meo excusserit rictum osculi et somn⟨i⟩um*]. (5) . . . But, hey, you see to it that you don't turn me in or testify against me to your daughter—as if I truly loved you more than her. For there's a danger that your daughter, riled up by this, since she's a severe and old-fashioned woman, might be quite angry over it and take away her hands and feet from me for kissing, or offer them only grudgingly; while I, good God! will as gladly kiss her tiny little hands and those fat little feet as your royal neck and your mouth, so sober and clever [*os probum et facetum*].[36]

This is yet another passage that is famous but not because of Fronto's feelings; it is famous because of the mention of the proliferation of royal images[37]— clearly not only posters or banners but tchotchkes, maybe souvenirs. But these Marcus action figures haunt Fronto; Marcus himself here is fetishized, specularized, the king of Fronto's dream life. Now Fronto's analogy between himself and Achilles, Marcus and Patroclus, sounds as stupid as Cicero's analogy between himself and Laelius, Pompey and Scipio.

And what Fronto dreams of is kissing him. In his dreams when he sees Marcus he inevitably kisses and embraces him, and each dream has its scenario, leading sometimes to weeping, sometimes to pleasure. When, waking, he walks through the city and sees the crude images of Marcus, with the same inevitability (*numquam est quin . . . ; numquam . . . accidit, ut non . . .*) they force his mouth open into the dream of a kiss. This odd phrase unfortunately lurks in a vexed text, much emended, but the Vatican palimpsest is reported to have *rictum* and *somnum*. Did Fronto write *rictum*? If so, his longing is opening him up in more ways than one. Fronto walking the streets, his lips parting at the sight of the image of his beloved, constitutes rhetoric undone, desire embodied, Achilles no more.

He is telling too much, more than he ever has before. The joke about kissing the baby's feet gives him an excuse to say what he really wants to do: he wants to kiss Marcus's neck and mouth, or face. His joke reverses ages, calling the baby a woman, and a serious, old-fashioned one at that; when he says "I'd rather kiss her than you," this is a tactic from flirtation; and the final phrase tells what Fronto really has in mind. The whole letter leads up to that phrase. Some of the writing in this letter is superb, as if forced out of Fronto by his need: the list of places in the city where Marcus's image can be found (the list a stylistic trait of Fronto's, but here so vividly evoking the peregrination of the city, the lover's feeling that everywhere he looks he sees the image); the final adjectives, *regias* (royal—a word he has never used of Marcus before—connoting cruelty, tyranny, archaic ritual) juxtaposed with the vulnerability of *cervices,* and *probum et facetum,* praise you might give to a clever boy, such a good student.

Time goes by, and then, evidently after a gap, Marcus has written Fronto a whole group of letters, and Fronto writes a long letter back to say how thrilled he is, the letters are written "so elegantly so lovingly so sweetly so effusively so burningly [*flagranter*]." The second section of the letter abruptly launches into a description of Marcus's kisses:

> (2) What is more delicious to me than your kiss? That delicious scent, that enjoyment is located for me in your neck and your kiss. And yet the last time

you were setting out, and your father had already gotten into the car, and a crowd of people saying goodbye and kissing you fondly was holding you back, it was better that I was the only one of all of them not to hug you or kiss you. . . . (3) . . . When I got your letters, I suffered just what a lover [*amator*] suffers who sees his darling [*delicias suas*] running toward him over a rough and dangerous road. For he's both glad to see him coming toward him and afraid of the danger at the same time. That's why I don't like the play so popular among actors, where the loving girl waits for her loving young man by night, with her lamp lit, standing in her tower while he's swimming in the sea. For I would rather be without you, although I burn with love for you, than let you swim so late at night in so deep a sea, lest the moon should set, lest the wind should put out the light, lest you should be seized there in the cold, lest the waves lest the shoals lest the fish somehow harm you. This strategy would be more becoming to a lover and better and more wholesome, not to pursue at the cost of another's deadly danger the use of a pleasure brief and to be regretted. (4) [Marcus is so loaded with work that Fronto would not want him to work one minute longer to write to him] . . . For I would rather that I lack all enjoyment of your love, than that you should undergo even the least bit of inconvenience for the sake of my pleasure.[38]

As in the letter that began with his dreams, here again Fronto goes into detail about kissing Marcus, and this time sensual traces leak out. Scent! This is a feature of erotic epigram; compare Martial 3.65, on the delicious scent of the kisses of a boy called Diadumenus.[39] Fronto also describes vividly a specific occasion on which he felt rejected. When everyone else goes to kiss Marcus (as part of the royal goodbye ritual), it is better that Fronto does not, because it means too much to him (it's not just a ritual to him).[40] His heart is broken.

Doomed, he goes on thanking Marcus for writing while protesting that he would not want Marcus to overburden himself by writing him letters. He uses explicitly amatory similes, like reminders, to describe the feeling of getting letters from a person who is usually too absorbed in his work to write; here he casts himself both in the male role (the lover seeing his *deliciae* running toward him) and in the female role, as Hero watching Leander swim the Hellespont. Despite Fronto's reputation as a poor stylist, this part of the letter is beautiful, the technique of listing again typical of his style; many have taken it to be a quotation, but if it is one, it is no idle ornament.[41] And when Fronto talks about Marcus swimming in the cold dark sea he is talking about more than his longing for Marcus or his fear that Marcus is working too hard; is he talking about a sea he knows too well himself? Is he wishing Marcus dead?

And when he talks about "another's deadly danger," is it Marcus's danger he means, or his own? The "pleasure brief and to be regretted"—is it just a letter, or something else?

But this letter did no good, there are no more love letters from Marcus, and the two go on apart.

◆ ◆ ◆

It has only been possible here to touch on some of the major letters; also of great interest are the way in which Fronto and Marcus circulate their love through women close to them (Marcus's mother, Fronto's wife) and the exuberant language they use both to figure their love and to bid each other farewell. Set in the context of Fronto's letters to his friends, and of the cultural history of the time, the Marcus letters can be seen to be extraordinary— though Fronto's later letters to Marcus's younger brother, Verus, also have their odd moments. The story remains to be told of how the letters were lost in late antiquity, found in the nineteenth century, received, used by Walter Pater in *Marius the Epicurean,* and then forgotten. Two hundred years after their recovery from oblivion, the letters are still waiting to be read.

· Notes

Translations throughout are my own. Thanks to Mathew Kuefler for inviting me to contribute to this volume, and to Henry Abelove, Mary Beard, Adam Blistein, Joseph Boone, David Konstan, Helen Morales, and James Tatum for getting me started and helping me to continue. Work on this essay was funded by the American Council of Learned Societies. I write in memory of John Boswell, a great scholar and a charming speaker.

1. Credit should also go to Robert Boughner for his paper, "The Sex Life of Marcus Aurelius," which was presented at the American Philological Association, San Francisco, December 30, 1990, and which he kindly let me see. Rictor Norton set a pair of letters between Fronto and Marcus at the start of his collection, *My Dear Boy: Gay Love Letters Through the Centuries* (San Francisco: Leyland, 1998); I am grateful to him for searching through his notes to find what had alerted him to the letters' existence, and it turned out to be Boswell's footnote. I would expect the same was the case for Foucault's brief allusion to the love letters in Luther Martin et al., *Technologies of the Self: A Seminar with Michel Foucault* (Amherst: University of Massachusetts Press, 1988) (thanks to Nancy Sorkin Rabinowitz for her eagle eye); in *The History of Sexuality,* vol. 3, *The Care of the Self,* Foucault refers to the correspondence only as an example of valetudinarianism, and it is not clear to me that he ever read the letters.

2. See Amy Richlin, "Eros Underground: Greece and Rome in Gay Print Culture, 1950–65," *Journal of Homosexuality,* special issue on Sexuality in Antiquity, ed. Beert Verstraete, forthcoming.

3. *The Correspondence of Marcus Cornelius Fronto,* ed. and trans. C. R. Haines, 2 vols. (London: Heinemann, 1919–20).

4. Edward Champlin, *Fronto and Antonine Rome* (Cambridge, Mass.: Harvard University Press, 1980), 8–20.

5. For Fronto's death-date, see Champlin, *Fronto and Antonine Rome,* 139–42.

6. On sentimental friendship in the eighteenth and nineteenth centuries, see Lillian Faderman, *Surpassing the Love of Men: Romantic Friendship and Love Between Women from the Renaissance to the Present* (New York: William Morrow, 1981); Karen V. Hansen, " 'Our Eyes Behold Each Other': Masculinity and Intimate Friendship in Antebellum New England," in *Men's Friendships,* ed. Peter M. Nardi (Newbury Park, Calif.: Sage Publications, 1992), 35–58.

7. See Richlin, "Eros Underground," on ideas of ancient sexuality in European and American gay popular culture from the 1880s to the 1960s.

8. Amy Richlin, *The Garden of Priapus,* rev. ed. (New York: Oxford University Press, 1992), 55.

9. Unfortunately, there are three standard numbering systems for Fronto's letters: (1) that of Samuel Adrianus Naber, ed., *M. Cornelii Frontonis et M. Aurelii Imperatoris Epistulae* (Leipzig: Teubner, 1867), which was used also by C. R. Haines in his Loeb edition, *The Correspondence of Marcus Cornelius Fronto;* (2) that of Edward Champlin, *Fronto and Antonine Rome,* which modified Naber's numbers; and (3) that of Michael P. J. van den Hout, *A Commentary on the Letters of M. Cornelius Fronto,* Mnemosyne Supplement 190 (Leiden: E. J. Brill, 1999), which references the page numbers of van den Hout, ed., *M. Cornelii Frontonis Epistulae* (Leipzig: Teubner, 1988), which also modified Naber's numbers. I will give four sets of references here, in this order: volume and page number in Haines; book/item number in Naber; page number and book/item number in van den Hout, *M. Cornelii Frontonis Epistulae;* book/item number in Champlin, Appendix A. I recommend Haines's Loeb edition to the general reader as accessible, clear, and reliable. The letters carry no dates; sometimes they can be dated by internal evidence, but most dating is conjectural. The *erōtikos logos* is Haines 1.20–31 = Naber *Epist. Graec.* 8 = van den Hout 250–55, Addit. 8 = Champlin *Ep. Var.* 8. The earlier letter is Haines 1.18–20 = Naber *Epist. Graec.* 6 = van den Hout 42, *M. Caes.* 3.9 = Champlin *M. Caes.* 3.9.

10. On gender and rhetorical training, see W. Martin Bloomer, "Schooling in Persona," *Classical Antiquity* 16 (1997): 57–78; Amy Richlin, "How Putting the Man in Roman Put the Roman in Romance," in *Talking Gender: Public Images, Personal Journeys, and Political Critiques,* ed. Nancy Hewitt, Jean O'Barr, and Nancy Rosebaugh (Chapel Hill: University of North Carolina Press, 1996), 14–35.

11. K. J. Dover, *Lysias and the Corpus Lysiacum,* Sather Classical Lectures 39 (Berkeley and Los Angeles: University of California Press, 1968), 69–71.

12. On antiphonal speech in Roman culture, see Thomas Habinek, *The World of Roman Song: From Ritualized Speech to Social Order* (Baltimore: Johns Hopkins University Press, 2005).

13. On the erotics of letter-writing in Rome, see Mary Beard, "Ciceronian Correspondences: Making a Book Out of Letters," in *Classics in Progress,* ed. T. P. Wiseman (Oxford: Oxford University Press, 2002), 103–44, esp. 130–41; Jennifer Ebbeler, "Pedants in the Apparel of Heroes? Cultures of Latin Letter-Writing from Cicero to Ennodius," Ph.D.

diss., University of Pennsylvania, 2001; Erik Gunderson, "Catullus, Pliny, and Love-Letters," *TAPA* 127 (1997): 201–31; Thomas Habinek, *The Politics of Latin Literature* (Princeton: Princeton University Press, 1998), 144–45; Patricia A. Rosenmeyer, *Ancient Epistolary Fictions: The Letter in Greek Literature* (Cambridge: Cambridge University Press, 2001). On the erotics of letter-writing in general, see Janet Gurkin Altman, *Epistolarity: Approaches to a Form* (Columbus: Ohio State University Press, 1982); Susan Stewart, *On Longing* (Baltimore: Johns Hopkins University Press, 1984).

14. Haines 1.30–33 = Naber *Epist. Graec.* 7 = van den Hout 249–50, Addit. 7 = Champlin *Ep. Var.* 7.

15. Michael P. J. van den Hout, *A Commentary on the Letters of M. Cornelius Fronto*, 560–61.

16. Diogenes Laertius wrote his biographies of the philosophers in the first half of the third century CE, but he incorporated much earlier material.

17. Amy Richlin, *The Garden of Priapus*, 111; see also Martial 11.6.14–16.

18. See Eve Kosofsky Sedgwick, *Epistemology of the Closet* (Berkeley: University of California Press, 1990); and, for the concept of "closeted writing," as in "deliberate concealment of one's same-sex erotic sympathies, desires, and activities from some observers, and coded communication of them to others," see extended discussion in David Michael Robinson, *Closeting and Continuity in the Literature of Homosexuality* (London: Ashgate, forthcoming), taking off from James Creech, *Closet Writing/Gay Reading: The Case of Melville's* Pierre (Chicago: University of Chicago Press, 1993). My thanks to David Robinson for allowing me to read his work in progress.

19. Richlin, *The Garden of Priapus*, 61.

20. Haines 1.74–79 = Naber *Ad M. Caes.* 4.2 = van den Hout 54–56, *M. Caes.* 4.2 = Champlin *M. Caes.* 4.2.

21. But compare the *Phaedrus*, where *philoi* are consistently both distinguished from and confused with *erastai* (232b, 232e–233a, 233c–d, 256c–d, e, and especially 255b, d–e). On the history of the concept of friendship in antiquity, see David Konstan, *Friendship in the Classical World* (Cambridge: Cambridge University Press, 1997).

22. Edward Courtney, ed., *The Fragmentary Latin Poets* (Oxford: Clarendon Press, 1993), 4–7.

23. Haines 1.12–15 = Naber *Ad M. Caes.* 3.11 = van den Hout 44, *M. Caes.* 3.12 = Champlin *M. Caes.* 3.12.

24. Haines 1.106–9 = Naber *Ad M. Caes.* 3.17 = van den Hout 50, *M. Caes.* 3.18 = Champlin *M. Caes.* 3.18.

25. Haines 1.128–31 = Naber *Ad M. Caes.* 2.3 = van den Hout 27, *M. Caes.* 2.6 = Champlin *M. Caes.* 2.3.

26. Haines 1.162–69 = Naber *Ad M. Caes.* 1.7 = van den Hout 13–16, *M. Caes.* 1.7 = Champlin *M. Caes.* 1.7.

27. James E. G. Zetzel, "*Emendavi ad Tironem:* Some Notes on Scholarship in the Second Century A.D.," *Harvard Studies in Classical Philology* 77 (1973): 227–45.

28. David M. Halperin, "Heroes and their Pals," *One Hundred Years of Homosexuality* (New York: Routledge, 1990), 75–87.

29. On heroic couples, see Halperin, "Heroes and Their Pals"; on the eroticization of the relationship between Achilles and Patroclus, K. J. Dover, *Greek Homosexuality* (Cambridge, Mass.: Harvard University Press, 1978), 197–99, where he also cites the myth about Hercules and his young comrade-in-arms Iolaus, who came to be known as lovers by the time of Aristotle. No such tales are told of Philoctetes, the lame hero who bore the bow of Hercules; on the other hand, he was not even Hercules's contemporary, and it is possible that Fronto here means to name Iolaus.

30. Haines 1.62–67 = Naber *Ad M. Caes.* 3.3 = van den Hout 36–38, *M. Caes.* 3.3 = Champlin *M. Caes.* 3.3.

31. Van den Hout, *A Commentary on the Letters of M. Cornelius Fronto,* 103. See also Myles McDonnell, "Writing, Copying, and Autograph Manuscripts in Ancient Rome," *The Classical Quarterly* 46 (1996): 469–91.

32. Fronto's hand, Haines 1.186–89 = Naber *Ad M. Caes.* 4.9 = van den Hout 64, *M. Caes.* 4.9 = Champlin *M. Caes.* 4.9; Marcus's pen, Haines 1.136–41 = Naber *Ad M. Caes.* 2.10 = van den Hout 28–29, *M. Caes.* 2.8 = Champlin *M. Caes.* 2.5.

33. Haines 1.116–17 = Naber *Ad M. Caes.* 2.4 = van den Hout 28, *M. Caes.* 2.7 = Champlin *M. Caes.* 2.4.

34. Haines 1.82–91 = Naber *Ad M. Caes.* 1.3 = van den Hout 2–5, *M. Caes.* 1.3 = Champlin *M. Caes.* 1.3.

35. Haines 1.214–19 = Naber *Ad M. Caes.* 4.13 = van den Hout 67–68, *M. Caes.* 4.13 = Champlin *M. Caes.* 4.13.

36. Haines 1.202–9 = Naber *Ad M. Caes.* 4.12 = van den Hout 65–67, *M. Caes.* 4.12 = Champlin *M. Caes.* 4.12.

37. Clifford Ando, *Imperial Ideology and Provincial Loyalty in the Roman Empire* (Berkeley and Los Angeles: University of California Press, 2000), 232–39.

38. Haines 1.218–23 = Naber *Ad M. Caes.* 3.13 = van den Hout 45–47, *M. Caes.* 3.14 = Champlin *M. Caes.* 3.14.

39. Richlin, *The Garden of Priapus,* 39–40.

40. On kissing ritual in Roman culture at this period, see Sebastiano Timpanaro, "Il 'Ius Osculi' e Frontone," *Maia* 39 (1987): 201–11.

41. Van den Hout gives references, with discussion, in *A Commentary on the Letters of M. Cornelius Fronto,* 125–26.

CHAPTER 7

Heterosexism and the Interpretation of Romans 1:18–32

Dale B. Martin

In the religious debate surrounding homosexuality Romans 1 has
commanded, perhaps unduly, a great deal of attention. It is not
my purpose in this chapter to offer yet another interpretation of
the passage, although I will in passing pose some exegetical arguments. Rather, I am interested in how modern heterosexism has
ruled interpretations of Paul's rhetoric. This chapter is thus less
an exegesis of Paul's text than an ideological analysis of modern
scholarship on Rom. 1:18–32.

According to Patricia Beattie Jung and Ralph F. Smith, *heterosexism* is "a reasoned system of bias regarding sexual orientation.
It denotes prejudice in favor of heterosexual people and connotes
prejudice against bisexual and, especially, homosexual people. . . .
It is rooted in a largely cognitive constellation of beliefs about
human sexuality." Heterosexism maintains that "heterosexuality
is *the* normative form of human sexuality. It is the measure by
which all other sexual orientations are judged."[1] In this article,
I analyze the logic of modern heterosexism as it has read Paul's
remarks on homosexual acts in Romans 1. My purpose is *not*
to argue that Paul approves of homosexual sex or would consider it acceptable behavior for Christians.[2] I will demonstrate,
however, that modern scholars are being disingenuous or self-
deluding when they claim that their position—the heterosexist
position—is simply an appropriation of "the biblical view." Their
reading of Paul is prompted not by the constraints of historical

130

criticism or their passive perception of the "clear meaning" of the text, as they claim, but by their inclination (not necessarily intentional) to reinforce modern heterosexist constructions of human sexuality. Although I refer in passing to several exegetes, I concentrate on two articles by my colleague Richard Hays, not because he represents a particularly egregious example of prejudice (his conclusions are less offensive than those of many others) but because the particular constellation of issues I wish to highlight can all be found in his work. Those issues are: (1) the claim that the etiology of homosexuality, according to Paul, lies in the corruption of universal human nature that occurred in the Fall; (2) the assumption that Paul is differentiating homosexual desire from heterosexual desire in Romans 1, ascribing the former to the Fall and the latter to pristine creation; and (3) the importation of a modern concept of acts "contrary to nature" when explaining Paul's term *para physin*.

The Origins of Homosexuality

Hays attempts the laudable task of convincing conservative Christians that Paul does not single out homosexuality as a particularly heinous sin. Believing he advocates a more compassionate position, Hays argues that Romans 1 refers to "the unrighteousness of fallen humanity," to "the human race in general."[3] Quoting Robin Scroggs, Hays agrees that "the whole passage is 'Paul's real story of the universal fall.'"[4] It is "an illustration of human depravity," an "apocalyptic 'long-view'" which indicts fallen humanity as a whole."[5] Homosexuality is no more (but no less) than a symptom of the depravity of all of human nature due to humanity's rebellion against God.

Hays is not alone in taking Paul's comments to refer to the beginning chapters of Genesis. Years ago, Helmut Thielicke similarly argued that homosexuality, according to Paul, is "a kind of symptomatic participation in the fate of the fallen world." Thus, in what is assumed to be a liberal stance, Thielicke insists that those with a homosexual orientation are no more sinful than other people: "We are all under the same condemnation."[6]

This inscription of homosexuality into "fallen human nature" is remarkable in light of the fact that Paul does not here mention Adam, Eve, Eden, the Fall, or the universal bondage of humanity to sin. Elsewhere, to be sure, Paul does cite Adam as the point at which sin entered cosmic and mythological history (Rom. 5:12), but, as many other scholars have noted, the scenario Paul sketches in Romans 1 has to do with the invention of idolatry and its consequences, not the Fall of Adam.[7] In Romans 1 Paul refers not to Adam or "he"—a single person—but to "they." Furthermore, we have no evidence that Paul considered Adam an idolater. I suggest that Paul's assumed narrative is as follows: Once upon a time, even after the sin of Adam, all humanity was safely and securely monotheistic. At some point in ancient history most of humanity rebelled against God, rejected the knowledge of the true God that they certainly possessed, willfully turned their collective back on God, made idols for themselves, and proceeded to worship those things that by nature are not gods. As punishment for their invention of idolatry and polytheism, God "handed them over" to depravity, allowing them to follow their "passions," which led them into sexual immorality, particularly same-sex coupling. Homosexual activity was the punishment meted out by God for the sin of idolatry and polytheism.

Paul apparently presupposes a Jewish mythological narrative about the origins of idolatry. Since the first chapters of Genesis do not explicitly recount the beginnings of idolatry and polytheism, Jews in Paul's day had filled in the missing data in different ways. Although accounts differ from one another, all of them place the beginnings of idolatry and polytheism at some point after the time of Adam: rabbinic sources variously ascribe the invention of idolatry to Kenan, Enosh (son of Seth), or the people of Enosh's generation.[8]

These Jewish accounts about polytheism's origins were part of a literary tradition that blamed many evils of contemporary Gentile civilization on some ancient turn in human history. A famous example is the story of the fall of the Watchers in *1 Enoch:* heavenly beings, the "sons of God" from Genesis 6, descend to earth, lust after women, mate with them, produce giants or monsters, and introduce the evils of civilization into the world: magic, astrology, warfare, cosmetics, etc. In these narratives, one result of the evil angelic influence is sexual immorality. None of the accounts I have examined explicitly names homosexuality as one of the "sins" introduced by the fallen angels, but sexual immorality in general, linked with impurity and corruption, is almost always mentioned, and Paul, along with other Jews, probably assumed that this "immorality" included same-sex intercourse. Stories such as these, which Stanley Stowers calls "decline of civilization narratives," were common in Greek, Roman, and Jewish circles; in the Jewish traditions, they usually function to set Israel off from the impurities and gross sins of the Gentiles.[9] For Jews, the stories served to highlight the fallenness not of Jewish culture or even of humanity in general, but of the Gentiles due to the corruption brought about by civilization. *Porneia,* as the sin of the Gentiles *par excellence,* is a polluted and polluting consequence of Gentile rebellion.

For example, the book of *Jubilees* offers a series of stories that depict the increasingly profound corruption of the world. In *Jubilees,* the introduction of idolatry occurs several chapters after the account of the sin of the Watchers.

According to this text, Ur built the city named after him, the citizens of which then began to make images and worship them. Heavenly beings encouraged them: "And cruel spirits assisted them and led them astray so that they might commit sin and pollution" (11:4). Here we have the usual constellation of motifs: civilization advances due at least in part to inspiration by evil heavenly beings; different aspects of urban culture (and empire) are introduced (in this case idolatry); impurity (often described as sexual) results; and strife (often including the invention of war itself) among human beings is intensified.

Accounts such as these provide the context for Paul's comments about the origins of homosexuality. The narrative flow of Paul's rhetoric mimics the linear structure of these "decline narratives." For Paul, knowledge of God has been available to human beings since the creation of the world (Rom. 1:20). The different peoples, however, willfully plunged themselves into foolishness and darkness of mind (vv. 21–22). They exchanged the glory of the immortal God for images of mortal humans, birds, beasts, and reptiles (v. 23).[10] *Therefore* (*dio*), that is, as a direct punishment for idolatry and polytheism, God handed over the nations to the "desires of their hearts," leading to uncleanness, pollution, and dishonoring of their bodies (v. 24). In vv. 25–32, Paul repeats the sequence: people exchanged monotheism for idolatry and polytheism (v. 25); *for that reason* (*dia touto*) God gave them over to passions of dishonor, leading to sexual actions "beyond nature" (*para physin,* v. 26).[11] The result of the corruption was further and deeper bondage to sin, strife, social conflict, and chaos (vv. 28–32).

That Paul is referring not to the "universal human condition" but to Gentile culture in particular is confirmed by a rhetorical analysis of the first few chapters of Romans. As Hays realizes, in Romans 1 Paul sets up a "sting" operation, first against the self-righteousness of Gentile moralists (2:1–16), and then against that of the Jewish moralist who puts himself forward as a teacher of the Gentiles (2:17–3:31).[12] He condemns first the Gentiles, and then turns his attention to the Jews. If Rom. 1:18–32 is taken as a depiction of the fallenness of human nature in general, the structure and power of Paul's argument collapse. As it is, Paul entices his "Jewish" hearer to nod in agreement with this traditional Jewish indictment of Gentile corruption, of which sexual impurity, as usual, is offered as a prime example.

My reading of Romans 1 as a reference to the origin of idolatry rather than to the Fall is not original or unusual. Even those scholars who read into the text the "fallen nature of humanity" often acknowledge that homosexual acts result as a punishment for idol worship.[13] Hays, for example, recognizes that Paul's contemporary readers would have heard the passage "as a condemnation of the pagan Gentiles."[14] This makes it especially notable when

Hays shifts the rhetoric from Paul's condemnation of Gentile polytheism to a general condemnation of perverse human nature.[15] Such inconsistencies betoken the ideological bias at work in the interpretations—a bias I identify as "heterosexist."

I will comment further below on possible reasons for reading Romans 1 as referring to the Fall, but some observations can here be offered. In the first place, modern scholars tend to read Paul through Augustinian lenses, seeking references to general theological anthropology in the most unlikely places.[16] Paul here makes a characteristic statement about Jewish ethnic purity—or rather, Gentile ethnic *impurity*—which is transformed by modern scholars, in good Augustinian fashion, into a statement about universal concupiscence.[17] Moreover, most modern scholars do not have the texts of *Jubilees* or the Rabbis foremost in their minds when they read Paul, but rather tend to see him as constantly alluding to or echoing the (Protestant!) Old Testament. More importantly, modern scholars read the Fall into Romans 1 because it renders the text more serviceable for heterosexist purposes.

Paul's own logic assumes a mythological structure unknown to most modern persons, Christians included. Most of us do not believe that all of humanity was once upon a time neatly monotheistic, only later, at a particular historical point, to turn to polytheism and idolatry; nor are we likely to believe that homosexuality did not exist until a sudden invention of polytheism. According to his etiology of homosexuality, Paul must not have believed that it ever existed among the Jews, at least those who abstained from idolatry. Importantly, when Paul finally indicts the Jews in Romans, he does not accuse them of idolatry or homosexual immorality; Jewish immorality is revealed, at most, in adultery and dishonesty regarding the property of temples (2:22). This is perfectly consistent with Paul's assumption that homosexuality is punishment for idolatry and polytheism: the Jews have not been so punished because they have not, in general, been guilty of that particular sin. If we were to follow Paul's logic, we would have to assume that once idolatry and polytheism were forsaken, homosexuality would cease to exist, which is probably what Paul believed; after all, he never even hints that any Jew or Christian engages in homosexuality. Even if we take the problematic terms *malakos* and *arsenokoitēs* in 1 Cor. 6:9 to refer to simple homosexual coupling (which is doubtful), Paul's point is "such *were* some of you"—in the past. The vice list functions again to characterize the Gentile world that these newly made "people of Israel" have left behind. Most of us, on the other hand, probably do not believe that the abolition of idolatrous cults and polytheism would spell the end of homosexuality. In sum, modern people, even Christians, do not believe the mythological structure that provides the logic for

Paul's statements about homosexuality in Romans 1. Heterosexist scholars alter Paul's reference to a myth which most modern Christians do not even know, much less believe (that is, a myth about the beginnings of idolatry) and pretend that Paul refers to a myth that many modern Christians do believe, at least on some level (the myth about the Fall). Heterosexism can retain Paul's condemnation of same-sex coupling only by eliding the supporting logic of that condemnation.

Natural Desire and Unnatural Acts

Another telling inconsistency in heterosexist scholarship on Romans 1 lies in its assumption that Paul is not only addressing the question of homosexual *activity* but also providing an explanation for the existence of homosexual *desire*. On the one hand, most of these scholars, in an attempt to be more "compassionate" and "liberal," point out that Paul condemns not homosexual orientation or desire but only homosexual acts. Thus gay and lesbian people should take comfort that, although their emotions are shameful, they are not exactly culpable. On the other hand, these scholars continue to read Romans 1 as offering an explanation for the existence of homosexual desire (that such an explanation is felt to be necessary is itself, of course, the result of heterosexism). Helmut Thielicke, for example, arguing against Karl Barth and others for a more "liberal" view of homosexuality, speaks of "the predisposition itself, the homosexual potentiality as such," and claims that it is "a kind of symptomatic participation in the fate of the fallen world." The "constitutional homosexual," therefore, should not be condemned any more than any other fallen human being.[18] According to a Church of England document, the "invert" is "an anomaly whose sexual disorientation bears its own tragic witness to the disordering of humanity by sin."[19] And Richard Hays, in spite of his insistence that Paul is condemning not homosexual desire or orientation but only homosexual activity, cannot in the end help but slip into reading Romans 1 as providing an etiology of homosexual orientation. "Paul, if confronted by a study demonstrating that (say) 10 percent of the population favor sexual partners of the same gender, would no doubt regard it as corroborative evidence for his proclamation that the wrath of God is being made manifest in rampant human unrighteousness."[20] Thus, though Hays insists (I think rightly) that Paul had no conception of homosexual orientation and thus no conception of homosexual people in the modern sense,[21] Hays nevertheless also insists that the presence of such people in the world is a sign of the wrath of God. All of these scholars, indeed, believe that Paul is *referring* to homosexual desire, even if he is not actually *condemning* it.[22]

To some extent, it is understandable that modern scholars read Paul's comments as a reference to homosexual desire; Paul does, after all, mention desire and passion in the passage. In v. 24 Paul says that God "gave them up in the desires [epithymiai] of their hearts to uncleanness with the result that they dishonor their bodies in themselves." Paul uses the term "passions of dishonor" (pathē atimias, v. 26), and he writes that males "burned in their yearning [orexis] for one another" (v. 27). But it is a mistake to read into these comments the kind of modernist dichotomy between homosexual and heterosexual desire, in which a difference in kind—between an unnatural, abnormal desire and a natural, normal desire—is assumed. The question is, Does Paul here assume a category of homosexual desire that is a different kind of desire from heterosexual desire?

First, it should be noted that Paul uses the term "contrary to nature" or "unnatural" only when referring to actions, not desires. In v. 26, Paul says that females exchanged the "natural use" (physikē chrēsis) for that which is "contrary to" or "beyond nature" (para physin). Paul also mentions males forsaking the "natural use of females" (v. 27). Paul does not, however, link the language of "nature" to "desire." The absence in Paul's language of any reference to "unnatural desire" is understandable when we place him in the context of ancient, rather than modern, notions of homosexual sex.

As has been often noted, ancient Greco-Roman moralists (and we should include most Jewish moralists of Paul's day) generally believed homosexual behavior sprang from the same desire that motivated heterosexual sex.[23] According to these moralists, some people, due to unrestrained sexual desire, grew bored with "basic" sexual activity and went cruising for new and untried pleasures. Women, no longer satisfied by sex with their husbands, would be led in their lasciviousness to experiment with bestiality.[24] Men were so enslaved to their lusts that they were eager to try activities out of the ordinary, such as sex with one another. The problem had to do not with a disoriented desire, but with inordinate desire. Degree of passion, rather than object choice, was the defining factor of desire.

This ancient logic surfaces in discussions about "unnatural" sex in the ancient texts. In a speech by Dio Chrysostom, for example, a rustic moralist bemoans the excesses of civilization and criticizes men who have gotten their fill of seducing women:

> The man whose appetite is insatiate in such things, when he finds there is no
> scarcity, no resistance, in this field, will have contempt for the easy conquest
> and scorn for a woman's love, as a thing too readily given—in fact, too
> utterly feminine—and will turn his assault against the male quarters, eager to

befoul the youth who will very soon be magistrates and judges and generals, believing that in them he will find a kind of pleasure difficult and hard to procure.[25]

As Victor Paul Furnish notes, the ancient moralists, and here we must include Paul, considered homosexual behavior to be "the most extreme expression of heterosexual lust."[26] Or as John Chrysostom put it, "You will see that all such desire stems from a greed which will not remain within its usual bounds."[27] In other words, a basically "natural" desire is taken to an "unnatural extreme."

It may be helpful here to note the analogy with eating. Ancient moralists often couple condemnations about sexual misdeeds with similar remarks about eating. Gluttony is "unnatural" because the glutton is insatiable: whereas "nature" intends human beings to be satisfied with a decent meal, gluttons stuff themselves until they become sick, even making themselves vomit so they can continue eating. Human beings should be content with basic nourishment—according to some of the more ascetic Greco-Roman traditions, bread, vegetables, and water; but gormandizers are never satisfied until they have searched out exotic and expensive delicacies. The glutton and gormand act "contrary to nature" not because they have perverted desires (for example, to eat things not found "in nature" or that will kill them) but because they have indulged their desires to excess, thus losing control of them. In this regard, it is significant that the Greek phrase *para physin,* usually translated "contrary to nature" or "unnatural," more exactly means "beyond nature" or "in excess of what is natural." For the ancient writers, certain behaviors were "contrary to nature" because they went beyond the proper limits prescribed by nature. Gluttony was "too much eating"; homosexuality was "too much sex."

We should compare this ancient logic of "unnatural acts" to modern heterosexist rhetoric about homosexuality as "unnatural." In modern discourse homosexuality is unnatural in that it results from disoriented desire, wrong "object choice": some people have perverted passions and desire things that are, in themselves, disgusting and harmful.[28] In this logic, homosexual desire is like a craving to eat excrement. This is, however, *not* what the ancients meant when they spoke of certain acts as "unnatural": for them, the actions could be "unnatural" but still sprang from basically natural desire. This is why the ancients had no notion of "homosexual orientation" or "homosexuals"; it was not a question of "disoriented desires" but of legitimate desires that were allowed illegitimate freedoms.[29]

It is true that Greco-Roman texts in rare cases speak of "unnatural desires," and an analysis of such cases reveals why some moralists considered same-sex intercourse "unnatural acts." What is at issue in these cases, however, is unlike anything modern discourse means when it sometimes labels same-sex eroticism "unnatural." For example, an Aristotelian discussion (the topic occurs in Aristotle's own texts and pseudo-Aristotelian accounts) ponders why some men, contrary to their nature as males, desire to *be* sexually penetrated. Males, by definition, are those "on top," those who penetrate. It is "unnatural," therefore, for a man to be willing—and even eager!—to allow himself to be penetrated.[30] The "unnaturalness" of the desire has nothing to do with one man's erotic interest in another, but with the "unnaturalness" of a man desiring to demean himself by enthusiastically assuming the despised, lower position appropriate for women. Sex in Greco-Roman society, as is well known, was hierarchical, and sex acts (whether the couple was male-male, male-female, female-female, or any combination of human and animal) were almost always inscribed by the assumed superiority of the penetrator to the penetrated. A man's desire to be penetrated was considered unnatural because he thereby renounced his natural position of male superiority and honor: his desire frustrated the gender hierarchy of "nature."[31]

This is precisely the argument mounted against homosexual sex by Plato: a man's *desire* for another male is assumed to be "natural"; but homosexual penetration affronts nature due to its disruption of the male-female cosmic hierarchy.[32] As Plutarch later puts it, homosexual sex is "contrary to nature," because of "the weakness and effeminacy on the part of those who, contrary to nature, allow themselves in Plato's words 'to be covered and mounted like cattle.'"[33] What is unspoken but clearly presupposed is that it is perfectly "natural" for *women* to be "covered and mounted like cattle."

Philo's writings demonstrate that Jews shared these Greco-Roman common senses about hierarchized sex roles, nature, and the implicit devaluation of the feminine. With the Greek and Roman authors, Philo also assumes an etiology of homosexual desire that is no different from heterosexual desire. Sexual desires exceed their bounds precisely like desires for food. In fact, an excess of indulgence in food may lead to an excess of sexual desire. Thus Philo writes:

> These persons begin with making themselves experts in dainty feeding, wine-bibbing, and the other pleasures of the belly and parts below it. Then sated with these they reach such a pitch of wantonness, the natural offspring of satiety, that losing their senses they conceive a frantic passion, no longer for human beings male or female, but even for brute beasts.[34]

Once led to act out their excessive sexual desire, people grow more and more brazen, and eventually "throw off nature" in their excess.[35] The aspects of same-sex intercourse Philo considers unnatural are the feminization of the penetrated man and the unfruitful expenditure of seed by the penetrator. The complex of desire and nature assumed by Philo is like that of other intellectuals of Greco-Roman culture: (1) male *attraction* to beautiful males is considered "natural" ("the natural offspring of satiety"), thus homosexual *desire* is not itself "contrary to nature"; (2) same-sex intercourse, however, may spring from an *excess* of desire, and allowing desire to exceed its bounds leads to actions "beyond nature"; (3) the aspects of same-sex intercourse assumed to be "unnatural" are (a) disruption of the male-female hierarchy and (b) sexual intercourse that does not have procreation as its goal.[36]

Paul, as a product of his culture, certainly shared many of these assumptions—with the exception that Paul shows no concerns for procreation whatsoever (see 1 Corinthians 7). Thus he describes homosexual activity in Romans 1 as inordinate passion.[37] As a possible objection to my argument one might note that Paul does speak of "dishonorable passions" (v. 26) as the motivation for homosexual activity. Does this not imply that Paul believed that homosexual acts sprang from a different kind of desire than heterosexual acts? This would be the case only if we could demonstrate that there was such a thing for Paul as "honorable passion," that is, heterosexual desire that was the positive counterpart of perverted homosexual desire. Such is not the case. Paul never has a positive word to say about sexual passion or desire.[38] The only other place in Paul's undisputed letters where the world *pathos* occurs is 1 Thess. 4:5, again linked with *epithymia* to denote sexual desire. Here also, passion is characteristic of Gentiles and must be avoided completely by Christians. Christian men are to have sex with their own wives *and thus avoid passion and desire.*[39] To be sure, Paul sometimes uses the term *epithymia* in a neutral or positive sense (Phil. 1:23; 1 Thess. 2:17), but never when referring to sexual desire. And when giving instructions to Christians in 1 Corinthians 7, Paul counsels people to get married—if they are too weak to control themselves otherwise—not so that they may have an arena for the proper expression of sexual desire but in order to *preclude* the possibility of it.[40] "It is better to marry than to burn" means, in spite of its incomprehensibility for modern persons, that Paul encouraged sex within marriage only as a prophylaxis against desire. Sex is not so much the problem for Paul as desire: marital sex acts thus assist in the precluding of passion. It is a mistake, therefore, for us to interpret Paul's phrase "passion of dishonor" as implying the possibility for him of "honorable passion," since for him *all* passion is dishonorable. For Paul, homosexuality was simply a further extreme of the corruption inherent in sexual passion itself. It did not spring from a different kind of desire, but simply from desire itself.

Doubtless, Paul also objects to same-sex intercourse due in part to his assumption about the cosmic hierarchy of male over female. While this is not made explicit in Romans 1, it is probably assumed.[41] Indeed, in only one other instance do we have an ethical argument from Paul based on "nature." In 1 Cor. 11:2–16 Paul argues that women should be veiled when they pray and prophesy. While there are several exegetical problems of this passage I cannot address here, certain points must be highlighted for what they tell us about Paul's concept of "nature."[42] In the first place, Paul is here concerned to maintain the male-female gender hierarchy assumed to exist in the cosmos. God is to Christ as Christ is to man as man is to woman (11:3). Man is the reflection of God, and woman is the reflection of man (v. 7).[43] To support his point, Paul offers an argument from "nature" to convince his readers that women "naturally" should be covered: "nature" teaches, according to Paul, that women are to have long hair and men short. Any disruption of that natural order results in "shame," either for the man with long hair or the woman with short. Paul assumes a cosmic hierarchy of male and female that is expressed in the "natural" facts of hair length. For men to wear long hair is "contrary to nature." And what makes such a situation "unnatural" is its disruption of gender hierarchy.[44]

It is not clear whether the modern apologists for heterosexism intend also to appropriate Paul's views about "nature" when it comes to the maintenance of patriarchal gender hierarchy. It is certain, however, that heterosexism has led them to introject their own modern conceptions of sexual desire and its relation to "nature" into the biblical text. Romans 1 offers no etiology of homosexual desire or orientation; its etiology of homosexual sex is one no modern scholar has advocated as factual; and its assumptions about "nature" and sex are not those generally held by the modern apologists for hetero-sexism.

The Power of Heterosexism

By now it should be clear that I am not arguing that Paul was pro-gay or even neutral on the topic of homosexual sex. My purpose, rather, has been to expose the radical difference between the logics of sexuality that underwrite Romans 1, on the one hand, and the modern logic, on the other, that rules virtually every current discussion, including those by people priding them-selves on being "true to the Bible." Whether we are talking about the origins of homosexuality, the mythological presuppositions of Paul's text, the nature of desire, or the logic of the "unnatural," I have highlighted the disjunctions between Paul's presuppositions and those of modern Christian heterosexism. In each case, contemporary scholars read Paul through the lenses of modern categories and assumptions, either ignoring, masking, or dismissing the logic of Paul's own account.

I am attempting, of course, to unmask what parades as "objectivity." Heterosexist scholars regularly impugn the motives of their foes, accusing them of seeing in the text only what they want to see (due, doubtless, to their disoriented nature). Richard Hays, for example, claims that others import anachronisms into the Pauline text; those who argue that the Bible does not condemn homosexuality (in the modern sense of the term) have simply "imposed a wishful interpretation on the biblical passages."[45] Hays criticizes John Boswell for "scrutiniz[ing] the text through the hermeneutical lenses of modern categories alien to the first-century historical setting."[46] Would Hays have us assume, then, that *he* is simply letting the texts "speak for themselves," that he is passively submitting to their penetrating word about homosexuality? Hays's rhetoric, of course, comes as no surprise; oppressive ideologies have always in the modern world masqueraded as objective descriptions of "the way things are."

I believe I have demonstrated, by using the same historical methods as these scholars who claim objectivity, that they are no more "objective" than the rest of us. Indeed, they construe Paul's argument the way they do because of the modern heterosexist assumptions they themselves bring to the text. As they see it, Paul inscribes disturbing desires and orientations into fallen human nature, and they see their own conceptions of "natural" and "unnatural" reflected back at them in the text—none of which would be possible apart from particularly modern forms of heterosexism. Ultimately, my purpose is to insist that modern scholars cannot blame *their* heterosexism on Paul precisely because the form *their* heterosexism takes—its assumptions, logics, ways of framing the question—is completely different from the form of *Paul's* heterosexism, as can be seen through my sketch of the different (indeed, conflicting) grammars of the ancient and modern ideologies.

Why have modern scholars read Romans 1 as a reference to universal fallen human nature? Why read the Fall into this text? Furthermore, why read Romans 1 as offering an etiology, not just of homosexual activity, but of homosexual desire? One possible explanation, though I recognize that it will be a controversial one, is that the modern accounts represent a classic case of homophobia.

Charges of homophobia should not be cast breezily or indiscriminately, so I will explain why I suggest it here. Homophobia is the loathing of homosexuality that arises from a deep-seated (and I think, irrational) fear of homosexuality, often including an unconscious or unacknowledged fear of one's own homoerotic tendencies.[47] Homophobia results when people (regardless of their orientation, for there are homophobic homosexuals) fear the homosexual within. Not all heterosexism springs from homophobia, any more than all sexism necessarily springs from misogyny, but some does.

Much scholarship on Romans 1 and religious writing on homosexuality in general could be read as a classic case of such internalized fear and loathing. I should be clear in making this point that I am unconcerned about the individual psychologies of particular biblical scholars. I am not claiming that these particular men are themselves homophobic. Rather, I would argue that their writings about homosexuality participate in a cultural homophobia, an irrational fear and loathing of homosexuality—and by extension (in spite of protestations to the contrary) lesbian, gay, and bisexual people—that pervades much of modern Western culture and expresses itself in discourses about sexuality, institutionalized marginalization of gay and lesbian people, and social structures that discriminate against them.

The homophobia of Hays's writing occurs in his stereotypical depiction of the "gay subculture" and "homosexual lifestyle" as depressing and loathsome. Hays introduces, as the spokesperson for gay experience, a self-loathing, conservative homosexual Christian who is dying of AIDS—and who had died by the time of the writing of the article, significantly rendering him unavailable for further discussion. His "condition"—referring to his identity as a homosexual man or to his medical diagnosis?—is "tragic." He experiences his homosexuality as "a compulsion and an affliction." (At this point, any distinction between his sexuality and his sickness has become blurred—or was perhaps never really possible at all.) He is "wracked" by his sexual orientation. (The language of torture is not accidental.) "Gary," the gay spokesman in the article, testifies that homosexual people tend (more than straights?) to "draw their identity from their sexuality." (It is a common heterosexist stereotype that gay men and lesbians are quintessentially defined by their sexual desires and activities, whereas the identities of "normal" heterosexuals are complex and constructed by many different aspects of personhood, such as relations, geographical origin, career, interests, hobbies, age, gender, talents, etc.) In the end, it seems, the only hope for gay Christians is the kind of miraculous healing of their homosexuality experienced by "Gary" at the end of his life; they must pray that the "great weight" of their sexuality be lifted off them. Through this amazing rhetorical sleight of hand and ventriloquism, Hays himself avoids explicitly accusing "gay subculture" of any of these faults and diseases; he simply lets the gay spokesman tell his own story about "the depressing reality of the gay subculture."[48]

This exclusively negative portrait of "gay subculture" and the tortured homosexual is surprising given the fact that Hays himself has for years known lesbian and gay Christians who have quite different, *positive* experiences of their sexuality and who have borne witness to the supportive alternative communities they have built outside heterosexist culture, including that of the church. The simultaneous presence of such persons in Hays's experience with the absolute absence of such voices in Hays's articles betrays the irrationality of ideological stereotype. Like racism and sexism, homophobia must construct and advance stereotypes of the "other" that are belied by the experiences of its very proponents.

Whereas Hays's article represents the *loathing* aspect of homophobia, irrational *fear* is the salient factor in an article published by a group of Jewish and Christian conservative scholars who call themselves the "Ramsey Colloquium." Although the article "The Homosexual Movement" does not attempt an exegesis of Romans 1, it also, like Hays, inscribes homosexual orientation into "humanity's fallen condition," thereby invoking fears of the "homosexual within" corporate humanity.[49]

The authors of the article question the famous claim that 10 percent of men experience predominantly or exclusively homosexual desires, insisting that such data "have now been convincingly discredited." Neglecting to cite the research to which they refer or to analyze it critically, they nevertheless continue: "Current research suggests that the percentage of males whose sexual desires and behavior are exclusively homosexual is as low as 1 percent or 2 percent in developed societies."[50] In spite of their claims that homosexuals are relatively insignificant demographically, however, the authors proceed with their argument by invoking fears that homosexuality, unless kept firmly in the closet, will destroy the existence of heterosexuality and the fabric of the heterosexually oriented nuclear family. They single out "the homosexual subculture" as particularly responsible for "sexual promiscuity, depression, and suicide and the ominous presence of AIDS." Even more broadly, they decry "the harm done to the social order when policies are advanced that would increase incidence of the gay lifestyle and undermine the normative character of marriage and family life." The mere presence of lesbians and gay men constitutes an "attack" upon "the heterosexual norm."[51] Invoking even the dangerous stereotype of the lecherous homosexual preying on and recruiting children, the authors advocate job "discrimination" (their word) "in education and programs involving young people." They argue: "Public anxiety about homosexuality is preeminently a concern about the vulnerabilities of the young. This, we are persuaded, is a legitimate and urgent public concern."[52]

One might reasonably expect that members of the Ramsey Colloquium would have settled on a coherent logic before going into print: is the incidence of homosexuality really as rare as they claim (in which case it is hard to imagine how dangerous an attack upon heterosexuality it could effectively mount), *or* is heterosexuality truly threatened (in which case we must imagine a far higher percentage of the population choosing exclusively homosexual relations)? Even if 20 or 30 percent of the population—a figure far higher than suggested by Kinsey's data—were in same-sex alternative families, it is difficult to imagine how that would disable the rest of the population from pursuing opposite-sex ones. Are the authors afraid that our society is on the brink of population extinction? *How* does the love of two men or two women for one another pose a significant threat to the existence of heterosexual relations or structures? The Ramsey Colloquium nowhere offers any reasoned arguments to demonstrate *how* even a large majority of gay men and lesbians could conceivably bring about the demise of heterosexuality; and the irrationality of their anxiety becomes even more glaring since they argue that only 1 or at most 2 percent of the population is homosexual. The homophobia of "The Homosexual Movement" is revealed, as is often the case with marginalizing ideologies, by its internal contradictions.

I have gone to such lengths to illustrate why I call certain positions homophobic (rather than simply heterosexist) for an important reason. Having denied that heterosexist scholars interpret Paul the way they do because they are simply "reading the text," I wished to propose other reasons to explain why they have misconstrued Paul's writings in the particular way they have. I suggest that a specifically modern form of homophobia—an irrational and exaggerated loathing and fear of homosexuality—has motivated many such interpretations.[53] By implanting homosexual desire into the body of universal, fallen human nature—which Paul does not do—conservative scholars closet homosexual desire in the deep recesses of humanity itself, manifesting the classic tendency of homophobia to portray the danger of homosexuality as that which threatens from within. Instead of representing homosexuality as something "they" do (for example, Paul's Gentiles), such modern readings curiously make it something "we" do—or that we (and our children!) may very well do if we are not careful to police our inmost urges and those of our fellow citizens. What for Paul functioned as a sign of the boundary separating idolatrous civilization from monotheistic faith has become a symptom *par excellence* of what is wrong with "all of us." Homosexual desire now lurks somewhere within us all. The fear of its outbreak motivates the current interpretive politics of heterosexism.

• *Notes*

1. Patricia Beattie Jung and Ralph F. Smith, *Heterosexism: An Ethical Challenge* (Albany: SUNY Press, 1993), 13–14.

2. Thus, my approach here differs from those scholars offering a more "pro-gay" reading of Paul, such as John Boswell, *Christianity, Social Tolerance, and Homosexuality: Gay People in Western Europe from the Beginning of the Christian Era to the Fourteenth Century* (Chicago: University of Chicago Press, 1980). My approach is perhaps closer to that of Klaus Wengst, "Paulus und die Homosexualität: Überlegungen zu Röm, 1,26f.," *Zeitschrift für evangelische Ethik* 31 (1987): 72–81.

3. Richard B. Hays, "Relations Natural and Unnatural: A Response to John Boswell's Exegesis of Romans 1," *Journal of Christian Ethics* 14 (1986): 184–215, at 189.

4. Hays, "Relations Natural and Unnatural," 190; Robin Scroggs, *The New Testament and Homosexuality* (Philadelphia: Fortress Press, 1983), 110.

5. Hays, "Relations Natural and Unnatural," 191, 200.

6. Helmut Thielicke, *The Ethics of Sex* (New York: Harper & Row, 1964), 282–83; for similar views, see also H. Kimball-Jones, *Toward a Christian Understanding of the Homosexual* (London: SCM Press, 1966), 77; William Muehl, "Some Words of Caution," in *Male and Female: Christian Approaches to Sexuality,* ed. Ruth Tiffany Barnhouse and Urban R. Holmes III (New York: Seabury, 1976), 167–74, at 174; Richard B. Hays, "Awaiting the Redemption of Our Bodies: The Witness of Scripture Concerning Homosexuality," in *Homosexuality in the Church: Both Sides of the Debate,* ed. Jeffrey S. Siker (Louisville: Westminster/John Knox, 1994), 3–17 (originally published in a edited version in *Sojourners* 20, no. 6 [July 1991]: 17–21; I cite the more recent, complete version); P. Michael Ukleja, "The Bible and Homosexuality, Part 2: Homosexuality in the New Testament," *Bibliotheca Sacra* 140 (1983): 350–58; S. Lewis Johnson Jr, "God Gave Them Up," *Bibliotheca Sacra* 129 (1972): 124–33; D. S. Bailey, ed., *Sexual Offenders and Social Punishment* (Church Information Board for Church of England Moral Welfare Council, 1956), 76, quoted in D. J. Atkinson, *Homosexuals in the Christian Fellowship* (Grand Rapids: Eerdmans, 1979), 62.

7. So also K. Wengst, "Paulus und die Homosexualität," 74. The most famous argument that Romans 1 refers to Adam is M. D. Hooker, "Adam in Romans I," *NTS* 6 (1959–60): 297–306; see also her "A Further Note on Romans I," *NTS* 13 (1966–67): 181–83. For refutations of Hooker's arguments, see Joseph A. Fitzmyer, *Romans* (Garden City, N.Y.: Doubleday, 1993), 274; and Stanley K. Stowers, *A Rereading of Romans: Justice, Jews, and Gentiles* (New Haven: Yale University Press, 1994), 86–94.

8. See Louis Ginzberg, *Legends of the Jews,* 7 vols. (Philadelphia: Jewish Publication Society of America, 1909–66), 1:123–24; 4:306; 5:150 n. 53, 151 n. 54; for Christian explanations of the origins of idolatry, see 5:150 n. 54.

9. Stowers, *A Rereading of Romans,* 85, 97–100. Stowers provides many parallels of such "decline narratives" and their hortatory use in Greek, Roman, and Jewish contexts. As Stowers points out, the particularly Jewish modifications of the commonplace are the condemnation of idolatry in particular as a degenerate and late invention of Gentile peoples and the blame placed on idolatry and polytheism for the other degenerate aspects of heathen civilization, such as rampant sexual immorality, warfare, pharmacology, and cosmetics.

10. This part of the narrative is one piece of evidence that Paul is not here referring to any rejection of knowledge of God by Adam and Eve nor to the Israelite sin of idolatry with the "golden calf." The particular description of the *kind* of idolatry here evident would evoke images not of Jewish rebellion but of the polymorphous polytheism of Gentile culture as depicted by contemporary Jews.

11. The Greek *para physin,* usually translated "contrary to nature" or "unnatural," more exactly means "beyond nature," the significance of which I explain below.

12. For a convincing argument that Paul is addressing a Gentile (rather than Jewish) moralist in Rom. 2:1–16, see Stowers, *A Rereading of Romans,* 100–109.

13. For example, Ukleja, "Bible and Homosexuality," 356.

14. Hays, "Relations Natural and Unnatural," 195.

15. Hays notes (at 195 and 200) that Paul is referring in Romans 1 to "pagan Gentiles" and "the whole *pagan* world" (emphasis added); he alters his language in several places, however, to take the passage as referring actually to the universal human condition: 189, 190, 191, 195, 200, 207, 211. See also "Awaiting the Redemption," 8–9, where Hays, in spite of realizing that Paul's initial subject is idolatry, continually slips into rhetoric about "the underlying sickness of humanity as a whole, Jews and Greeks alike," "the universal fall of humanity," "human fallenness," and "humanity's tragic confusion and alienation from God the Creator." It may be true that Paul's argument takes idolatry to be one expression of the fallenness of humanity, an expression particular to Gentiles. In that case, however, homosexual activity, as an example of the depravities caused by idolatry, would be a subset of a set: homosexual sex came from idolatry, which came from the Fall. But this is a long way from using homosexuality itself as a special symptom of the universal fallenness of human nature, which Hays takes Paul to do.

16. The classic critique of this practice is Krister Stendahl, "The Apostle Paul and the Introspective Conscience of the West," *Harvard Theological Review* 56 (1963): 199–215.

17. Stowers labels Paul's portrait an "ethnic caricature" of non-Jewish civilization (*A Rereading of Romans,* 95), and "what moderns would call an ethnic cultural stereotype" (109). The redundancy (in Paul's thought) of "Gentile sinners" comes naturally to Paul's pen (Gal. 2:15).

18. Thielicke, *Ethics of Sex,* 282–83.

19. Bailey, ed., *Sexual Offenders,* 75–76, quoted in Atkinson, *Homosexuals,* 62.

20. Hays, "Relations Natural and Unnatural," 208.

21. Note Martha Nussbaum's succinct description of the difference between ancient and modern notions: "[T]here was for the ancient Greeks no salient distinction corresponding to our own distinction between heterosexuality and homosexuality: no distinction, that is, of persons into two profoundly different kinds on the basis of the gender

of the object they most deeply or most characteristically desire. Nor is there, indeed, anything precisely corresponding to our modern concept of 'sexuality'—a deep and relatively stable inner orientation towards objects of a certain gender" ("Therapeutic Arguments and Structures of Desire," *Differences* 2 [1990]: 46–66, at 49). Among the many treatments of the modern invention of homosexuality, perhaps the most famous are Michel Foucault, *The History of Sexuality,* vol. 1: *An Introduction* (New York: Random House, 1978); idem, *The History of Sexuality,* vol. 2: *The Use of Pleasure* (New York: Random House, 1985); David M. Halperin, *One Hundred Years of Homosexuality* (New York: Routledge, 1990); see also the collection of essays, written from a social-constructionist point of view, in David M. Halperin et al., eds., *Before Sexuality: The Construction of Erotic Experience in the Ancient Greek World* (Princeton: Princeton University Press, 1990). See also John Boswell's response to those critics who label him an "essentialist": "Concepts, Experience, and Sexuality," *Differences* 2 (1990): 67–87. For an excellent account of "constructionism," "history," and the problem of knowledge, see Eve Kosofsky Sedgwick, *Epistemology of the Closet* (Berkeley and Los Angeles: University of California Press, 1990), esp. 1–63.

22. This is the necessary implication of Hays's connection of an admission of sexual orientation in perhaps 10 percent of the population (a figure he yet questions without providing contrary evidence) to his statements that Paul would respond to such information by pointing to it as "evidence" for "the wrath of God." See also "Awaiting the Redemption," 12, where Hays imagines Paul responding to "sexual orientation" as proof that "the power of sin is rampant in the world" (see also Atkinson, *Homosexuals,* 58.) Hays admits that he himself accepts the reality of "homosexual orientation" (14). It is baffling to me that Hays can admit such an important difference between his own beliefs and Paul's (that there is such a thing as "sexual orientation") and then act as if the difference is irrelevant. For an excellent theological critique of both progressive and conservative assumptions of the modernist "sexed identity" (which includes the modern notion of sexual orientation), see Mary McClintock Fulkerson, "Gender—Being It or Doing It? The Church, Homosexuality, and the Politics of Identity," *Union Seminary Quarterly Review* 47 (1993): 29–46.

23. See, for example, Victor Paul Furnish, "The Bible and Homosexuality: Reading the Texts in Context," in *Homosexuality in the Church,* 18–35, at 27. I disagree, however, with Furnish's claims that in the Greco-Roman world "it was universally presupposed that anyone who sought intercourse with a partner of the same sex was willfully overriding his or her own 'natural' desire for the opposite sex" (26; see also 31). As I explain below, ancient persons considered same-sex eroticism to be simply one expression of "desire" in general—perhaps taken to an undue extreme, but not different in kind from opposite-sex eroticism. In fact, one *reason* the ancients had no conception of homosexual orientation in the modern sense is that they did not differentiate the different sexual activities into a bimorphic dichotomy framed by two different *kinds* of desire. They considered same-sex desire completely "natural," even if they did sometimes consider same-sex *intercourse* "unnatural."

24. Apuleius, *The Golden Ass,* Book 16, contains a famous fictitious account of a noblewoman's insatiable lust. See the parallel story in (Pseudo?-) Lucian, *Lucius, or the Ass,* 51.

25. Dio Chrysostom 7:151–52; see 7:135 for Dio's remark indicating that he took

male-female intercourse within the family to represent sex "according to nature" (*kata physin*). Since I will presently compare notions of "natural" sexual activity with "natural" use of food, it is interesting that, just after his quotation as given above, Dio compares insatiable appetites in sex to those in wine-drinking: "His state is like that of men who are addicted to drinking and wine-bibbing, who after long and steady drinking of unmixed wine, often lose their taste for it and create an artificial thirst by the stimulus of sweatings, salted foods, and condiments" (7:152). Importantly, Hays knows and even quotes this passage from Dio; I am puzzled that he does not perceive the radical difference between the ancient logic of the "natural" and the modern.

26. Victor Paul Furnish, "The Bible and Homosexuality," in *Homosexuality: In Search of a Christian Understanding,* ed. Leon Smith (Nashville: Discipleship Resources, 1981), 6–21, at 13; see also Furnish's comments in "The Bible and Homosexuality: Reading the Texts in Context," in *Homosexuality in the Church,* 18–35, esp. 26–28. Hays, it should be noted, knows of this material (see "Relations Natural and Unnatural," 193). I generally offer as examples ancient texts known to Hays himself; Hays's failure to discern the radical difference between his and Paul's notions about "nature" and "desire" is due not to ignorance of the ancient sources but ideological misconstrual or elision of the ancient logics of sex and desire.

27. *Homily IV on Romans.* This translation is by Boswell, *CSTH,* 361. An English translation of the homilies is also available in *The Homilies of S. John Chrysostom,* 3d ed. rev. (Oxford: James Parker, 1877), and in the *Nicene and Post-Nicene Fathers* series.

28. Interestingly, as Jeff Siker reminded me in personal conversation, the heterosexist inclination to compare homosexual orientation with a propensity towards alcoholism (which Hays in particular does, see "Awaiting the Redemption") has more in common with the ancient notion that "unnatural" action springs from a basically "natural" activity taken to an extreme. Also interestingly, however, modern scholars do not label alcoholism "unnatural."

29. Importantly, commentators on Romans 1 writing in the nineteenth century do *not* look to the passage as providing an etiology of homosexual desire. Much more akin to ancient conceptions, they generally assume that the same-sex *desire* is an extension of desire in general, not a different *kind* of sexuality. They offer not an etiology of homosexual *desire* but an etiology of homosexual *sex* that is assumed to spring from lust in general given too much latitude. This makes perfect sense once we realize that they were writing before the common currency of the concepts of "homosexuality" as opposed to "heterosexuality" in terms of orientation or personhood. See, for example, Albert Barnes, *Notes, Explanatory and Practical, on the Epistle to the Romans* (New York: Leavitt, Lord, 1835), 40–42; M. F. Sadler, *The Epistle to the Romans, with Notes Critical and Practical* (London: George Bell, 1888), 22–23; William G. T. Shedd, *A Critical and Doctrinal Commentary on the Epistle of St. Paul to the Romans* (Grand Rapids: Zondervan, 1967 [1879]), 25–29; Moses Stuart, *A Commentary on the Epistle to the Romans* (Andover: Flagg and Gould, 1832), 104, 108. Martin Luther also does not speak of homosexual *desire* as different; it is simply excessive indulgence in lust in general: *Commentary on the Epistle to the Romans,* trans. J. Theodore Mueller (Grand Rapids: Zondervan, 1954), 31. According to one study, the culture of colonial New England also knew of no particular *kind* of "homosexual" desire; see Jonathan Ned Katz, "The Age of Sodomitical Sin, 1607–1740," in *Reclaiming Sodom,* ed. Jonathan Goldberg (New York:

Routledge, 1994), 43–58, originally published, in a longer version, in Katz, *Gay/Lesbian Almanac* (New York: Harper and Row, 1983), 31–65.

30. See *Nichomachean Ethics* 1148b15–9a20; *Problemata* 4.26; Kenneth J. Dover, *Greek Homosexuality* (Cambridge, Mass.: Harvard University Press, 1978), 168–69.

31. In female-female intercourse, it was generally assumed that one of the women would have to penetrate the other, and the "penetrating woman" was more than an oxymoron; she was a monster—contrary to nature. Descriptions and analyses of the importance of gender hierarchy for Greco-Roman sexuality are now quite numerous. For starters, see Michel Foucault, *The History of Sexuality,* vol. 3: *The Care of the Self* (New York: Pantheon, 1986), 18–20, 84–88, *et passim;* Halperin, *One Hundred Years of Homosexuality,* 22–24, 130; Boswell, "Concepts, Experience, and Sexuality," 72–73; John J. Winkler, *The Constraints of Desire* (New York: Routledge, 1990), 39–40, 51, *et passim* (see index under "penetration"). I deal at length with the subject of gender hierarchy, penetration, and the construction of the feminine in my *The Corinthian Body* (New Haven: Yale University Press, 1995), esp. 177, 240, 247–48. Penetration framed in terms of gender hierarchy is of course not limited to the Greco-Roman world. For comparison with similar situations from anthropological studies, see Gerald W. Creed, "Sexual Subordination: Institutionalized Homosexuality and Social Control in Melanesia," in *Reclaiming Sodom,* 66–94 (originally published in *Ethnography* 23 [Pittsburgh: Department of Anthropology, University of Pittsburgh, 1984]: 157–76); J. W. M. Whiting, *Becoming a Kwoma* (New Haven: Yale University Press, 1941), 51; S. Brandes, "Like Wounded Stags: Male Sexual Ideology in an Andalusian Town," in *Sexual Meanings: The Cultural Construction of Gender and Sexuality,* ed. S. Ortner and H. Whitehead (Cambridge: Cambridge University Press, 1981), 216–39, at 232–33. I do not mean to imply that *all* homosexual relations were rigidly constructed along the lines of dominance/subordination; only that that was the way sexual relations in general were ideologically constructed. For the variety of possible constructions of homosexual relations, see John Boswell, *Same-Sex Unions in Premodern Europe* (New York: Villard, 1994); it is not hard to imagine that in many cases same-sex relations provided opportunity for more equality between lovers than opposite-sex ones. I also do not wish to imply that our modern society is free from the misogynous tendency to degrade the person penetrated. Common derogatory language and insults no longer even considered obscene by most people ("This sucks!") derive their meaning from assumptions about the despised role of the penetrated in intercourse, implicating therefore the feminine in the inferior.

32. *Laws* 636a–c; 836c–e.

33. *Dialogue on Love (Moralia)* 751d.

34. *Special Laws* 3:43; see also 3:37.

35. *On Abraham* 133–36.

36. See also *Special Laws* 1:325; *The Contemplative Life* 59–62.

37. Although agreeing with many points made by David L. Bartlett, "A Biblical Perspective on Homosexuality," *Foundations* 20 (1977): 133–47, my position on the nature of desire in Paul's thought puts me at odds with his statement that Paul condemns homosexual *lust* rather than homosexual love in Romans 1 (140). I would say, rather, that Paul considers *any* homosexual activity necessarily to spring from lust in general (that is, the "lust" is the same thing whether directed towards persons of the same or opposite sex). This

does not mean, however, that Paul had some other notion of desire that would be appropriate—either homosexual or heterosexual.

38. This constitutes an important difference between Paul's position and that of most others of his time who wrote on desire and sex. Philosophers and physicians, for example, believed that "moderate" desire and passion were necessary for sexual activity; some "burning" was necessary to induce sex and provide the semen for ejaculation. Their moralism extended only to urging people to moderate their passion. Paul, on the other hand, never gives "moderated passion" as a possible solution to the problems of desire (see, further, *The Corinthian Body,* chap. 8).

39. See also Colossians 3:5. In Galatians *pathēma* is linked with *epithymia* in a context that refers to various sexual "impurities" as "works of the flesh" that have no place among Christians (Gal. 5:16, 19, 24).

40. See Dale Martin, *The Corinthian Body,* 209–17.

41. Significantly, most early Christian commentators on Romans take the references to women to refer *not* to lesbian activity but to heterosexual intercourse considered "unnatural" due to the female's assumption of the "male" role. Again, the concern is about "natural" gender hierarchy—in these cases related to heterosexual rather than lesbian sex. See Bernadette J. Brooten, "Patristic Interpretation of Romans 1:26," in *Studia Patristica XVIII,* ed. Elizabeth A. Livingstone (Kalamazoo, Michigan: Cistercian Publications, 1985), 1:287–91.

42. In *The Corinthian Body,* 229–49, I offer a fuller argument that Paul is reinforcing, rather than challenging, an assumed Greco-Roman gender hierarchy.

43. Some have tried to interpret vv. 11–12 to depict Paul as backing off a rigid hierarchy and providing an opening for egalitarian mutuality. In the ancient world, however, interdependence (whether economic, social, or sexual) did not in any way imply equality. See, further, *The Corinthian Body,* 229–49.

44. Wengst, "Paulus und die Homosexualität," 75. Joseph Fitzmyer recognizes that Paul's comment about "nature" in 1 Cor. 11:14 "creates a problem" for an uncritical acceptance of Paul's argument from "nature" in Romans 1. In an astonishing instance of double-speak, however, he insists that the reference to nature in 1 Cor. 11:14 is actually a reference to culture and that it has, in any case, no relevance for the function of Paul's argument from nature in Romans 1: "In this instance [1 Cor. 11:14], *phusis* hardly refers to the natural order of things, but the social convention. That use of *phusis,* however, is said to be 'of no theological significance' [citing the *Theological Dictionary of the New Testament,* 9:273]; but it is a problem for the interpretation of 1 Corinthians. Yet what is meant there has little relevance for this context in Romans" (*Romans,* 286–87). Fitzmyer never explains *why* the only other instance of a Pauline argument "from nature" is irrelevant for the interpretation of the same kind of argument in Romans 1. Having noted, correctly, that appeals to "nature" are actually appeals to social constructions, Fitzmyer does not seem to realize that "nature" is *always* socially constructed—or, put differently, that "culture" is always "natural." At this point, it seems to make little difference which option one takes; the real objective should be to dispense with the modernist culture/nature dichotomy as an explanatory, hermeneutical trick. See, for example, Bruno Latour, *We Have Never Been Modern* (Cambridge: Harvard University Press, 1993). It should come as no surprise that

"nature" in Paul's world may differ radically from "nature" in ours (assuming, perhaps too rashly, that there is an "us" that *has* a common construction of nature).

45. Hays, "Awaiting the Redemption," 4, 9; "Relations Natural and Unnatural," 200.

46. Hays, "Relations Natural and Unnatural," 204.

47. For various discussions of heterosexism, homophobia, and the problematics of such terminology, see Warren J. Blumenfeld, ed., *Homophobia: How we All Pay the Price* (Boston: Beacon Press, 1992).

48. Hays, "Awaiting the Redemption," 3–4, 15.

49. For the full text, see "The Homosexual Movement: A Response by the Ramsey Colloquium," *First Things* no. 41 (March 1994): 15–20. An excerpt appeared in *The Wall Street Journal* on 24 February 1994. I quote from the *First Things* article. For the reference to the Fall, see p. 18.

50. "The Homosexual Movement," 18.

51. The article, as is typical in heterosexist literature, nowhere explains exactly what is meant by calling heterosexuality "normal" or "the norm." This could conceivably be rather innocuous (though it seldom if ever is) if it means no more than that most people are straight rather than gay, just like most people are right-handed. One may believe, that is, that it is "normal" to be right-handed without believing that there is anything "wrong" with left-handed people or that society or right-handedness is threatened by the availability of commodities like left-handed scissors or drinking cups. It is, in my opinion, heterosexist but not necessarily homophobic to consider heterosexuality "the norm." I believe, in other words, that it is heterosexist in our *current* cultural situation to hold up heterosexuality as "normal" even if one does not mean by that that homosexuality should be prohibited. What is homophobic is the belief or fear that the very existence of homosexuality or gay men and lesbians threatens the existence of heterosexuality or the social structures supporting it.

52. "The Homosexual Movement," 19.

53. This should not be taken as a claim that I have offered here a completely sufficient and final "explanation." Having granted that these interpretations are instances of cultural homophobia, one might then pose the further question, "So why does homophobia exist in our culture?" My suggestions, however, may perhaps be useful to introduce new directions for discussion and analysis.

CHAPTER 8

My Sister, My Spouse: Woman-Identified Women in Medieval Christianity

E. Ann Matter

An inquiry into the history of lesbians in medieval Christian Europe faces double jeopardy. First, there is the difficulty of speaking about women's lives in a society which was solidly patriarchal in both its Roman and Teutonic roots, and which made very little provision for women except as objects for or possessions of men. Secondly, the inquiry must confront the problem of speaking about sexual mores in a culture essentially hostile to sexuality, particularly nonprocreative sexuality. These realities have necessarily limited my research and shaped my interpretations. This is, then, by no means a statistically valid study; it is rather a venture into a realm of silence and contradiction.

Scholars have by now reached accord about the great contributions of women to Christian monastic culture.[1] Similarly, we are increasingly aware of the advantages offered to women by life in the cloister, and of the ways in which women's life in religion was changed by and helped to change medieval Christian society.[2] No other group of medieval women, not even queens and other aristocrats, enjoyed the economic, political, and intellectual autonomy of nuns. It is no wonder that so many women who achieved power in secular life (Eleanor of Aquitaine is the obvious example) chose to retire to monasteries. Nuns also had the great advantage of literacy; only in the cloister could a medieval woman attend a school or live in an intellectual environment. One consequence of this, from a modern perspective, is that we know very

little about the lives of medieval lay women. It is not clear whether generalizations from sources about women in monastic life might also suggest
patterns for women's lives in the secular world. It is, nevertheless, striking
that many of the women mystics, and most of the female literary figures of
the Middle Ages, were in religious life. The three most famous, Hroswitha,
Hildegard, and Heloise, were all nuns; although, of course, it is not for her
vow of chastity that Heloise is primarily remembered.

Men, even priests, were limited in their contacts with nuns, but many
close intellectual and emotional relationships developed between men and
women in religious life—and, of course, sexuality could not be summarily
dismissed. Cloistered women expressed their longings for (and knowledge of)
physical intimacy in outbursts such as the entry of a nun of Auxerre on the
mortuary role of Matilda, daughter of William the Conquerer:

> All Abbesses deserve to die
> Who order subject nuns to lie
> In dire distress and lonely bed
> Only for giving love its head
> I speak who know, for I've been fed
> For loving, long on stony bread.[3]

Several monastic manuscripts from south Germany record what has been
called a "magnificent chaos" of literary fragments, including a number of
love-lyrics and epistolary poems from lover to beloved. Many of these poems
speak in the voice of a woman; as Peter Dronke says, they "show us beyond
any doubt that a number of cultivated, witty, and tender young women in
an eleventh-century convent in south Germany imposed on the clerics who
frequented their society the values of an *amour courtois*."[4]

In a series of remarkable poems found in a twelfth-century manuscript
from the monastery of Tegernsee, this courtly amorousness is directed by a
woman poet to a woman beloved. Tegernsee, a men's community, was in
the thick of a poetic flowering of twelfth-century Bavaria, being the mother-
house of Benediktbeuern, the home of the famous *Carmina Burana* manuscript. These poems were probably written at a women's monastery in the
region. One has received particular attention from John Boswell, who considers it "perhaps the most outstanding example of medieval lesbian literature."
Boswell translates it in this way:

> To G.; her singular rose
> From A. the bonds of precious love

What is my strength, that I may bear it,
That I should have patience in your absence?
Is my strength the strength of stones,   5
That I should await your return?
I who grieve ceaselessly day and night
Like someone who has lost a hand or a foot?
Everything pleasant and delightful
Without you seems like mud underfoot.   10
I shed tears as I used to smile,
And my heart is never glad.
When I recall the kisses you gave me,
And how with tender word you caressed my little breasts,
I want to die   15
Because I cannot see you.
What can I, so wretched, do?
Where can I, so miserable, turn?
If only my body could be entrusted to the earth
Until your longed-for return   20
Or if passage could be granted to me as it was to Habakkuk
So that I might come there just once
To gaze on my beloved's face—
Then I should not care if it were the hour of death itself.
For no one has been born into the world   25
So lovely and full of grace,
Or who so honestly
And with such deep affection loves me.
I shall therefore not cease to grieve
Until I deserve to see you again.   30
Well has a wise man said that it is a great sorrow for [one] to be
     without that
Without which [one] cannot live.
As long as the world stands
You shall never be removed from the core of my being.
What more can I say?   35
Come home, sweet love!
Prolong your trip no longer;
Know that I can bear your absence no longer.
Farewell,
Remember me.[5]

This poem elicited from Dronke the observation that it "seems to pre-suppose a passionate physical relationship."[6] Yet it is stylistically quite tradi-tional. The poem is made up of rhymed couplets (untranslatable), but with no discernable rhyme scheme or meter. It echoes the spirituality of medieval Christian readings of the Song of Songs, and the passionate friendships of Jerome and Alcuin.[7] Both Boswell and Dronke are careful to set it within the sophisticated and venerable tradition of spiritual friendship—the *amicitia* discussed so tenderly by Aelred of Rievaulx.[8] Whether the poet thought of herself in any way we would recognize as a "lesbian identity," she certainly celebrated a deep homoerotic orientation.

The poem which precedes this one in the Tegernsee manuscript is more elliptical, but just as erotic. Here the poet says to her beloved:

> You are sweeter than milk and honey
> You are peerless among thousands.
> I love you more than any.
> You alone are my love and longing,
> You the sweet cooling of my mind,
> No joy for me anywhere without you.[9]

This theme of longing for the absent beloved, sometimes expressed in courtly love language, is a recurrent theme of medieval monastic au-thors, male and female. It is poignantly found in the letters of Hadewijch, a thirteenth-century Flemish Beguine.[10] We know very little of the life of Hadewijch. It is debated, for example, whether she lived in Brussels or Antwerp, what sort of family she came from, or where she was educated. What we do know about Hadewijch is gleaned from the poems, letters, and visions which make up her collected works. She was not a nun, but a Beguine, one of the many women in the thirteenth century who chose to live in piety and apostolic poverty without taking monastic vows. Beguine communities were especially popular in the low countries and the Rhineland, so popular, in fact, as to arouse ecclesiastical fear and restrictions.[11]

Hadewijch gained a reputation for spiritual authority among the Beguines of Flanders both because of her remarkable series of visions and the elegant prose and poetry in which she recorded them. She certainly ranks as one of the leading figures of medieval Dutch literature. Her consistent theme was love—*Minne*—the same word celebrated in the secular poetry of medieval Germany and Flanders. God is experienced by Hadewijch as *Minne*, in a love relationship with parallels to human love. The passion of Hadewijch for her spiritual spouse, Christ, is expressed in ravishingly sensual language.

And yet, these writings stress that only through the imperfect experience of earthly love can union with the heavenly lover be glimpsed.[12] The letters of Hadewijch urge her fellow Beguines to strive for this mystical love, while giving us glimpses of her very human love relationships and of the pain of a prolonged separation from her sisters.

Letter 25 is an excellent example of the power of *Minne,* at once divine and intimately human:

> Greet Sara also in my behalf, whether I am anything to her or nothing.
>
> Could I be fully all that in my love I wish to be for her, I would gladly do so; and I shall do so fully, however she may treat me. She has very largely forgotten my affliction, but I do not wish to blame or reproach her, seeing that Love [*Minne*] leaves her at rest, and does not reproach her, although Love ought ever anew to urge her to be busy with her noble Beloved. Now that she has other occupations and can look on quietly and tolerate my heart's affliction, she lets me suffer. She is well aware, however, that she could be a comfort to me, both in this life of exile and in the other life in bliss. There she will indeed be my comfort, although she now leaves me in the lurch.
>
> And you, Emma and yourself—who can obtain more from me than any other person now living can, except Sara—are equally dear to me. But both of you turn too little to Love, who has so fearfully subdued me in the commotion of unappeased love. My heart, soul, and senses have not a moment's rest, day or night; the flame burns constantly in the very marrow of my soul.
>
> Tell Margriet to be on her guard against haughtiness, and to be sensible, and to attend to God each day; and that she may apply herself to the attainment of perfection and prepare herself to live with us, where we shall one day be together; and that she should neither live nor remain with aliens. It would be a great disloyalty if she deserted us, since she so much desires to satisfy us, and she is now close to us—indeed, very close—and we also so much desire her to be with us.
>
> Once I heard a sermon in which Saint Augustine was spoken of. No sooner had I heard it than I became inwardly so on fire that it seemed to me everything on earth must be set ablaze by the flame I felt within me. Love is all![13]

The love that Hadewijch bears for Sara is particularly interesting. Sara, the best beloved, returns Hadewijch's fervor with indifference; yet Hadewijch urges her on to new heights of *Minne* for "her noble beloved," that is, the heavenly bridegroom, Christ. Yet, the author's mourning for Sara's *human* love spills out between the lines: "whether I am anything to her or nothing . . . however she may treat me" Hadewijch will "fully be all that in my love I wish to be for her," without "blame or reproach." The intensity, awkwardness, and sublimation of this love should be recognized by all who have read the collection of memoirs, *Lesbian Nuns: Breaking Silence.*[14] Certainly Hadewijch did not see herself as a "lesbian" in any modern understanding of the term. And yet, whether or not their relationship was explicitly sexual, it seems a possible interpretation that Hadewijch and Sara were "Particular Friends."

From the same period as Hadewijch, but another corner of Europe, the courts of Provence, comes the only medieval lesbian voice I have found outside of the religious life: the poem attributed to Bieris de Romans, addressed to the Lady Maria.[15] We know nothing at all about either the poet or the object of her poem. But in the worldly tradition of Provence, where the ladies at court sang alongside the more famous male troubadours, at least one trobairitz, as the women poets were called, addressed her praises to another woman.

The poem begins with a catalogue of lady Maria's finer points; then in the second stanza, the lover pleads more directly:

> Thus I pray you, if it please you that true love
> and celebration and sweet humility
> should bring me such relief with you,
> if it please you, lovely woman, then give me
> that which most hope and joy promises
> for in you lie my desire and my heart
> and from you stems all my happiness,
> and because of you I'm often sighing.[16]

We've heard these sighs already, in the poems of an anonymous nun of south Germany, and in a letter of a Flemish Beguine. The relative sophistication and freedom of courtly Provençal society allows the love message to be expressed more directly, without the monastic habit of spiritual *amicitia*. Yet, all of these medieval lesbian voices speak within the courtly tradition of longing, separation, and hope for union with the object of love.

These voices assure us that there was passionate love between women in medieval Europe, love which could sometimes be expressed in the elite, discreet, and rarified air of the cloister, community, or court. This brings us to the second consideration of my paper: the interpretation and reception of this love in the context of medieval Christian social mores. For this inquiry, it is necessary to consider far less pleasing material: penitential and juridical attention to love between women.

A good deal of the scholarship on homosexuality in the Middle Ages is concerned with the writings know as "penitentials," handbooks for confessors which catalogue sins and their respective penances. Penitentials originated in the British Isles in the sixth century; until the twelfth century, they were increasingly found in continental Europe as well.[17] John Boswell (CSTH, 180–85) has rightly cautioned against the use of penitential literature as an index to popular attitudes towards sinful acts. Medieval penitentials are anything but standardized, and their credibility is further brought into question by the scorn with which they were regarded by some well-known ecclesiastics. Yet, it is worth noting that disapproval of the penitentials was usually on account of their *laxity;* this is certainly the case in Peter Damian's *Liber Gomorrhianus,* a vituperative denunciation of homosexuality among the clergy of the mid-eleventh century.[18]

The penitentials were a product of the missionary activity of early medieval Europe. As Vern Bullough put it, they "give us a picture of the attempts of the Christian Church to impose its will upon a society that, though nominally Christian, had not yet accepted Christian morality."[19] The burden of this missionizing was carried out by monks and nuns; many medieval monasteries, especially in Germany, were outposts of Christianity in essentially pagan rural areas. The penitentials, then, belong to the same monastic culture as the poems of the Tegernsee manuscript. As such, they deserve some consideration as evidence of lesbian activities, at least in the cloister.

In the penitentials, sins are roughly categorized by type and seriousness; often the status and spiritual record of the sinner are brought into account in assigning a penance. The penances listed are units of time—so many days, months, or years for a given act of theft, irreverence, or fornication, for example. The punishment consisted of fasting (on bread and water, with normal food on Sunday and feast days); but provision was made to work off the penance more quickly by means of prayers, vigils, or giving of alms.[20]

Except as objects of male lust, women are of little interest to the authors of the penitentials. Sections on heterosexual fornication typically go into great detail about the status of the woman as part of assigning a penance to a man. Was she a virgin? A nun? Someone's wife? (Whose wife?) Was she related by blood? Did she resist? Was there conception? What happened to the child? The greatest detail on women's sexual penances has, in fact, to do with abortion and infanticide.[21]

The details of penances for sexual acts between men are given in almost obsessive detail. In the penitential attributed to Bede, an eighth-century document from England, male sodomy is adjudicated according to the age of the participants, the clerical status (lay, monk, priest, deacon—other texts add bishop) and the nature of the intimacy. There is a certain fascination in these discussions. A penitential ascribed to the Irish abbot Cummean, in circulation in seventh-century Frankland, even goes into prurient detail on the subject of kisses between boys:

> Those who kiss simply shall be corrected with six special fasts; those who kiss licentiously without pollution, with eight special fasts; if with pollution or embrace, with ten special fasts.
>
> But after the twentieth year (that is, adults) they shall live at a separate table (that is, in continence) and excluded from the church, on bread and water.[22]

Amid this profusion of pastoral concern for the sexual practices of men are only a few comments about lesbian acts. The earliest is found in the *Penitential of Theodore* (ascribed to Theodore of Tarsus, Archbishop of Canterbury) and it is relatively simple:

> If a woman practices vice with a woman, she shall do penance for three years.
>
> And if she practices solitary vice, she shall do penance for the same period.[23]

The penance is actually quite light; the same document prescribes a penance of ten years for male homosexual acts.[24]

Homosexual men suffer heavier punishments than lesbians in other Anglo-Saxon penitentials as well. The document ascribed to Bede lists a four-year penance for male sodomites, but only three years for "fornication" between women.[25] A Carolingian conflation of this text with the *Penitential of Egbert* returns to the old formula: ten years for a man, only three for a woman who "fornicates with herself or another by whatever means possible."[26] But this Bede-Egbert text adds another consideration: women (nuns are specified) who fornicate "per machina," by means of some device, must do penance for seven years rather than three.[27]

Sex between women by means of "machines" is also mentioned by Hincmar, the ninth-century Archbishop of Rheims. His treatise on the divorce of Emperor Lothar defends the decision of a Carolingian monarch to put aside his wife in order to marry his concubine.[28] Hincmar's argument is dependent on the belief that women practicing witchcraft (*maleficio*) can render men impotent.[29] This subject gives Hincmar, one of the most flamboyant of Carolingian authors, an excellent opportunity to hold forth about sexual deviance of all kinds. It is a diabolical force, he says, that controls human sexual desires. Therefore:

> Even females have this sordid appetite, as Ambrose says in expounding the Apostle (Romans 1:26) on the subject of females engaging in filthy acts. They do not put flesh to flesh in the sense of the genital organ of the one in the body of the other, since nature precludes this, but they do transform the use of the member in question into an unnatural one, in that they are reported to use certain instruments (*machinas*) of diabolical operation to excite desire. Thus they sin nonetheless by committing fornication against their own bodies.[30]

Boswell has taken this as a comment "specifically on lesbianism" (*CSTH*, 204). This may be so, but there is a derivative quality about the passage, in Hincmar's testimony that such acts "are reported" and in the echoes of the penitentials, which may bring any real knowledge of lesbianism into question. About Hincmar's attitude towards the possibility, though, there can be no doubt. We will again see the charge of diabolical intervention in the case of a seventeenth-century nun, Benedetta Carlini. It should also be noticed that Hincmar's denunciation of women who use such *machinas* evokes the only reference we have seen so far to Paul's supposed denunciation of lesbians in Romans 1:26.[31]

In any case, sex between women involving imitation of male genitalia was considered a far more serious sin than simple "fornication" between women. This gives us a different glimpse of the attitude of medieval ecclesiastics towards lesbians: the condemnation of women perceived to be conducting themselves, especially sexually, in ways reserved "by nature" for men. A remarkable number of references to lesbians before the modern era list instances of women acting like, even posing as, men. Just as remarkable is the fact that scholars have neglected this nuance in evaluating lesbian history.

A poem from sixth-century France serves as an excellent example:

> You, strange mixture of the female gender,
> Whom driving lust makes a male,
> Who love to fuck with your crazed cunt.
> Why has pointless desire seized you?
> You do not give what you get, though you service a cunt.
> When you have given that part by which you are judged a woman,
> Then you will be a girl.[32]

To contrast this bit of misogynist verse with the poems of the gay clerical underground which flourished in the same culture, or the celebratory "Ganymede" literature of the twelfth century, is to be brought face to face with the unpleasant possibility that intimate relations between women were most despised—and perhaps only noticed—when they challenged male cultural prerogatives. Nor was this zeal for safeguarding male privilege limited to the realm of sexuality. The tenth-century *Decretals* of Burchard of Worms, which does not mention sexual acts between women, nonetheless stipulates:

> If any woman because of continence (as she may think) changes her habit, and for that customary to women puts on a male garment, let her be anathema.[33]

This prohibition seems oddly harsh in view of such Christian ascetic heroines as Mary of Egypt and Pelagia the Harlot, although it does add to our understanding of the harsh condemnation of Joan of Arc.[34]

I would like to conclude by considering two documented trials which bear out my hypothesis. Both date from the early modern period, but they are so unusually detailed as to provide important evidence about magisterial attitudes towards lesbians.

The 1721 trial and execution of Catherina Margaretha Linck in Halberstadt, Germany, involves action against a woman who posed successfully as a man, in military and private life, for many years. The accused married another Catherina Margaretha, surnamed Mühlhahn, in 1717. Catherina Linck escaped detection by her fellow soldiers, even by her wife, by the skillful use of "a penis of stuffed leather with two stuffed testicles made from pig's bladder attached to it."[35] The death sentence was deemed appropriate as much for her religious apostasy as for sexual crimes. Linck was in the habit of affiliating with the religious sect of each town in which she lived, professing by turn Lutheranism and Catholicism; she and Mühlhahn were actually married twice, in Lutheran and Catholic ceremonies. So, the trial document states:

> Since the outrages perpetrated by the Linck woman were hideous and nasty, and it can furthermore not be denied that she engaged in repeated baptism for which she should be punished, the jurists are also of the opinion that a woman who commits sodomy with another woman with such an instrument could therefore be given *poena ordinaria* [that is, capital punishment.][36]

There was some question, however, as to how the sentence should be carried out. The penalty for sodomy, the magistrates note, is ordinarily burning, "since because of them [sodomites] God let fire and brimstone rain from the sky and whole cities be destroyed." But this case presented special difficulties, since "it might appear that no genuine sodomy could be committed with a lifeless leather device, in which case capital punishment would not apply." The magistrates settled on a compromise: death by the sword. Catherina

Mühlhahn, "who let herself be seduced into depravity," was sentenced to three years in the penitentiary or spinning room, followed by banishment.[37]

Equally striking is the case of the Italian nun, Benedetta Carlini, Abbess of the Convent of the Mother of God in Pescia. Ecclesiastical records from 1619–23 document (in explicit detail) her sexual relations with another nun, Bartolomea Crivelli. Benedetta defended herself by claiming that she had been repeatedly possessed by an angel: "She always appeared to be in a trance while doing this. Her Angel, Splenditello, did these things, appearing as a boy of eight or nine years of age."[38] In commenting on this account, Judith Brown has noted: "In this double role, as male and as angel, Benedetta absolved herself from any possible wrongdoing."[39] This brings to mind the fourteenth-century French romance of Princess Ide, where the heroine, disguised as a man, marries the daughter of the emperor, but is exposed. On the brink of being burned by her furious father-in-law, Princess Ide is saved by the miraculous intervention of the Virgin Mary, who turns her into a man.[40]

Brown's study of Benedetta Carlini raises very pertinent questions about the applicability of the term "lesbian" to any case before the late nineteenth century. Brown acknowledges the imprecision of the term for Benedetta Carlini, but uses it nonetheless in the subtitle of her book.[41] The difficulty lies in the paucity of information about women's sexuality in general:

> Although medieval theologians and other learned men were not totally un-
> aware of sexual relations between women, they for the most part ignored
> them. The world of the Middle Ages and Renaissance was not prudish. It was
> a world that was fully cognizant of human sexuality, but it was also phallo-
> centric. The thought that women could bring sexual pleasure to each other
> without the aid of a man occurred to very few theologians and physicians.[42]

These observations are certainly reinforced by the medieval ecclesiastical material examined in this paper. I further suggest that sexual activities between women primarily came to the notice of medieval ecclesiastics when the women implicated seemed to be appropriating recognized male sexual roles. In those cases, the response could be, literally, deadly. But it must be noted that this was the penalty for male posturing, not for what we recognize today as "a lesbian relationship."

And yet, turning away from the penitentials, trials, inquisitors and executions, we have still the charm of the poems and letters with which this essay began. We have the first-person testimony of "a number of cultivated, witty and tender young women" who wrote to each other of their love and longing. Perhaps it is not anachronistic to consider here Adrienne Rich's thesis of a "lesbian continuum" marked primarily by emotional orientation.[43] Perhaps Hadewijch and the twelfth-century German poets would echo the twentieth-century provincial quoted in *Lesbian Nuns* on the thorny subject of Particular Friendships: "Let them go to it! Thank God somebody loves somebody!"[44]

· Notes

1. Lina Eckenstein, *Women under Monasticism* (New York: Russell and Russell, 1896); Eileen E. Power, *Medieval English Nunneries c. 1275 to 1535* (New York: Biblo and Tannen, 1922).

2. Carolyn Walker Bynum, *Jesus as Mother: Essays in Medieval Spirituality* (Berkeley and Los Angeles: University of California Press, 1982); Brenda Bolton, "Mulieres Sanctae," *Women in Medieval Society,* ed. Susan Stuard (Philadelphia: University of Pennsylvania Press, 1976) and idem, "Vitae Matrum: A Further Aspect of the Frauenfrage," *Medieval Women,* ed. Derek Baker (Oxford: Basil Blackwell, 1978); Shulamith Shahar, *The Fourth Estate: A History of Women in the Middle Ages* (London: Methuen, 1983); John A. Nichols and Lillian Thomas Shank, eds., *Distant Echoes: Medieval Religious Women,* vol. 1 (Kalamazoo, Mich.: Cistercian Publications, 1984); Suzane Fonay Wemple, *Women in Frankish Society: Marriage and the Cloister, 500 to 900* (Philadelphia: University of Pennsylvania Press, 1985).

3. Quoted by R. W. Southern, *The Making of the Middle Ages* (New Haven: Yale University Press, 1953), 24.

4. Peter Dronke, *Medieval Latin and the Rise of European Love-Lyric,* 2 vols. (Oxford: Clarendon Press, 1968), 1:225–26.

5. John Boswell, *Christianity, Social Tolerance, and Homosexuality: Gay People in Western Europe from the Beginning of the Christian Era to the Fourteenth Century* (Chicago: University of Chicago Press, 1980), 220–21; Dronke, *Medieval Latin,* 2:480–81. Lines 31, 32, my emendations. On this manuscript, München clm 19411, see also H. Plechl, "Studien zur Tegernseer Briefsammlung des 12 Jahrhunderts 1," *Deutsches Archiv für Erforschung des Mittelalters* 11 (1955): 422–661, and "Die Tegernseer Handschrift Clm 19411," *Deutsches Archiv* 18 (1962): 418–501.

6. Dronke, *Medieval Latin,* 2:482.

7. Compare line 17, "Quid faciam, miserrima" to the eleventh-century poem "Quis est hic?" in *The Oxford Book of Medieval Latin Verse,* ed. F. J. E. Raby (Oxford: The Clarendon Press, 1959), 158. Invoking the journey of Habakkuk to bridge the distance between an author and a loved one is an "extravagant conceit" of both Jerome and Alcuin; see Dronke, *Medieval Latin,* 1:198–99.

8. Boswell, *CSTH,* 221–26; Dronke, *Medieval Latin,* 1:192–221.

9. Dronke, *Medieval Latin,* 2:478–79. Compare "cooling" (*refrigerium*) in line 33 with "caressed" (*refrigerasti*) in the poem discussed above.

10. Mother Columba Hart, ed. and trans., *Hadewijch: The Complete Works* (New York: Paulist Press, 1980).

11. See E. McDonnell, *The Beguines and the Beghards in Medieval Culture: With Special Emphasis on the Belgian Scene* (New Brunswick, N.J.: Rutgers University Press, 1954), and, for the letters of Jacques de Vitry, R. Röhrich, "Briefe des Jacobus de Vitriaco," *Zeitschrift für Kirchengeschichte* 14 (1984).

12. For a discussion of this concept in Hadewijch, see the preface of Paul Mommaers in Hart, *Hadewijch*, xiii–xxiv; for the Latin tradition behind it, see Dronke, *Medieval Latin*, 1:192–221.

13. Hart, *Hadewijch*, 105–106. The influence of Augustinian notions of love is worthy of further study.

14. Rosemary Curb and Nancy Manahan, eds., *Lesbian Nuns: Breaking Silence* (Tallahassee, Fla.: Naiad Press, 1985).

15. Meg Bogin, ed. and trans., *The Women Troubadours* (New York: Norton, 1976), 132–33; note on the text, 176–77. Bogin describes the length to which scholars have gone to interpret this as anything *but* a poem by a woman to a woman.

16. Bogin, *The Women Troubadours*, 133.

17. The classic English discussion of penitential literature is John T. McNeill and Helena Gamer, *Medieval Handbooks of Penance* (New York: Columbia University Press, 1938). See also John T. McNeill, *The Celtic Penitentials* (Paris: Champion, 1923). Many of the texts are found in A. W. Hadden and W. Stubbs, *Councils and Ecclesiastical Documents Relating to Great Britain and Ireland*, vol. 3 (Oxford: The Clarendon Press, 1871), and Herm. Jos. Schmitz, *Die Bussbücher und die Bussdisciplin der Kirche*, 2 vols. (Mainz: Verlag von Franz Kirchheim, 1883). A more recent discussion of this literature is Pierre J. Payer, *Sex and the Penitentials: The Development of a Sexual Code, 500–1150* (Toronto: University of Toronto Press, 1984).

18. *Patrologiae cursus completus, series Latina*, ed. J.-P. Migne (Paris, 1844–55), 145:172; hereafter, PL; translated by McNeill and Gamer, *Medieval Handbooks of Penance*, 411. See discussions in Boswell, *CSTH*, 210–13; Derrick Sherwin Bailey, *Homosexuality and the Western Christian Tradition* (London: Longmans, Green, and Co., 1955), 111–17; and Vern Bullough, *Sexual Variance in Society and History* (New York: John Wiley and Sons, 1976), 363–64. Peter Damian's treatise does not mention lesbianism.

19. Bullough, *Sexual Variance in Society and History*, 357.

20. See especially the so-called *Roman Penitential of Haligar of Cambrai* (ca. 830), preface and directions to confessors, in Schmitz, *Die Bussbücher und die Bussdisciplin der Kirche*, 1:471–74; English trans. in McNeill and Gamer, *Medieval Handbooks of Penance*, 297–301.

21. See the so-called *Penitential of Bede*, "De fornicatione," in Hadden and Stubbs, *Councils and Ecclesiastical Documents*, 327–29; *Penetential of Egbert*, "De machina mulierum," in Schmitz, *Die Bussbücher*, 1:535–37; Eng. trans. in McNeill and Gamer, *Medieval Handbooks*, 196–197.

22. Schmitz, *Die Bussbücher*, 1:661; Eng. trans. in McNeill and Gamer, *Medieval Handbooks*, 112–13. See also the tenth-century *Decretals* of Burchard of Worms, 17.56 (PL 140:931–33).

23. Schmitz, 1:526; Eng. trans. McNeill and Gamer, 185. The Latin verb "fornicare" is used in canon 12; "solitary vice" is in the Latin "sola cum se ipsa coitum habet."

24. Schmitz, 1:526; Eng. trans. McNeill and Gamer, 185.

25. Haddan and Stubbs, 328.

26. Schmitz, 2:688: "mulier qualicunque molimine aut in se ipsa aut cum altera fornicaverit, iii annos peniteat."

27. Haddan and Stubbs, 328: "si sanctaemoniales cum sanctaemoniale per machinam annos vii." Schmitz, 2:688: "si sanctaemoniales femina cum sanctaemoniali per machinam fornicatur, vii annos peniteat."

28. PL 123:619–722. I am indebted to an unpublished study of this text by Burton Van Name Edwards of the John Carter Brown Library, "Hincmar of Rheims and the Relationship Between Women and Witchcraft in Medieval Culture," 1974.

29. PL 125:707.

30. PL 125:692–93; Eng. trans. from "they do not" to end, Boswell, *CSTH*, 204.

31. The ninth-century commentary on Romans by Hrabanus Maurus also glosses 1:26 with a reference to Satan (PL 111:1301).

32. Boswell's translation (*CSTH*, 184), with notes on the textual difficulties.

33. "Si qua mulier propter continentiam quae putatur, habitum mutat, et pro solito muliebri amictu virilem sumit, anathema sit" (8.60; PL 140:805).

34. Joan's androgyny and the impact of her masculine attire are considered by Anne Llewellyn Barstow, "Joan of Arc and Female Mysticism," *Journal of Feminist Studies in Religion* 1 no. 2 (Fall 1985): 29–42, esp. 40–42. See also Kelly DeVries, *Joan of Arc: A Military Leader* (Stroud: Sutton, 1999), and Ann W. Astell and Bonnie Wheeler, eds., *Joan of Arc and Spirituality* (New York: Palgrave, 2003).

35. Brigitte Eriksson, "A Lesbian Execution in Germany, 1721: The Trial Records," in *Historical Perspectives on Homosexuality*, ed. S. J. Licata and R. P. Petersen, reprint of a special issue of *Journal of Homosexuality* 6 (1980–81): 27–40, at 31. The quotation is from the trial record, dated 13 October 1721.

36. Eriksson, "A Lesbian Execution," 31.

37. Eriksson, "A Lesbian Execution," 38, 40.

38. Judith C. Brown, "Lesbian Sexuality in Renaissance Italy: The Case of Sister Benedetta Carlini," *Signs: Journal of Women in Culture and Society,* The Lesbian Issue, 9, no. 4 (Summer 1984): 751–58, at 757.

39. Brown, "Lesbian Sexuality in Renaissance Italy," 756.

40. Related by Louis Crompton, "The Myth of Lesbian Impunity: Capital Laws from 1270 to 1791," *Historical Perspectives on Homosexuality*, 11–25, at 13. Crompton does not consider the significance of Ide's male disguise.

41. Judith C. Brown, *Immodest Acts: The Life of a Lesbian Nun in Renaissance Italy* (New York: Oxford University Press, 1986), see 17–20. The book relates the outcome of the Carlini case, life imprisonment. The book gives a much broader context for the visionary career of Benedetta Carlini. It should be noted that the angel's name, "Splenditello," was transcribed as "Splendidiello" in "Lesbian Sexuality," and changed here without explanation.

42. Brown, "Lesbian Sexuality," 754.

43. Adrienne Rich, "Compulsory Heterosexuality and Lesbian Existence," *Signs* 5 (1980): 631–60; critiqued as anachronistic for historical inquiry by Brown, "Lesbian Sexuality," 756.

44. Curb and Manahan, *Lesbian Nuns*, 92. *Lesbian Nuns* has been especially illuminating in providing firsthand documentation of theories and interpretations for which medieval evidence is sparse: for example, that nuns entered convents in search of social mobility, education, and to avoid contact with men; and that confessors and spiritual guides often considered the emotional attachments between nuns as unthreatening and inconsequential.

CHAPTER 9

R. W. Southern, John Boswell, and the Sexuality of Anselm

Bruce O'Brien

While historians resist the maxim that the times make the man, as well as its opposite, that the man makes the times, we can at least agree that the times helps us understand the man. With this in mind, I want to consider one of the sharper exchanges between John Boswell and one of his critics, in this case R. W. Southern, fellow of Balliol College, Chichele Professor of Modern History, and then President of St. John's College, Oxford. Their point of disagreement was Anselm of Canterbury's alleged homosexuality. But Anselm's sexuality is, in some ways, irrelevant to their dispute. Their disagreement is neither strictly based on interpretations of the evidence, nor on the changing climes of twentieth-century academic history in England and the United States. Rather, it grew out of a difference in their fundamental attribute as historians: their historical imaginations.

About Anselm's life, little need be said. He was born in Aosta, in northern Italy, in 1033, left home in his twenties, and wandered France before becoming a student of Lanfranc at the abbey of Bec in Normandy in 1059. It was there, while prior of the abbey, that he composed his most famous work, the *Proslogion* (1077–78). He became archbishop of Canterbury in the time of William II and remained in that post, despite two exiles, until his death in 1109. During the entire time, Anselm wrote not only theological or spiritual treatises but also letters.[1] These letters are filled with words conveying Anselm's many passionate loves. Both Boswell and

Southern quote from these letters extensively. Here are two samples. First, Boswell's translation of Anselm's letter to one Gilbert: "Sweet to me, sweetest friend, are the gifts of your sweetness, but they cannot begin to console my desolate heart for its want of your love. Even if you sent every scent of perfume, every glitter of metal, every precious gem, every texture of cloth, still it could not make up to my soul for this separation unless it returned the separated other half. The anguish of my heart just thinking about this bears witness, as do the tears dimming my eyes and wetting my face and the fingers writing this."[2] Now Southern's translation of another letter to Gilbert: "If I were to describe the passion of our mutual love, I fear I should seem to those who do not know the truth to exaggerate. So I must subtract some part of the truth. But you know how great is the affection that we have experienced—eye to eye, kiss for kiss, embrace for embrace. I experience it all the more now when you, in whom I have had so much pleasure, are irretrievably separated from me."[3] The talk in the many letters of this type is all of kisses, embraces, tears, longing, desire. This language is not in all the letters, but it is in a distinct group of the early ones. And there it is pronounced.

R. W. Southern, born in 1912, found Anselm first.[4] Southern pulls Anselm out of the mists of the sources and turns him, as is often the case with those Southern chose to study, into a tangible figure, an archbishop of spiritual ideals and physical failings. It was Anselm's letters, though, that first caught Southern's attention back in the 1930s. The letters of Anselm, almost 150 in number, offer not only a guide to the archbishop's actions but also an outpouring of emotive language in letters to his friends, colleagues, and brothers.[5] Southern interpreted these remarks as nonsexual but *sui generis*. Anselm created his own expressions for his friendships because he was a special individual.[6] Southern developed this view in several publications stretched out over twenty years, but drawing on the work of twice that, from his early postgraduate days in the early 1930s to the 1970s.[7] It was the 1960s that saw his most extensive publications: a dual biography of sorts, delivered as the 1959 Birkbeck lectures at Cambridge, and published in 1963 as *St. Anselm and His Biographer,* just after publication of his edition of Eadmer's *Vita Anselmi* in the Nelson Medieval Texts series.[8]

It is in *St. Anselm and His Biographer* that we hear Southern's earliest extended discussion of Anselm's language of friendship. What he said was that the principal purpose of these letters was for Anselm to communicate who he was—his essence as it were—to his friends. The language Anselm used was at times surprisingly emotional. Southern said that Anselm wrote to his friends "in language which now seems to us, who are accustomed to read quite different meanings than he intended into the words which he uses, enormously overdone" (69). This language reveals, Southern said, that Anselm's friendships are different from ours because, according to Southern, love at the time "was essentially an intellectual concept" (70).[9] The early letters were not private but were meant to be shared. This was a not uncommon practice of letter writers in the Middle Ages as well as in antiquity. Nevertheless, the emotive words of Anselm's letters could be misunderstood by those "who did not understand that the fire was primarily intellectual and that it fed on an incorporeal ideal. It was a product of philosophy rather than of feeling" (74). Last, Southern argued that "in intention Anselm's extravagance of language has nothing in common with the contrived fancifulness of the language of romantic love. . . . Even Anselm's contemporaries seem to have been disappointed to find that he meant something less or something different than appeared on the surface" (75–76).

In the late 1970s, John Boswell, a young scholar fresh from graduate study at Harvard and coming up for tenure at Yale, read these letters differently. He thought that perhaps the letters revealed Anselm's sexuality. Boswell's 1980 book, *Christianity, Social Tolerance, and Homosexuality,* made, of course, quite a splash. Martin Duberman, writing in the *New Republic,* called it "revolutionary." "Boswell's study," he wrote, "is indubitably one of the most profound, explosive works of scholarship to appear within recent memory. His book will inaugurate controversies bound to rage for years."[10] The book, as Duberman anticipated, made what had been seen as a controversial claim that Christianity was not responsible for medieval intolerance, and that the late eleventh and twelfth century saw the creation of a self-conscious community of gay intellectuals in Western Europe, centuries before most scholars were willing to consider such a consciousness possible. These claims ignited the debates of Duberman's review. These debates rage on. But they rage on the frontiers between gay and straight, between Christian and non-Christian.[11] It is the territory between camps that is contested. It is in this territory that John Boswell placed Anselm.

The analysis of Anselm was not a significant element in *CSTH.* Anselm is mentioned on five pages treating the 1102 Westminster Council and Anselm's letters of friendship (215–16, 218–20). First, the council. Boswell argued that there were no statutes in England against homosexuality before the 1102 council. The council legislated principally against married clergy and simony, but included as its last and longest chapter, legislation against sodomy. The chapter claimed that sodomy was thought to be very common in England, and that no one knew how serious a sin it was. So the council said. Boswell noted that the council's decisions were never published, and he claimed that they had been suppressed by Anselm. Why did he suppress them? Boswell opined that Anselm in part had done this because the severity of the edict violated the papal decree of Leo IX from 1051 forbidding extreme measures against sodomites (*CSTH*, 215).

But that was not all Boswell wrote. He said that Anselm "may also have had personal reasons for suppressing the council's decree" (*CSTH*, 215–16). Anselm participated in "the first efforts to formulate a theology which could incorporate expressions of gay feelings into the most revered Christian lifestyle, monasticism" (218). Anselm's contribution to this was his tradition of passionate friendship. Admitting that Anselm was "devoted to the monastic ideal of celibacy," Boswell nevertheless heard in Anselm's letters to his old master Lanfranc and to a succession of students and friends the sound of "extraordinary emotional relationships," some of which, he argued, "appear erotic by any standards."[12] To get from these erotic letters to theology, Boswell used the stepping stone of Southern's short sketch of Anselm in *Medieval Humanism*. Boswell has Southern tell us that "[f]rom these friendships, and the discussions which cemented them, came the theological treatises."[13]

Southern's revision of *St. Anselm and His Biographer,* published in 1990 as *Saint Anselm: A Portrait in the Landscape,* but worked on from at least the 1970s, became the forum for his response to Boswell's claims. Southern did not take Boswell's claims lightly—the response in *Portrait* was not an afterthought. Note that the only new section Southern signaled in his preface was one dealing with the issue of Anselm's alleged homosexuality.[14] Southern thought Boswell had misinterpreted both council and letters. When addressing the 1102 council that Boswell had seen as evidence of Anselm thwarting the unforgiving mandates of reformers, Southern insisted at some length that Anselm determined to do all that the council set out to do: it was Anselm who called the council and he and only he who drafted the canons before the actual meeting.[15] Anselm is no reluctant enforcer of other bishops' zeal against sodomites. Southern acknowledged that this canon was secondary to the rest (though it is longest, even if last), and that Anselm had foolishly expected the support from the council in the main effort to enforce clerical celibacy. Southern also situated the letters in a thicker context than before of friendship, love, and letter writing. Again, the love in those letters was an intellectual concept and the friendship a spiritual ideal, expressed in the unusual but understandable metaphoric language of human passion.

Southern did concede that the young Anselm may have had a predisposition to homosexuality.[16] Southern inverted Boswell's interpretation of the 1102 council, suggesting that its very vehemence against sodomy may be Anselm's guilty response to previous sins. This is how Southern would explain Anselm's extremism on this issue, where otherwise he is gentle with sinners.[17]

Southern suggested that Anselm's horror at the sodomy he found in the English royal court and his prospective legislation of 1102 against sodomy (and,
Southern added, "its accompaniments of long hair and effeminate habits")
"may suggest that these subjects touched a raw spot in his own past."[18] Both
Boswell and Southern used the council to say the same thing—that Anselm
might have been homosexual. Southern, however, rejected the Anselm of
Boswell's interpretation—a sympathizer working behind the scenes to divert
the forces of oppression. The only Anselm Southern is prepared to allow
to be gay is the one he also thought we could never know—Anselm the
young, premonastic lad.[19] About these years, Eadmer, Anselm's biographer,
says only that after his mother's death, Anselm "began to give attention to
youthful pleasures [ludi]"; about the period from the time Anselm fled his
father in 1056 until he arrived at Bec in 1059, Eadmer tells us nothing at all.[20]

Why had they disagreed? The immediate grounds seem and are obvious:
the nature and history of Anselm's sexuality. In many instances, historical
disagreement is rooted in the evidence itself. This is only partly the case
here. Southern's and Boswell's words on Anselm's sexuality are not really
the cause of the dispute, but rather a symptom of much deeper issues in
their respective lives and eras. My explanation begins not where I might be
expected to start—with a closer analysis of Southern's and Boswell's words
on Anselm, or with Anselm's own words and actions. I am going to start
someplace rather different. In 1977, Southern delivered the Rede Lecture
at the University of Cambridge.[21] He chose as his topic those imaginative
epiphanies that constitute formative moments for how we understand the
past, what he called the historical experience. Here he spoke not only of
those nineteenth-century figures who so captured his admiration—Charles
Darwin, John Henry Newman, Friedrich Engels, and Ernest Renan—but also
about his own personal experience of history. The historical experience was
one that Southern thought we all must have had at some point—an "experience of a sudden perception which gradually makes sense of a whole
large area of the past," an experience that brought an "extraordinary sense of
peace and satisfaction" which was "never diminished."[22] Southern said that
the perception had to be "very sharp and vivid"; it had to have "a private
and personal significance"; and it had to work.[23] Southern's description of a
historical perception privileges imagination over facts or truth, because he
would worry that—and this was the case for Darwin—the existing truth was
so very wrong.[24] Southern likened having had such an experience of historical
perception to seeing a ghost. Once you have seen it, you cannot not see it.

The historical experience brought what Southern called "pleasure."[25] This
is not a word often used to describe the end result of what we historians do.

But for Southern, it was crucial, both for becoming a historian in the first place and for all his subsequent work. Perhaps pleasure was the only result we could count on, because historical truths were in the end so personal. The days when history was publicly purposive were gone—gone with the Victorians who trained those who trained Southern, gone with the old syllabus of parliamentary history that Southern put to rest at Oxford in the 1960s.[26] He wrote that "we must not expect too much of history. It will not tell us what to believe or how to act; it will not make us more tolerant or more ecumenical or more peaceful." What then will it do? "The historical experience," Southern concluded, "is first for pleasure, but it is also a warning." The warning was especially for the sciences, to remind them that their truths were not timeless but products of historical circumstances, and so they should remain humble and open to new truths.[27]

Southern saw this process as one of empathy. Take, for example, what he told us in the same Rede Lecture of 1977 about John Henry Newman. What Southern wants to trace is the path to, moment of, and aftermath of Newman's epiphany—his historical experience. That moment came in 1839, when Newman, while reading fifth-century Christian texts, found his own age's religion reflected in the past and realized that he was in fact a Monophysite. Southern quotes Newman's words: "I saw my face in that mirror, and I was a Monophysite."[28] According to Southern, Newman's historical understanding of the Christian past was shaken; what was unchanged and unchanging "turned out to represent only a peculiar and repugnant variant." What Newman had done, and what Southern thought all historians should do, was to look to the past and "to seek congruity also with our own experience of the possible."[29] And here Southern's formulation is inversely *Proslogion*esque: "It must not be beyond our powers to conceive that we might ourselves have thought or behaved thus in the circumstances and under the pressures which our observations of the past have brought to light."[30] We—suitably tempered by immersion in the past's customs and ideas—are the measure of action and thought in those we study.

I could say much more about their different worlds. How Southern's was a repressed age where homosexuals were criminals (a word he used when talking about homosexuality), and where the fog of the inherited sensibilities of the Victorians about sex had not been dissipated by the rising sun of the discipline of psychology; and how Boswell's world was an age of sexual revolution and intellectual fervor and, most importantly here, of strident and victorious social activism for civil rights.[31] But these are necessary and not sufficient causes. I would rather say a few words about each man's Christianity, which is where the solution of this puzzle lies.

Here let me take John Boswell first. Boswell came of age in Virginia during the 1950s and 1960s and so witnessed great shifts in the sensibility of the country. The rhetoric of civil rights was to convince the unknowing and unwilling that Black Americans (and later others) deserved the same dignity and rights as all Americans. And in this struggle, some of the churches had been very visible fighters—most notably in concert with the Southern Christian Leadership Conference and Martin Luther King Jr. The church that made the deepest impression on young John's mind, however, was the Catholic Church. Boswell began life as an Episcopalian. When he was a teen, he told his parents he intended to convert. They assumed, he told me, that it was to Judaism—he had been learning Hebrew from the local rabbi for some time by then—and this would not have bothered them much since Judaism was also a high status religion. But Boswell converted to Roman Catholicism as a teenager because, in large part, the archdiocese of Baltimore had voluntarily desegregated its schools, without a court order, solely because it was the right thing to do. I don't think it a stretch to see this perception as part of the historical experience that led him to write *CSTH*. Here was born Boswell's faith in a religious institution's morality and opposition to intolerance, argued with verve years later in the book. This was the historical experience that set the mold of his historical imagination. That the book's physical genesis came in the 1970s when local churches asked Boswell to give public lectures on Christianity and homosexuality reinforces this interpretation.[32]

R. W. Southern, on the other hand, did not think much about the social activism of the church, and he felt no good knowledge of the past would come from examining it with an eye to affecting the condition of the present.[33] Southern's own conversion—or I should say return—to Christianity, in his case Anglicanism, came not through Christianity's moral challenge to public authority but through its meditative powers, its inner appeal. Southern as a young teen, just about the age when Boswell became a Catholic, was busy leaving his religion.[34] What offended his sensibilities was the church's unwillingness to come the distance to modern science. As a result, in 1927 he dropped out of his confirmation class, stopped praying, and, once away from home and at university, stopped attending church. In his obituary of Southern, Sandy Murray points to 25 March 1937 as the date of Southern's return. Evicted from the library at Corpus Christi because it was Good Friday (after ten years away, he had forgotten the sacred calendar), he killed time by going to a Cambridge church where a German anti-Nazi pastor was speaking. At the end of the *Benedictus,* when Southern heard "to give light to them that sit in darkness and in the shadow of death and to guide our feet into the way of peace," Southern, as he put it years later, "found himself a Christian."[35]

Southern in the late 1960s told one of his students—Brian McGuire—that "it was the reading of the *Prayers and Meditations* of St. Anselm (which was probably during the 1930s) that had given him back his Christianity."[36] This reading was probably from the days in the 1930s when Southern was first contemplating a scholar's life, and either prepared the way for his epiphany or gave the faith that came from it a context afterwards. From this faith, he was never shaken.

For a man like Southern who believed in historical empathy as the means of understanding people of the Middle Ages, and who had rediscovered his own faith through or in Anselm, and whose own worldview consciously or unconsciously excluded sex and sexuality as topics of historical merit, Boswell's arguments must have seemed a personal affront. Although homosexuality never appeared in his writings, Southern was able to think about the issue of sexuality, even with respect to Anselm's. Brian McGuire remembers asking Southern in the late 1960s why he didn't say Anselm was homosexual. Southern smiled and replied that they wouldn't understand back at Oxford.[37] While he might think about it, he would not write about it.[38] Boswell not only was willing to write about sexuality, but also considered doing so something like a moral and religious duty. His questions were different than Southern's; his willingness to consider such things as sexuality and homosexuality in particular were in step with a new age. Southern's imaginative leap was to take us inside the minds of early scholastics and show us things we hadn't seen before. Sandy Murray wrote that for Southern, "faith was to be understood in the light of the world of flesh and blood."[39] If this is so, and I think it is, then it is a flesh and blood with some very serious limitations of action. Boswell's leap was to add the issue of sexuality to morality, faith, and reason—his interests are truly body and soul. As Southern had enlarged the portrait of his subjects from what he had received, so too Boswell in his time enlarged the scope of understanding like that found in Southern's work.

That Southern was able, despite his own imaginative limitations, to follow Boswell some of the way, objecting all the time, correcting and revising Boswell's points, is a sign of his intellectual strength. That Boswell was willing to amend and explain and take the cascades of criticism his book unleashed is a sign of his as well.

One thing we will, I think, not be able to answer is the question of Anselm's sexuality, preferences, or identity.[40] The very fact that I have to say it several ways points to the principal problem we have with such issues as these. The current debate between constructionists and essentialists is, as Boswell pointed out in the 1980s, strangely parallel to that between nominalists and realists.[41] That medieval debate about universals was resolved not by reason but by the force of coercive authority. The current impasse on what is and is not gay (and by implication anything at all) will likewise not be resolved by any arguments we might muster. Southern in the end concluded that the question may be unanswerable. I don't think in the case of Anselm that John Boswell would have disagreed.

· Notes

I would like to thank many students and friends of both R. W. Southern and John Boswell for their help with this essay. In particular, I would like to thank Rob Bartlett, Brian McGuire, and Ralph Hexter for sharing with me their memories and unpublished works.

1. *S. Anselmi Opera Omnia,* ed. F. S. Scmitt, 6 vols. (Edinburgh, 1946–61). Our understanding of the collection and dissemination of these letters is still a work in progress: see R. W. Southern, *Saint Anselm: A Portrait in a Landscape* (Cambridge, 1990), 394–403 and 458–81; hereafter Southern, *SAPL.*

2. Boswell, *CSTH,* 219, translating Anselm, *Epistle* 84 (*S. Anselmi Opera,* 3:208–209).

3. Southern, *SAPL,* 145, translating Anselm, *Epistle* 130 (*S. Anselmi Opera,* 3:272–73).

4. One gets the impression reading Southern's first biography that there wasn't much previous biographical scholarship on Anselm. Southern has the new editions of Anselm's works, edited by F. S. Scmitt, but little beyond that. He cites F. Liebermann, "Anselm v. Canterbury und Hugo v. Lyon," *Historische Aufsätze dem Andenken an G. Waitz gewidmet* (1886), 156–203; A. Wilmart, *Auteurs spirituels et textes dévots du moyen âge: Études d'histoire littéraire* (Paris, 1932); A. Porée, *Histoire de l'Abbaye du Bec,* 2 vols. (Évreux, 1901); J. McIntyre, *St. Anselm and His Critics: A Reinterpretation of the Cur Deus Homo* (Edinburgh, 1954); and Aubrey Gwynn, "St. Anselm and the Irish Church," *Irish Ecclesiastical Record* 59 (1942): 1–14, but not, for example, Johann Adam Möhler, *The Life of Saint Anselm, Archbishop of Canterbury,* trans. Henry Rymer (London, 1842); Martin Rule, *Life and Times of St. Anselm: Archbishop of Canterbury and Primate of the Britains* (London, 1883); J. M. Rigg, *Saint Anselm of Canterbury: A Chapter in the History of Religion* (London, 1896); Enrico Rosa, *Saint Anselm de Cantorbérey: La vie et l'ame du saint* (Paris, 1929), let alone Arrigo Levasti, *Sant Anselmo: Vita e Pensiero* (Bari, 1929); Joseph Clayton, *Saint Anselm: A Critical Biography* (Milwaukee, 1933); Anselm Stolz, *Anselm von Canterbury* (Munich, 1937); or R. W. Church, *St. Anselm* (London, 1937). It is not always easy to tell from Southern's notes what he has read other than primary sources.

5. Southern initially began to prepare an edition of Anselm's letters in the 1930s, before abandoning the project once he discovered F. S. Scmitt was doing the same. See R. W. Southern, *Saint Anselm and His Biographer: A Study of Monastic Life and Thought* (Cambridge, 1963), xiii.

6. Southern, *Saint Anselm and His Biographer,* 68–69, 75–76.

7. This and a good deal of biographical information comes from Alexander Murray, "Richard William Southern, 1912–2001," *Proceedings of the British Academy* 120 (2003): 413–42.

8. Eadmer, *The Life of St. Anselm, Archbishop of Canterbury,* ed. and trans. R. W. Southern (Oxford, 1962).

9. See also Jean Leclercq, *Monks and Love in Twelfth-Century France: Psychohistorical Essays* (Oxford, 1979), and Giles Constable, *Letters and Letter-Collections,* Typologie des sources du Moyen Âge occidental, fasc. 17 (Turnhout, 1976).

10. Martin Bauml Duberman in *The New Republic,* 18 October 1980, 32–35.

11. For a sense of the debates, see Martin Bauml Duberman, "Reclaiming the Gay Past," *Reviews in American History* 16 (1988): 517–19, and Steven Epstein, "A Queer Encounter: Sociology and the Study of Sexuality," *Sociological Theory* 12 (1994): 188–202, who locates Boswell and many others within the broader trends in the field.

12. In *Kindness of Strangers,* Boswell returned to the issue briefly and here attributed Anselm's solicitous attitude toward oblates to paternal feelings and excluded pedophilia on scientific grounds of frequency. It is more likely that Anselm saw them as his children and very unlikely that he saw them as sex objects: *The Kindness of Strangers: The Abandonment of Children in Western Europe from Late Antiquity to the Renaissance* (New York, 1988), 308–9 and n. 46.

13. Boswell, *CSTH,* 219, citing R. W. Southern, *Medieval Humanism* (New York, 1970), 13.

14. Southern, *SAPL,* xvi.

15. Southern, *SAPL,* 148–49, 348–50. Anselm's authorship of the council's capitula is stated directly by Eadmer: "Cuius concilii seriem, sicut ab eodem patre Anselmo descripta est, huic inserere non incongruum existimavimus" ("This list of recommendations, just as it was composed by the same father Anselm, we think it not irrelevant to add here"): *Eadmeri Historia Novorum in Anglia,* ed. Martin Rule, (London, 1884), 141. All selections related to this council were published in modern editions in *Councils and Synods with Other Documents Relating to the English Church,* vol. 1: *871–1204,* ed. D. Whitelock, M. Brett, and C. N. L. Brooke (Oxford, 1981), 672–88. This edition appeared after the publication of Boswell's *CSTH.*

16. Southern, *SAPL,* 151.

17. *SAPL,* 152.

18. Southern said there were "several indications in Anselm's words and attitudes of an exaggerated sensitivity on this subject, which may point to a violent rejection of his past" (*SAPL,* 152).

19. This might be interpreted as a displacement of sexuality to protect Anselm's integrity for the period after he had taken his monastic vows. Southern could not see Anselm as having betrayed them. But before that was open territory, not least because the sources tell us so little: Eadmer, *The Life of St. Anselm,* 1.1–4, pp. 3–7; Southern, *SAPL,* 3–13, tries to work out from the fragments in the *Vita* and letters. Anselm's entrance into the Benedictine Order at Bec "suggests a revolt from the past rather than a simple change of direction" (*SAPL,* 152).

20. " . . . ac juvenilibus ludis coepit operam dare": Eadmer, *Life,* 1.4, p. 6, and 1.5, p. 8. *Ludus,* when linked with age, may also mean sexual pleasure: Charlton T. Lewis and Charles Short, *A Latin Dictionary* (Oxford, 1879), *s.v.* at II.C.

21. Published as "'The Historical Experience," in the *Times Literary Supplement* (24 June 1977), 771–74. It has been republished in a collection of Southern's works on the doing of history: R. W. Southern, *History and Historians,* ed. R. Bartlett (forthcoming).

22. Southern, "Historical Experience," 771.

23. Ibid.

24. Ibid., 771–72: "'Truth comes from error more easily than from confusion. It is only by having a vivid perception that an energetic search can begin; without it there is only languid and aimless confusion."

25. Ibid., 774.

26. Murray, "Richard William Southern, 1912–2001," 432–33.

27. Ironically, Southern fled the church because of its stance on science and lists nineteenth-century scientists as his model historians. Boswell joined the church because of activism, but fought in scholarly work against coldly scientific views of sexuality like those of Alfred Kinsey, William Masters, and Virginia Johnson. For more on the development of science during this time and its impact on society, see *The Cambridge History of Science,* ed. David C. Lindberg and Ronald L. Numbers (Cambridge, 2003–); John Henry, *The Scientific Revolution and the Origins of Modern Science* (New York, 1997); Brian Silver, *The Ascent of Science* (New York, 1998); and William Irvine, *Apes, Angels, and the Victorians: The Story of Darwin, Huxley, and Evolution* (New York, 1955).

28. John Henry Newman, *Apologia Pro Vita Sua* (London, 1864), 208–10, quoted by Southern, "Historical Experience," 772.

29. Southern, "Historical Experience," 771.

30. Ibid.

31. For homosexuality in Britain, see H. Montgomery Hyde, *The Love that Dared not Speak its Name: A Candid History of Homosexuality in Britain* (Boston, 1970); Jeffrey Weeks, *Coming Out: Homosexual Politics in Britain from the Nineteenth Century to the Present* (London, 1977); Hugh David, *On Queer Street: A Social History of British Homosexuality, 1895–1995* (London, 1997); and Angus McLaren, *Twentieth-Century Sexuality: A History* (Oxford, 1999), chap. 5. Havelock Ellis published his revolutionary *Studies in the Psychology of Sex,* 4 vols. (New York, 1936) first in 1910, vol. 2 of which dealt with "sexual inversion." That England was hostile of homosexuality in the twentieth century, see McLaren, *supra,* and Michael S. Foldy, *The Trials of Oscar Wilde: Deviance, Morality, and Late-Victorian Society* (New Haven, 1997). David Sweetman's eloquent biography of Mary Renault gives this a personal dimension: *Mary Renault: A Biography* (New York, 1993), 138–52. The tide had begun to turn after World War II. See Alfred Kinsey, Wardell B. Pomeroy, and Clyde E. Martin, *Sexual Behavior in the Human Male* (Philadelphia, 1948); William H. Masters and Virginia E. Johnson, *Human Sexual Response* (Boston, 1966); and idem, *Homosexuality in Perspective* (Boston, 1979). On the influence of Christianity on the civil rights movement in the United States, see, e.g., Taylor Branch, *Parting the Waters: America in the King Years, 1954–1963* (New York, 1988).

32. Personal communication from Ralph Hexter, May 2004.

33. This point he emphasized in an as yet unpublished lecture, "The Truth about the Past," delivered to the St. John's College Historical Society in 1988. It will be published in Southern, *History and Historians,* ed. Bartlett.

34. Murray, "Richard William Southern, 1912–2001," 416.

35. Ibid., 426.

36. Personal communication, May 2004.

37. Ibid.

38. Southern does not treat sexuality, even by oblique reference, anywhere outside of his response to Boswell in *Portrait*. On twelfth-century humanists like Marbod of Rennes and Baudri of Bourgueil, whose sexuality was thoroughly integrated into their works, Southern has almost nothing to say. His only references to Marbod are as a famous school teacher and as a talented bishop. He never refers to Baudri.

39. Murray, "Richard William Southern, 1912–2001," 439.

40. Neither Southern nor Boswell considered the evidence in detail: this consideration has been undertaken by Brian McGuire, "Love, Friendship, and Sex in the Eleventh Century: The Experience of Anselm," *Studia Theologica* 28 (1974):11–52; and Glenn W. Olsen, "Anselm and Homosexuality," *Anselm Studies* 2 (1988): 93–141.

41. John Boswell, "Revolutions, Universals, and Sexual Categories," in *Hidden from History: Reclaiming the Gay and Lesbian Past,* ed. Martin Duberman, Martha Vicinus, and George Chauncey Jr (New York, 1989), 17–36.

CHAPTER 10

Male Friendship and the Suspicion of Sodomy in Twelfth-Century France

Mathew Kuefler

Scholars have long recognized the attention paid in the literature of the twelfth century to intimate bonds between men. There are numerous instances, on the one hand, of the favorable depiction of men whose loyalty and devotion to each other overcome all obstacles. There is, on the other hand, a concerted effort to condemn men whose intimacy involved a sexual component. Attempts to historicize this double reaction have not been successful, however, mostly because literary scholars tend to focus on the narrative role played by depictions of male friendships and their implied homoeroticism, while religious scholars tend to emphasize the prohibition of sexual connections between men and the intellectual background from which that prohibition emerged. The key to contextualizing both the homoerotic implications of male friendships and the hostility to sodomy, though, is to understand the traditions of male solidarity and friendship among the military aristocracy of medieval France and the reasons that existed for undermining those traditions in the twelfth century. I will argue that throwing suspicion on male friendships as breeding-grounds for sodomitical behavior suited the goals of the men of the ecclesiastical and royal hierarchies, who were attempting large-scale social and political reforms that required the subversion of male solidarity and the abandonment of earlier patterns of men's friendships in favor of new patterns of support for lineage and obedience to authority.

Almost two decades ago, historian John Boswell described what he called an "efflorescence" of gay male culture in the period before the twelfth century, using the term "gay" to refer "to persons who are conscious of erotic inclination toward their own gender as a distinguishing characteristic or, loosely to things associated with such people, as 'gay poetry'" (*CSTH*, 44). He also documented the end of this gay culture in the period after the twelfth century, and a shift from tolerance of sexual difference to intolerance. Nonetheless, he was unable to historicize the pattern he perceived and unable to explain why this shift occurred in the twelfth century. His hypothesis was that it was related to urbanization, yet even he described such a hypothesis as "largely unsatisfactory" and expressed the opinion that "advances in knowledge in many disciplines will probably be necessary to clarify the nature of so large and complex a development" (*CSTH*, 243–44).

Since that time, few scholars have taken up Boswell's challenge. Most historians have contented themselves with undermining the first part of Boswell's thesis, dismissing Boswell's claim that certain historical individuals can be characterized as "gay" and rejecting the evidence for a "gay" culture in the Middle Ages.[1] Indeed, in a book on the theological development of the notion of sodomy in the eleventh and twelfth centuries, historian of theology Mark Jordan maintains forcefully that his work "is not a social history of 'medieval homosexuality'" and doubts "whether such a history is possible . . . [or] desirable."[2] Historian R. I. Moore stands apart in accepting Boswell's claim for the disintegration of a subculture based on homoeroticism and in attempting an explanation of that disintegration. Moore argues that:

> during the eleventh, twelfth and thirteenth centuries, Jews, heretics, lepers, male homosexuals and in differing degrees various others were victims of a rearrangement . . . which defined them more exactly than before and classified them as enemies of society. But it was not only a matter of definition. In each case a myth was constructed, upon whatever foundation of reality, by an act of collective imagination. A named category was created—Manichee, Jew, leper, sodomite and so on—which could be identified as a source of social contamination, and whose members could be excluded from Christian society and, as its enemies, held liable to pursuit, denunciation and interrogation, to exclusion from the community, deprivation of civil rights and the loss of property, liberty and on occasion life itself.[3]

It is a powerful and compelling argument—that society defined itself through a process of social exclusion—but it still does not explain why male homoeroticism should be listed among the categories for exclusion. As Jordan so neatly demonstrates, "the category 'sodomy' had been vitiated from its invention by fundamental confusions and contradictions," and the "sodomite" as represented by Christian theologians did not and could not exist.[4] Even as historians generally have repudiated the possibility of a sexual identity based on homoeroticism and any premodern conscious recognition of erotic difference that Boswell defined as "gay," however, literary scholars increasingly point to homoerotic elements in writings about male friendship of the twelfth century.[5]

My project is to try to cut through this Gordian knot, precisely by attempting to historicize these literary and theological expressions of male intimacy, praised as friendship or condemned as sodomy, and to situate them among the inhabitants of the twelfth century and within a period of social change. Indeed, I maintain that such a project is key to understanding both the nature of those expressions of male intimacy and their implications for a history of sexuality, and also key to taking up Boswell's unanswered question of explaining the rise of intolerance of male homoeroticism.[6] I would also argue, *pace* Jordan, that the uncovering of the historical context in which the "invention of sodomy" took place is a prerequisite for denaturalizing that invention, a denaturalization that I deem both possible and desirable.[7]

As part of that historicizing process, moreover, the relationships between men need to be seen within a broader context than the clerical subculture that forms the basis for much both of Jordan's and of Boswell's work. Any attempt to historicize must include the connections between that subculture and the aristocratic military culture around it. For even if virtually all of the writings which survive from the twelfth century come from clerical or monastic hands, these writings form part of a larger relationship between the religious and the secular, in which the former was not only critical of but also deeply influenced by the latter. As part of that relationship, the twelfth-century clerical and monastic writers on male friendship and on sodomy replied directly to the traditions of masculinity among the military aristocracy, even if they attempted to parody or to subvert those traditions.

In particular, these ecclesiastical writers worked to weaken the bonds of male solidarity encouraged by military culture in favor of ties of obedience to church and state, a movement well recognized by historians and often called the "taming" of the nobility. As part of that "taming," ecclesiastical writers of the twelfth century problematized male friendships in a new way, using the suspicion that these friendships were nothing more than a cover for sodomy as a means of undermining their social importance. Moreover, as will be shown, this suspicion was also associated with the performance of male gender identity among the military aristocracy to the extent that to be a sodomite was to be no longer a man, linking the suspicion of sodomy with men's misogynistic fears of effeminacy.

The literary tradition of male friendship may seem an odd place from which to begin a "historicizing" account of men's relationships, but for the twelfth century, literary sources provide the clearest images of those relationships, images which can then be supplemented by and verified against other sources. Northern France provides a rich deposit of literary and other historical sources, and forms a culturally cohesive unit. By using a variety of the texts spanning the twelfth century, moreover, we can more easily mark the progress of the suspicion of sodomy in male friendships over the course of that century. While it is impossible to pinpoint an exact date at which men's friendships became suspect, it is possible to demonstrate a broad shift in attitudes from early twelfth-century texts to later twelfth-century ones, and it is in several mid-century texts that the new problematics of male intimacy can first be seen.

Many early twelfth-century sources from northern France preserve a record of emotional intimacy between men. John Boswell documented numerous examples in his study, including such ecclesiastical figures as Anselm of Bec, Baudri of Bourgeuil, and Marbod of Rennes.[8] These are among the writers who have fallen under the scrutiny of scholars after Boswell.[9] Historian Stephen Jaeger, who rejects Boswell's argument that the writings of these men demonstrate a physical eroticism, suggests that the "language of the erotic shows innocently that the illicit is proximate [*proche*] but avoided or ignored, . . . mastered, controlled, maintained in its place."[10] Such language, he counters, owes more to the epistolary and philosophical traditions of ancient writers than to a "gay" identity. The erotic could not have been articulated, he argues, if it had been physicalized.

Jaeger is certainly correct in asserting that before the middle of the twelfth century love between men might be depicted without awkwardness or embarrassment. Consider Peter Abelard's early twelfth-century poetic version of the lament of the biblical king David for Jonathan, a traditional model of male friendship:

> Jonathan, more than a brother to me, one in spirit with me, what sins, what crimes have sundered our hearts? . . . For you, my Jonathan, I must weep more than for all the others. Mixed in all my joys there will always be a tear for you. . . . Alas, why did I agree to the wretched advice that I not defend you in battle? Stabbed like you, I should have died happily, for love can do nothing greater than this, and to outlive you is to die at every moment: half

a soul is not enough for life. I should have paid friendship's single obligation then, at the time of greatest need; as sharer in victory or companion in ruin, I should have either rescued you or fallen with you, ending for you the life you so often saved. Then death would have joined us even more than it parted us.[11]

His poem borrows not only from biblical antecedents but also from classical ones, such as the lament of Nisus for Euryalus in Virgil's *Aeneid,* another traditional model of male friendship.

By the end of the twelfth century, however, writers of northern France displayed a new awkwardness in depicting male friendships and a new desire to downplay the devotion between male friends. The erotic was no longer so "innocent." The praise of male friendship continued, but only when it insisted on its spiritual and not carnal nature.[12] Take, for instance, the example of Alain of Lille, writing near the end of the twelfth century, whom we will have occasion to discuss in greater detail below. Alain put the praise of male friendship in the mouth of personified Nature herself:

Indeed, she desires that he be thus embraced by love [*amor*] and by inviolate loyalty [*fides*], that his love might gain the love of another. . . . She desires that he might believe anything of him, wish to declare himself to him, and to reveal to him all of his thoughts. Let him commit to him the secrets hidden in his heart, so that to him, keeping the treasure of his mind in him, there is no secret that might not be revealed to him, that his friend might measure by such a sign the weight of his friendship, which might equally be weighed in return.[13]

When Alain remarked on the devotion between David and Jonathan and between Nisus and Eurylaus, he admitted the possibility of real intimacy between men:

For David and Jonathan are two there but yet are one; although they are separate individuals, they are not two in soul but one; they halve their souls and each gives part to the other. . . . Another Nisus appears in Euryalus and another Euryalus flourishes in Nisus; thus either one of them reflects the other and from one of these companions a judgment can be made on both.[14]

Nonetheless, Alain also made sure to clarify that he was writing about "those whom chaste love, uncomplicated friendship, unclouded trust, true affection have joined together."[15] Significantly, Alain dedicated another treatise, his *De planctu naturae* ("Nature's Lament"), to personified Nature's condemnation of sodomitical relationships between men. Alain thus demonstrates that the awkwardness of twelfth-century writers about male friendships was directly connected to the suspicion of sodomy between men.

The anonymous reworking of Virgil's *Aeneid*, written shortly before the mid-point of the twelfth century in the Norman French dialect and called the *Roman d'Énéas*, serves as an excellent example of the suspicion of male friendship and as a useful starting-point. The *Roman d'Énéas* is a particularly interesting source, because it was both situated in the past and the present: set in a distant Roman past and borrowing from an ancient Latin literary tradition, but also written in the midst of the changes of the twelfth century and in the new written vernacular. As such, its anonymous redactor had both a model for male friendship and the liberty to manipulate that model. The figure of Eneas, moreover, was already marked with a certain effeminacy even in the Latin text because of his eastern Mediterranean origins, a typical Roman conceit, and as we will see, the accusation of effeminacy formed an integral part of the accusation of sodomy in the twelfth century.

Male friendship is at the heart of the *Roman d'Énéas*. The text includes the story of the male companions Nisus and Euryalus, and even elaborates on Virgil's description of the men's devotion to each other:

> They loved each other with such a love that they might not have a greater. Never was there a truer love than theirs, as long as they lived. One did not know anything without the other, nor had any joy nor good thing.[16]

Another episode of male intimacy in the *Roman d'Énéas*, also borrowed from Virgil, involves Eneas himself and a young man named Pallas, who was killed in the conquest of Italy. Eneas holds the dead youth in his arms, uttering a long and poignant lament before fainting away from grief:

> Pallas, said he, flower of youth [*jovente*], . . . you were so handsome yesterday morning, that under the sky there was no more comely youth [*meschin*], but in a short time I see you changed. . . . Handsome figure, comely thing, just as the sun withers the rose, so has death quickly all defeated and all withered and changed you.[17]

Eneas's grief is reiterated through physical description:

After that he was silent, he could say no more, in his heart was grief and very great anguish, he fell on the deceased in pain, and when he rose back up, all weeping, he kissed the corpse.[18]

Indeed, Eneas exhibits more grief and more emotion here than at any other place in the text.

The *Roman d'Énéas* also complicates male friendship. Later in the text, in an episode barely present in Virgil's poem but much elaborated by the twelfth-century author, Eneas falls in love with Lavine, who is betrothed to his political rival. Their love is opposed by Lavine's mother, who attempts to dissuade Lavine from her love for Eneas in a manner worth quoting at length, because it makes clear how the suspicion of sodomy within male friendship worked:

This villain is of such a nature [*de tel nature*] that he has never a care for women. He prefers the opposite practice [*mestier*]. He does not want to eat the female animal [*biset*], for he loves very much the flesh of a male one [*char de maslon*]. He would rather take a boy [*garçon*] than be near to you or any other. . . . How is that you have not heard that he treated Dido badly? No woman had any good from him, nor will you have, if he is, as I think, a traitor and a sodomite [*sodomite*]. Always he will announce that he is leaving you, if he has any debauched young thing [*godel*], and it will seem to him good and well that he leave to seek his pleasures [*druz*]. And if he can use you to attract the boy, he will not find it too strange to let the boy do his thing [*son bon*] with you so that the boy will let him do it to him [*lo sofrist de soi*]; he will let the boy mount you, if he can in turn ride the boy.[19]

When Eneas abandons Lavine for the male companionship of a military campaign, she begins to have her own doubts about him:

It is the truth, said she, what my mother told me about him. A woman is very little to him, he would rather sport with a boy [*deduit de garçon*], he loves none but male whores [*males putains*]. His Ganymede he has with him, little of me is enough for him. He has been rutting for a very long time, in the middle of sporting with a boy. . . . He has enough boys with him, and loves the worst of them better than me. He makes their clothes ripped [*fandue trove lor chemise*]. Many of them he has in his service, and their breeches are lowered: thus they earn their wages.[20]

It is not only Lavine who is forced to re-evaluate the virtue of Eneas's relationship with Pallas, however, but the audience of the poem along with her, and this is reinforced by her words which generalize this episode:

> Be cursed today such a type of man [*tel nature d'ome*] who has no care for women; and he who is all accustomed to that. For this practice [*mestiers*] is very bad, and he is thinking very much like a fool who leaves a woman and takes a man.[21]

Here is a new and self-conscious admission of the possibility of a sexual element in male friendships.

The *Roman d'Énéas* also demonstrates that what was being challenged in the twelfth century, through the suspicion of sodomy, was military culture and the bonds of solidarity between men that were necessary for the cohesion of military culture. The anonymous redactor of the *Roman d'Énéas* was asserting that the service of young warriors to a war-leader might be as much a sexual as a military service. If we accept, at least for the moment, the assertion of the anonymous redactor of the *Roman d'Énéas* that sodomy might have formed part of military culture, and if we also accept that the redactor was commenting not only about the ancient conventions of pederasty but also about contemporary society and its sexual mores, we now have a point from which to begin to historicize sexual relations between men and to consider, in the words of Jonathan Goldberg, "the ways in which normative bonds that structured society also allowed for sexual relations."[22]

How often sexual relations may have resulted from the cohabitation of men during times of military service is of course impossible to say. Many writers of the twelfth century implied a real physical intimacy between men of the military class, and sources throughout the period describe the erotic charms of youthful males, or what Sally North calls a "combination of manly stature and strength with a girlish face."[23] This physical intimacy certainly included an appreciation of male beauty. The *Chanson de Roland,* for example, which survives from the beginning of the twelfth century, describes the warrior Ganelon in these words: "Noble was his body and his torso was broad, and so handsome was he that all his peers stare at him."[24] Likewise, the physical side to male intimacy included touches and embraces between men. The *Couronnement de Louis,* for example, written in the mid-twelfth century, includes this description of the meeting of two aristocratic friends: "The noble count embraced him on both sides and kissed him four times on his face."[25] Physical intimacy between men is also directly connected to their emotional intimacy, as depicted in the French legend of two knights, called *Ami et Amile,* written probably at the very end of the twelfth century:

> And he saw him who had already recognized him. Toward him he turned when he had also recognized him in turn. With such sweetness [*vertu*] did they greet each other, so forcefully did they kiss and so softly did they embrace, that not long after they were done in and overcome. [26]

In other words, a physical component to male friendship was expected and celebrated.

It would be presumptuous simply to read these expressions of physical intimacy in male friendships as overtly homoerotic. [27] Nonetheless, writers of the twelfth century seeking to undermine the solidarity between men by accusing them of sodomitical practices may have used these physical expressions of friendship as part of their attack. And it is not difficult to imagine that these physical expressions may also have reflected a type of homoeroticism that might sometimes have included sexual intimacy. Indeed, sexual intimacy between men must sometimes have happened, if the accusations made by the author of the *Roman d'Énéas* and other writers of the twelfth century hoped to carry any real weight. So we are left to interpret in a variety of possible ways the ambiguous statements of the twelfth century, such as that by the anonymous author of the mid-century *Prise d'Orange,* who remarks that better than the love of a beautiful woman was that of "a young bachelor [*bacheler*] with his first beard, who knows how to live well in fun [*deport*] and in arms." [28]

The adolescent male, the "bachelor with his first beard," figures prominently in virtually all twelfth-century discussions of sexual intimacy between men. Georges Duby has discussed the sexual adventurousness of the bands of adolescent males, but assumes it to have taken place entirely within a heterosexual framework. "The sexuality of the bachelors had always been meandering," he writes:

> They freely availed themselves of peasant women, servant girls, and the many whores who were apt to relieve the champions of most of their winnings on the night after the tournament; they also took advantage of the widows whom they consoled and the 'maidens' who so graciously received the heroes of the Breton romances at each nightly pause of their wanderings. [29]

Duby implies that the bachelors indulged their sexual needs entirely with women, but contemporary writers—and not only the author of the *Roman*

d'Énéas—suggested otherwise. Hildebert of Lavardin, archbishop of Tours
in the middle of the twelfth century, used the classical myth in which Jove
abducted the youth Ganymede for his sexual and domestic service as the
basis for his attack against the sexual arrangements of the military aristocracy.
Hildebert railed against what he called *Ganymedes crimen* ("Ganymede's sin")
in his own society:

> A boy [*puer*] is not at all a safe thing; do not devote yourself to any of them.
> Many a house is reported to have many Joves. But you should not hope for
> heaven through Ganymede's sin: no one comes to the stars through this type
> of military service. A better law consecrates heavenly castles to Junos alone:
> a male wife [*masculus uxor*] has the underworld.[30]

If Hildebert is to be believed, these sexual practices were rampant throughout
the noble households of northern France:

> Above all other sexual crimes is the sodomitical plague, and males [*mares*] give
> to males [*mares*] the debts due their spouses. Innumerable Ganymedes tend
> innumerable hearths, and that which she was used to enjoying, Juno grieves.
> Boys [*puer*] and men [*vir*] and even frail old men [*senex*] debase themselves
> with this vice and no manner of life [*conditio*] ceases from this vice. Whoever
> of you change the honor of nature to this practice [*mos*] and neglect the licit
> Venus for the forbidden, do you not remember that you are taught by [the
> example of] Sodom that you should beware this crime, lest you perish by
> sulphur?[31]

About the same time, Bernard of Cluny also complained about the "innumerable Ganymedes" of his day.[32] It is impossible to gauge the extent to which the
comments of Bernard and Hildebert reflected the realities of male sexuality
and how much was exaggerated for rhetorical effect. Still, the suspicion of
sexual relationships between men and adolescent boys was reinforced by
worries about its prevalence among the military aristocracy.

   If male sexuality involved some sexual experimentation with other males
within the war-band and noble household, and if it took the form of an
older man's sexual interest in a younger man, as these sources imply, the
likeliest site for such sexual behaviors was in the institution of fostering.
Through fostering, groups of noble sons were raised in the household of a
military associate of their father, learning the arts of war and serving as his
companions and assistants. In the twelfth century, foster-sons remained with
their foster-fathers until they reached adulthood and were given their own

arms, an event that typically occurred at about the age of fifteen.[33] Fostering is well attested in the sources of the eleventh and twelfth centuries. In the early twelfth-century romance of *Tristan* by Béroul, for example, the hero says that he should have "a hundred young men [*danzeaus*] with me, who serve me in order to take arms and who render me their service."[34] In many ways, fostering formed the backbone of early medieval military culture, since the loyalties established and cultivated through fostering provided the cohesion to the military band. Fostering also provided much of the social context for male friendship in the period before the twelfth century.

The institution of fostering also provided the context for attacks on male intimacy by writers, beginning in the middle of the twelfth century. The guardianship of Pallas and the other young men by Eneas in the *Roman d'Énéas,* for example, was implied to be that sort of fostering arrangement. Hildebert's complaint against "this type of military service" (*hac modo militia*) also relies on a play-on-words linking pederasty and fostering. The image of Jove and Ganymede itself depends on the parallels between the mythical rapture of the adolescent male by an adult male for domestic and sexual service and the contemporary "theft" of boys into the military household as foster-sons. In fact, several writers of the twelfth century refer to the younger partners in alleged sexual relationships as *catamitae* ("catamites"), a medieval Latin variant of Ganymede.

Even writers who do not attack the homoeroticism of the fostering household seem to have considered the adult male's appreciation of adolescent male beauty as one of the characteristics of the institution. Consider the remark made regarding the arrival of Richard, the future duke of Normandy, at the court of King Louis IV of France, a twelfth-century reference from the *Gesta Normannorum ducum* ("Deeds of the Dukes of the Normans") to a tenth-century event:

> Sending for the boy [*puer*] Richard he had him presented for his inspection, and, having seen that he was endowed with handsome features [*egregia forma perspiciens decoratum*], decided that he should be brought up with other boys of his own age [*cum coetaneis pueris*] in his own court.[35]

Consider also the description of the fostering of Amicus and Amelius, two young men of a hagiographical legend from the early twelfth century, but again, referring to an earlier age, the age of Charlemagne:

> The two pledged their faith to each other and made their way together to the court of Charles the king, where he perceived them to be modest, wise,

and very handsome [*pulcherrimi*] young men, peers alike in their education as in their appearance [*vultus*], loved by all and honored by all. What more can I add? Amicus was made the king's treasurer and Amelius his cup-bearer [*dapifer*].[36]

Amelius as cup-bearer to Charlemagne cannot help but bring to mind the myth of Ganymede and Jove. It is not impossible to view these descriptions of the role played by physical attraction in fostering in earlier eras as part of the critique by twelfth-century writers, although the appreciation of the boys' beauty may also be related to medieval notions of the connection between physical beauty and moral goodness.

We have yet to understand why it was in the twelfth century that male intimacy became so problematic. As I see it, the problem was two-fold. First was a social problem. Loyalty and intimacy between men, of the sort described as typical for men of the warring classes and encouraged by the institution of fostering, distracted men from what was being promoted as their primary responsibility to the family. Men's duties to the lineage were an obsession of twelfth-century writers. The requirements of the family included first and foremost its perpetuation through the fathering of male heirs to take up its titles and lands, and were interpreted as necessitating a single-minded pursuit of procreation.[37] These requirements reflected in turn the shift of the economic basis of Western Europe, from wealth derived from the capture and circulation of booty stolen by the warring band to a wealth calculated on the incomes of cultivated lands and the inheritance of those lands. The delayed ages of marriage of men in the noble classes and their long absences away from their wives in the warrior band to support the earlier system of wealth had to be brought to an end for the sake of family continuity, which supported the new system of wealth.[38]

One sees how commonplace the concern for lineage was in the writings against sodomy from the twelfth century, which frequently condemned the "sterile unions" between men. In an anonymous poem of debate from the end of the twelfth century, Helen, who represents the love of women, provokes Ganymede, who represents the love of boys, with these words: "Venus mixes males [*masculi*] in sterile unions."[39] Alain of Lille complained of the sodomitical male that "he hammers on an anvil which issues no seeds," and that "his ploughshare scores a barren strand."[40] The same concern for lineage can also be seen in the *chansons de geste*. The central theme of the *Roman d'Énéas*, like that of Virgil's *Aeneid* on which it is based, is the descent of Eneas, but in the twelfth-century version, this descent is made possible only by Eneas's abandonment of the military band and his "sodomitical tendencies" for the love of Lavine. Her mother clarifies the issues at stake, after calling Eneas a sodomite:

> It would be all over with this age if all men [*home*] were like this throughout the world. Never would a woman conceive, there would be a great loss of people, no one would ever have children. The age would fail in a hundred years.[41]

The very existence of such arguments implies that the emphasis on lineage did not necessitate an abandonment of the homosocial war-band, but ecclesiastical writers of the twelfth century worked hard to link the one with the other.

In place of the devotion which men offered each other, moreover, twelfth-century writers offered to men the possibility of an equal devotion to women through the promotion of courtly love. As modern scholars have pointed out, to love a woman became such a central focus of male identity beginning in the twelfth century that not to love a woman brought into question a man's right to call himself a man.[42] This idea is sprinkled through the twelfth-century literature of courtly love. Chrétien de Troyes had a knight say that:

> Whoever kisses a woman and does nothing more, when they are all alone together, then I think there is something remiss [*remaint*] in him.[43]

But this idea was also closely linked with the contemporary attack on intimacy between men and the accusation of sodomy. In the *Lai de Lanval*, Marie de France had Guinevere give this retort to a man who rejects her sexual advances:

> I have been told often enough that you have no inclination [*talent*] toward women. You love young men [*vaslez*] who are well built [*bien afaitiez*] and you sport [*dedulez*] together with them.[44]

A man's refusal to devote himself to a woman is here linked to his illicit devotion to other men.

A recurring theme in all of these texts praising the love of women is the unnaturalness of sex between men. Lavine's mother includes it in her harangue against Eneas: "he who acts against nature, who takes men [*homes*], who leaves women, undoes the natural coupling."[45] In the debate between Helen and Ganymede, the same accusation is made: "You openly despise sex with women [*sexum mulieribus*]. The order of things is overturned and its law perishes through you."[46] To call sexual relations between men unnatural was to imply that a natural form of sexual relations existed, and twelfth-century writers worked hard to assert a sexual complementarity between men and women, part of a larger reformulation of gender relations in that period that has been skillfully delineated by Jo Ann McNamara.[47] It is true that courtly love sometimes worked counter to the support of the lineage. Even then, however, courtly love furthered the project of the reorientation of men's affections away from each other to someone outside the "system" of male solidarity. If that someone, moreover, was a woman with lands of her own or was heiress to her father's lands, lineage might still be promoted. Most importantly, through the conventions of courtly love, writers of the twelfth century insisted that every man give his love, both devotion and sexual interest, to a woman. In the *Roman d'Énéas,* Eneas moves from his homosocial band and his devotion to the boy, Pallas, to the love of the woman, Lavine. Even Ganymede, in his debate with Helen, eventually accepts her viewpoint that love of a woman is better than love of a boy.

The legend of Amicus and Amelius or Ami and Amile serves as an excellent example of the twelfth-century shift from devotion to male friendship and the military band to devotion to a woman and the lineage. According to the earlier, hagiographical form of the legend, written anonymously in the early twelfth century, Amicus and Amelius begin their friendship when they are baptized together as children, and strengthen that friendship when they serve together as young men in Charlemagne's army, although they eventually separate to marry and raise families. When Amicus is stricken with leprosy, however, he approaches his former companion with a story that an angel has appeared to him and told him that he will be cured only by being bathed in the blood of his friend's sons. After some deliberation, Amelius's loyalty to Amicus overcomes his loyalty to his family: he slaughters his children, bathes his dear friend in their blood, and his dear friend [*carissimus*] is healed. But because of God's mercy, his sons are brought back to life, and in thanksgiving, the two men leave their wives and take vows of chastity. They rejoin Charlemagne's army and are killed together in battle. Even in death their devotion to each other is affirmed by means of another miracle:

> Those whom God had joined in the concord of one spirit and in love [*unanimi corcordia et dilectione*] in life, so in death he did not want them to be sep-arated. . . . There were made therefore two churches . . . [and t]he remains of their bodies were buried, the one here, the other there. In the morning, however, and done according to divine disposition, the body of Amelius was found with his sarcophagus next to the sarcophagus of Amicus in the king's

church. What an admirable association of these two friends, what ineffable love between them [*o admiranda duorum societas amicorum, o ineffabilis caritas amborum*], which not even in death deserves separation![48]

Near the end of the twelfth century, however, a new version of this legend was written in the vernacular. The lives of the two men, now called Ami and Amile, follow roughly the same pattern, but after the miraculous cure from leprosy, the story takes a new turn. Amile remains with his wife and his resurrected sons, and Ami, who is now free of the pollution of leprosy, is able to rejoin his wife and son. In this version, notably, it is not the male bond that is reinforced by the divine intervention, but the family bond. The final episode of their death and burial together is entirely omitted. Reginald Hyatte, who has examined the theme of friendship in the later version, remarks that the two men's "pursuit of absolute friendship . . . does not have a place in the social order of family and feudal state."[49] Although the exact relationship between the two versions of the legend is uncertain, it is tempting to see the latter as a redaction of the former more in keeping with the sentiment of the later twelfth century, when traditions of male friendship were being subverted in favor of familial ties.

Male friendship was not only a social problem, however, but a political one. The devotion of men of the military classes to each other also undercut their loyalty to the church and state. Placing suspicion on male solidarity as sodomitical also suited a larger agenda of reorienting the personal loyalties of the male nobility away from each other and towards their obligations of obedience as subjects of royal and ecclesiastical power, both of which were being greatly extended in the twelfth century. R. I. Moore, for example, argues that accusations of sexual and religious unorthodoxy were "means of suppressing resistance to the exercise of power . . . and of legitimizing the new regime in church and state."[50] Christopher Baswell also sees the extension of royal power behind the suspicion of sodomy in the *Roman d'Énéas*.[51] The numerous ecclesiastical regulations on marriage of the twelfth century have also been typically seen as attempts by church leaders to control the sexuality of the noble classes and as part of the efforts to "tame" them. Simon Gaunt, for example, sees the twelfth century as a "historical flashpoint" for the "renegotiation of sexuality amongst the French aristocracy which may well be related to the impact of the Church's attempt to control the adjudication of marriage," in which the antipathy to homoeroticism in texts such as the *Roman d'Énéas* provided "a means of regulating male homosocial bonds, of imposing normative models of heterosexuality and gender on all men."[52]

The accusation of sodomy was useful to both royal and ecclesiastical authorities. Given the right political circumstances, any man's friendships might be accused of being a cover for unnatural acts, and this accusation would then justify the regulations of men's lives which both church and state imposed. This is not to say that church and state worked in concert. Indeed, they often worked against each other, but both used the same methods since both were also working within the same cultural context, and implicated even as they complicated each other. Alan Bray has noted the political uses of the suspicion of male intimacy at work in texts of the sixteenth century, but it can also be seen as early as the twelfth.[53]

The accusation of sodomy was also politically useful on another level, by deflecting anxiety about its prevalence away from the clergy and monastic orders and onto the secular nobility. The anonymous clerical writer who penned the *Roman d'Énéas,* as well as the other ecclesiastical writers of the twelfth century, were doubtless aware of the campaigns of the Gregorian reformers, men like Peter Damian, who believed that sodomy was a serious problem for the clergy and that men guilty of the offense should be permanently removed from clerical ranks.[54] In the wake of the Gregorian reforms, moreover, especially after the imposition of clerical celibacy in the early twelfth century, clerics faced accusations that they were sodomites, forbidding to other priests sexual relationships with women only because they themselves were uninterested in them.[55] Serlo of Bayeux, for example, writing at the beginning of the twelfth century, called the celibate clerics "men of foul, adulterous, and sodomitical [*turpis, mechi, sodomite*] lives."[56] Linking sodomy with military culture, then, also served to refocus the accusation of sodomy and to acquit the clergy of the charge that they were the twelfth century's true sodomites.

An excellent example of these varied social and political uses of the suspicion of sodomy is Orderic Vitalis's account of the Norman king of England, William Rufus, from his *Historia ecclesiastica.* According to Orderic, who wrote before about 1140 from his monastery in Normandy, William was an undisguised enemy of the Christian religion, a fact that made all of his interactions suspect on some level. It was the group of young men at William's court, however, that triggered Orderic's fiercest denunciations. William's courtiers were purely wicked, he wrote:

> They rejected the traditions of honest men, ridiculed the counsel of priests, and . . . frivolled away their time, spending it as they chose without regard for the law of God or the customs of their ancestors. They devoted their nights to feasts and drinking-bouts, idle chatter, dice, games of chance, and other sports, and they slept all day.[57]

It was hardly surprising, Orderic seemed to suggest, that at that same court sodomy was rampant:

> Then the effeminates [*effeminati*] throughout the realm ruled supreme, and carried on their debaucheries without restraint, and loathsome Ganymedes [*catamitae*], who ought to be consumed by flames, abused themselves with foul sodomite-things [*sodomitica*].[58]

It is true that William Rufus never married, despite being over forty years of age at the time of his death in 1100, and he seems to have preferred to spend his time in the company of young men, hunting and warring with them. William was by no means unique in these pursuits, but such a lifestyle could serve to raise suspicions of sodomitical behavior, given the right circumstances, as Orderic attempted to do in his history. William Rufus thus served as an excellent if negative example, according to Orderic, of the sodomitical dangers inherent in this unmarried and impious lifestyle. Through his presentation of William, Orderic advocated for both a conscious dedication to family and lineage and a conscious devotion to ecclesiastical authority. Through William, Orderic also presented the risk to those who refused such dedication and devotion: the descent into effeminacy, that combination of gender and sexual perversion.[59]

If William is placed alongside one of his contemporaries, Geoffroi, the count of Perche, whom Orderic depicts as a model of manhood, the contrast that Orderic implied becomes much starker:

> He was a distinguished count, handsome and brave, God-fearing and devoted to the church, a staunch defender of the clergy and God's poor; in time of peace he was gentle and lovable and conspicuous for his good manners; in time of war, harsh and successful, formidable to the rulers who were his neighbors, and an enemy to all. He stood out among the highest in the land because of the high birth of his parents and his wife Beatrice, and kept valiant barons and warlike castellans in firm subjection to his government. He gave his daughters in marriage to men of high rank . . . from whom sprang a worthy line of noble descendants. So Count Geoffrey, being blessed with such descendants and supported by arms and men, wealth and friends, and, most important of all, filled with the fear of the Lord, feared no man and advanced [into battle] bold as a lion.[60]

Geoffroi is obedient to God and his church and careful of his lineage, and it was this obedience and care as much as his prowess in war that distinguished him as a real man in Orderic's eyes. Orderic included Geoffroi's marriage and the resulting children as part of his masculine "success"; the role of aristocratic wives in the "taming" process advocated by ecclesiastical writers such as Orderic should not be underestimated, and it served as yet another reason for encouraging marriage among the noble classes.[61] Orderic had another good reason for praising Geoffroi: he was allied through marriage with the closest neighbor and greatest benefactor of Orderic's abbey.[62]

It is true that there were other men disliked by Orderic Vitalis, men not painted as sodomites by him. Hugh of Chester, for example, was "a great lover of the world and worldly pomp," and was "always surrounded by a huge household [familia], full of the swarms of boys [numerosa puerorum] of both high and humble birth."[63] Hugh was married, but also had many concubines. Indeed, Hugh seems yet another example of the "untamed" sexuality of the military aristocracy. Still, Hugh had several children, even if all but one of them were by his concubines and not by his wife. Hugh, moreover, permitted good priests like Gerold of Avranches to preach freely and to win converts for the ascetic life from among the young men attached to his household.[64] So Hugh had a fecundity, both physical and spiritual, that William Rufus lacked.

William Rufus's brother, Robert Curthose, who became duke of Normandy, narrowly escaped a condemnation at Orderic's hands similar to that of his brother. In his history, Orderic included a holy man's prophecy that Robert would "give himself up to lust and indolence," and that "Ganymedes and effeminates [catamitae et effeminati] will govern [in his duchy], and under their rule vice and wretchedness will abound."[65] And indeed, when Robert became duke, Orderic continued, he was at first "led astray by the evil counsel of degenerate youths [peruersi iuuenes]."[66] But Robert repented of his evil ways, sought the advice of churchmen, and later even participated in the First Crusade, being transformed in the process from Christian reprobate to Christian hero. Ultimately, as the example of Robert Curthose demonstrates, Orderic's vituperation against the nobility formed part of a larger ecclesiastical project: the pacification of military culture, or at least its redirection toward more acceptable ends.

The means by which the prohibition against sodomitical relations between men and youths was enforced was by associating such sexual activity with effeminacy, which in the twelfth century implied the perversion of sexuality and gender. For if to be a man necessitated devotion to a woman or to the lineage which marriage to her might provide, men who were devoted to each other could hardly be men. To reject these social aims, then, was to make oneself vulnerable not only to attacks of sexual unorthodoxy but also of gender unorthodoxy. Such an association can be seen in Orderic Vitalis's writing against the "effeminates," but he was not the only twelfth-century writer to do so. Bernard of Cluny, when attacking sodomy, linked the two in this fashion:

> The law of kind [*genus*] perishes, and common custom is destroyed by this plague. It is unknown to cattle, or dogs, or horses, but to man [*homo*] entirely [alone]. I call them half males [*semimares*] and judge them half men [*semivires*], polluting themselves, giving to each other—alas!—what they owe to those of the inferior sex [*sexibus inferioribus*].[67]

The nature which was violated by sodomy, Bernard implied, was not only human nature but also especially masculine nature. Helen describes it in this way in her debate with Ganymede:

> Males [*masculi*] should blush, nature should mourn; of nature's bonds, no concern is shown by men [*vires*]. . . . You who attach yourselves, males to males [*maribus mares*], who wastefully unman men [*devirare vires*], at night you pollute yourselves and boys [*pueri*].[68]

Nowhere was the objection to sodomy on the basis of the natural order more clearly linked to the loss of masculinity than in one of the twelfth-century's greatest advocates of nature, the churchman Alain of Lille. His *De planctu naturae* begins:

> I turn from laughter to tears, from joy to grief, from merriment to lament, from jests to wailing, when I see the decrees of Nature fall silent, when a shipwrecked multitude perishes by a monster of Venus, when Venus fighting with Venus makes "hes" into "shes," and when she unmans men [*devirare vires*] with magic art. . . . The sex of the active gender [*activi generis sexus*] trembles thus to degenerate shamefully into the passive gender [*passivum genus*]. A man [*vir*] is made female [*femina*]. He blackens the honor of his sex. The art of magic Venus hermaphrodites [*hermaphroditare*] him. . . . He denies being a man [*vir*].[69]

Alain's use of grammatical similes to back up his argument about the unnaturalness of same-sex coupling has been carefully analyzed by Jan Ziolkowski, who compares them with those of several other contemporary authors.[70] Nevertheless, the similes work not because human correspondences should follow grammatical rules—in fact, the opposite argument is being made—but because in both, masculine and feminine are separate categories and there should be no confusion between the two. Indeed, Gautier de Coincy in his *Miracles de Nostre Dame* argued for the distinction between grammar and sex:

> Grammar couples "him" to "him" [*hic a hic*], but nature curses this coupling. Eternal death is born to him who loves the masculine gender [*masculin genre*] rather than facing the feminine, and God effaces him from his book. Nature laughs, it seems to me, when "him" and "her" join together, but "him" and "him" is a lost cause [*chose perdue*]. Nature is so aghast, she beats her fists and wrings her hands.[71]

Curiously, the same authors who condemned men becoming women also described women becoming men in praiseworthy tones and without concern for the damage done to the natural categories of gender. Even Alain of Lille, in another work, congratulated the goddess Minerva for her virile wisdom: "a man in mind [*sensus*], a woman in body [*sexus*], thus both a man and a woman, and in spirit [*anima*] not a she but a he."[72] The *Roman d'Énéas* also celebrates the manly martial prowess of the warrior-woman, Camille.[73]

The gap left between the condemnation of men-who-become-women and the praise of women-who-become-men reveals much about the categories of gender as understood by twelfth-century writers. Obviously it was not the crossing of gender boundaries that defined the transgressive act; indeed, women who so behaved were seen as improving themselves. Rather, it was because the boundary between gender and sexual difference was situated on an incline: women who became men elevated themselves, but men who became women degraded themselves. The underpinnings of this belief are obvious: the misogyny of twelfth-century culture which assumed the inferior status of women, and the "deep-seated ambivalence" for women, such as Penny Gold describes for the period.[74] As so often has been demonstrated about many medieval writers, women represented carnality and men spirituality. Sexual desire was always therefore effeminizing to men on some level, at least according to ecclesiastical writers. But twelfth-century writers regarded sodomy as particularly abhorrent because men were believed to take on feminine sexual roles, in addition to giving into an effeminizing desire. Behind this idea is the assumption that a man who interacts sexually with another man must do so by acting as a figurative woman, and behind that idea, another assumption, that there can be no sexual relations without a gendered hierarchy. Neither of these were new ideas of the twelfth century, and both were as entrenched in Western culture as misogyny and tied directly to it.[75]

Writers of the twelfth century exploited these ancient fears to lend weight to their prohibitions. They maintained that masculine identity itself depended on the rejection of affectional solidarity between adult and adolescent males in favor of devotion to women. There was a certain irony to suggesting that fostering, the institution whose primary purpose was to initiate a boy into manhood, was instead the occasion for the perversion of masculine identity and the making of the boy into a woman, it is true. But linking the loyalty that these young men had for each other with the perversion of masculine nature resulting from sodomy was part of the "taming" of the military nobility.

Associating male intimacy with the loss of masculine identity worked both at the level of external prohibition and at that of internal self-regulation. The one subjected to the power of surveillance became the principle of his own subjection and assumed responsibility himself for the constraints of that power.[76] Probably the most famous treatise on courtly love, that written by Andreas Capellanus near the end of the twelfth century, serves as an excellent example of this self-policing trend. He began his treatise with the declaration:

> Now, in love you should note first of all that love [*amor*] cannot exist except between persons of different sexes. Between two males [*mares*] or two females [*feminae*] love can find no place, for we see that two persons of the same sex are not at all fitted for giving each other the exchanges of love or for practicing the acts natural to it. Whatever nature denies, love blushes to embrace.[77]

Here is both the argument of the complementarity of men and women, and the claim of the unnaturalness of love between men. Andreas repeated the idea later in his treatise, to support his claim that all men long for sexual union with a woman:

> And if you want to deny the truth of this, you will be forced to admit that two males [*masculi*] can give each other the solaces of love, a thing which would be disgraceful [*nefandus*] enough to speak of and criminal [*criminosus*] to practice.[78]

Nevertheless, and even before this declaration, Andreas stated in the dedicatory prologue that

> I am greatly impelled by the continual urging of my love [*dilectio*] for you, my revered friend Walter, to make known by word of mouth and to teach you by my writings the way in which a state of love [*amor*] between two lovers

may be kept unharmed. . . . Because of the love [*affectus*] I have for you I can
by no means refuse your request.[79]

Despite Andreas's careful choice of synonyms for love—*dilectio* and *affectus*—this prologue must surely undo on some level Andreas's subsequent remarks insisting that men can only love women. Andreas, moreover, ended his treatise by undermining the "naturalness" of courtly love altogether and by affirming that true affection is best found between male friends, concluding that true love was impossible between men and women, in part, because by it

> one friend [*amicus*] is estranged from another and serious unfriendlinesses grow up between men [*homines*]. . . . For what do we find so necessary or so useful to men [*homines*] as to have reliable friends?[80]

Andreas returned to the praise of marriage at the end of his treatise, it should be noted, bringing his work into conformity with the new emphasis on family and lineage. Nonetheless, the tension caused by Andreas's ambivalent recognition of male intimacy remains.

The suspicion of sodomy in the twelfth century by no means put an end to male friendship, as is obvious, even if it questioned the purpose of male intimacy. Even in the midst of attacks against sodomitical desire, erotic desire for men could still be expressed, if in indirect ways. Chrétien de Troyes frequently described the masculine appeal of his heroes, for example, and placed an appreciation of their beauty in the minds of other men:

> Meleagant was extremely noble [*genz*] and capable, and well built [*bien tailliez*] in his arms, legs, and feet; and his helmet and shield which hung from his neck suited him perfectly. But at [first sight of the] other [knight, who was Lancelot], all fell silent—even those who wished to see him shamed—and all said that Meleagant was nothing compared to him.[81]

Alain of Lille also paused longingly on the image of the ideal man as he appears before his mystical wedding to the personification of nature, even in the midst of his treatise against sodomy and while ostensibly repudiating that longing:

> On his face there showed no signs of feminine softness [*feminea mollitia*]; rather the authority of manly dignity [*virilis dignitas*] alone held sway there. . . . [H]is hair lay in orderly fashion to prevent it from appearing to degenerate into feminine softness. . . . His face, as manly dignity demanded, was missing in no grace of beauty [*pulchritudinis gratia*].[82]

This passage suggests the same sort of ambivalence in Alain of Lille's writing about the relationship between nature and homoeroticism that Jordan has described in Alain's writings.[83] But it shows an equal ambivalence about the meaning of a gendered sexuality, since if the man has no *feminea mollitia,* which might be translated as "effeminacy" as easily as "feminine softness," then what is most desirable about him is his masculinity, which lies at the heart of his *pulchritudinis gratia* ("grace of beauty").

The fear of male intimacy beginning in the mid-twelfth century did mean, however, that it became impossible to represent openly passionate friendships between men. In some ways, the only truly unproblematic passion that could be shared between men was a mutual desire for the same woman, because it lay beyond the suspicion of sodomy. Eve Sedgwick has pointed out that in nineteenth-century literature "the bond that links the two rivals is as intense and potent as the bond that links either of the rivals to the beloved," and Marjorie Garber has discussed the polymorphous sexuality of the love triangle in modern literature.[84] Such potent configurations of desire were not unknown to medieval writers. Andreas Capellanus suggested that the passion of rivalry even improved love:

> If you know that someone is trying to win your beloved away from you, that will no doubt increase your love and you will begin to feel more affection for her. I will go further and say that even though you know perfectly well that some other man is enjoying the embraces of your beloved, this will make you begin to value her solaces all the more.[85]

Nothing typifies the vestiges of homoeroticism in this new relationship of rivalry better than *Le Chevaliers au lyeon* ("The Knight of the Lion"), the legend told by Chrétien de Troyes of Yvain and his longtime companion, Gawain. Despite their sincere devotion to each other, they come to blows in defending a woman's honor, ignorant of each other's identity. Chrétien detailed at length how they both love and hate each other with equal passion at that moment.[86] The passage parallels an earlier description of the love and hate between Yvain and his lady.[87] When Chrétien began his depiction of the battle between the two men, he could not resist returning to the irony of their ignorance of each other's identity, saying that if they had known who they were fighting, "they would have permitted each other to kiss and embrace and not to bruise, they who were bruising and wounding each other."[88] When the two men finally recognize each other, they do exactly as Chrétien had predicted: "each threw his arms around the other's neck and they embraced."[89] Yvain and Gawain had been fighting over a woman, and her presence inserts itself between them as the cause of their breach. Nevertheless, the two men surmount this obstacle to their love and regain it in the end. As this example demonstrates, male intimacy was rescued somewhat by being recast as rivalry, and this sort of love triangle proved an especially fruitful conjunction for writers from the twelfth century on.[90]

It is important, finally, to add something about the consequences of the ambivalence surrounding male friendships for male sexual identity. For the reluctance to address devotion between men in literary sources after the twelfth century, as seen in the love triangle, can also be historicized, situated in the historical aftereffects of the problematization of male friendships. Even as the promotion of the lineage and the conventions of courtly love made men's sexual desire for women an essential component of male identity, it also constructed its opposite, the sodomite, the "other" that a man could never permit himself to be and still be a man. R. I. Moore briefly alludes to the formation of a sodomite identity in this period, but it was John Boswell who first suggested that *something* important happened in this period, even if he did not understand what that *something* was.[91] Boswell's work has been dismissed by some as essentialist; that is, presupposing a transhistorical gay identity without which his interpretation of homoerotic texts is meaningless.[92] Nonetheless, it is possible to view the writings that condemned male intimacy in the twelfth century as part of the construction of a new sexual identity for men.

Indeed, concomitant to the historical changes of the twelfth century was a major shift in the categories of male sexuality. A magnifying glass had been turned on men's relationships, both social and sexual. Alain of Lille could, as a result of this intensified examination of men's sexual roles, desire to make the following precise classifications, again by using a grammatical metaphor:

> Of those men [*homines*] who acknowledge the grammar of Venus, some closely embrace those of masculine gender [*genus*] only, others, those of feminine gender, others, those of common, or indiscriminate [*promiscuus*] gender. Some, indeed, if belonging to the heteroclite gender, decline irregularly, in the winter with the feminine, in the summer with the masculine gender. There are some, who, disputing in the logic of Venus, in their conclusions get [*sortiri*, to obtain by chance] a law of interchangeability of subjects and predicates. There are those who take the part of the subject and cannot function as predicate. There are some who function as predicates only but have no desire to have the legitimate subject submit to them.[93]

These are odd categories of sexual identity from a modern perspective, perhaps, but the attempt at classification itself is not unfamiliar to us.

Not even the detailed groupings of sexual acts in penitential literature, which provides the best precedent to Alain's remarks from an earlier age, demonstrates an equivalent desire to create different categories of identity based on sexual preferences. The *Decretum* of Yves of Chartres, for example, which collected together different opinions on penances for sin at the turn of the previous century also in northern France, only alludes to such classificatory possibilities, and with a much more limited scope of vision. The *Decretum* suggests harsher penances for someone who is "in the habit of" (*in consuetudine est*) committing sodomy, and for a cleric or monk who is "a pursuer of boys" (*parvulorum insectator*) or one who "plays with boys and has friendships [with boys] of tender age" (*ludere cum pueris et habere amicitiae aetatis infirmae*).[94] Sodomy has by no means the same implications as in the texts we have examined, where it functions as much as a violation of masculine identity as of sexual morality, and where being a sodomite represented a male person who was a failure as a man.

Appreciating the historical context of the twelfth-century literary sources, we can now see that the fluidity of sexual identities in premodern Europe, emphasized in much of the current historiography on the history of homosexuality, began to be lost in the twelfth century. We are not viewing the creation of a "sexual minority" or the construction of a "third sex," by any means, but the writers of the twelfth century did begin to open a conceptual space for such later developments through their notion of a man who became an "unman" by means of his sexual practices. Indeed, the very content of masculinity, what it meant to be a man, was changed by this fear that intimacy between men could cause men to fall out of the category of being men. Jordan's documentation of a terminological shift from "Sodom" to "sodomy" to "sodomite" is particularly useful, when situated in this context, because it confirms the development of a new sexual identity for men, if only as a mental image, as he suggests in his conclusion.[95] Such a conclusion also parallels that of R. Howard Bloch, who demonstrates the complex interplay between the courtly and misogynistic literature of the later Middle Ages and its central role both as response to and in the construction of a new social identity for women.[96] Gender, one's sense of oneself as "male" or "female" and the social meaning attached to that sense, and sexuality, the spectrum of desires between love and sexual pleasure, thus regulated each other in turn.

· *Notes*

1. On this debate, see the various essays collected in *Forms of Desire: Sexual Orientation and the Social Constructionist Controversy,* ed. Edward Stein (New York: Garland, 1990).

2. Mark D. Jordan, *The Invention of Sodomy in Christian Theology* (Chicago: University of Chicago Press, 1997), 8.

3. R. I. Moore, *The Formation of a Persecuting Society: Power and Deviance in Western Europe, 950–1250* (Oxford: B. Blackwell, 1987), 99.

4. Jordan, *Invention of Sodomy,* 9.

5. See, for example, Reginald Hyatte, *The Arts of Friendship: The Idealization of Friendship in Medieval and Early Renaissance Literature* (Leiden: E. J. Brill, 1994), 130.

6. In this project, I am grateful to the groundbreaking research of Eve Kosofsky Sedgwick, who, in her study of men in nineteenth-century English literature, created a useful new terminology for writing about male intimacies, "homosociality." She called a similar suspicion of male friendships in the nineteenth century a "homosexual panic," and linked it to new gender arrangements which brought into question men's "homosocial desires." I argue that a similar process was at work in the twelfth century, a process one might even call "sodomitical panic." See Sedgwick's *Between Men: English Literature and Male Homosocial Desire* (New York: Columbia University Press, 1985).

7. Jordan never asks, for example, why it was in the eleventh century that Peter Damian coined the term "sodomy," nor why it was used by so many theologians after him in the twelfth as a helpful category. Still, Jordan's is a fascinating and innovative work of intellectual history and one grounded in a profound knowledge of the intellectual history of the Middle Ages.

8. Boswell, *CSTH,* esp. chap. 8, "The Urban Revival," and chap. 9, "The Triumph of Ganymede."

9. See, for example, Gerald A. Bond, *The Loving Subject: Desire, Eloquence, and Power in Romanesque France* (Philadelphia: University of Pennsylvania Press, 1995).

10. C. Stephen Jaeger, "L'amour des rois: Structure sociale d'une forme de sensibilité aristocratique," *Annales E.S.C.* 46 (1991): 547–71: "Le langage de l'érotique montre innocemment que l'illicite est certes proche mais évité ou ignoré. Il est maîtrisé, contrôlé, maintenu à sa place." Unless otherwise indicated, all translations are mine.

11. Peter Abelard, *Dolorum solacium,* in *Medieval Latin Poems of Male Love and Friendship,* ed. and trans. T. Stehling (New York: Garland, 1984), ll. 45–8, 61–64, 69–92: "Plus fratre mihi, Ionatha, / in una mecum anima, / quae peccata, quae scelera, / nostra sciderunt viscera! / . . . / Tu mihi, mi Ionatha, / flendus super omnia, / inter cuncta gaudia / perpes erit lacrima. / . . . / Heu, cur consilio / adquievi pessimo, / ut tibi praesidio / non essem in proelio? / vel confossus pariter / morerer feliciter, / cum, quid amor faciat, / maius hoc non habeat, / et me post te vivere / mori sit assidue, / nec ad vitam anima / satis sit dimidia. / Vicem amicitiae / vel unam me reddere / oportebat tempore / summae tunc angustiae, / triumphi participem / vel ruinae comitem, / ut te vel eriperem / vel tecum occumberem, / vitam pro te finiens / quam salvasti totiens, / ut et mors nos iungeret / magis quam disiungeret."

12. See Jean Leclercq, *Monks and Love in Twelfth-Century France* (Oxford: Clarendon, 1979); Hyatte, *Arts of Friendship,* chap. 2.

13. Alain of Lille, *Anticlaudianus,* in *The Anglo-Latin Satirical Poets and Epigrammatists of the Twelfth Century,* ed. T. Wright, vol. 2 (1872; Wiesbaden, 1964), 7.7: "Quaeret quem vero sic complectatur amore, / Illaesaque fide, quod amor lucretur amorem / Alterius. . . . / . . . / Quaerat cui possit se totum credere, velle / Declarare suum, totamque exponere mentem. / Cui sua committat animi secreta latentis, / Ut sibi, conservans thesaurum mentis in illo, / Nil sibi secretum, quod non develet eidem, / Ut suus in tali signo mensuret amicus / Pondus amicitiae, quam lance rependat eadem."

14. Alain of Lille, *Anticlaudianus,* translated here by J. Sheridan (Toronto: University of Toronto Press, 1980), 2.4: "Nam David et Jonathas ibi sunt duo, sunt tamen unum; / Cum sint diversi, non sunt duo mente, sed unus. / Dimidiant animas; sibi se partitur uterque, / . . . / Alter in Euryalo comparet Nisus, et alter / Eurialus viget in Niso, sic alter utrumque / Reddit, et ex uno comitum pensatur uterque."

15. Alain of Lille, *Anticlaudianus,* trans. Sheridan, 2.4: "quos castus amor, concordia simplex, / Pura fides, vera pietas, conjunxit."

16. *Énéas, roman du XIIe siècle,* ed. J.-J. Salverda de Grave, 2 vols. (1925; Paris: E. Champion, 1983), ll. 4913–18: "amoient soi de tele amor / qu'il ne pooient de greignor: / unques plus voire amor ne fu / que d'aus, tant com il ont vescu; / l'uns ne savoit sanz l'autre rien, / ne ne avoit joie ne bien." I have based my translation of *Énéas* here and below in part on the translation of J. Yunck (New York: Columbia University Press, 1974).

17. *Énéas,* ll. 6147, 6187–89, 6193–96: "Pallas, fait il, flor de jovente, / . . . / tant estïés biaus ier matin, / sos ciel n'avoit plus gent meschin, / en po d'ore te voi müé, / . . . / Bele faiture, gente chose, / si com soloil flestist la rose, / si t'a la morz tot tost plessié / et tot flesti et tot changié."

18. *Énéas,* ll. 6209–13: "Atant se tolt, ne pot plus dire, / au cuer ot duel et molt grant ire, / desor lo mort chaï pasmez, / et quant il s'an fu relevez, / lo mort baisa tot an plorant."

19. *Énéas,* ll. 8567–73, 8579–92: "Cil cuiverz est de tel nature / qu'il n'a gaires de femmes cure; / il prise plus lo ploin mestier; / il ne velt pas biset mangier, / molt par aimme char de maslon; / il priseroit mialz un garçon / qui toi ne altre acoler; / . . . / N'as tu oï comfaitemant / il mena Dido malemant? / Unques feme n'ot bien de lui, / n'en avras tu, si com ge cui, / d'un traitor, d'un sodomite. / Toz tens te clamera il quite; / se il avoit alcun godel, / ce li seroit et bon et bel / quel laissasses a ses druz faire; / s'il lo pooit par toi atraire, / nel troveroit ja si estrange / qu'il ne feïst son bon de toi / por ce qu'il lo sofrist de soi; / bien lo lairoit sor toi monter, / s'il repuet sor lui troter."

20. *Énéas,* ll. 9130–38, 9159–64: " 'Ce est,' fait ele, 'verité, / que ma mere m'a de lui dit; / de feme lui est molt petit, / il voldroit deduit de garçon, / n'aime se males putains non. / Son Ganimede a avec soi, / asez li est or po de moi; / il est molt longuement an ruit, / a garçon moine son deduit; / . . . / Il a asez garçons o soi, / lo peor aime mialz de moi, / fandue trove lor chemise; / maint an i a an son servise, / lor braies sovant avalees: / issi deservent lor soldees.' "

21. *Énéas,* ll. 9165–70: "Maldite soit hui tel nature / d'ome qui de femme n'a cure; / il est de ce toz costumiers. / Molt par est malvés cist mestiers / et molt par a fol esciant / qui feme let et homo prent."

22. Jonathan Goldberg, *Sodometries: Renaissance Texts, Modern Sexualities* (Stanford,

Calif.: Stanford University Press, 1992), 23. He calls this project "reading for sodomy—and for sodomites."

23. Sally North, "The Ideal Knight as Presented in some French Narrative Poems, c.1090–c.1240: An Outline Sketch," in *The Ideals and Practice of Medieval Knighthood*, ed. Christopher Harper-Bill and Ruth Harvey (Bury St. Edmunds: Boydell and Brewer, 1986), 123.

24. *Chanson de Roland*, ed. P. Jonin (Paris: Gallimard, 1979), ll. 284–85: "Gent out le cors e les costez out larges; / tant par fut bels tuit si per l'en esguardent."

25. *Couronnement de Louis*, ed. E. Langlois (Paris: Champion, 1925), ll. 1766–67: "Li gentilz cuens par mi les flans l'embrace, / si le baisa quatre feiz en la face."

26. *Ami et Amile*, ed. P. Dembowski (Paris: Champion, 1969), ll. 177–81: "Et cil le vit qui l'ot ja avisé. / Vers lui se torne quant il l'ot ravisé, / Par tel vertu se sont entr'acolé, / Tant fort se baisent et estraingnent soef, / A poi ne sont estaint et definé."

27. See Yannick Carré, *Le baiser sur la bouche au moyen age: Rites, symboles, mentalités* (Paris: Léopard d'Or, 1992).

28. *Prise d'Orange*, ed. C. Régnier (Paris: Klincksieck, 1970), ll. 625–26: "Un bacheler juene de barbe prime, / Qui de deport et d'armes set bien vivre."

29. Georges Duby, *Medieval Marriage: Two Models from Twelfth-Century France*, trans. E. Forster (Baltimore: Johns Hopkins University Press, 1978), 13. See also Georges Duby, "Youth in Aristocratic Society: Northwestern France in the Twelfth Century," in *The Chivalrous Society*, trans. C. Postan (Berkeley and Los Angeles: University of California Press, 1977).

30. Hildebert of Lavardin, *Ad S. nepotem*, in *Hildeberti Cenomannensis episcopi carmina minora*, ed. A. Brian Scott (Berlin: B. G. Teubner, 1969), 20–21: "Res male tuta puer, nec te committe quibusdam; / multa domus multos fertur habere Joves. / Non tamen expectes Ganymedes crimine coelum; / hac modo militia nullus ad astra venit. / Consecrat aethereas solis junioribus arces / lex melior; manes masculus uxor habet."

31. Hildebert of Lavardin, *De malitia saeculi*, in *Medieval Latin Poems of Male Love and Friendship*, ed. T. Stehling (New York: Garland, 1984), ll. 35–44: "Omnibus incestis superst est sodomitica pestis, / dantque mares maribus debita conjugibus. / Innumeras aedes colit innumerus Ganymedes, / hocque, quod ipsa solet sumere, Juno dolet. / Hoc sordent vitio puer et vir cum sene laeno, / nullaque conditio cessat ab hoc vitio. / Quisquis ad hunc morem naturae vertis honorem / et Venerem licitam negligis ob vetitam, / nonne recordaris quod per Sodomam docearis / hoc scelus ut caveas, sulphure ne pereas?"

32. Bernard of Cluny, *De contemptu mundi*, in *Medieval Latin Poems of Male Love and Friendship*, ed. T. Stehling (New York: Garland, 1984), l. 15: "Lex Sodomae patet, innumerus scatet heu! Ganymedes."

33. Jean Flori, *L'essor de la chevalerie, XIe-XIIe siècles* (Geneva: Droz, 1986), 15. See also Maurice Keen, *Chivalry* (New Haven: Yale University Press, 1984), 66–69.

34. Béroul, *Tristan*, ed. N. Lacy (New York: Garland, 1989), ll. 2174–76: "Et cent danzeaus avoques moi, / Qui servisent por armes prendre / Et a moi lor servise rendre."

35. *Gesta Normannorum ducum*, ed. and trans. E. van Houts, vol. 1 (Oxford: Clarendon, 1992), 4.2: "Mittens enim Ricardum puerum suis iussit aspectibus presentari, quem egregia forma perspiciens decoratum cum coetaneis pueris in suo palatio decreuit educandum."

36. *Vita Amici et Amelii carissimorum,* in *Amis and Amiloun,* ed. E. Kölbing, Altenglische Bibliothek, vol. 2 (Heilbronn: Henninger, 1884); trans. M. Kuefler, *Life of the Dear Friends Amicus and Amelius,* in *Medieval Hagiography: An Anthology,* ed. T. Head (New York: Garland, 2000): "utrique fidem inter se spoponderunt et ad curiam Karoli regis simul ingrediuntur, ubi cerneret juvenes moderatos, sapientes, pulcherrimos, pares uno cultu et eodem vultu, ab omnibus dilectos et ab omnibus honoratos. Quid referam? Factus est Amicus thesaurarius regis et Amelius dapifer." Note that Kölbing's edition, which contains numerous typographical errors, has *cerneres* where I read *cerneret.*

37. An early study is that by Georges Duby, "Lineage, Nobility and Knighthood: The Mâconnais in the Twelfth Century–A Revision," in *The Chivalrous Society,* trans. C. Postan (Berkeley and Los Angeles: University of California Press, 1977). For a recent examination, see Theodore Evergates, "Nobles and Knights in Twelfth-Century France," in *Cultures of Power: Lordship, Status, and Process in Twelfth-Century Europe,* ed. T. Bisson (Philadelphia: University of Pennsylvania Press, 1995).

38. The contemporary shift in land inheritance from partitive inheritance to primogeniture did not detract from this emphasis on procreation and family continuity. First, primogeniture did not always and everywhere triumph over other forms of inheritance. See the example of continued competing systems of land inheritance in Blois-Chartres by Amy Livingstone, "Kith and Kin: Kinship and Family Structure of the Nobility of Eleventh- and Twelfth-Century Blois-Chartres," *French Historical Studies* 20 (1997): 419–58. Second, even when younger sons were excluded from the primary landholding of the family, they were often given secondary landholdings, from maternal, dotal, acquired, or border estates. See Andrew W. Lewis, *Royal Succession in Capetian France: Studies on Familial Order and the State* (Cambridge, Mass.: Harvard University Press, 1981), especially 29–32, 37–42, and 162–63. Third, younger sons might be needed to take up the primary landholding of the family in the event of the death of the eldest son and principal heir, a not infrequent event in the period.

39. *Altercatio Ganymedis et Helene,* in *Medieval Latin Poems of Male Love and Friendship,* ed. T. Stehling (New York: Garland, 1984), l. 155: "Miscet Venus masculos sterili iunctura."

40. Alain of Lille, *De planctu naturae,* in *The Anglo-Latin Satirical Poets and Epigrammatists of the Twelfth Century,* ed. T. Wright, vol. 2 (Wiesbaden: Kraus, 1964; orig. publ. 1872), translated here by J. Sheridan (Toronto: Pontifical Institute of Medieval Studies, 1980), 1.1: "Cudit in incudem quae semina nulla monetat, / Torquet et incudem malleus ipse suam. / Nullam materiam matricis signat idea, / Sed magis et sterili litore vomer arat."

41. *Énéas,* ll. 8596–8602: "De cest sigle seroit tost fin, / se tuit li home qui i sont / erent autel par tot lo mont; / ja mes feme ne concevroit, / grant sofraite de gent seroit; / l'an ne feroit ja mes anfanz, / li siegles faudroit ainz cent anz."

42. For discussion of the assumption of sexual desire and devotion to women as an integral part of masculinity by later medieval writers, see David Aers, "Masculine Identity in the Courtly Community: The Self Loving in *Troilus and Criseyde,*" in *Community, Gender, and Individual Identity: English Writing, 1360–1430* (New York: Routledge, 1988); or Susan Crane, "Masculinity in Romance," chap. 1 in *Gender and Romance in Chaucer's Canterbury Tales* (Princeton: Princeton University Press, 1994).

43. Chrétien de Troyes, *Li contes del Graal,* ed. R. Pickens (New York: Garland, 1990), ll.

3826–28: "Qui beise fame et plus n'i fet, / Des qu'il sont seul a seul andui, / Dons cuit ge qu'il remaint an lui."

44. Marie de France, *Lai de Lanval*, ed. K. Warnke (Geneva: Slatkine, 1974; orig. publ. 1925), ll. 281–84: "Asez le m'a hum dit sovent, / que de femme n'avez talent. / Vaslez amez bien afaitiez / ensemble od els vus dedulez."

45. *Énéas*, ll. 8606–08: "et qui se fet contre nature, / les homes prent, les fames let, / la natural cople desfait."

46. *Altercatio Ganymedis et Helene*, ll. 114–15: "sexum mulieribus invides aperte. / Ordo rerum vertitur et lex perit per te." See also Boswell, *CSTH*, 381–89.

47. Jo Ann McNamara, "The *Herrenfrage*: The Restructuring of the Gender System, 1050–1150," in *Medieval Masculinities: Regarding Men in the Middle Ages*, ed. Clare Lees (Minneapolis: University of Minnesota Press, 1994).

48. *Vita Amici et Amelii carissimorum*, cix–cx: "Quos Deus sicut unanimi concordia et dilectione in vita coniunxit, ita et in morte eos separari noluit. . . . Fabricate sunt ergo due ecclesie . . . reliqua vero corpora hic atque illic sepulta sunt. Mane autem facto dispositione divina inventum est corpus Amelii cum suo sarchofago juxta sarchofagum Amici in ecclesia regali. O admiranda duorum societas amicorum, o ineffabilis caritas amborum, que nec in morte dividi meruit!"

49. Hyatte, *Arts of Friendship*, 130. On the versions of the legend, their dating and relationships, see the introduction to MacEdward Leach, *Amis and Amiloun* (London: Oxford University Press, 1937), ix–xxxii.

50. Moore, *Formation of a Persecuting Society*, 144.

51. Christopher Baswell, "Men in the *Roman d'Énéas:* The Construction of Empire," in *Medieval Masculinities*, ed. Clare Lees, Baswell explores these questions further in his *Virgil in Medieval England: Figuring the Aeneid from the Twelfth Century to Chaucer* (Cambridge: Cambridge University Press, 1995), 200–10.

52. Simon Gaunt, *Gender and Genre in Medieval French Literature* (Philadelphia, 1995), 74, 81. See also the earlier work of Georges Duby, *The Knight, The Lady, and the Priest: The Making of Modern Marriage in Medieval France*, trans. B. Bray (New York: Pantheon, 1983); and Christopher Brooke, *The Medieval Idea of Marriage* (Oxford: Oxford University Press, 1989), 56–60.

53. Alan Bray, "Homosexuality and the Signs of Male Friendship in Elizabethan England," *History Workshop* 29 (1990): 1–19.

54. See Jordan, *Invention of Sodomy*, chap. 3.

55. See Anne Llewellyn Barstow, *Married Priests and the Reforming Papacy: The Eleventh-Century Debates* (New York: Edwin Mellen, 1982), especially 112–14, 120, and 134–36.

56. Serlo of Bayeux, *Defensio pro filiis presbyterorum*, in *Monumenta Germaniae Historica, Libelli de lite imperatorum et pontificum*, 3:580–83; quoted in Barstow, *Married Priests*, 240: "homines vite turpis, mechi, sodomite." Barstow also provides information on the authorship of the text, 240, n. 53. Cf. the anonymous *Nos uxorati*, quoted and translated in Boswell, *CSTH*, 398–400.

57. Orderic Vitalis, *Historia ecclesiastica*, ed. and trans. M. Chibnall, vol. 4 (Oxford: Clarendon, 1973), 8.3.324: "Ritus heroum abiciebant, hortamenta sacerdotum

deridebant. . . . Omne tempus quidam usurpabant, et extra legem Dei moremque patrum pro libitu suo ducebant. Nocte comesationibus et potationibus uanisque confabulationibus aleis et tesseris aliisque ludibriis uacabant, die uero dormiebant."

58. Orderic Vitalis, *Historia ecclesiastica* (my translation here), 8.3.324: "Tunc effeminati passim in orbe dominabantur indisciplinate debachabantur sodomiticisque spurciciis foedi catamitae flammis urendi turpiter abutebantur."

59. See also Frank Barlow, *William Rufus* (Berkeley and Los Angeles: University of California Press, 1983), especially chap. 3, "The Bachelor King and his Domestic Servants," for his discussion of the accusation of sexual unorthodoxy made against William.

60. Orderic Vitalis, *Historia ecclesiastica*, trans. Chibnall, vol. 4, 8.3.302: "Erat idem consul magnanimus, corpore pulcher et ualidus, timens Deum et aecclesiae cultor deuotus, clericorum pauperumque Dei defensor strenuus, in pace quietus et amabilis bonisque pollebat moribus; in bello grauis et fortunatus, finitimisque intolerabilis regibus et inimicus omnibus. Hic nobilitate parentum suorum et coniugis suae Beatricis inter illustres spectabilis erat; strenuosque barones et in armis acres oppidanos suae ditioni subditos habebat. Filias quoque suas consularibus uiris dedit in matrimonio . . . ex quibus orta est elegans sobolis generosae propago. Goisfredus itaque comes tot stemmatibus exornabatur; et armis animisque cum diuitiis et amicis fulciebatur; et quod est super omnia timore Domini stipatus neminem timens ut leo progrediebatur."

61. See Sharon Farmer, "Persuasive Voices: Clerical Images of Medieval Wives, " *Speculum* 61 (1986): 517–43, especially 522–23 on Orderic Vitalis.

62. See Marjorie Chibnall, *The World of Orderic Vitalis* (Oxford: Clarendon, 1984), 24–26. A similar description is given of Helias of Maine: see Orderic Vitalis, *Historia ecclesiastica*, 8.3.332; 10.4.35–39.

63. Orderic Vitalis, *Historia ecclesiastica*, trans. Chibnall, vol. 3, 6.3.4: "Hic nimirum amator fuit seculi seculariumque pomparum quas maximam beatitudinum putabat esse portionem humanarum. Erat enim in militia promptus in dando nimis prodigus gaudens ludis et luxibus, mimis, equis et canibus aliisque huiusmodi uanitatibus. Huic maxima semper adherebat familia in quibus nobilium ignobiliumque puerorum numerosa perstrepebat copia."

64. See Orderic Vitalis, *Historia ecclesiastica*, 4.2.220 on Hugh's children and 6.3.4–17 on the preaching of Gerold and its effects.

65. Orderic Vitalis, *Historia ecclesiastica*, trans. Chibnall, vol. 3, 5.2.385: "Ipse uelut uacca lasciuiens libidini pigriciaeque seuiet, et ipse primus aecclesiasticas opes diripiet spurcisque lenonibus aliisque lecatoribus distribuet. Talibus principatum suum porriget et ab his consilium in necessitatibus suis exiget. In ducatu Rodberti catamitae et effeminati dominabuntur sub quorum dominatione nequitia et miseria grassabuntur." I have replaced Chibnall's "catamites" with "Ganymedes."

66. Orderic Vitalis, *Historia ecclesiastica*, trans. Chibnall, vol. 3, 5.2.388: "Prauo peruersorum monitu iuuenum Rodbertus iuuenis male deceptus est et inde multis ingens discrimen et detrimentum exortum est."

67. Bernard of Cluny, *De contemptu mundi*, ll. 31–34: "Lex genii perit, usus et interit hac lue notus; / nescit ea pecus, aut canis, aut equus, ast homo totus. / Semimares voco, semiviros probo, se maculantes; / debita sexibus inferioribus heu! sibi dantes."

68. *Altercatio Ganymedis et Helene,* ll. 153–34, 209–11: "Erubescant masculi, doleat natura; / de nature vinculo non est viris cura. / . . . / Vos qui vobis maribus mares applicatis, / qui prodigialiter viros deviratis, / nocte vos et pueros fede maculatis."

69. Alain of Lille, *De planctu naturae,* 1.1: "In lacrimas risus, in luctus gaudia verto, / In planctum plausus, in lacrimosa jocos, / Cum sua Naturae video decreta silere, / Cum Veneris monstro naufraga turba perit; / Cum Venus in Venerem pugnans illos facit illas; / Cumque suos magica devirat arte viros. / . . . / Activi generis sexus se turpiter horret / Sic in passivum degenerare genus. / Femina vir factus, sexus denigrat honorem, / Ars magicae Veneris hermaphroditat eum. / . . . / Se negat esse virum." I have relied in part here on Sheridan's translation.

70. Jan Ziolkowski, *Alan of Lille's Grammar of Sex: The Meaning of Grammar to a Twelfth-Century Intellectual* (Cambridge, Mass.: The Medieval Academy of America, 1985).

71. Gautier de Coincy, *Les Miracles de Nostre Dame,* ed. V. F. Koenig, vol. 2 (Geneva: Droz, 1961), ll. 1233–43: "La grammaire *hic* a *hic* acopple, / Mais nature maldist la copple. / La mort perpetuel engenre / Cil qui aimme masculin genre / Plus que le feminin ne face / Et Diex de son livre l'esface. / Nature rit, si com moi samble, / Quant *hic* et *hec* joinnent ensanble, / Mais *hic* et *hic* chose est perdue; / Nature en est tant esperdue / Ses poins debat et tuert ses mains."

72. Alain of Lille, *Anticlaudianus,* 3.4: "vir sensu, femina sexu; / Sic vir, sic mulier, animo non illa, sed ille est."

73. See *Énéas,* ll. 3959–76.

74. Penny Schine Gold, *The Lady and the Virgin: Image, Attitude, and Experience in Twelfth-Century France* (Chicago: University of Chicago Press, 1985), 3.

75. For examples of the fear of effeminacy in men from late ancient texts, see the Christian author, Prudentius (*Amartigenia,* ll. 279–307), or the pagan author, Ammianus Marcellinus (*Res gestae,* 14.6.9–10). A useful overview of the ambivalence toward women and sexuality in the Western Christian tradition is provided by Uta Ranke-Heinemann, *Eunuchs for the Kingdom of Heaven: Women, Sexuality, and the Catholic Church,* trans. Peter Heinegg (London: Penguin, 1990).

76. This social-psychological process is discussed by Michel Foucault, *Discipline and Punish: The Birth of the Prison,* trans. A. Sheridan (New York: Random House, 1995; orig. publ. 1975), 202–3.

77. Andreas Capellanus, *De amore,* ed. P. Walsh (London: Duckworth, 1982), trans. J. Parry (New York: Columbia University Press, 1990), 1.2: "Hoc autem est praecipue in amore notandum, quod amor nisi inter diversorum sexuum personas esse non potest. Nam inter duos mares vel inter duas feminas amor sibi locum vindicare non valet; duae namque sexus eiusdem personae nullatenus aptae videntur ad mutuas sibi vices reddendas amoris vel eius naturales actus exercendos. Nam quidquid natura negat, amor erubescit amplecti."

78. Andreas Capellanus, *De amore,* trans. Parry, 1.539: "Et si huic vultis resistere veritati, necessitatis cogit ratio profiteri duos masculos sibi adinvicem posse amoris solatia exhibere, quod satis esset narrare nefandum et agere criminosum."

79. Andreas Capellanus, *De amore,* trans. Parry, *praefatio:* "Cogit me multum assidua tuae dilectionis instantia, Gualteri venerande amice, ut meo tibi debeam famine propalare

mearumque manum scriptis docere qualiter inter amantes illaesus possit amoris status conservari. . . . propter affectum quo tibi annector, tuae nullatenus valeo petitioni obstare."

80. Andreas Capellanus, *De amore,* trans. Parry, 3.9: "Nam exinde unus ab altero divertitur amicus, et inimicitiae inter homines capitales insurgent. . . . Quid enim tam necessarium tamve utile hominibus invenitur quam amicos habere securos?"

81. Chétien de Troyes, *Le Chevalier de la charette,* ed. W. Kibler (New York: Garland, 1981), ll. 3540–49: "Molt estoit genz et bien aperz / Melïaganz, et bien tailliez / de braz, de janbes, et de piez; / et li hiaumes et li escuz / qui li estoit au col panduz / trop bien et bel li avenoient. / Mes a l'autre tuit se tenoient – / nes cil qui volsissent sa honte – / et dïent tuit que rien ne monte / de Melïagant avers lui."

82. Alain of Lille, *De planctu naturae (Patrologia Latina* 210, col. 471–72), 16.8: "Hujus in facie nulla femineae mollitie vestigia resultabant, sed sola virilis dignitatis regnabat auctoritas. . . . moderatae tamen comptionis libramine jacebat ornata, ne si comptionibus vagaretur anomalis, in femineam demigrare videretur mollitiem. . . . Hujus facies, prout virilis dignitas exposcebat, a nulla pulchritudinis gratia deviabat." This passage is omitted in the Wright edition without explanation.

83. Jordan, *Invention of Sodomy,* chap. 4.

84. Sedgwick, *Between Men,* 21; Marjorie Garber, *Vice Versa: Bisexuality and the Eroticism of Everyday Life* (New York: Simon and Schuster, 1995), chap. 18.

85. Andreas Capellanus, *De amore,* 2.2: "Sed et, si cognoveris aliquem ad tuae amantis subversionem laborare, illico tibi sine dubio augmentatur amor, et maiori eam incipies affectione diligere. Immo amplius tibi dico: etsi manifeste cognoveris quod alius tuae coamantis fruatur amplexu, magis ex hoc eius incipies affectare solatia." Andreas later contradicts himself, ibid., 2.6.16, but this is not unusual.

86. See Chrétien de Troyes, *Le Chevaliers au lyeon,* ed. W. Kibler (New York: Garland, 1985), ll. 6002–27.

87. Chrétien de Troyes, *Le Chevaliers au lyeon,* ll. 1453–65.

88. Chrétien de Troyes, *Le Chevaliers au lyeon,* ll. 6119–21: "entrebeisier et acoler / s'alassent einz quë afoler, / qu'il s'antr'afolent et mehaingnent."

89. Chrétien de Troyes, *Le Chevaliers au lyeon,* ll. 6316–17: "s'a li uns a l'autre tandu / les braz au col, si s'antrebeisent."

90. The homoerotic element of men's rivalry over a woman in thirteenth-century romance texts is skillfully described by Christiane Marchello-Nizia, "Amour courtois, société masculine et figures du pouvoir," *Annales E.S.C.* 36 (1981): 969–82.

91. See also Colin Morris, *The Discovery of the Individual, 1050–1200* (Toronto: University of Toronto Press, 1987; orig. publ. 1972), 96, who also seems to link in a vague way the new attitude toward male friendship and sexual love: "The growth of a keen self-awareness was naturally accompanied by a fresh interest in close personal relationships. The twelfth century has been called the century of friendship, and it occupies an important, if controversial, place in the history of the Western idea of sexual love."

92. Boswell defended his position in his final book, *Same-Sex Unions in Pre-Modern Europe* (New York: Vintage, 1995), but refused to see it as essentialist. See also my introductory essay to this collection, chapter 1, "The Boswell Thesis," for more on his position.

93. Alain of Lille, *De planctu naturae,* 8.4: "Eorum siquidem hominum qui Veneris profitentur grammaticam, alii solummodo masculinum, alii femininum, alii commune, sive genus promiscuum, familiariter amplexantur. Quidam vero, quasi hetrocliti genere, per hiemen in feminino, per aestatem in masculino genere, irregulariter declinantur. Sunt qui, in Veneris logica disputantes, in conclusionibus suis subjectionis praedicationisque legem relatione mutua sortiuntur. Sunt qui vicem gerentes suppositi, praedicari non norunt. Sunt qui solummodo praedicantes, subjecti termini subjectionem legitimam non attendunt." Again, I have relied in part here on Sheridan's translation.

94. Yves of Chartres, *Decretum (Patrologia Latina* 161, col. 682), 9.92–95: "Qui fornicatus fuerit sicut Sodomitae, si servus est, scopis castigabitur et 2 annos poeniteat; si liber est conjugatus, 10 annos; si privatus, septem annos poeniteat. Puer 100 dies, si in consuetudine est; laicus conjugatus, si in consuetudine habet, 15 annos poeniteat. . . . Clericus vel monachus ut parvulorum insectator, vel qui osculo vel aliqua occasione turpi deprehensus fuerit, publice verberetur, et comam amittat, decalvatusque turpiter sputamentis oblinitus in facie, vinculisque arctatus ferreis, carcerali 6 mensibus angustia maceretur, et triduo per hebdomadas singulas ex pane hordeaceo ad vesperam reficiatur. . . . Si deprehensus fuerit aliquis frater ludere cum pueris, et habere amicitias aetatis infirmae, tertio commoneatur ut memor sit honestatis, atque timoris Dei; si non cessaverit, severissime corripiatur."

95. Jordan, *Invention of Sodomy,* passim. Jordan writes (163–64): "The invention of the homosexual [in the nineteenth century] may well have relied on the already familiar category of the Sodomite. The idea that same-sex pleasure constitutes an identity of some kind is clearly the work of medieval theology, not of nineteenth-century forensic medicine." This is much like the conclusion that I also reached (independently), although I would emphasize the interplay of social and political forces with theological categories.

96. R. Howard Bloch, *Medieval Misogyny and the Invention of Western Romantic Love* (Chicago: University of Chicago Press, 1991).

PART III

Innovations

CHAPTER 11

Impossible Translation: Antony and Paul the Simple in the *Historia Monachorum*

Mark Masterson

The desert literature of the fourth and early fifth centuries CE presents the desert as primarily a place for men. There was the occasional woman in this homosocial space,[1] but she would have been the exception.[2] Of interest, then, is the sensible assertion that homosocial environments increase the incidence of homosexual desire.[3] But the testimony of the literature of the desert features relative silence about male homosexual behavior.[4] Observe some exceptional moments of talk about homosexual behavior in the desert (buried in the many rules Pachomius wrote to supervise behavior in his establishment):

> Rule 94: No one should speak to another after lights out. No one should sleep with another on a rush mat. No one should hold another's hand; but whether he stands, walks, or sits, let him be separated from another by one cubit.[5]

> Rule 95: No one will dare remove a thorn from the foot of another, with the exception of the head of the house, or in the second place, another who has been ordered to do so.[6]

Clearly what is at issue here is the emergence of homosexual desire. Why else, really, would the removal of a thorn from a foot attract such attention? But as I have noted, these rules are exceptional. Much of what we have in the literature from the desert is depiction of self-denial not at all invested in telling what I imagine to be a truth about the realities of sexual desire in the desert and the probable effects of homosociality.

Perhaps a scholar's focus on desire in the desert can seem somewhat beside the point in the face of this literature that does have additional things on its mind.[7] Athanasius's *Vita Antoni,* for example, played an important role in his political objectives as bishop.[8] In a work to be considered below, Rufinus's translation of the *Historia monachorum,*[9] Rufinus arguably intervened in the Origenist controversy through alterations he made to the text as he translated it from Greek to Latin.[10] But all the same, politics are only a part of the story (albeit an important one). As these texts help secure a bishop's episcopal throne or intervene to favor a particular construal of doctrine, they also are always reaching out to the reader. Indeed, we commonly see at the beginning of works from the desert explicit awareness that the readers of these works will (and should) be moved to imitate what they are reading.[11] This stress on imitation must be read for the powerful thing it is. Resonantly reaching back to Paul (e.g., 1 Corinthians 4:16),[12] and perhaps even further back to Platonic discussions of mimesis, the injunction to imitation powerfully inscribes hierarchy and, simultaneously, both valorizes sameness and devalues difference.[13] The offering of a model for imitation, as an injunction to mold oneself to the measure of an ideal, holds out the promise of identity, a melding of wish and reality to be realized at some point in the future.[14] And the management of desire of all kinds plays an important part in the consolidation of identity in this hierarchical scene of imitation.

I would like to discuss my method before we begin in earnest. To some readers my mode of argumentation may at times seem (very nearly) intolerably speculative. Indeed, since I am endeavoring to demonstrate the presence of something, homosexual desire, which we cannot measure directly, my method *is* inescapably speculative. Virginia Burrus speaks of avoiding "a particular performative mode of interpretation that tends, in the service of directly reproducing a 'world,' to elide the creative work of texts and the critical agency of (other) readers and writers."[15] To get at the play of homosexual desire at and just beyond the margins of these texts we need to think of creative and critical readers and writers. Not doing so, we run the risk of presenting the norms and idealized personages contained in a text as the total reality, when they are surely only part of it.[16] In looking at these interventionist texts, with their mimetic injunctions an inheritance from prior centuries, we must therefore consider how the individual who may have felt such desire (or who thought others could feel such desire) might have received these

texts. Furthermore, we are lucky because we have access to an actual contemporary reception with which to supplement my more speculative moves.
In arguments to come, I will be investigating the story of Antony of the desert
and Paul the Simple in an anonymous Greek text, the *Historia monachorum in
Aegypto* ("The Narration of the Monks in Egypt"; henceforth *HM*) with the
goal of revealing the action of homosexual desire. I will also be comparing
this Greek text to a contemporary Latin translation of it. Written about 400
CE, the *HM* is a resume of a journey through Egypt, a sort of travelogue,
filled with stories of monks who are remarkable in various ways. Within ten
or so years, Rufinus, one of the Latin fathers, made a translation of the *HM*
into Latin. His translation significantly alters the content of the story of Paul
and Antony and thus provides a way into judging the way the Greek text was
received on at least one occasion.

In section 24 of the *HM* we read the story of Antony and his disciple Paul
the Simple. Once Antony established himself as an exemplar of monastic self-
discipline, he attracted the attention of others. One such—on the testimony of
anonymous—was Paul the Simple. Paul catches his wife in adultery and goes
immediately to the desert to be with Antony. He begs Antony to be allowed
to stay with him. Antony agrees, provided Paul display total obedience:

> Having caught his wife in the very act of adultery, saying nothing to anybody,
> he headed out to the desert to Antony. Falling to Antony's knees, he declared
> that he wanted to reside with him because he wanted to be saved. Antony
> answered him: "You can be saved provided you have obedience and whatever
> you hear from me, this you must do." Paul answering said, "whatever you
> order, I will do it all."[17]

And Antony means what he says; he is full of orders and is so demanding that
the story is unbelievable.

To test Paul's obedience and mental devotion (*gnōmē*, 24.2) to monastic
discipline, he makes Paul stand in the same place for a week and it is specified
that it is the hot season. Neither food nor water is mentioned. At the end
of the week, Antony sets a table with food and drink and makes Paul sit at
it without eating or drinking. Then he sends Paul off to bed. Antony then
awakens Paul for prayers in the middle of the night. After the prayer session,
Paul is allowed to eat a little but is given no water. Antony subsequently
sends Paul to wander in the desert for three days. When Paul comes back
from the desert Antony makes him serve some visiting brothers food. He is
not allowed to eat or speak. Three weeks later—three weeks!—when Paul has

eaten nothing and said nothing, the brothers ask Paul why he says nothing. Paul will not answer. He is obedient. Intervening, Antony asks Paul why he is quiet and then, without waiting for an answer, Antony tells Paul to converse with the visiting brothers. Being the obedient one that he is, Paul converses:

> Finally, when the third week had passed and Paul had eaten nothing, the brothers kept asking him why he was silent. Since he wouldn't answer, Antony said to him: "Why are you silent? Converse with the brothers." He conversed.[18]

In addition to these impossible demands on Paul's actual physical being, Antony requires Paul to perform ostensibly meaningless tasks—further tests of Paul's commitment to obedience. Antony makes Paul break open a jar of honey, pour the honey out onto the ground and then gather it up again without bringing up any dirt with it. Other tasks include weaving baskets and then unweaving them, drawing water all day, and stitching and unstitching Antony's cloak (24.8–9).

But in the end Paul has such obedience that God gives him powers that are greater than Antony's own:

> And to so great an extent did the man [sc. Paul the Simple] possess obedience, that a grace from God, the power to drive out demons, was bestowed on him. The demons the blessed Antony was not able to drive out, these he sent to Paul and they were cast out immediately.[19]

A usual way the story of Paul and Antony can be understood, and it's sensible—I see what I am doing in this paper as supplementing such a reading—is that this story is a hyperbolic representation of the ideal relationship between a master/*abba* and his disciple. The hyperbole is to be understood as clarifying the respective positions of mastery and subservience that master and disciple occupy. The disciple learns from his master/*abba* how to transform himself into a successful faster/prayer who will have the ability to spend time alone in the uninhabited places. To accomplish the transformation, the disciple makes the *abba* privy to his most inward thoughts. He also shows absolute obedience. He also endeavors to increase his endurance in fasting, to cultivate silence, to limit food and water intake, and to extinguish sexual desire to the extent possible. The disciple also utterly suppresses his self-will and does not presume to believe that he can assess his own spiritual progress.[20]

The story of Paul and Antony can be profitably understood in this way. Present are obedience, endurance, and a refusal to judge one's progress for oneself. There is omission of the confession of inmost thoughts, but since Paul seemingly arrives without a thought in his head, he arguably models the complete mental surrender desirable in the disciple throughout the story. We are liable, however, to miss something if we see the odd story of Paul and Antony as primarily an allegory of obedience. Given that the final destination in this story is the homosocial sphere of the desert, I have questions about homosexual desire. And since this story has an intended audience that is larger than men of simple demeanor who have caught their wives with another man *in flagrante delicto,* we should consider the wider tastes, propensities, and life experiences of the audience too. How would have others read this story? Would they ask whether the sublimation of one desire stands for all; whether homosexual desire's sublimation is assured by a sort of general law to be drawn from this account that *all* sexual desires will be left behind in the retreat to the desert? And what about the sexual tensions that will arise in the homosocial environment of the desert? These questions destabilize the default heterosexuality that can all too easily be assumed in accounting for possible receptions of this story. With these questions in mind, let's pull the homosexual out of the homosocial in the story of Antony and Paul. So, from the top again, and this time subversively.

Paul witnesses his wife's adultery and, traumatized by the sight, says goodbye to home, wife, and sex once and for all. In the emphatic first position in the story, the traumatizing sight of Paul's wife's adultery and all he is leaving behind stays in the mind of the reader. It is possible, of course, to view Paul's past life with the climactic betrayal as providing both comment on the inherent depravity of the *saeculum* and spur to Paul's immediately commenced life of sanctity. But the fact that it took the betrayal to break Paul out of his prior married life encourages another approach to the two halves of Paul's life. While not denying the critique of the *saeculum,* I suggest that we additionally view Paul's new life as a reconstruction and replication of the wholeness (though illusory it may have been) that he lost at the moment of his wife's betrayal. Viewing Paul's new life with Antony as a sort of replication of prior married life leads, then, to questions about desire—questions that the Greek employed in the story encourages.

Passages discussed above contain suggestive verbs. When Paul asks to "reside" with Antony and when Antony tells Paul to "converse" with the bothers, it is well to remember that the verbs used (*syneinai* and *homilein* respectively) can function as euphemisms for sexual activity. The sexual meanings of "reside"/*syneinai* (and the related *synousia*) and "converse"/*homilein* (and *homilia*) are in use from the classical period on.[21] Hence, the combination of suggestive language with the notion that marriage is replicated in the desert suggests that perception of homosexual desire is possible in ancient reception of this text. Furthermore, the notion that homosexual desire would have been perceived in ancient reception of this text is strengthened when we consider the miraculous abilities of Paul. The impossibility of these actions of course provides an ideal, but it also has the effect of highlighting the all too human nature of any reader of the text, since the model on offer is inimitable.

The superhuman exploits in the account will cause a reader to reject it as being strictly applicable to him- or herself. Paul's surviving seven-day exposure to the hot Egyptian sun and living so long without food and water are unbelievable. Paul is capable of so much! We mere humans of so little. So how do we humans (ancient and modern) make sense of this account? One way to do so is to regard the story of Paul as a model for emulation, an ideal model transcending of human weakness. This ideal model is ever there to urge on and ever there to find fault. Hence, if we think of the story in this way, the impossibilities perhaps enhance the story's value—the impossibilities enfigure for the ascetic the impossibility of ever ceasing from his or her practice.

But at the same time, when the model is revealed as so excessive of human capability, the reader rejects it as a literal human truth and discontinuity between reader and story results. This rejection and the resultant discontinuity both encourage allegorical interpretation and forcefully emphasize the reader's insufficiency; compelled to look through the surface of the account for other meaning by the impossibility of replicating Paul's acts and with a feeling of lack continually reinforced through the mere fact of allegory's inevitably divisive presence, the reader inhabits a place forever alienated from Paul's. Furthermore, the effort to interpret a miracle connected to desire has the counterproductive result of increasing desire's hold on the reader. To illustrate these effects of the inimitable model, I will now perform a thought experiment. I will read the scene of Paul with his honey (in the context of my larger concern with homosexual desire) with sections of Porphyry's *On the Cave of the Nymphs in the Odyssey* (henceforth *On the Cave*) and the Old Testament. These comparative readings will suggest how the effort to allegorize the impossible can increase desire's power and thereby sabotage the drive for sublimation.

We now return to the scene of the useless tasks Antony sets for Paul:

> On another occasion, when he had given Paul a jar of honey, Antony said to him, "break the container and let the honey pour out." Paul did so. Then

Antony said to him, "bring the honey back up from the ground with a little spoon so that you don't gather up any dirt with it."[22]

Here we have an instance of the miraculous; how in the world can honey be brought up from the Egyptian dust clean of dirt? It cannot and so the account compels interpretation. Following Averil Cameron, I suggest that we focus on the fact that what Paul does here *is* miraculous. Cameron suggests that instances of the miraculous should be read as a late-ancient/Christian rhetorical device that directs the reader to look at the text symbolically:

> Miracle, the suspension of normal laws of nature, is to be seen less as an example of "irrationality" or credulity than as an instance of the symbolic interface of human and divine: it functions as a rhetorical device to express what is otherwise inexpressible.[23]

The question to which the miracle directs the reader, then, centers on that which is inexpressible and, as a result, symbolized.[24] A possible reception of this scene will surely suggest that Paul's miraculous mastery of the honey is a symbolization of God's ineffable and transcendent consideration for Paul's piety. But to a reader fallible, weak, and aware of the presence of homosexual desire, the honey will stubbornly symbolize the desire that will stubbornly persist as surely as it is impossible to fast for three weeks.

Writing at the end of the third century CE, Porphyry associates bees and honey with souls and the joys/enticements of embodiment respectively in his *On the Cave*.[25] The reader will see this association clearly in Porphyry's discussion of Zeus, Kronos, and Ouranos:

> Suggesting the trick of the honey, Night says the following to Zeus: "When you see him (Kronos) under the high-leafed oaks drunk on the labor of the loud-buzzing bees, bind him." Kronos suffers this and, bound, he is castrated, just as Ouranos was. The theologian tells in riddling fashion here how divine principles are bound through pleasure and bring themselves down to genesis and how, dissolved into pleasure, they emit their powers as semen. So in this way Kronos castrates Ouranos who came down to Gaia through desire for intercourse. To the ancients the sweetness of the honey with which Kronos was deceived before his castration expresses the same idea as the pleasure of intercourse.[26]

Honey designates the *telos* of male sexual desire. Success in realizing this *telos* means castration according to the story (and, temporarily, according to the bodily mechanics to which the human male is subject). Sweet honey also symbolizes the pleasure divine principles feel when they join themselves to the world of things that are born and die (*genesis*). Elsewhere, speaking generally of souls, Porphyry notes that "blood and moist semen are dear to them," again closely associating embodiment with the pleasure of intercourse.[27]

If the reader of the *HM* turns his or her attention from honey's association in Porphyry with sexual desire and intercourse (*and* post-coital disorientation and two castrations) back to Paul and his honey, what might he or she make of Paul's abilities now? Paul's superhuman glamor is surely reinscribed as he succeeds in handling that which defeated the all too carnal archaic gods. (And Christianity, incidentally, triumphs yet again.) We may also interpret Paul's ability to overcome the adhesive qualities of honey as an ability to transmute desire in spite of itself into something else; Paul dissolves dusty dirty desire for a wife (and / or for Antony) into a cleanly adhesive and sweetly pure obedience in the context of sublime homosociality.

While seeing the honey in terms similar to Porphyry's suggests that a desirable sublimation of Paul's prior way of being has occurred (and as such it harmonizes nicely with the notion that Paul's new life is in some sense a replication), a paradox has now been substituted for the forbidding miracle. If we allegorize the honey as Porphyry does, the desire that moves Paul in his new life is one whose *telos* is no longer carnal and yet this desire is allegorically (and paradoxically) related to carnally directed desire. Paul's desire to be the perfect disciple leads him to handle that which defeated the semen-spewing, archaic father-gods. At a symbolic level, then, Paul embraces unchastity to secure chastity. At this point, any reader envisioning his or her life in the desert will see it as a place surely infused with desire that will, it would seem, take a miracle to manage. This particular effort to interpret Paul's miracle, even as it suggests the power of God's favor, also hints at a desert full of desire. One might say that a symbolization of the inexpressible action of divine grace coexists with a symbolization of unspeakable carnal desire.

The search for meaning could also lead a reader to an episode from the life of Samson in Judges 14 of the Old Testament. As he is on the way to meet his future wife (an unnamed woman of the Philistines [14:1–3]), Samson bare-handedly kills a lion (14:5–6). Later, returning to take his new wife home, he discovers bees and honey in the lion's carcass (14:8). Samson consumes some of the honey. Later, he uses this miracle in a wager with some Philistines. He poses a riddle, "what edible thing came from the eater, what sweet thing from the strong" (14:14)? At a loss, the Philistines threaten Samson's new wife. She extorts the answer to the riddle from Samson through tears and the Philistines, told by her, are able to give Samson an answer: "What is sweeter than honey and what is stronger than the lion?" (14:18). Realizing he has been betrayed, he responds with more riddling words: "If you had not plowed with my heifer, you would not know my riddle" (14:18). Samson then disavows his new wife, giving her to one of his friends (14:20).

If we think of Samson's honey in terms of desire, we can with ease connect the miracle of the carcass-born honey to Samson's repudiation of his wife. Samson's destruction of the lion, equivalent to the mastering of his bestial impulses, brings him a sweet reward. Such mastering prefigures the rejection of his wife, whom he compares to a farm animal and who, it could be argued, is the site for the play of bestial impulses. And so, Samson, now a paragon of self-control, prefigures the ascetic who enjoys chastity's sweetness. Such an interpretation is strained in the face of the phallic man-of-action Samson (and Delilah waits in the wings!), but such a reading was a way of approaching this text in the fourth century. In a recent discussion of Ambrose's reception of this passage (*De sancto spiritu 2 praef.*), Virginia Burrus notes that Ambrose sees a rejection of masculine assertion and a valorization of (a surely feminine) receptivity:

> . . . as he was going to his marriage, about to enjoy the wished-for wedlock, Samson discovered in the sundered leonine body of his hypermasculine desire a habitation for bees and a receptacle for honey's yielding sweetness.[28]

Later in her discussion of Ambrose's works (and Paulinus's *Vita Ambrosii*), Burrus identifies honey with the virginity that Ambrose idealized in women and himself:

> . . . we understand that the body of Ambrose's masculinity has, like Samson's . . . lion, been transformed in Paulinus's text into a receptacle for bees, a producer of virginity's sweet honey.[29]

Following Ambrose and Paulinus (and Burrus) as they read Judges 14, the reader of the *HM* may find in Paul's honey chastity realized through *askesis*. It is also possible, however, that the use of this story, with Samson's brawny insistence on marriage and the spectacle of a wife handed off to be the wife of another, may provoke desire more than calm it. Furthermore, the discovery of a "yielding sweetness" in a male body may suggest a man ready to give his body for penetration to another.

Both resorts to text outside of the *HM* in an effort to understand the significance of the honey (and thereby put Paul's miracle to use for the purpose of imitation) proliferate desire. Furthermore, any symbolization of the honey effected to interpret Paul's miracle sabotages imitation of Paul. The symbolization of the honey, insinuating more difference (the honey is no longer just honey, it is something else too), *ipso facto* disrupts imitation's drive toward the production of sameness and drives the model farther out of reach. Indeed, the mere fact of trying to understand the miracle in symbolic terms perhaps makes the verbs "converse" and "reside" more susceptible to double-entendre; things quickly become other than what they seem. Paul can gather up his honey and get about his business while we, trying to understand, deal with a sticky dirty mass of meanings that we will never get straight. Homosexual desire's possibility in the actual space of homosocial monastic withdrawal is emphasized as the model, inaccessible, ever drives the reader to fall back on his or her own resources in vain attempt to effect a miraculous and paradoxical conversion of desire. It is at this point that I want to bring in my second text, Rufinus's translation of this story.

Rufinus's Latin translation of the Greek text we have been discussing appeared within a few years of the original. Comparison of Rufinus's translation to the Greek original is revealing; Rufinus alters the text in ways that I see as sensitive to the effect the account could have had on the reader. He takes steps, seemingly, to circumvent the readings I just performed. Before proceeding to his translation, however, consideration of some of Rufinus's remarks on translating is to the point, for they most definitely open up a space for my interpretation.

Rufinus does not reflect on translation as an activity in his translation of the *HM* (he in fact almost completely effaces himself except for a mention of the eleventh book of his *Ecclesiastical History* at 29.5.5), but he does offer programmatic statements on translation elsewhere in his works. In general terms, a "practico-ethical aim" motivates Rufinus to give "useful works . . . suitable presentation."[30] This "practico-ethical aim" licenses a number of procedures on the part of Rufinus the translator. To begin with, Rufinus believes that some looseness in translation is allowed:

> I have been asked to show to those who speak Latin how [this text] is understood among Greek speakers. I merely have given Latin words to Greek thoughts.[31]

He is not looking to translate merely word for word. Taking the thought as a whole instead, Rufinus endeavors to reproduce it in Latin. Indeed, with his goal the recreation of the impression the words would have made in Greek, Rufinus looks for conceptual frameworks that will guide periphrasis:

Accordingly then I—on account of the sparseness of our language, the novelty of these matters, and . . . because the speech of the Greeks has more words and their language is more fertile—I will not try so much to translate word for word (which is impossible) as I will try to tease out the force of the words in a certain roundabout way.[32]

In this teasing out, in this explication in a circuitous manner combined with the need to attend to the sense as well, the original in Greek to varying degrees is left behind.

Concern for sense was not the only possible standard to which Rufinus appeals. The needs of orthodoxy could license more invasive alterations than mere periphrasis:

In the short prefaces to each of those two works, however, and especially in the one to the booklet for Pamphilus (which I translated first), I put on display first of all my faith and bore witness to the fact that I believe according to the catholic faith; I also bore witness to the fact that if anything were read or translated by me I did such activity in harmony with my faith. And truly in those volumes of [Origen's] *Peri Archōn,* I served notice there that, while in those very volumes some things might be found to be written according to the dictates of the catholic faith (as the church prescribes), certain other things, however, may be found to be contrary to the teachings of the church, although they may be speaking about the same thing. It seemed best to me that those matters [in Origen] ought to be offered to readers according to the constant standard that he offered in his exposition of orthodoxy and it also seemed best to me that I remove those things which might be discovered to be contrary to catholic doctrine on his own testimony—things either added by others . . . or without a doubt [contrary to orthodoxy], so that I omit nothing constructive in the matter of supporting faith.[33]

After Rufinus's initial assertion of his unwavering orthodoxy, which he insists he manifests in his faith, reading, and translating, he explains how it guides him in his handling of the text of the notoriously controversial Origen. Rufinus notes that he will change Origen's text merely to remove the appearance of unorthodox doctrine. When such smoothing of superficialities will not work, Rufinus resorts to excision from the text on the basis of what he identifies as an internal contradiction, which he then resolves in favor of making the text orthodox in its assertion. He blames others for tampering with the text or even grants that Origen was at fault. (There is a "good" Origen and a "bad"

Origen as far as Rufinus is concerned.) Rufinus will alter the text as he sees fit, and an appeal to *fides catholica* justifies all. Rufinus's procedures here are similar to the ones he employs in his translation of the *Historia ecclesiastica* by the doctrinally suspect Eusebius of Caesarea. There, his cannily adjusting translation produces "a more orthodox Eusebius."[34]

On another occasion, Rufinus views translation as a sort of clarifying exposition:

> . . . as I have done in the homilies or in the short prayers on Genesis or Exodus, or especially in those passages that are spoken in the style of a prayer by him [Origen] on the book of Leviticus, the words have been translated by me with the goal of making the content manifest.[35]

Eschewing reproduction of Origen's prayers or prayer-like passages, Rufinus brings to the fore (presumably) Origen's interpretations of the Old Testament that he perceives as underlying the prayers. Rufinus also sees his work as translator as one of making the texts he is translating as *useful* as possible:

> It was not my goal to seek out the applause of readers but rather benefit for those who are making [moral] progress.[36]

Virtuosic reproduction is not Rufinus's goal. He is concerned, instead, with the place of his translation in an economy of moral improvement. Indeed in pursuing his goals of reproducing sense (as opposed to words), remaining faithful to orthodoxy, clarifying, and being useful to those on their spiritual journeys, Rufinus flat out states that he had to use whatever means necessary:

> . . . I have thus attempted through certain words taken away, changed, or added to render the sense of the author with the objective of providing a straighter path for understanding.[37]

The objective here, understanding, we must view as already implicated in a moral economy. The straighter path to this goal is one inflected by the needs of orthodoxy and moral improvement. Another objective a translation could serve was a polemical one. Elizabeth Clark has discussed additions made to the translations of the *Cogitationes* of Sextus and the *HM* that seemingly are driven by Origenist partisanship.[38]

On his own testimony, then, Rufinus intervenes when he translates more than we might expect a translator to. But as his goal was not to provide a copy, our possibly unmet expectations are our problem. Rufinus's goals, rather, included making the text function in a similar fashion among those who spoke Latin *and* rendering the text useful in matters of both orthodoxy and spiritual improvement of readers. So with Rufinus's faceted and invasive approach to translation in mind, we now pass to his translation of the story of Paul and Antony.

The beginning of the story shows some indicative alterations, especially in the matter of attributing agency to Paul:

> When Paul had seen with his own eyes his wife having sex with another man, saying not a thing to anyone he left the house. Driven by heartsickness, he gave himself [to wander] into the desert, where, while he was wandering agitatedly, he came to Antony's monastery and there through the suggestion [arising seemingly of its own accord] from the place and through the happenstance of being there, he adopts the plan [of living there with Antony].[39]

Not the virtual automaton we see in the Greek original, Rufinus's Paul has an interior life. Rufinus presents Paul's heartsickness and agitation. Furthermore, Paul's initial goal is not Antony. The need to get away is. The final goal of being the disciple of Antony only emerges when he comes upon Antony's establishment.

There are other differences between the Greek original and Rufinus's translation. Rufinus excises mention of the three weeks of no food or water and the seven days and nights outside. In Rufinus's version, Antony merely tells Paul to stay outside for a day and a night (31.4). Certainly there was no pleasure in this, but it would have been possible. Nor does Paul have to bring up honey from the dirt with a little spoon. The plaiting/unplaiting of baskets and the stitching/unstitching of Antony's cloak do remain (31.13) however. In sum, Rufinus has written the impossible out of the account.

Elsewhere in Rufinus's version (and only in Rufinus's version), Antony instructs Paul in labor that will make the solitude less onerous (*quomodo opere manuum solitudinem solaretur*, 31.5), perhaps by making rope.[40] Antony also schools Paul in the old monastic standby of not eating too much or drinking too many liquids before bedtime; wet dreams may result:[41]

> Antony also directed Paul to consume food at twilight but to have a care lest his eating come to a point of satiety and especially in the matter of drink; Antony stressed that *fantasias* [i.e. dreams that cause nocturnal emissions] of the soul happen through an abundance of water just as through wine the body's heat increases.[42]

In this passage, Paul receives instruction that will enable him to live on his own. Paul's eventual independence is imagined and prepared for. Later, in still another passage not in the Greek, when Antony's instruction of Paul is at an end, he sends Paul to live some distance away from him:

> And when Antony had fully instructed Paul in how he should act in the case of individual matters, he designated a cell for him in the neighborhood (i.e., three miles away), and he ordered him to practice what he had learned. Coming to see him frequently, Antony rejoiced to discover him persevering with total concentration and care in those things that had been taught to him. [43]

If we consider all the divergences between the two versions of the story of Antony and Paul, it seems as though Rufinus wants to pry Paul and Antony apart. Rufinus's Paul possesses more personhood; he has the interior life that his Greek counterpart lacks. We also see Rufinus's Paul acquire skills (labor and canny habits concerning drink and food) that will enable him to live and make decisions on his own. Also, crucially, Paul will be able to imitate Antony—and the reader will be able to imitate Paul. In the process of making his translation, Rufinus has made the Greek text more of a "benefit for those who are making [moral] progress" (*fructum proficientium*). [44]

The possibility for homosexual desire / behavior is to be found in this story, however, and this in spite of Rufinus's seeming determination to ensure that it does not emerge through making Antony *not* Paul's first goal as he flees the sight not to be seen and through his specification of a separation between them. The making of the famous Antony the un-goal of Paul's non-search raises a question as to why it is that such an obvious objective has been covered up. It seems to me that Rufinus is sensitive to the spectacle (emerging, as I have argued, in the reception of the Greek version) of an unseemly closeness between Paul and Antony because of the immediate substitution of Antony for the wife. Furthermore, the homosociality of life in the desert likewise remains; it will generate at least the suspicion of homosexual desire, and this desire's possibility may explain Rufinus's specification of a three mile separation between Antony and Paul and Paul's training in skills that will help him live on his own. Finally, the frank discussion of the possibility of nocturnal emissions makes Rufinus's desert a place where sexual desire survives and with it the possibility of homosexual desire.

In conclusion, then, the Greek version of the story of Paul and Antony counsels *via* miracle (and therefore problematically) that perfect sublimation of erotic desires is possible. On offer is a perfect model that compels imitation for the length of the imitator's life. Because this version uses the miraculous, however, it has the effect of proliferating desire at the point of reception as the reader is made acutely aware of his or her own mortal insufficiency. Furthermore, the homosocial sphere of the desert, as pure and golden as it is in the account, will surely be impossible to realize as even the effort to interpret the miracle fails; the symbol of Paul's success, a miraculous act legible as evidence of God's grace, can also be read as a symbol of possibility for failure by mere humans living in an all too real desert.

Rufinus, on the other hand, excises Paul's miraculous feats and increases his agency. In Rufinus's account sexual desire does not vanish into miraculous sublimation. We see it directly in Antony's directions to Paul about nocturnal emissions. And reception of the text reveals specifically homosexual desire in Rufinus's care to make Antony *not* Paul's initial goal and Antony's care to move Paul to a cell three miles away. A scene in which measures need to be taken in response to homosexual (and other) desire replaces the certainty of the Greek version that sexual desire can be converted without remainder into a new life of perfect sublimation. Or put differently, with the arrival of Paul's agency, humanity, and the real possibility of imitation by the readership, the guarantee of a sexuality-free homosocial sphere is lost—a guarantee that the utopian absoluteness and inaccessibility of the Greek version problematized anyway.

• *Notes*

All translations, except where noted, are my own. Citations of PG and PL are, respectively, to *Patrologiae cursus completus, series Graeca,* and *series Latina,* ed. J.-P. Migne (Paris, 1857–66 and 1844–91, respectively), with volume and section numbers.

For readers wishing to read the *Historia Monarchorum* in English, Norman Russell has translated it under the title *The Lives of the Desert Fathers* (Oxford: Mowbray, 1980).

This chapter began its life as one of the papers in the Lambda Classical Caucus Panel at the 2002 meeting of the American Philological Association. I thank Georgia Franks and Steven Smith for their valuable advice and Amy Richlin for her unfailing encouragement. I am most grateful to Mathew Kuefler for asking me to contribute to this volume. Timothy Heartt and Niels, as usual, were most helpful.

1. I must say a word here about my use of the word "homosocial" in this paper. Eve Kosofsky Sedgwick, in *Between Men: English Literature and Male Homosocial Desire* (New York: Columbia University Press, 1985), writes: " 'Homosocial' is a word occasionally used in history and the social sciences, where it describes social bonds between persons of the same sex; it is a neologism, obviously formed by analogy with 'homosexual,' and just as obviously meant to be distinguished from 'homosexual' " (1). Reaction to homosexuality since the nineteenth century marks this word indubitably. Indeed, David Van Leer, in "The

Beast of the Closet: Homosociality and the Pathology of Manhood," *Critical Inquiry* 15 (Spring 1989): 587–605, sees in "homosocial" not merely dependence on but hostility to homosexuality: "[T]he term 'homosocial' moves in conflicting directions. Constructed after and in answer to the term 'homosexual,' it is simultaneously parasitic on the word and hostile to the sexual preference. Thus, as a category, it contains by definition what it means to deny. As always, the etymological paradox is resolved in favor of the socially normative, until there is no positive place within 'homosociality' for 'homosexuality' " (603). In the face of these issues, I debated whether this word is more trouble than it is worth in the context of an investigation into late antiquity. I decided to keep "homosocial" precisely because of its association with desire between men that it ever tries to keep at bay—the desert was a space in which men were not supposed to be having sex with each other, after all. I also don't agree with Van Leer's pessimistic estimation that there can be no positive place for homosexuality within homosociality. I think rather that we should insist that the resistance to the sexual contained in the term predisposes any future subversion to be a homosexual one.

2. The sayings of three desert mothers (Theodora, Sara, and Syncletica) are preserved in the *Apophthegmata patrum* (PG 65 201A–204B, 420B–21A, and 421A–28A, respectively). See, too, Susanna Elm, *Virgins of God: The Making of Asceticism in Late Antiquity* (Oxford: Oxford University Press, 1994), and Rebecca Krawiec, *Shenoute and the Women of the White Monastery: Egyptian Monasticism in Late Antiquity* (Oxford: Oxford University Press, 2002) for further discussion.

3. See, e.g., Henning Bech, *When Men Meet: Homosexuality and Modernity,* trans. Teresa Mesquit and Tim Davies (Chicago: University of Chicago Press, 1997), 20–25, or Steven Zeeland, *Sailors and Sexual Identity: Crossing the Line between "Straight" and "Gay" in the U.S. Navy* (New York: Harrington Park, 1995), 6, 8–9.

4. When I use the term "homosexual" in this paper, I am referring to sexual behavior and / or desire between persons of the same sex and that is all; there is no presumption of identity effects.

5. Jerome *Interpretatio regulae Sancti Pachomii* (PL 23 78A–B), 94: "Nemo alteri loquatur in tenebris: nullus in psiathio cum altero dormiat: manum alterius nemo teneat; sed sive steterit, sive ambulaverit, sive sederit, uno cubito distet ab altero."

6. Jerome *Interpretatio regulae Sancti Pachomii* (PL 23 78B), 95: "Spinam de pede alterius, excepto domus praeposito, et secundo, et alio cui iussum fuerit, nemo audebit evellere."

7. But thanks in large part to John Boswell's *CSTH,* issues of same-sex desire, both in the desert and in other early-Christian contexts, are never less than secondary and are often central. His book called into being important discussions which still continue and with which this paper engages.

8. Athanasius, *Vita Antoni (Vie d'Antoine),* ed. and trans. G. J. M. Bartelink, Sources Chrétiennes, no. 400 (Paris: Les Éditions du Cerf), 1994. A salient feature of the *Vita Antoni* is its demonstrable status as an intervention against the Christians Athanasius terms "Arians"; Athanasius repeatedly portrays Antony as a staunch defender of Nicene Christianity (see sections 68–69, 82, 86, 89, and 91). As a leading bishop on the side of Nicene orthodoxy, Athanasius was always working to delegitimate the "Arians," who more than once were able to secure his banishment from the Alexandrian episcopal throne. See

David Brakke, *Athanasius and the Politics of Asceticism* (Oxford: Oxford University Press, 1995) for discussion of Athanasius's political use of asceticism; see Virginia Burrus, *Begotten, Not Made: Conceiving Manhood in Late Antiquity* (Stanford: Stanford University Press, 2000), 69–70, and Robert C. Gregg and Dennis Groh, *Early Arianism: A View of Salvation* (Philadelphia: Fortress Press, 1981), 131–59, for discussion of Athanasius's portrayal of Antony as a defender of Nicene Christianity.

9. Tyrannus Rufinus, *Historia monarchorum sive de vita sanctorum patrum,* ed. Eva Schulz-Flügel (Berlin: Walter de Gruyter, 1990); hereafter Rufinus *HM*.

10. Elizabeth A. Clark, *The Origenist Controversy: The Cultural Construction of an Early Christian Debate* (Princeton: Princeton University Press, 1992), 184.

11. E.g., see *Historia monachorum in Aegypto,* critical edition of the Greek text, ed. A.-J. Festugière (Brussels: Société des Bollandistes, 1961; hereafter, *HM*), *praef.* 2: "trusting the prayers of those [who were asking for this account] I have dared to apply myself to this narrative so that (even for me) some benefit from their [i.e., the monks'] service should eventuate—through imitating their way of life, their complete withdrawal from the world, and their stillness acquired through virtues' steadfast endurance, endurance which they keep at until the end of life." (" . . . ταῖς αὐτῶν εὐχαῖς καταπιστεύσας ἐτόλμησα πρὸς τὴν διήγησιν ταύτην τραπῆναι, ἵνα κἀμοί τι κέρδος γένηται τῆς αὐτῶν ὠφελείας, μιμησάμενον αὐτῶν τὴν πολιτείαν καὶ τὴν παντελῆ τοῦ κόσμου ἀναχώρησιν καὶ ἡσυχίαν διὰ τῆς ὑπομονῆς τῶν ἀρετῶν, ἧς μέχρι τέλους κατέχουσιν.") See also Athanasius *Vita Antoni praef.* 3, 89.1, 89.4; *Apophthegmata patrum praef.* (PG 65 72A); Rufinus *HM, praef.* 2.

12. "Παρακαλῶ οὖν ὑμᾶς, μιμηταί μου γίνεσθε."

13. Elizabeth Castelli, in *Imitating Paul: A Discourse of Power* (Louisville: Westminster/John Knox Press, 1991), persuasively illuminates connections between Paul's injunctions to his followers to imitate him and the construction of his authority. Paul's emphasis on mimesis creates an "economy of sameness" (or an "hegemony of the identical") that both provides a powerful source of legitimization to hierarchy and produces a coercive understanding of the nature of identity as inimical to difference (120, 124–25; see also 16–17). Or, in other words, through his emphasis on mimesis, Paul elaborates an "ideology of imitation . . . within the fields of both social relations (power) and metaphysics (identity)" (22) that offers the promise of identity (and the threat of abjection to those who refuse [cf. Judith Butler, *Bodies That Matter: On the Discursive Limits of Sex* (New York: Routledge, Chapman and Hall, Inc., 1993), 14–15]) in the context of asymmetrical social relations.

14. Of course, that future never comes because the ideal "is" in an eternal "present" beyond time and space while the ascetic must act in time and space. This ultimate failure of mimesis recalls what Judith Butler has to say about the ultimate failure haunting the efforts to be a man or a woman: "The 'real' and the 'sexually factic' are phantasmatic constructions—illusions of substance—that bodies are compelled to approximate, but never can . . . and yet this failure to become 'real' and to embody 'the natural' is, I would argue, a constitutive failure of all gender enactments for the very reason that these ontological locales are fundamentally uninhabitable" (*Gender Trouble: Feminism and the Subversion of Identity* [New York: Routledge, Chapman and Hall, Inc., 1990], 146).

15. Burrus, *Begotten, Not Made,* 11.

16. That norms and idealized representations are only part of the story is increasingly recognized. Peter Brown notes that he "fell into the trap prepared . . . by the disciples of the holy man" (*Authority and the Sacred: Aspects of the Christianisation of the Roman World* [Cambridge: Cambridge University Press, 1995], 63) when he presented the holy man as a patron in 1971, in "The Rise and Function of the Holy Man in Late Antiquity," *Society and the Holy in Late Antiquity* (Berkeley and Los Angeles: University of California Press, 1982), 103–52. Brown now recognizes that the various accounts' tales of holy men scolding the rich and interceding on behalf of the poor left out an economic reality: the holy man and his establishment were in fact a "costly amenity" that many regions could ill afford (*Authority and the Sacred*, 62)—cf. Elizabeth Castelli's remarks ("Gender, Theory, and the 'Rise of Christianity': A Response to Rodney Stark," *Journal of Early Christian Studies* 6, no. 2 [1998]: 227–57, at 257) on Rodney Stark's offering the rhetorical presentation of Christian womanhood as the reality of it (*The Rise of Christianity: A Sociologist Reconsiders History* [Princeton: Princeton University Press, 1996]). Criticizing Michel Foucault's reliance on didactic texts that resulted in the presentation of the norms of elite men as the sexual reality of the first- and second-century CE Roman empire, Simon Goldhill, in *Foucault's Virginity: Ancient Erotic Fiction and the History of Sexuality* (Cambridge: Cambridge University Press, 1995), suggests that we consider the Greek novels and their readers in addition to the texts Foucault privileged (and this advice is valid for other genres as well). These narratives create their effects through a complicit reader whose "hesitations, appropriations, fantasies and blindnesses" interact with a narrative that presents and undercuts norms at the same time (*Foucault's Virginity*, 44–45). Indeed, examples of readerly complicity and agency are to be found in late antiquity. By way of an example, the emperor Julian, in his eighth oration, "To the Mother of the Gods," most probably written in 362 CE, sees the role of the reader as crucial whenever he or she is faced with the paradoxical contents of myths (Julian [emperor], *Oeuvres complètes*, ed. and trans. Gabriel Rochefort [Paris: Les Belles Lettres, 2003], vol. 2, pt. 1). Julian remarks that men of old "clothed" the truths of the universe "in paradoxical myths, so that through paradox and incongruity the fiction, detected, might turn us toward the search for truth" (8.170A–B: "ἐσκέπασαν . . . μύθοις παραδόξοις, ἵνα διὰ τοῦ παραδόξου καὶ ἀπεμφαίνοντος τὸ πλάσμα φωραθὲν ἐπὶ τὴν ζήτησιν ἡμᾶς τῆς ἀληθείας προτρέψῃ . . ."). The great unwashed will accept the myths as they are, of course (8.170B), but those who are wiser, because they recognize that these myths are a riddling representation of a higher reality, will search for meaning beyond them (8.170B: " . . . διὰ μὲν τῶν αἰνιγμάτων ὑπομνησθεὶς ὅτι χρή τι περὶ αὐτῶν ζητεῖν . . ."). And Julian most assuredly sees this work of interpretation as involving an engaged and active reader: "He should not be modest and he should not put faith in the opinion of others more than he does in his own mental powers" (8.170B–C: " . . . οὐκ αἰδοῖ καὶ πίστει μᾶλλον ἀλλοτρίας δόξης ἢ τῇ σφετέρᾳ κατὰ νοῦν ἐνεργείᾳ").

17. *HM* 24.1: "Οὗτος τὴν ἑαυτοῦ γαμετὴν ἐπ' αὐτοφώρῳ καταλαβὼν μοιχευομένην μηδενὶ μηδὲν εἰπὼν ἐπὶ τὴν ἔρημον πρὸς Ἀντώνιον ὥρμησεν. Καὶ προσπεσὼν αὐτοῦ τοῖς γόνασιν παρεκάλει συνεῖναι αὐτῷ σωθῆναι βουλόμενος. Ἔφη δὲ πρὸς αὐτὸν ὁ Ἀντώνιος· 'Δύνῃ σωθῆναι ἐὰν ἔχῃς ὑπακοήν, καὶ ὅπερ ἂν παρ' ἐμοῦ ἀκούσῃς, τοῦτο ποιήσῃς.' Ὁ δὲ Παῦλος ἀποκριθεὶς εἶπεν· 'Πάντα ποιήσω ὅσαπερ ἂν προστάξῃς.'"

18. *HM* 24.7: "Ὡς δὲ λοιπὸν τρίτη ἑβδομὰς ἐπληρώθη μὴ βεβρωκότος τοῦ Παύλου, οἱ

ἀδελφοὶ ἠρώτων αὐτὸν τίνος ἕνεκεν σιωπᾷ. Τοῦ δὲ μὴ ἀποκρινομένου λέγει πρὸς αὐτὸν ὁ Ἀντώνιος· Τί σιωπᾷς; ὁμίλησον τοῖς ἀδελφοῖς.' Ὁ δὲ ὡμίλησεν."

19. *HM* 24.10: "Καὶ τοσαύτην ὁ ἀνὴρ ἐκτήσατο ὑπακοήν, ὥστε καὶ χάριν αὐτῷ δεδόσθαι θεόθεν τὴν κατὰ τῶν δαιμόνων ἐλασίαν. Οὓς γὰρ οὐκ ἠδύνατο ὁ μακάριος Ἀντώνιος ἐκβάλλειν δαίμονας, τούτους πρὸς Παῦλον ἀπέστελλεν καὶ αὔθωρον ἐξεβάλλοντο."

20. See Graham Gould, *The Desert Fathers on Monastic Community* (Oxford: Oxford University Press, 1993), 26–87, for more on the pedagogical aspect of the relationship between *abba* / master and disciple.

21. Ὁμιλέω is found with sexual meaning in classical sources (*LSJ* IV), as is the related noun ὁμιλία (*LSJ* I.2). Classical sources also feature sexual meaning associated with both σύνειμι (*LSJ* [συνεῖναι] II.2) and its related noun, συνουσία (*LSJ* I.4). Sexual meanings continue to be associated with these words later in the empire: ὁμιλέω (G. W. Lampe, ed., *Patristic Greek Lexicon*, A4; *Apophth. patr.*, Paphnutius 1 [PG 65 377C]; John Chrysostom *Oppugn.* 2.10 [PG 47 346]; Athanasius *Ar.* 3 [348B7; Guido Müller, *Lexicon Athanasianum* (Berlin: Walter de Gruyter, 1952), 984]); ὁμιλία (Lampe A2a; John Chrysostom *Oppugn.* 3.15 [PG 47 375]); συνεῖναι (Lampe 4; Saloustios *De deis* 4.7 [Saloustios, *Des dieux et du monde*, ed. and trans. Gabriel Rochefort (Paris: Les Belle Lettres, 2003)]); συνουσία (Lampe 2; John Chrysostom *Oppugn.* 1.3 [PG 47 323], 2.3 [PG 47 335], 2.10 [PG 47 346]; Athanasius *De incarnatione* 8.23 [Robert W. Thomson, *Athanasius* Contra Gentes *and* De Incarnatione (Oxford: Oxford University Press, 1971), 152]; Porphyry *Antr.* 16).

22. *HM* 24.8: "Ἄλλοτε δὲ στάμνου μέλιτος αὐτῷ ἐνεχθέντος εἶπεν ὁ Ἀντώνιος πρὸς αὐτόν· Κλάσον τὸ ἀγγεῖον καὶ ἐκχυθήτω τὸ μέλι.' Ἐποίησεν δὲ οὕτως. Καὶ λέγει αὐτῷ· Σύναξον πάλιν τὸ μέλι μυακίῳ ἄνωθεν, ἵνα μὴ ῥυπαρίαν τινὰ συνεισενέγκῃς.' "

23. Averil Cameron, *Christianity and the Rhetoric of Empire: The Development of Christian Discourse* (Berkeley and Los Angeles: University of California Press, 1991), 60.

24. Cameron elsewhere notes that a mix of manifest meaning and hidden significance was expected in literature meant to inspire imitation by ascetics: "Like visual art, early Christian discourse presented its audience with a series of images. The proclamation of the message was achieved by a technique of presenting the audience with a series of images through which it was thought possible to perceive an objective and higher truth. That the images carried a meaning, whether hidden or not, was not in doubt: 'now we see though a glass darkly, but then face to face; now I know in part, but then shall I know even as also I am known' [1 Cor. 13: 12]" (*Christianity and the Rhetoric of Empire*, 57).

25. Robert Lamberton, "Sweet Honey in the Rock: Pleasure, Embodiment, and Metaphor in Late-Antique Platonism," in *Constructions of the Classical Body*, ed. James I. Porter (Ann Arbor: University of Michigan Press, 1999), *passim*, but see 321–23.

26. Porphyry *On the Cave* 16; translation, altered slightly, is from L. G. Westerlink et al., *Porphyry, The Cave of the Nymphs in the Odyssey: A Revised Text with Translation*. Arethusa Monographs, 1. (Buffalo: State University of New York, 1969):

"Φησὶ . . . ἡ Νὺξ τῷ Διὶ ὑποτιθεμένη τὸν διὰ μέλιτος δόλον·

'εὖτ' ἄν δή μιν ἴδηαι ὑπὸ δρυσὶν ὑψικόμοισιν

ἔργοισιν μεθύοντα μελισσάων ἐριβομβέων,

δῆσον αὐτόν.' Ὁ καὶ πάσχει ὁ Κρόνος καὶ δεθεὶς ἐκτέμνεται ὡς ὁ Οὐρανός, τοῦ θεολόγου δι᾿ ἡδονῆς δεσμεῖσθαι καὶ κατάγεσθαι τὰ θεῖα εἰς γένεσιν αἰνισσομένου ἀποσπερματίζειν τε δυνάμεις εἰς τὴν ἡδονὴν ἐκλύθεντα· ὅθεν ἐπιθυμίᾳ μὲν συνουσίας τὸν Οὐρανὸν κατιόντα εἰς Γῆν ἐκτέμνει Κρόνος· ταὐτὸν δὲ τῇ ἐκ συνουσίας ἡδονῇ παρίστησιν αὐτοῖς <ἡ> τοῦ μέλιτος, ὑφ᾿ οὗ δολωθεὶς ὁ Κρόνος ἐκτέμνεται."

27. "Αἷμά τε γὰρ ταύταις καὶ ὁ δίυγρος γόνος φίλος . . ." (Porphyry On the Cave 10).

28. Burrus, Begotten, Not Made, 163.

29. Burrus, Begotten, Not Made, 181.

30. Sister M. Monica Wagner, Rufinus, the Translator (Washington D.C.: The Catholic University of America Press, 1945), 6. I have found Wagner's presentation of Rufinus's reflections on his practice as translator to be most helpful. See especially 4–11.

31. Rufinus Apol. ad Anastasium 7 (PL 21 626C): "Sicut in Graecis habetur, rogatus sum ut Latinis ostenderem. Graecis sensibus verba dedi Latina tantummodo."

32. Rufinus Apol. adv. Hier. 1.25 (PL 21 563C): "Unde et nos propter paupertatem linguae et rerum novitatem, et . . . quod Graecorum et sermo latior et lingua felicior sit, conabimur non tam verbum ex verbo transferre, quod impossibile est, quam vim verbi quodam explicare circuitu."

33. Rufinus Apol. adv. Hier. 1.12 (PL 21 549A–B): "In praefatiunculis tamen utriusque operis et maxime in Pamphili libellum, quem primum transtuleram, exposui primum omnium fidem meam, et protestatus sum me quidem ita credere sicut fides catholica est; si quid autem vel legeretur vel interpretaretur a me, id me salva fidei meae facere ratione. In istis vero Περὶ Ἀρχῶν libellis, etiam illud admonui, quod, cum in ipsis libris invenirentur quaedam de fide ita catholice scripta, ut Ecclesia praedicat, quaedam autem his contraria, cum de una eademque re dicantur: mihi visum sit haec secundum illam semper regulam proferenda, quam ipse catholicae sententiae expositione protulerat, et ea quae a semetipso invenirentur esse contraria, vel inserta ab aliis . . . abicerem, vel certe, ut nihil aedificationis in fide habenda praeterirem."

34. Clark, The Origenist Controversy, 181.

35. Rufinus In explan. Origen. super Epist. ad Rom., peror. ad Heraclium (PG 14 1293–94): " . . . sicut in homiliis sive in oratiunculis in Genesim et in Exodum fecimus, et praecipue in his quae in librum Levitici ab illo quidem perorandi stilo dicta, a nobis vero explanandi specie translata sunt."

36. Rufinus In explan. Origen. super Epist. ad Rom., peror. ad Heraclium (PG 14 1293–94): "Nobis enim propositum est non plausum legentium, sed fructum proficientium quaerere."

37. Rufinus Apol. adv. Hier. 2.46 (PL 21 622A): " . . . ita et nos vel ademptis, vel immutatis quibusdam vel additis, sensum auctoris adducere conati sumus ad intelligentiae tramitem rectiorem."

38. Clark, The Origenist Controversy, 168, 184.

39. Rufinus HM 31.2: "Cum uxorem suam oculis suis cum altero cubitantem vidisset, nulli quicquam dicens egressus est domum et maestitia animi actus in eremum semetipsum dedit, ubi cum anxius oberraret, ad monasterium pervenit Antonii ibique ex loci admonitione et opportunitate consilium capit."

40. See, e.g., the seventh of Pachomius's rules: "No one should look at another while he is making a rope, or praying; he should be intent in his work with his gaze averted." (VII.

"Nemo aspiciat alterum torquentem funiculum, vel orantem; sed in suo defixis luminibus opere sit intentus" [Jerome *Interpretatio regulae Sancti Pachomii* PL 23 69A]).

41. These directions make Rufinus's Antony sound much more like John Cassian in *De nocturnis illusionibus* 22 (*Collationes*, Sources Chrétiennes, no. 64 [Paris: Éditions du Cerf, 1959]) than the Antony of the Greek original. See David Brakke, "The Problematization of Nocturnal Emissions in Early Christian Syria, Egypt, and Gaul," *Journal of Early Christian Studies* 3, no. 4 (1995): 419–60, and Kenneth C. Russell, "John Cassian on a Delicate Subject," *Cistercian Studies Quarterly* 27 (1992): 1–12, for further discussion of nocturnal emissions in the desert.

42. Rufinus *HM* 31.6: "Cibum quoque sumere in vesperam praecepit, sed observare, ne usque ad saturitatem veniret et praecipue in potu, confirmans non minus per aquae abundantiam fantasias animae fieri quam per vinum calorem corporis increscere."

43. Rufinus *HM* 31.7: "Et ubi plene eum, qualiter in singulis agere deberet, instruxit, in vicino ei, hoc est a tribus milibus, cellulam constituit ibique eum exercere quae didicerat iubet, ipse tamen frequentius visitans gratulabatur deprehendens eum in his, quae sibi tradita fuerant, tota intentione et sollicitudine permanentem."

44. Rufinus *In explan. Origen. super Epist. ad Rom., peror. ad Heraclium* (PG 14 1293–94).

CHAPTER 12

Beauty and *Passion* in Tenth-century Córdoba

Jeffrey A. Bowman

In July 925, a Christian hostage named Pelagius was executed at the command of the emir of Córdoba. Within a few years of the execution, the emir assumed the caliphal title and proceeded to govern al-Andalus as 'Abd al-Raḥmān III until his death in 961. From early in his reign, he was the most powerful ruler not only on the Iberian peninsula but in all of Europe. According to a *passion* composed by a priest named Raguel soon after Pelagius's execution, Bishop Ermogius of Tuy had been taken captive during one of the raids that Andalusi leaders regularly made in the Christian north during the ninth and tenth centuries. The bishop's health deteriorated in captivity and he arranged to have his ten-year-old nephew, Pelagius, take his place in prison.

Pelagius saw the privations of prison life as a way of absolving his sins. He spent more than three years praying and studying, before a jailor noticed his remarkable beauty. Thinking the young Christian might make a welcome addition to his master's court, the jailor dressed Pelagius in elegant clothes and presented him during a lavish banquet to the "king" (as Raguel describes the Andalusi ruler). Pelagius's good looks did indeed impress the future caliph, who offered to release Pelagius from captivity and to shower him with gifts and honors if he would renounce Christ and declare Muhammad the true Prophet. Court minions whispered in Pelagius's ears that he was fortunate that his beauty had raised him to such a lofty position. Pelagius brusquely refused the generous offer. The caliph's attempt to seduce his prisoner encompassed not only freedom, power, and wealth, but also physical pleasure: he reached out to caress Pelagius. The phrase Raguel uses here (*tangere joculariter*) might be translated literally as something like "to touch playfully," but it is clear that Raguel meant to indicate that the caliph's intentions were sexual; words like "fondle" or "grope" might more aptly convey Raguel's outrage. Pelagius responded violently; he cried, "Get back, you dog! Do you think I am effeminate like yourselves?" and tore off his splendid robe. The caliph's mood turned and he ordered a slow and painful execution. The calm endurance Pelagius displayed during his own dismemberment made his martyrdom, in Raguel's eyes, particularly glorious. His body parts were thrown into the Guadalquivir river, where other Christians recovered them. Pelagius's cult soon attracted eager adherents both in Córdoba and in his native northern Spain.[1]

When the *passion* was read as part of the liturgical office on his feast day, listeners doubtless found the account of Pelagius's confrontation with the caliph gripping. The turning point in the story is the moment at which the Pelagius rejects the caliph's invitation to riches and his overtures of physical intimacy, but the significance of this aborted caress and of Pelagius's violent reaction are far from obvious. It is hard to shake from Raguel's account a very satisfying sense of the hopes and fears that motivated the caliph or the fetching Galician youth.

The *passion* is emblematic of two interpretive challenges faced by historians of premodern Europe: (1) the challenge of understanding the value of hagiographic texts as historical evidence and (2) the challenge of deciphering references to sexual activity. Hagiographic texts rely heavily on traditional models and often include references to miraculous phenomena that modern historians find hard to credit. References to sexual behavior pose a similarly intractable set of difficulties. Modern terms used to describe human affective experience or sexual behavior rarely coincide with medieval categories. Many references to sexual behavior, like Raguel's to the caliph's touch, are penned neither by enthusiastic participants nor by neutral observers but by hostile critics. Prescriptive sources such as law codes or penitentials often contain the most explicit references to varieties of sexual behavior, but they probably tell us more about the anxieties of lawmakers than about the emotional lives and sexual practices of medieval people. Other varieties of evidence present similar puzzles: Do the polemical works of churchmen (Peter Damian's *Book of Gomorrah* or Alan of Lille's *Plaint of Nature*) reflect widespread attitudes or the refined anxieties of a small minority? Do literary sources (*The Canterbury Tales*, *Libro de Buen Amor*, the *fabliaux*, or the *Decameron*) tell us about the domestic negotiations of husbands, wives, and lovers or merely about the authors' sense of humor? Do the poems of Aelred of Rievaulx and Baudri of Bourgueil afford modern readers genuine glimpses of medieval passions or are these professions of love so stylized that they tell us only about poetic conventions?

Raguel's account of the caliph's touch becomes no easier to understand when considered alongside other evidence about the political and religious landscape of al-Andalus. In general, the caliph did not arbitrarily persecute the many Christians living under his rule.[2] Raguel's *passion* purports to give its readers a glimpse of the lavish and licentious life of the caliphal court. Other textual and archaeological evidence can confirm the opulence of the Umayyad court, but these sources neither confirm nor refute Raguel's suggestion that the caliph especially enjoyed the company of handsome hostages. The vast preponderance of evidence related to 'Abd al-Raḥmān III focuses on his seasonal military campaigns and his consolidation of political power in al-Andalus.[3] Raguel's depiction of the amorous caliph is an engaging one, but it is hard to determine what, if anything, we can learn from it. Rumors about the sex lives of powerful people seem to have been a subject of scandal then as now, and determining the veracity of such rumors was no less a challenge.

But if Raguel's account of the caliph's thwarted seduction of Pelagius cannot satisfy our more prurient interests in who made love to whom in the palaces of al-Andalus, the incident might teach us something of greater value about the intellectual, cultural, and religious world inhabited by the priest, the martyr, and the caliph.

To grasp why Raguel describes Pelagius's confrontation with the caliph in the way he does, we should look at the *passion* alongside two textual traditions. The first of these is Latin hagiography and, in particular, earlier *passions* of Iberian martyrs. The second is that of Arabic *belles lettres* from al-Andalus and elsewhere. The works of Andalusi poets can help us to understand the world that Raguel observed, criticized, and absorbed. At the very start of his *passion*, Raguel insists that good authorship entails scrupulous adherence to models: "Every written work corresponds to some clear model."[4] Some curious features of Pelagius's *passion,* including the caliph's touch, might be explained by acknowledging that it was informed by several distinct models.

Raguel's composition owes many debts to hagiographic conventions. Pelagius's early manifestations of holiness, his placid endurance of diverse tortures, and the scramble of other Christians to recover his carelessly disposed of remains all have close analogues in other *passions*. Since the caliph's touch is the curious turning point in the story, it is worth looking at the ways in which Raguel's "king" resembles his precursors. Erratic and bloodthirsty persecutors were a common feature of Iberian hagiography long before Pelagius's jailers lifted him from the squalor of his cell to the splendor of the court. In his *Peristephanon,* composed around the year 400, Prudentius recounts in gory detail the suffering of martyrs at the hands of tyrants. The most notorious of these is a Roman prefect named Dacian who subjects Vincent of Saragossa to a dizzying range of bloody tortures.[5] Later hagiographers followed precedents established by Prudentius and others. In the seventh-century *Vitae patrum emeretensium,* Bishop Masona of Mérida overcomes numerous obstacles in his devotion to Saint Eulalia and in defense of her shrine. King Leovigild, an Arian Christian, orders the Trinitarian Masona to appear before him in Toledo, to relinquish control of Eulalia's relics, and to embrace Arianism. Masona reproaches the king and criticizes his heretical beliefs. Leovigild first tries to win Masona's conversion and allegiance with splendid gifts. When these blandishments fail to have their intended effect, he resorts to threats. Masona responds to both with the same composed resistance displayed by Raguel's Pelagius. He suggests that the most prized of Eulalia's relics (her tunic) would be polluted by contact with Arian heretics. The Visigothic king (by now, a *crudelissimus tyrannus*) embarks on a campaign of persecution. He threatens Masona with diverse tortures and eventually consigns the bishop to a bleak three-year exile.[6]

The struggle between the resolute Masona and the foaming Leovigild is, of course, not so much a battle of personalities as it is a reflection of interwoven religious and political tensions between Trinitarian and Arian Christians, between Hispano-Romans and Visigoths, and between Mérida and Toledo. The set of relevant oppositions in Raguel's world differed (Christian versus Muslim, Galicia versus al-Andalus, Latin versus Arabic, austerity versus luxury), but the same rudimentary model of confrontation between placid saint and rabid tyrant allowed hagiographers to chart a wide range of divides; one of the reasons that hagiographic models are so successful is that they are so elastic. The basic narrative of the martyr's *passion* allowed hagiographers to articulate varied and shifting ethnic, sexual, moral, political, and religious oppositions. Pelagius's *passion* is, among other things, the story of a resolute Christian confronting manifold differences. There were, of course, vast differences between the Visigothic King Leovigild and the Umayyad caliph 'Abd al-Raḥmān III, but the logic of the saint's *passion* accommodated both in similar roles.[7] Like Dacian in Prudentius's *Peristephanon* and Leovigild in the *Vitae patrum emeretensium,* Pelagius's persecutor was wrathful and vindictive when disappointed. Like these earlier persecutors, he resorted to threats and torture only after failing to convert or seduce his victims with riches and honors. The hagiographers even rely on similar animal metaphors to characterize persecutors; both the caliph and King Leovigild are described as dogs.

Hagiographic conventions do not, however, explain why Raguel makes the caliph's touch—his thwarted caress, his apparent appetite—the hinge of the story. In most *passions,* the only hands laid on martyrs are those of nameless subalterns who apply clanking instruments of torture. Dacian and Leovigild both issue instructions to their henchmen and both harass their martyrs verbally, but they do not try to touch them, *joculariter* or otherwise. What explains this apparent enrichment of the conventions that Raguel otherwise embraced so enthusiastically and so literally?

The Córdoba where Pelagius spent the final years of his short life was a rich, sophisticated, polyreligious city, boasting, in some accounts, more than 60,000 mansions, hundreds of private libraries, and over 900 public bathhouses.[8] In Raguel's world, the greatest threats to the Christian community were neither the idolatry of Roman magistrates nor the ambitions of Arian kings, but rather the power and sophistication of Muslim elites. For the better part of a century, some Christian leaders in al-Andalus had despaired at the fact that their co-religionists were being drawn away from the Christian community, attracted to convert not only by Islam's religious appeal but also by opportunities for economic and political advancement, and by the thriving literary and artistic environment so lavishly patronized by leaders like ʿAbd al-Raḥmān III.[9] While not persecuted, the Christian community was sorely tested and Christians were often deeply divided about how to respond to these tests.

In his depiction of the caliph, Raguel articulates a set of virtues that stand in stark opposition to what he sees as the depravity of the caliphal court and, by extension, Andalusi society. Among other things, Raguel is giving his co-religionists a vivid portrait of why the conjoined economic, spiritual, cultural, and physical seductions of Umayyad society were worth resisting. The effeminacy of the caliph is juxtaposed with the athleticism of the adolescent Pelagius; the opulence—the *luxuria*—of the caliphal court is opposed to Pelagius's austerity.

But while critical of Andalusi society, the *passion* of Pelagius fully participates in the world of tenth-century Córdoba. The *passion* is indebted in many respects to earlier saints' *passions,* but Raguel's text also echoes the narrative and thematic concerns of contemporary *belles lettres,* written in Arabic by Muslims. Raguel's modest work thus reminds us that while the inhabitants of al-Andalus were in certain respects divided by religion, they often shared habits of mind, literary preoccupations, and patterns of spiritual reasoning.

Medieval literature in Arabic includes countless episodes in which powerful men are overwhelmed by the sheer beauty of their social inferiors, male and female. Wazirs, caliphs, and religious leaders express their deep attachment to and physical desire for slaves, domestic servants, and prisoners (like Pelagius).

Andalusi author Ibn Ḥazm composed his *The Ring of the Dove,* a catalog of the joys and follies of lovers, in Córdoba within a century of Pelagius's death. The collection includes many anecdotes about men who are passionately attached to other men. While Ibn Ḥazm and Raguel would have disagreed about whether there was something troubling about these attachments, both acknowledged that mature, powerful men were sometimes smitten by attractive youths *and* that beautiful young men did not always welcome the attention. In one episode reminiscent of Pelagius's rebuff of the caliph, Ibn Ḥazm describes a desperate lover who begins to frequent the mosque attended by a handsome young page in order to be able to gaze on the page without hindrance. The irritated page is eventually driven to slap his older admirer.[10]

Ibn Jubayr includes a similar anecdote in his twelfth-century travelogue. In a passage praising the outstanding educational and health-care facilities in Damascus, he tells the story of a great religious teacher who became so infatuated with a beautiful young man that he was driven to distraction. Authorities saw this passionate attachment as a medical disorder grave enough to warrant the teacher's hospitalization. The story troubled Ibn Jubayr not because the attachment in question involved two men or two people of different ages, but rather because it led the scholar to neglect his vast store of Quranic wisdom. For Ibn Jubayr and for the inhabitants of Damascus, the loss of such wisdom was cause for lamentation, but the source of the scholar's undoing (i.e., his emotional attachment to a young man) was an occasion for humor rather than stern condemnation.[11]

Ibn Ḥazm and Ibn Jubayr both had keen eyes for detail, and their works occasionally give modern readers the pleasant sense of eavesdropping on the negotiations of daily life in eleventh-century al-Andalus or twelfth-century Syria, but poets pursued the theme of the beautiful youth and the desperate lover even more exhaustively. Poems describe dreamy, seductive worlds in which passionate attachments end not with comical slaps or therapeutic interventions, but with intoxication, ecstasy, and (eventually) sleep. In the ninth century, Abū Nuwās wrote poems celebrating sensual pleasure which, in his estimation, resided chiefly in wine (sweet and abundant) and men (young and compliant). One short poem might stand as an epitome of his exuberant philosophy:

> Don't worry when people say
> "That is not allowed and that is not permitted."

> Obey your passion and, in the early morning, bring it a yellow
>   wine spraying fire.
> Make love to boys in their youth, when their beards begin to
>   sprout, and in ripe old age.[12]

Building on the themes Abū Nuwās championed, Andalusi poets of the tenth, eleventh, and twelfth centuries wrote poems about myrtle-scented gardens where judicious and powerful men are broken by gentle breezes, sweet wine, and the pale skin of nimble cupbearers. Poets lavished attention on attributes of male adolescent beauty: sword-like glances,[13] golden complexions,[14] slim waists,[15] cheeks like "white marble" or "apples of gold" or "gleaming roses,"[16] throats like white jewels,[17] breasts like golden pomegranates,[18] or a single mole that "enchants every man free to love."[19] Their teeth are like pearls, their waists are slim, and their saliva is sweet as wine. Facial hair inspires an entire subgenre devoted to the question of whether the arrival of a youth's first beard marked the end of his desirability of simply its transformation.[20] The bodies of adolescent boys begin to sound like the jeweled orchards through which they gracefully move.

This poetic tradition (always sensual, frequently erotic, and occasionally pornographic) was alive and well in Raguel's Córdoba.[21] Ibn 'Abd Rabbihī, encyclopedist and court poet to 'Abd al-Raḥmān III, composed homoerotic poems in which otherwise powerful men are transfixed by the beauty of adolescents.[22] One of the caliph's sons composed a poem in which the poet's voice pledges eternal love to a boy whose lithe figure, rosy cheeks, and dark pupils drove men wild.[23] The love poems of one of the caliph's grandsons, al-Sharīf al-Ṭalīq, often focused on women (especially blonde women), but he also wrote verses celebrating the perfect beauty of young men, particularly cupbearers.[24] In one poem, he describes how a youth's careless lock of blonde hair might fall over his face in the shape of an Arabic letter. In some respects, al-Sharīf al-Ṭalīq's biography resembles that of Pelagius himself. Imprisoned at the age of sixteen, the beauty of his face inspired older admirers.[25] One of his own poems described the robing and unrobing of a splendid, slim-waisted cupbearer, whose cheeks are flushed with wine. Raguel's Pelagius is, of course, not nearly so wanton. But he is, in Raguel's account, first clothed and then strips himself bare before admiring observers. Pelagius's removal of his robes is a sign of protest—an emphatic rejection of the caliph's hospitality and robes of honor—but in both cases a beautiful youth achieves the upper hand by taking his clothes off.[26]

Arabic *belles lettres* offered to Andalusi readers many encounters something like the encounter that reportedly took place between Pelagius and the caliph.

In the logic of this tradition, it is fully natural for mature men to gaze in admiration at young men. It is inevitable that some men will want to do more than gaze, even though many poets and moralists agreed that moving beyond the gaze might entail moral and legal consequences that gazing alone did not. As James Monroe, Everett Rowson, and others have pointed out, in many places in the medieval Islamic world, the desire to engage in some homosexual acts was not considered unnatural, even if the acts themselves occasionally met with varying degrees of censure.[27] Poets, intellectuals, and moralists, might, in other words, distinguish the "permitted gaze" from the "forbidden pleasure," or, if particularly scrupulous, between a first glance (permitted) and a second (prohibited).[28]

Like the innumerable cupbearers of medieval Arabic and Hebrew poetry, Pelagius is both beautiful and athletic.[29] Like the others, Pelagius's admirer seeks to weaken his resistance with gifts, delicacies, and promises of wealth.[30] Ibn Shuhayd suggests that it was helpful to get adolescents drunk and, although Raguel does not mention it, we might imagine that someone in the caliphal court would have offered Pelagius a cup of wine along with all the other enticements.[31] In Pelagius's *passion*, as in many Arabic poems, the passions described are asymmetrical in more than one way. Beloved youths are often not only a different age ('Abd al-Raḥmān III was in his early thirties at the time of Pelagius's execution, Pelagius was thirteen), but also of a different social status. Attachment to young men was taken in some circles as a sign of sophistication, polish, and good manners, but the boys were themselves often from the other side of the river.[32] A twelfth-century Zaragozan poet apologized for his ferocious attachment to a frisky weaver: "If my passion were mine to control, I would have chosen otherwise, but it was not up to me."[33] Some poets apparently took pleasure in the musky quality of their downmarket younger lovers: "What matter if his robe is coarse? The rose has thorns on its calyx / The wine is covered in pitch and musk is carried in crude vessels."[34] The eleventh-century ruler of Seville confessed that passion had made him the subject of his own slave, incidentally a Christian: "I made him my slave, but the coyness of his glance has made me his prisoner, so that we are both at once slave and master to each other."[35]

Passions that crossed religious boundaries also carried a special erotic charge.[36] A tenth-century Andalusi poem describes a man so smitten with a Christian boy that he begins to adopt Christian practices.[37] A poem by Ibn Sahl describes the convictions of a lover in spiritual turmoil, who admits that all his religious beliefs center around loving a youth with red lips; while a Muslim in his heart, he confesses that the pupils of his eyes were Zoroastrian because they adored his beloved's cheeks.[38] A poem attributed to a near contemporary of Raguel's living at the other end of the Mediterranean tells of a stationer in Edessa named Sa'd who falls in love with the son of a Christian merchant and writes love poems to him. When the boy, "the most attractive of people facially, the most agreeable in stature, and the most delicate in nature and speech," enters a monastery, Sa'd plunges into sorrow and madness. He sits just outside the monastery, continuing to write poems about his beloved.[39]

Pelagius is linked to these other boys not only by his youth, his athleticism, his status as a prisoner, and his Christianity, but also by his response to the caliph's courtship. Although the seductions described in poems reach diverse conclusions from blissful consummation to desolate sorrow, many of the weavers, cupbearers, and slaves do not reciprocate the passions of their social superiors. If the poets are to be believed, the beautiful adolescents of the Islamic world, from Baghdad to Córdoba, were coy. They rarely responded with the anger and hostility shown by Pelagius, but they often resisted their admirers or, at the very least, teased them before accepting their gifts and embraces.[40]

The *passion* of Pelagius shares with this poetic corpus something more important than common plot elements: the notion that physical beauty (particularly the beauty of male adolescents) has a spiritual significance. For both Raguel and Muslim poets, the beauty of young men was not merely erotically charged (although it was that), it was also an especially brilliant reflection of the beauty of God's creation. Raguel sees in Pelagius's beauty a sign of his sanctity: "It was not without reason that he (Pelagius) appeared outwardly beautiful, since he had been made still more beautiful within by Lord Jesus Christ." Pelagius's beauty praised his master, Christ, and reflected his imminent departure for the kingdom of heaven: "For who would not applaud this natural quality which adorns the beautiful appearance of those destined for paradise?" Some Muslim poets made similar claims about the spiritual import of the beauty of cupbearers. Ibn Khafājah, for example, confesses to worshiping the fire in a boy's cheeks and describes his face as "a Ka'ba of beauty wherever he turns."[41] Al-Kharā'iṭī, a contemporary of Pelagius, included in his treatise on profane love a chapter entitled, "The Excellence of Beauty, the Privileges Which God Has Accorded to Those Who Are Provided with It, and the Duties He Has Imposed on Them."[42] Like the Achmad of one poem whose mole drove all sensate men wild with passion, Pelagius was an ambassador from paradise.[43]

If Raguel's "king" resembles in some respects the persecutors of earlier hagiography, he also resembles the love-sick caliphs of Arabic *belles lettres*. And while Pelagius appears in some ways like earlier martyrs who responded with saucy resolve to their enraged persecutors, he also resembles the lithe adolescents who populated the lavish gardens of Andalusi cities. To be sure, Raguel was alarmed by the sexual mores that, in his imagination, obtained at the caliphal court and he almost certainly would have disapproved of poems that celebrated sensuality and passionate love between men across religious boundaries. But while Raguel's sexual morality was not that of Abū Nuwās or Ibn Sahl, he did equate adolescent male beauty with the promise of paradise. As Mark Jordan suggests, it is an irony of Raguel's *passion* that he should praise in such heated terms the unparalleled beauty of the young Pelagius while so vividly condemning the caliph and members of his court who show the same appreciation of his beauty.[44] The priest and the caliph would have found many things to disagree about, but they both knew a handsome young man when they saw one. Raguel apparently would have agreed with many poets that beautiful adolescents were, as Lévi-Strauss might put it, "good to think with."

While we can say little about the caliph's emotional life, we can say that the literary traditions that he did so much to support celebrated passionate, affective relations between men *and* devoted special attention to those relations in which older men are smitten by beautiful adolescents.[45] But, as Raguel's "king" was acutely aware, admiring that which is beautiful is not quite the same as having sex, just as poems are not practices. The poetic traditions I have described so briefly do not mean that the inhabitants of al-Andalus (Christian or Muslim) shared unified or constant attitudes toward sexual behavior or that Muslim elites universally approved of or engaged in homosexual relations while Christians deplored them and refrained from engaging in them. In some cases, poets wrote about lithe compliant cupbearers to evoke a paradise on earth. In others, they wrote to warn that the mighty and wise could be undone by their desires. In some the attitude was sincere and enthusiastic, in some comical or disappointed. While some poets applauded or at the very least winked at all manner of physical pleasure, others were more restrained. Some poets generated enchanting descriptions of breezy gardens and tipsy cupbearers, but many sources reminded readers that such passions were not without dangers.[46]

We must imagine that ʿAbd al-Raḥmān III would have been, if not amused, indifferent to an obscure priest's attack on what we might call, for lack of a better term, his personal life. The opinions of his own jurists and spiritual authorities were probably a different matter. Roughly contemporary *fatwas* show that authorities were concerned with the caliph's sexual behavior, although their concern focused less on whether he was seducing adolescent Christian hostages at luxurious banquets than with whether he was having sexual intercourse during Ramadan.[47]

Raguel's hostility toward the caliph's touch may have been out of step with the mores of the court, but broadly speaking, the sexual behavior of rulers was a subject of concern to their subjects.[48] In the late eleventh century, 'Abd Allah, the last Zīrid amir of Granada, defended himself from widespread accusations of libertinage and indulgence. His detractors condemned his dual addiction to wine and young men, and his apparent indifference to the company of women.[49] While suggesting that pleasure and leisure might contribute to a long and healthy life, he insisted that he "never threw off all restraints nor did I resort to leisure entailing neglect of my duties as other kings have done before me."[50] He dismissed the charges against him as trivial and ill-founded: "So all you can say now is that the prince of Granada coveted money and was fond of good-looking boys and of their company as boon companions. [But in saying this] you have not given the matter careful consideration or due deliberation. For don't you know, ignoramus that you are, that money is of no value to a king unless it comes in vast amounts?"[51] While some poets celebrated the company of "good-looking boys" as a *desideratum* in its own right, 'Abd Allah explained that he had surrounded himself with attractive young men for purely political reasons. No ruler, however personally uninterested in carousing or caresses, could neglect the adornment of his court:

> As for taking boys as boon companions, they were not employed for wine-bibbing and caresses as this would have entailed the use of some wine from which God has turned me away. It was not, however, a question of some decision-making council for which older people should have been chosen, nor a deliberative assembly in which men of learning had to be consulted, nor was it a battlefield to which brave horsemen had to be summoned. There is a time and place for everything, and a man would indeed be deemed an ignoramus if he did not have the right person for the right occasion. However that may be, I never sought their advice on any serious matter, nor did I entrust them with any authority or charge them with any task beyond their scope.
>
> Besides, great dynasties have always employed boys and artisans—young and old, slaves and free men. They adorn a ruler's court and are there to assist him. A young person can handle tasks which do not become an older person. Each has his own position and rank. And is not kingship or wealth intended for enjoyment and adornment? And is it not its purpose to choose handsome servants for whom splendid attire and swift mounts are becoming?[52]

In other words, having beautiful young men at court is a political necessity rather than a personal pleasure. In describing two otherwise quite different

Andalusi courts for different reasons, Raguel and 'Abd Allah agreed that there is a constellation of political power, adornment, and youthful (male) beauty that was the hallmark of courtly life. For both authors, this constellation at times provoked suspicions of lascivious behavior. People sought to discredit their enemies and rivals by suggesting that they were addicted to vices, to indulgence, or to luxury. In many cases, these accusations cut across religious lines. Some ninth-century Mozarab authors associated Islamic rule with sexual promiscuity, just as Raguel seems to.[53] But in many other cases, such insinuations and accusations might circulate without crossing religious boundaries. Later Muslim writers saw similar connections between libertinage and incompetent rule, attributing the collapse of the Umayyad caliphate in the early eleventh century to, among other things, lapses in religious orthodoxy and personal morality. While Raguel's praise of Pelagius's beauty echoes Andalusi poets, his critique of the indulgence of the caliphal court anticipates by several decades Almohad and Almoravid attacks on the moral laxity of the Umayyad regime. In other words, accusations of indulgence and sexual deviance were a part of political life across religious boundaries and within them.[54]

Poems describing luxuriant gardens populated by lovely boys are probably not better guides to mundane historical realities than saints' *passions*. We know the gardens themselves existed, and even the battered remains of the Small Garden constructed for the caliph at the Madīnat al-Zahrā', to this day look like an ideal location for a tryst.[55] But contemporaries acknowledged that compliant cupbearers appeared more often in dreams than in the actual gardens of Damascus, Cairo, or Córdoba.[56] And, when poets wrote about sex and seduction, they may well have had others things on their minds. Abū Nuwās's poems about anal penetration, domination, and obliging youths may have more to do with his attitude toward prevalent political structures than with the poet's own desires.[57] Neither *passions* nor poems can serve as literal guidebooks to the Andalusi cities of the tenth century. Just as they share some narrative elements and some thematic preoccupations, both varieties of evidence have in common the fact that they traffic in ideals and exemplars. They are less guides to the churches, courts, markets, and mosques of Córdoba than they are clues about the mental furniture of the city's inhabitants. Our goal should not be to privilege particular varieties of evidence (bawdy poems, saint's *passions,* charters, *fatwas*, excavated gardens) as giving an especially accurate picture of the past, but rather to learn to read the sources in concert—to see how, in this case, Arabic poetry might help us understand Latin hagiography.

Raguel's *passion* ultimately tell us little about the caliph's affective life. We cannot determine whether he liked boys and boys alone as sexual partners, or whether he preferred Christian adolescents, or prisoners, or the nephews of bishops, or Asturians to other sexual partners.[58] We cannot say with certainty whether military hostages were frequently subjected to the unwanted attentions of their jailors, although we do know that large numbers of hostages and slaves from the Christian north were taken to Córdoba during the tenth century, and common sense may be not an altogether unreasonable guide here. But while we might not depend on Raguel to provide a reliable picture of the Andalusi ruler and his court, we can see in this *passion* a reflection of how some Mozarab Christians perceived the dazzling caliphal court and, more broadly, the dominant society around them.[59] The *passion* tells us less about the caliph's sexual exploits or about the young Galician's good looks than it does about religious and cultural difference in tenth-century al-Andalus.

Pelagius's *passion* reflects the anxieties of beleaguered Christian communities confronting the wealth, power, and sophistication of Andalusi culture. It is less the record of a thwarted sexual advance than it is evidence both of a pervasive anxiety among Mozarabs about the manifold forms of seduction they saw threatening their community *and* of the ways in which Christian priests and Muslim poets might share certain ideas. The *passion* also dramatizes how depictions of sexual activity are inevitably bound up with other forms (religious, ethnic, cultural) of difference. Raguel, like some other early medieval Christian writers, drew on a complex set of ideas about wealth, luxury, and effeminacy to warn against the dangers of falling into hell through prosperity.[60] In Raguel's eyes, the court's *luxuria* was as dangerous as and inseparable from its sexual morality, and his attitudes toward Muslim elites were probably shared by many (though by no means all) members of Córdoba's Christian community.

If, in the past twenty five years, we have achieved some greater understanding of the emotional and affective lives of medieval people in general and of gay people in particular, we owe a debt to John Boswell for clearing a vast field that we are gradually learning to cultivate. Boswell's *CSTH* dramatized the difficulty of understanding what had long been accepted as straightforward scriptural and patristic condemnations of all forms of homosexual activity. He turned our attention to a vast corpus of understudied texts, such as the homoerotic writings of twelfth-century churchmen and medieval Arabic poetry. And, he began to show how historical evidence about sexuality is invariably embedded in very particular political, economic, social, and religious conditions. In *CSTH* and elsewhere, Boswell helped us to explore and to understand the fraught sites of contact and the longstanding patterns of dialogue between different groups, whether the groups in question are gay churchmen and their critics or the Mudejars of the Crown of Aragón and their Christian neighbors.

When Raguel describes Pelagius being brought before the caliph's gaze, he wrote with unrelenting hostility. The caliph's touch does not appear, as it might in contemporary poetry, as an understandable expression of admiration or a pardonable peccadillo. But while Raguel was bitterly critical of what he saw as the religious and moral shortcomings of elite Umayyad society, the *passion* he composed is fully a product of the distinctive culture of tenth-century Córdoba. Raguel associates his "king" with depraved indulgence, but he shared with the poets whose culture he criticized a similar attitude toward the significance of beauty.

Raguel's *passion* reflects the porousness of the very boundaries he was trying to reinforce. Raguel's "king" is caught between two genres; he is both the foaming persecutor of Latin hagiography and the love-struck caliph of Arabic poetry. His Pelagius is both defiant martyr and comely cupbearer. These two apparently contradictory roles are integrated in the idea of the witness. Martyrs were, etymologically and theologically, witnesses to Christ's redemptive power. Similarly, in certain strains of Islamic literature, the beauty of adolescent boys is a witness to God's glory.[61] Some Islamic mystics contemplate the beauty of adolescent boys as a meditative practice and consider the boy a " 'witness' (*shāhid*) to the beauty of God and the glory of His creation."[62] Pelagius is a double witness, both martyr and *shāhid*. For, as Raguel explains, it was not without reason that he was so beautiful.

- ### Notes

1. Celso Rodrígues Fernández, *La Pasión de S. Pelayo: Edición crítica con traducción y comentarios* (Santiago de Compostela, 1991). A thorough discussion of the texts can be found in Manuel C. Díaz y Díaz, "La Pasión de S. Pelayo y su difusión," *Anuario de Estudios Medievales* 6 (1969): 97–116; for an English translation, see Jeffrey A. Bowman, "The Martyrdom of Saint Pelagius," in *Medieval Hagiography: A Sourcebook*, ed. Thomas Head (New York, 2000), 227–36. John Boswell mentions Raguel's *passion* of Pelagius and Hrosvit of Gandersheim's dramatic adaptation of it in *CSTH*, 198–200; The permutations in Pelagius's *passion* are the subject of the first chapter of Mark D. Jordan's *The Invention of Sodomy in Christian Theology* (Chicago, 1997). Jordan places these different versions in the context of Christian theology. My goal here is to place Raguel's *passion* in the context of Andalusi culture.

2. The martyrs of Cardeña, executed by the caliph's officers less than a decade after Pelagius's execution, are probably better considered war casualties than persecuted

minorities. See G. Martínez Díez, "Los Mártires de Cardeña (6–VIII–934)," *Hispania Sacra* 34 (1982): 321–28.

3. By one account, the caliph made jaunty jokes related to anal penetration based on confusions in Arabic and Roman vocabulary. R. Menéndez Pidal, *Orígenes de Español: Estado Lingüístico de la península ibérica hasta el siglo xi* (Madrid, 1926), 442, note 2.

4. Raguel, "Martyrdom of St. Pelagius," 231.

5. For Dacian, see Baudouin de Gaiffier, "Sub Daciano Praeside," *Analecta Bollandiana* 72 (1954): 378–96.

6. *Vitas sanctorum patrum emeretensium,* ed. A. Maya Sánchez (Turnhout, 1992), 64–65, 67.

7. Some ninth-century Mozarab Christians distinguished between earlier martyrs (who had been brutally persecuted by Roman authorities) and the martyrs of Córdoba (who had needlessly provoked a legitimate and tolerant regime). See Kenneth Baxter Wolf, "The Earliest Spanish Christian Views of Islam," *Church History* 55 (1986): 281–93.

8. Robert Hillenbrand, "The Ornament of the World: Medieval Cordoba as a Cultural Centre," in *The Legacy of Muslim Spain,* ed. Salma Khadra Jayyusi (Leiden, n.d.), 119.

9. See Kenneth Baxeter Wolf, *Christian Martyrs in Muslim Spain* (Cambridge, 1988); Jessica Coope, *The Martyrs of Córdoba: Community and Conflict in an Age of Mass Conversion* (Lincoln, Nebr., 1995).

10. Ibn Ḥazm's page emerges from this contretemps rather better than Pelagius does from his encounter with the caliph. Unlike the caliph, Muqaddam ibn al-Asfar happily endures the blows of his beloved. Ibn Ḥazm places the story in a section of his work celebrating lovers' acts of compliance. The incident has no long-term consequences for either party. The lover's infatuation with the page does not prevent him from attaining a high social and political position and the page is not tortured and executed for his insolence. Ibn Ḥazm, *Ring of the Dove,* trans. A. J. Arberry (London, 1994), 90; See also Boswell, *CSTH,* 194–97. The collection of essays edited by J. W. Wright Jr and Everett K. Rowson, entitled *Homoeroticism in Classical Arabic Literature* (New York, 1997), and dedicated to the memory of John Boswell, provides a valuable overview of the topic.

11. *The Travels of Ibn Jubayr,* trans. R. J. C. Broadhurst (London, 1952), 296.

12. J. W. Wright Jr, "Masculine Allusion and the Structure of Satire," *Homoeroticism in Classical Arabic Literature,* 13; see also Michael Sells, "Love," in *The Literature of al-Andalus,* ed. María Rosa Menocal, Raymond P. Scheindlin, and Michael Sells (Cambridge, 2000) 135–36; see also Philip Kennedy, *The Wine Song in Classical Arabic Poetry: Abū Nuwās and the Literary Tradition* (Oxford, 1997), J. E. Montgomery, "For the Love of a Christian Boy: A Song by Abū Nuwās," *Journal of Arabic Literature* 27 (1996): 115–24, and idem, "Revelry and Remorse: A Poem of Abū Nuwās," *Journal of Arabic Literature* 25 (1994): 116–34.

13. Ibn 'Abd Rabbihī, *Banners of the Champions: An Anthology of Medieval Arabic Poetry from Andalusia and Beyond,* selected and translated by James A. Bellamy and Patricia Owen Steiner (Madison, 1989), no. 64, p. 66; and Ibn Rashīq al-Qayrawānī in *Banners of the Champions,* no. 65, p. 67; For another mortal glance, see Franz Rosenthal, "Male and Female: Described and Compared," in *Homoeroticism in Classical Arabic Literature,* 34.

14. *Banners of the Champions,* no. 65, p. 67.

15. Abū Bakr al-Abyad, in Tova Rosen, "The Muwashshah," in *The Literature of al-Andalus*, 165–89, at 173.

16. A. R. Nykl, *Hispano-Arabic Poetry and its Relations with the Old Provençal Troubadours* (Baltimore, 1946), 22; the same themes appear frequently in contemporary Hebrew poetry, see Norman Roth, "Deal Gently with the Young Man: Love of Boys in Medieval Poetry in Spain," *Speculum* 57 (1982): 20–51, and *idem*, "The Care and Feeding of Gazelles: Medieval Arabic and Hebrew Love Poetry," in Moshé Lazar and Norris J. Lacy, eds., *Poetics of Love in the Middle Ages* (Fairfax, Va., 1989), 96–118; and Jefim Schirmann, "The Ephebe in Medieval Hebrew Poetry," *Sefarad* 15 (1955): 55–68.

17. Cola Franzen, *Poems of Arab Andalusia* (San Francisco, 1989), 21.

18. Roth, "Deal Gently with the Young Man," 41.

19. *Banners of the Champions*, no. 57, p. 59.

20. See, for example, *Banners of the Champions*, no. 65, p. 67; Norman Roth, "Boy-Love in Medieval Arabic Verse," *Paidika* 3, no. 3 (1994): 12–17, at 13.

21. Roth, "Boy-Love in Medieval Arabic Verse," 14.

22. *Banners of the Champions*, no. 64, p. 66.

23. Nykl, *Hispano-Arabic Poetry*, 22.

24. *Banners of the Champions*, no. 192, p. 193; See Harry Neale, "The *Diwan* of al-Sharīf al-Ṭalīq," *Journal of Arabic Literature* 34 (2003): 20–44.

25. *Banners of the Champions*, no. 192, p. 193; Richard Serrano, "Al-Sharīf al-Ṭalīq, Jacques Lacan, and the Poetics of Abbreviation," in *Homoeroticism in Classical Arabic Literature*, 142–43.

26. For some examples, see Neale, "The *Diwan* of al-Sharīf al-Ṭalīq," 24–25.

27. James T. Monroe, "The Striptease that Was Blamed on Abū Bakr's Naughty Son: Was Father Being Shamed, or Was the Poet Having Fun? (Ibn Quzmān's *Zajal No. 133*)," in *Homoeroticism in Classical Arabic Literature*, 117–18.

28. Lois Anita Giffen, *Theory of Profane Love Among the Arabs: The Development of the Genre* (New York, 1971), 11, 123–25; "That love and desire are awakened by gazing was more than a commonplace; it was an occasion for religious and legal discussion." Everett K. Rowson, "Two Homoerotic Narratives from Mamluk Literature," in *Homoeroticism in Classical Arabic Literature*, 165–66.

29. For beloved youths as athletes and wrestlers, see Rowson, "Two Homoerotic Narratives," 178.

30. Ahmad al-Tifachi, *Les Délices des coeurs, ou ce que l'on ne trouve en aucun libre*, trans. René R. Khawam (Paris, 1981), emphasizes the importance of gifts, including money and dried fruit, for attracting young men.

31. Nykl, *Hispano-Arabic Poetry*, 104; for another translation, *Banners of the Champions*, no. 177, p. 188.

32. Ibn Sahl wrote of a friend who gave up women to pursue boys in the hopes of being considered more elegant. J. M. Continente Ferre, "Aproximación al estudio del tema de amor en la poesía hispano-árabe de los siglos XII y XII," *Awraq* 1 (1978): 12–28, at 19.

33. *Banners of the Champions*, no. 178, p. 189; for another translation of the same poem, see Roth, "Boy-Love in Medieval Arabic Verse," 14.

34. *Banners of the Champions*, no. 187, p. 198.

35. Boswell, *CSTH*, 196.

36. Paul Sprachman, "Le beau garçon sans merci," *Homoeroticism in Classical Arabic Literature*, 193–94.

37. Nykl, *Hispano-Arabic Poetry*, 59; for other examples of attachment to Christian boys, see Ross Brann, *Power in the Portrayal: Representations of Jews and Muslims in Eleventh- and Twelfth-century Islamic Spain* (Princeton, 2002), 96–97. See also Rosenthal, "Male and Female: Described and Compared," 36–37.

38. Continente Ferrer, "Aproximación al estudio del tema de amor," 20.

39. Sprachman, "Le beau garçon sans merci," 194–95; For other lovers who go mad, see Giffen, *Theory of Profane Love*, 108.

40. Monroe, "The Striptease that Was Blamed on Abū Bakr's Son," 95–97.

41. Johann Christoph Bürgel, "Man, Nature and Cosmos as Intertwining of Elements in the Poetry of Ibn Khafājah," *Journal of Arabic Literature* 14 (1983): 31–45, at 33; Magda M. al-Nowaihi, *The Poetry of Ibn Khafājah: A Literary Analysis* (Leiden, 1993) 13–15, 52.

42. Giffen, *Theory of Profane Love*, 75. In his discussion of al-Sharīf al-Ṭalīq, Harry Neale writes, "We may conclude that this idealization of beauty is representative of the nobility (*majd*) and glory (*fakhr*) that were once the defining features of the poet's ancestors, rather than the features of the body of the beloved" ("The *Diwan* of al-Sharīf al-Ṭalīq," 25).

43. *Banners of the Champions*, no. 57, p. 59.

44. Jordan, *Invention of Sodomy*, 28.

45. As John Boswell points out (*CSTH*, esp. chaps. 8 and 9), some Christian authors cultivated a similar set of literary interests. He describes, for example, twelfth-century churchmen who wrote amorous verses to younger men.

46. See Giffen, *Theory of Profane Love*, 28, 118–23.

47. Maribel Fierro, "Caliphal Legitimacy and Expiation in al-Andalus," in *Islamic Legal Interpretation: Muftis and Their Fatwas*, ed. Muhammad Khalid Masud, Brinkley Messick, and David S. Powers (Cambridge, Mass., 1996), 55–62.

48. Fierro, "Caliphal Legitimacy." Twelfth-century *hisba* manuals also legislate sexual purity. Pedro Chalmeta Gendrón, "El kitāb fī ādāb al-ḥisba (El libro de buen gobierno del zoco) de al-Saqaṭī," *Al-Andalus* 32 (1967): 125–62, 359–97; 33 (1968): 143–95, 367–434; and *Sevilla a comienzos del siglo XII: El tratado de Ibn 'Abdūn*, ed. E. Lévi-Provençal and Emilio García Gómez (Madrid, 1948), no. 170. See, in general, Everett K. Rowson, "The Categorization of Gender and Sexual Irregularity in Medieval Arabic Vice Lists," in *Body Guards: The Cultural Politics of Gender Ambiguity*, ed. Julia Epstein and Kristina Straub (New York, 1991), 50–79.

49. Amin T. Tibi, *The Tibyān: Memoirs of 'Abd Allāh B. Buluggīn, Last Zīrid Amīr of Granada* (Leiden, 1986), 189.

50. *Tibyān*, 191.

51. *Tibyān*, 192.

52. *Tibyān*, 192.

53. See Kenneth B. Wolf, "Muhammad as Antichrist in Ninth-century Córdoba," *Christians, Muslims, and Jews in Medieval and Early Modern Spain: Interaction and Cultural Change*, ed. Mark D. Meyerson and Edward D. English (Notre Dame, Ind., 1999), 9–10.

54. *Taifa* kings were similarly criticized by their co-religionists for their addiction to wine, their intimacy with Christians, and, occasionally, their "effeminacy." See Hanna Kassis, "Muslim Revival in Spain in the Fifth/Eleventh Century," *Der Islam* 67 (1990): 81–83; in one case, in the context of Shi'ite threat, a missionary was accused of improper worship, homosexuality, and libertinage. Farhat Dachraoui, "Tentative d'Infiltration Sī'īte en Espagne Musulmane sous le règne d' al-Ḥakam II: Le Procès d'un missionaire sī'īte d'après Ibn Sahl," *Al-Andalus* 23 (1958): 96–106, at 100. See also Maria Isabel Fierro Bello's account of the trial of Abū l'Hayr, in which concerns about sexual and doctrinal purity were intermixed, in her *La heterodoxia en al-Andalus durante el periodo omeya* (Madrid, 1987), 149–55.

55. D. Fairchild Ruggles, *Gardens, Landscape, and Vision in the Palaces of Islamic Spain* (University Park, Penn., 2000), 74–75 and color plate 1.

56. Monroe, "Striptease," 95–97.

57. So argues J. W. Wright Jr, "Masculine Allusion and the Structure of Satire," in *Homoeroticism in Classical Arabic Literature*, 1–23.

58. Pelagius was an unwilling sexual partner to the caliph, but other Christians from the North actively sought the attention of Andalusi rulers. 'Abd al-Raḥmān III's mother and grandmother were both aristocratic Christian women from northern Spain. The caliph's son, al-Hakam II, married a woman from Navarre. For other examples of peaceful exchange between al-Andalus and the Christian north, see Fernando de la Granja, "A propósito de una embajada cristiana en la corte de 'Abd al-Raḥmān III," *Al-Andalus* 39 (1974): 391–406.

59. See, for example, Peter Heath, "Knowledge," in *The Literature of al-Andalus*, ed. María Rosa Menocal, Raymond P. Scheindlin, and Michael Sells (Cambridge, 2000), 110–11. One source describing the sack of Evora in 913, for example, claims that the Andalusi forces took 4,000 prisoners: *Una crónica anónima de 'Abd al-Rahmān III Al-Nasir*, ed. E. Lévi-Provençal and Emilio García Gómez (Madrid-Granada, 1950), 111.

60. John V. Tolan, *Saracens: Islam in the Medieval European Imagination* (New York, 2002), 63.

61. "Whether homoerotic or heteroerotic elements prevail in direct comparisons or are analyzed in separate chapters or separate essays, these collections present a shimmering, albeit solid and encompassing, picture of a society in which a significant segment of the intellectual leadership tried to teach seeing love as beauty was the indispensable means for its true fulfillment" (Rosenthal, "Male and Female: Described and Compared," 43). See also Jim Wafer, "Vision and Passion: The Symbolism of Male Love in Islamic Mystical Literature," in *Islamic Homosexualities: Culture, History, and Literature*, ed. Stephen Murray and Will Roscoe (New York, 1997), 87–96.

62. Rowson, "Medieval Arabic Vice Lists," 62. See also Giffen, *Theory of Profane Love*, 101–12.

CHAPTER 13

Sexual Mutilation and Castration Anxiety: A Medieval Perspective

Jacqueline Murray

The publication of *Christianity, Social Tolerance, and Homosexuality* marked the beginning of serious historical study of homosexualities in the past, but it did much more, as well. With it John Boswell became one of the founders of the history of sexuality. In the course of his book, he demonstrated the significance, indeed, the critical importance, of studying the Middle Ages to reach a nuanced understanding of the origins and development of Western values about sex. Boswell's long historical sweep, his broad evidential base, and his insistence that the medieval experience was part of the history of twentieth-century gay people combined to make the work much criticized and much read. Controversial and groundbreaking, *CSTH* proposed a myriad of topics that subsequent scholars have explored in greater detail.

With increasing attention on the construction of masculinities in past and present, historians have also begun to focus on the male genitalia and such issues as impotence or nocturnal emissions. Castration, as a fundamental assault on the male sexed body, has also garnered significant attention. Between 1999 and 2003, some six full-length studies and essay collections appeared on aspects of castration, ranging from an overarching "cultural history"[1] to the study of an obscure Russian Orthodox sect of self-castrators,[2] to the more predictable studies of Byzantine eunuchs,[3] early Christian saints,[4] and the castrati of the papal choirs.[5] Among medievalists, Abelard has become a veritable cottage industry with about half a dozen articles in as many years that focus on his castration and the accounts of that event.[6] Far from being an esoteric area of research, this focus on male genitalia is helping historians to understand some very complex aspects of Western psycho-social history. This can be seen as an extension of the history of sexuality into the realm of the history of embodiment. It also provides a means to examine something of the psycho-sexual experience of embodiment so that it is possible to move beyond the history of acts to contemplate the history of the sexed body and of bodily experiences, an agenda of which John Boswell would surely have approved.

Arguably, there was an attitude of fear among men in the Middle Ages that might be identified as "castration anxiety," much as Boswell found evidence of "gay people."[7] Castration, and fear of castration, occupied a central place in theological, legal, and popular discourses precisely because it was a real issue for medieval men.[8] Much thought was given to interpreting and understanding Jesus' words in the Gospel of Matthew (19:12):

> For there are eunuchs who were born thus from their mother's womb; and there are eunuchs who are made by men; and there are eunuchs who make themselves eunuchs on account of the kingdom of heaven.

The early Christian fathers understood this passage to refer to the containment of the body and the rejection of lust and sexual desire. For example, Augustine observed: "I might have more carefully listened to these words [about chastity] and, thus made a eunuch for the kingdom of heaven's sake, I might have more happily awaited Thy embraces."[9] In a similar vein, Jerome employed the metaphor to distinguish freely chosen spiritual eunuchism, or chastity, from physical castration. He wrote: "It is necessity that makes another a eunuch, my own choice makes me so."[10]

While for many, even most, early Christians, "eunuchs for God" was understood metaphorically, there were nevertheless opportunities for a literal, bodily interpretation as well. Physiological eunuchs, however, were also part of the cultural landscape of late antiquity, and not only as part of the imperial court. Origen was neither the first nor the only Christian devotee believed to have demonstrated his own purity by means of self-motivated mutilation.[11] While observers and commentators such as Eusebius tended to present critical, or at least ambivalent, views of such acts, castration continued to be presented as a positive metaphor for chastity and the individual's control over his disobedient genitals. For example, writers of the stature of Cassian and Gregory the Great contributed to a body of religious literature that described holy men being mystically castrated—usually in dreams—which ended their struggles with both their sexed body and their sexual desire.[12] Such stories about shadowy, semi-legendary saints endured, and the motif of mystical castration eventually was included in the lives of historical figures such as Hugh of Avalon in the twelfth century and Thomas Aquinas in the thirteenth century.

While castration and eunuchism, either actual or mystical, may have attained a specifically spiritual meaning, physical castration was also a real, bloody, painful fact of medieval life. For example, Boswell cited the case of two Byzantine bishops whom Justinian persecuted on account of their homosexual activities. Their punishments were harsh and uncompromising:

> They were brought to Constantinople by imperial order and were tried and deposed by the city prefect, who punished them, exiling Isaiah after severe torture and exposing Alexander to public ridicule after castrating him. Shortly after this, the emperor ordered that those found guilty of homosexual relations be castrated. Many were found at the time, and they were castrated and died. From that time on, those who experienced sexual desire for other males lived in terror. (Cited in *CSTH*, 172)

Justinian's hostility and punishment for homosexual activity was widely disseminated, and for most of the Middle Ages castration was one of the common penalties for men caught in homosexual acts. This was detailed in the thirteenth-century French law code, *Li Livres de jostice et de plet*[13] and also in the Castilian *Fuero real* promulgated by Alfonso X in the thirteenth century. The *Fuero real* states:

> Although we are reluctant to speak of something which is reckless to perform, terrible sins are nevertheless sometimes committed, and it happens that one man desires to sin against nature with another. We therefore command that if any commit this sin, once it is proven, both be castrated before the whole populace and on the third day after be hung by the legs until dead, and that their bodies never be taken down. (Cited in *CSTH*, 288)

The harsh recommendations of secular law codes were also reflected in popular attitudes, not only towards sodomites but also towards men who committed sexual transgressions with women. Moreover, such men were just as likely to face castration at the hands of informal justice as in formal courts.

Castration was also a penalty exacted for a variety of heterosexual crimes. Peter Abelard, who was castrated by a gang of thugs for his seduction of

Heloise, was perhaps better prepared than most men to come to terms with violent and involuntary emasculation. His assailants were tried and themselves castrated and blinded as punishment for their attack. Abelard, in his turn, lamented the cruelty done to him and left the world for a more monastic existence. Yet, Abelard was by no means the only seducer to be castrated as punishment for seduction or rape.

Matthew of Paris recorded a case of seduction followed by vigilante justice in 1248.[14] A knight from Norfolk, Godfrey de Millers, wanted to seduce the daughter of another knight, John the Briton. This could not have been a spontaneous or unplanned act, since the woman herself revealed that Godfrey was going to come to her father's house in order to have sex with her, although it is unclear whether this assignation was their first or if they had already engaged in sexual relations on previous occasions. Matthew asserts that she "was afraid of being thought a married man's mistress." As a result of her betrayal, a gang of men was waiting for Godfrey when he crept into the house. The men seized him and beat him up. "After this he was suspended from a beam, with his legs stretched apart, and, when thus exposed to the will of his enemies, he was disgracefully mutilated to such a degree that he would have preferred decapitation. And thus wounded and mutilated, he was ejected, half-dead, from the house." This exaction of informal justice, however, did not end the matter. The mechanisms of formal justice were also invoked. Matthew of Paris reports that John the Briton was tried subsequently for his men's attack on Godfrey de Millers. Upon being found guilty, the court disinherited John and banished him in perpetuity, and sent his henchmen into exile.

It is interesting to note that in his roughly contemporary redaction of English law, Bracton asks: "What is to be said where a man cuts off another's testicles and castrates him on account of debauchery?" The answer was that sometimes the perpetrator was executed and sometimes he forfeited his property and was exiled.[15] Thus, John the Briton received the appropriate sentence, as prescribed by English law, for someone who castrated a debaucher. The situation differed elsewhere in Christendom. For example, on the Iberian Peninsula various *fueros,* including that of Cuenca, permitted a man to castrate the lover of either his wife or daughter, providing the culprit was caught *in flagrante* and the castration occurred in the heat of the moment.[16]

On the crudest level, castration could be viewed as a case of the punishment fitting the crime. It was frequently the penalty recommended for the rape or seduction of virgins and not only according to the rough justice of vigilante mobs. Bracton observed that if a man were convicted of the rape of a virgin he was to be punished by:

the loss of members, that there be member for member, for when a virgin is defiled she loses her member and therefore let her defiler be punished in the parts in which he offended. Let him thus lose his eyes which gave him sight of the maiden's beauty for which he coveted her. And let him lose as well the testicles which excited his hot lust.[17]

This is a fascinating and highly charged statement about the equivalency between hymen and testicles and the role of the sense of sight in exciting lust. Other sources, such as the Welsh *Chronicle of the Princes,* provide numerous examples of a defeated opponent, often a male relative such as an uncle or nephew, who was both castrated and had his eyes put out.[18] Thus, blinding was frequently linked with castration in the context of both judicial proceedings and vigilante justice.

Adultery was another sexual crime that could warrant the punishment of castration. A case from fourteenth-century Manosque, in southern France, reveals the extent to which a judge could interpret the facts of a case in reaching his decision. In 1341 Alaxia Carllanda, a Christian wife and mother, appeared before the local court, accused of having an affair with Crescan, a Jewish physician.[19] Alaxia asserted that she had been blackmailed by Crescan, who refused to treat her ill daughter unless she had sex with him. After he was so presumptuous as to grab her hand and place it on his erect penis and declare he wanted to have sex with her while standing up, she went to the local authorities for assistance. When Crescan returned he took her upstairs and threw her on the bed. Alaxia testified that, in order to avoid being touched by his Jewish penis, she put her petticoat between them, which was ruined when the overexcited Crescan ejaculated prematurely. Eventually, Crescan admitted to the attempted seduction and threw himself on the court's mercy. The usual secular penalty for adultery was a fine or, for those who could not pay, a beating, so no doubt the physician saw no reason to fear the court unduly. The prosaic court record does not reveal Crescan's reaction when he heard the judge's sentence that he be castrated. This punishment was anomalous for simple adultery, even if accompanied by blackmail. It is possible that the judge viewed the situation not so much as adultery as the rape of a respectable matron by an unscrupulous physician. This case may also, however, reflect contemporary fears about sexual transgression across religious boundaries. In urban communities in which Christians and Jews lived side by side, engaged in commerce and may even have socialized together, the fear of sexual mixing could have elicited a harsh penalty to serve as a warning.[20] Unfortunately, the record ends with a simple notation of the verdict and sentence without rationale or commentary, nor does it indicate whether the sentence was carried out.

The academic jurisprudence of Bracton, the spare records of the court clerk, the theological reflections of Abelard, and even the evident disapproval of Matthew of Paris all sanitize what was, in actuality, a bloody and violent act. This is illustrated in the account of a case at Worcester in the 1220s that highlights the macabre circumstances that could attend castration even in the relatively controlled environment of a judicial proceeding. An adulterous man was sentenced to be blinded and castrated publicly. Afterwards, his eyes and testicles were tossed around by the youths and girls (*mulierculas*) before they were thrown far away into a field.[21] Thus, the emasculation was accompanied by a certain levity among the crowd who seemed untouched by the suffering of man before them.

Nor was the Worcester case an isolated example of indifference. Benedict of Peterborough included an astonishing account of castration in his *Miracles of Thomas Becket*.[22] The miracle involved a man unjustly accused of theft. Having failed trial by water, he was sentenced to be blinded and castrated. The account is gory and quite appalling. The man's left eye was cut out whole, but the right was lacerated and cut into pieces. Finally, with difficulty, the eyes were gouged out. The man's testicles were then cut off and buried in a thicket. Benedict reports: "A not small crowd had gathered for the spectacle, some compelled by public power, some drawn by curiosity." The unfortunate man bled so profusely that they sent for a priest, fearing he would bleed to death. Gradually, however, the flow of blood lessened and the man survived. This account, as part of a miracle story, continues past the violence and torture of the mutilation. Becket, to whom the man had prayed while in prison, appeared to him and, afterwards, the man's eyes slowly began to regenerate until once again he was able to see. Then, while the man was en route to Canterbury to give thanks to Thomas for restoring his eyes, his scrotum began to itch. When he scratched it, he realized that his testicles were also being restored, gradually regenerating and growing and increasing in size. Benedict of Peterborough concludes that the man did not hesitate to allow anyone who wanted to stroke his miraculously restored testicles.

This miracle story presents a less sanitized view of castration than that afforded by more theoretical texts. It also presents some historical and contextual details that help us to understand better the cultural meaning and the actual practice of castration in medieval society. Classical medical texts, such as that by Paul of Aegina, identified two methods of castration.[23] One method was suitable for use on prepubescent boys and was commonly used in Byzantium. This involved compression of the testicles by squeezing them while they were still quite small and underdeveloped. This is the method that ensured the steady supply of eunuchs so necessary to the functioning of the Byzantine imperial court and, much later, for the angelic voices of the papal choirs. The other method involved what is more commonly understood by the term castration: the excision of the testicles of an adult man. In this procedure the scrotum was cut open and the testicles were removed. If the elastic skin of the scrotum were pulled sufficiently taut, it would then snap back, helping to close the wound and staunch the flow of blood. The bleeding could have lasted for about seven days and death from bleeding would certainly have been common, but so, too, would survival.[24] Thus, Benedict of Peterborough's account exhibits some knowledge of what might have been expected as a result of castration. He describes the victim's bleeding, which slowed and was followed by the gradual healing of the wound, and the man's eventual recovery. Castration was not a procedure hidden away from public view, but was as aspect of daily life. People witnessed judicial castration, just as they witnessed executions and other forms of corporal punishment. It was part of their cultural landscape.

For medieval people, castration could also perceived as a form of divine punishment. Although some saints followed Thomas Becket and restored the genitals of men who had been deprived of them unjustly, others wielded castration as a form of divine retribution. For example, one of the miracles attributed to Gerald of Aurillac involved a woman who, while returning from praying at Gerald's tomb, was attacked by a horseman. She appealed to the predator, declaring that she was a woman devoted to St. Gerald, but the man did not care and proceeded to rape her. "When he had risen from lying with her, the man was struck through divine vengeance in the groin or the testicles, or, as I should say, in the genitals, which putrefied and fell off him."[25] Thus, the famously chaste Gerald left no doubt that this was a punishment suited to the wretched man's crime.

In another miracle story, a band of men were pursing St. Marculph. Suddenly, all but one of the men were struck motionless. The man who retained his mobility was particularly contemptuous of Marculph. As he was mounting his horse, however, he banged his groin against the high saddle with such force that his scrotum was sliced open and his testicles dangled out. As a result the man was left half-dead. His friends begged the saint to have mercy on him. "So the man of God, moved to pity by their prayers, ordered the masculine parts, which had fallen down outside the natural sack of skin, to reconceal themselves in nature's proper place."[26] The wound was healed presumably as miraculously as it had been caused.

The treatment accorded to the excised testicles in such stories suggests that medieval people had conflicted responses to bodily mutilation. Sometimes people were moved to pity; other times they were utterly dispassionate, or worse. This is evident in Guibert of Nogent's assertion that Thomas of Marle hung up his prisoners by their testicles, which were often torn off by the victim's own body weight.[27] In the Becket miracle, the testicles were taken away and buried, while in the Worcester case the crowd tossed around the testicles and then threw them away.[28] Jean Froissart described how, before Hugh le Despenser was executed, both his penis and testicles were cut off and burned in front of him.[29]

Nor were the dead safe, as the posthumous mutilation of Simon de Montfort so clearly demonstrates. In 1265 de Montfort was killed in the Battle of Evesham. Numerous chroniclers, from both the royalist side and the baronial side, report that the victors, motivated by some sense of bloody revenge, dismembered de Montfort's body, cutting off his head, arms, and legs.[30] A number of sources also state that his genitals were cut off as well.[31] The *Annals of London* provide one of the most graphic descriptions: "After he had died they wickedly cut off his head, arms, legs, and also his shameful parts [*pudibunda*], with his trunk alone remaining, placing the aforementioned masculine organs [*virilia*] in his mouth."[32] According to Walter of Guisborough, when the head and genitals *(membris)* were removed from the body, the king's army carried these body parts with them as the spoils of war. Ultimately, they sent the head, possibly with the amputated genitals still in its mouth, to Maud, the wife of Roger Mortimer of Wigmore.[33]

These examples suggest an almost ritualistic desire to desecrate, defile, and destroy the testicles. A similar reaction is presented in one of Caesarius of Heisterbach's miracle stories, which reveals the deep psychological fear that attended castration, real or imagined. In *The Dialogue on Miracles,* Caesarius discussed a monk who was struggling with the vow of chastity. He had resolved to return to the world and marry but his abbot asked him not to leave until the next day. That night the monk dreamt that he saw

> a horrible man, in the likeness of an executioner, hastening towards him, holding in his hand a long knife and with a huge black dog following him. At this sight he trembled. And no wonder. The man, seizing him violently, cut off his genitals and threw them to the dog, which immediately devoured them.[34]

This story echos the mystical castrations of holy men such as Serenus and Equitius, but with a darker twist. The dreams of mystical castration that visited holy men were considered signs of grace. This dream, however, reveals more of the anxiety that could attend an average man, not a saint, as he interposed the horror of literal castration into the discourse of spiritual castration. The fate of the severed genitals is more horrific than burying, discarding, or burning. Given the disrespect with which these organs were treated in some of the examples already discussed, the suggestion they were eaten by a dog reflects a fear that was not beyond the realm of possibility.

Part of the motivation behind the handling of the castrated body parts may have been destruction as much as desecration. There had been much debate about whether a castrated man's genitals would be restored at the resurrection, giving him a complete body, or whether he would remain a eunuch even in the afterlife. The question of the materialism of resurrection attracted the attention from writers as Guibert of Nogent in the eleventh century, Peter Lombard and Hugh of St. Victor in the twelfth century, and the discourse continued on through the thirteenth century. Various aspects of bodily resurrection were debated, including the question of whether the severed parts of the body, especially those that were lost or misplaced, could be reassembled in the afterlife. Thomas Aquinas concluded that even bodily matter that had been consumed and digested remained of the original substance and so would be returned as part of a person's resurrected body, but this conclusion was not well disseminated.[35] Given the interest of theologians in this topic, it is reasonable to suspect that there may have been popular concerns about the fate of lost, destroyed, or digested body parts. If castration were accompanied by the destruction of the amputated organ, the mutilation would have been even more serious and debilitating because the fear was that the mutilated body would not be rendered whole and perfect at the resurrection.[36] Castration, a realistic fear for medieval men, could be exacerbated by the destruction or defiling of the amputated organs. Perhaps because of this immediacy, and because it was such a profound violation of the individual's body, it also occasioned deep-seated psychological anxiety in men and bizarre, almost ritualistic, behavior in both men and women.

Among the most famous and problematic accounts of castration is that associated with the Gilbertine community of Watton in the mid-twelfth century. This incident is known from a report of the event prepared by Aelred of Rievaulx, at the request of Gilbert of Sempringham. Aelred was asked to investigate the case of a rebellious nun who had been seduced by one of the lay brothers and become pregnant. While imprisoned for her scandalous behavior, her pregnancy miraculously disappeared. This story has most often been read as that of a fallen nun who was miraculously restored to purity after disgracing herself and her community by having a sexual liaison and becoming pregnant.[37]

One aspect of the Watton story that has been glossed over is the fate of the wayward brother and the meaning of the inconceivable behavior of the fallen nun's sisters, who plotted his capture and punishment. After consultation with the men of the community, one of the brothers impersonated the nun by dressing in a habit. He then awaited a prearranged assignation, while the other brothers hid nearby:

> Aflame with desire, as soon as he [the paramour] spied the veil, he threw himself like a brainless horse or mule upon the man whom he thought to be a woman. Those who were there, using their sticks as a bitter medicine, extinguished the fever at its source.[38]

The wording suggests that the unfortunate man was beaten around the genitals, which were doubtless the "source" of the fever. While accounts often describe a gang beating the captive during the general struggle that accompanied his capture, they do not stipulate any focus for the beating. For example, Matthew of Paris used only general language to discuss the beating that Godfrey de Millers received before he was castrated. It is also worth noting how the man was characterized as like a horse or mule. This same analogy was used in the miracle of Gerald of Aurillac, which described the rapist as "made like a horse and a mule in which there is no reason." Horses and mules have proportionately larger penises, especially when erect, than other domesticated animals. Moreover, they are particularly violent and aggressive in their mating activities. This sexual analogy, then, would have resonated immediately for medieval people.

According to Aelred, after the brother was apprehended, the nuns asked that he be turned over to them. The account suggests that the women merely wanted to interrogate him. What subsequently happened, however, was quite different and cannot have been spontaneous:

> They took him up and he was laid out and bound. She who was the cause of all the evils was brought forth as to a spectacle. His instrument was placed in her hand and she was unwillingly compelled to amputate the man with her own hands. Then one of the women standing there seized what had been taken and thrust it all stinking with blood into the mouth of the sinning woman.[39]

On first reading, this description might suggest that both the man's penis and testicles had been amputated. Aelred notes, however, that "[t]he *castratus* was restored to the brothers," and he disappears from the report.[40] This disappearance suggests that only his testicles were removed since, if the man had bled to death, as would be almost certain from a penectomy, Aelred would of necessity have passed a much harsher judgement on the nuns who perpetrated the act. As it was, he contented himself to state: "I do not praise the deed but the zeal; nor do I approve the shedding of blood but I extol the holy virgins' great offensive against turpitude."[41] Castration was not an uncommon punishment for rape and seduction, especially of a nun; murder by a group of nuns, however, would arguably have elicited a stronger reaction from Aelred and would likely have left other traces in the historical record.

Another troubling aspect of this thoroughly troubling incident is the highly symbolic nature of the castration. The nuns planned in advance what they were going to do since they had the rope ready to bind the man and the knife to cut him. In this, the nuns were informally implementing the prescriptions of formal law, much like the henchmen of John the Briton had done. Perhaps forcing the disgraced nun to perform the deed was seen as an appropriate form of expiation for her transgression. Most troubling of all, however, is that the nuns put the testicles in their sister's mouth. While there would seem to be some similarity between this act and the manner in which Simon de Montfort's corpse was defiled, there are numerous points of divergence, points which would seem to be at the crux of the symbolic meaning of this act. There are various examples of similar sorts of acts including putting amputated genitals in the mouths of enemies killed in war or of the victims of lynchings. There are also numerous cases of men being compelled to castrate themselves. This case, however, appears without any immediate parallels in anthropological or historical literature.

The meaning of castration and other forms of genital mutilation such as penectomy was directly related to how medieval men were understood as embodied beings.[42] Masculine gender definition was focused on the male genitals, the organs that symbolized men's generative power, the organs that represented their natural superiority over women, with their less perfect interiorized genitals, and the organs that allowed men to dominate women and other men, through rape or the production of heirs.[43] Yet, the genitals were also dangerous and irrational organs. They moved—or didn't—seemingly of their own accord.[44] This accounts for the rich medieval discourses on nocturnal emissions, spontaneous erections, and impotence. But, perhaps most troubling of all, male genitals were vulnerable. They could be diseased, wounded, or amputated, depriving a man of the sexual prowess so fundamental to his gender identity. Consequently, the locus and symbol of men's patriarchal power was also the site of their spiritual weakness and physical vulnerability. The genitals, then, the penis and testicles, were at once symbols of power and of vulnerability, and they must figure into any understanding of medieval masculinities. The man who misused his genitals, desired sexual relations with another man, or chose the wrong woman to seduce or rape could be deprived of them by formal or informal justice or by divine intervention. Similarly, miracle stories that described the return or regeneration of the amputated and mutilated genitals provided some solace to the frightened man or the grieving *castratus*.

The psychologically disturbing aspects of castration were expressed in other ways as well. For example, some historians contend that Guibert of Nogent was preoccupied with genital mutilation and castration.[45] And indeed, Guibert is a compelling example of a man troubled by the disobedient nature of the genitals, but arguably even more so by their vulnerability. This is illustrated in his retelling of the well-known story of the pilgrim of Compostela.[46] While en route to the shrine, the devil, in the shape of the apostle James, begins to torment the unfortunate pilgrim about his sexual sins. After berating the man, the devil finally convinces him that the only way to demonstrate his repentance is to "cut off that member with which you have sinned—that is, your penis—and afterwards take your very life." Later that night, "he first cut off his penis and then plunged the knife into his throat."[47]

This account, although based on an earlier poem that was known across Europe, is wholly Guibert's. He modified it extensively, transforming a mere suicide by throat-slitting into a dramatic scene of anguish and self-mutilation.[48] This is made all the worse by the fact that the pilgrim's sexual sins were nothing more than conjugal relations, which Guibert characterized as "not . . . proper but . . . improper love."[49] Was Guibert implying that the man had had sexual relations after he had assumed the pilgrim's cloak and such activity was prohibited? Or was he referring to earlier acts involving simple sexual pleasure or non-procreative sex, or unnatural sexual positions? Or, perhaps the most disturbing possibility of all, was this an assault on conjugal relations *per se,* no matter how chaste and well intentioned? It is impossible to resolve this interpretive conundrum. Another of Guibert's additions was to have the pilgrim cut off his penis, not just his testicles. What purpose was served in this story by exceeding the usual mode of castration? Why have the pilgrim amputate his penis, an act of certain death that was rendered superfluous by the throat-slitting?

Part of the explanation for the penectomy could be that the penis and the testicles had different symbolic meanings. The testicles were understood to be the site of men's generative power, perhaps even the organ that defined manliness. Therefore, the excision of the testicles unsexed a man. The penis, by contrast, may have had another, deeper meaning. Caroline Bynum has argued that the representation of Christ's penis in medieval art was a symbol of his humanity.[50] If this were the case, Guibert's deliberate interpolation of a penectomy could be a means of signaling that the pilgrim has lost his humanity. There are a number of possible reasons that could account for this. The pilgrim listened to the Devil. He apparently despaired and succumbed to the temptation of suicide. Or perhaps his sin was having sex with his wife in a de-humanized way, *contra naturam*. Or, as with the rapist in the Gerald of Aurillac miracle and the victim of Watton, had lust dehumanized him "like a horse or mule without reason"?

If there were a difference in the symbolic meaning of testicular castration and penectomy, it might help to explain some of the truly bizarre rantings found in the fifteenth-century *Malleus Maleficarum,* in particular the sections that describe how witches were able to steal men's penises. Book One asks: "Whether Witches may work some Prestidigitary Illusion so that the Male Organ appears to be entirely removed and separate from the Body."[51] The ensuing discussion affirms that, with the devil's help, witches can "really and actually remove the member" as opposed to only apparently doing so by an illusion. God allows witches more power over the genital functions, including the actual removal of the genital organ, because this is where sin originated. If the devil were not there to help, however, the witch could only excise the organs by a glamour, "although it is no illusion in the opinion of the sufferer. For his imagination can really and actually believe that something is not present, since by none of his exterior senses, such as sight or touch, can he perceive that it is present."[52] Thus, the penis and testicles, although still present on the body, would be rendered invisible to the afflicted man who "can see and feel nothing but a smooth body with its surface interrupted by no genital organ."[53] Through diabolical machinations, then, the victim's very humanity is threatened by the disappearance of his genitals. He is both desexed and rendered sexless, in defiance of the order of creation and the order of nature. As Genesis made explicit, "male and female he created them" (Gen. 1:28). There was no place in this world or the next for a sexless aberration, and no possibility that a man whose genitals had been stolen by a witch might be confused with a "eunuch for God."

There is a sense in which women's invisible genitals were the sign of women's dangerousness just as men's genitals were a sign of their vulnerability and weakness.[54] Men's genitals were superior because they were visible. Women's inferior genitals were interiorized because women lacked the requisite heat to externalize them. But men's superior genitals were also the source of their fear of impotence, of spontaneous erections, of the sight of a woman's face, or the threat of the ligature. Castration, the removal of the outward, visible sign of manhood, made the male body more closely resemble the female body and stripped a man of his manliness. As Abelard would argue, a castrated man was saved from lust and could resist women and sexual temptation, albeit at the terrible cost of being deprived of the genitals, the exterior sign of manhood and of full humanity.

Castration was not an unreasonable fear for the poacher, the thief, the prisoner of war, the sodomite, the rapist, or the adulterer. But castration was not only punitive, it was also an assault on the visible sign of masculine identity. As a result, it can be traced to the prevailing discourse of misogyny. Sodomites overturned nature and were feminized by virtue of their sex acts. Weak men, dominated by lust, became like horses or mules. Devils or saints could castrate a man or return his amputated testicles, seemingly at random. With diabolical aid, witches could steal men's genitals and render them less than human. In a society in which masculinity was genitally defined, mutilation, by oneself or another, real or imagined, existed as an omnipresent threat to the concept of manhood. Fear of castration, not unreasonably, lay buried in the medieval psyche, bursting forth in miracle stories or acted out in the destruction or desecration of amputated testicles. From our historical vantage point, it is possible to catch glimpses of this complex medieval manifestation of what, in the twentieth century, came to be called castration anxiety.

· *Notes*

Research for this essay was supported by a grant from the Social Sciences and Humanities Research Council of Canada. I am grateful to Dyan Elliott, Alastair Summerlee, Mathew Kuefler, Jill McCutcheon, and Steve Bednarski who each offered critical advice at various stages of this project.

1. Piotr O. Scholz, *Eunuchs and Castrati: A Cultural History* (Princeton: Markus Wiener, 2001). See also the literary and cultural study by Gary Taylor, *Castration: An Abbreviated History of Western Manhood* (New York: Routledge, 2000).

2. Laura Engelstein, *Castration and the Heavenly Kingdom: A Russian Folktale* (Ithaca: Cornell University Press, 1999).

3. For example, the collection *Eunuchs in Antiquity and Beyond,* ed. Shaun Tougher (London: Gerald Duckworth, 2002).

4. Mathew Kuefler, *The Manly Eunuch: Masculinity, Gender Ambiguity, and Christian Ideology in Late Antiquity* (Chicago: University of Chicago Press, 2001).

5. See the discussions in Scholz, *Eunuchs and Castrati,* and in Valeria Finucci, *The Manly Masquerade: Masculinity, Paternity and Castration in the Italian Renaissance* (Durham, N.C.: Duke University Press, 2003).

6. Among these are: Martin Irvine, "Abelard and (Re)writing the Male Body: Castration, Identity and Remasculinization," in *Becoming Male in the Middle Ages,* ed. Jeffrey Jerome Cohen and Bonnie Wheeler (New York: Garland, 1997), 87–106; Bonnie Wheeler, "Origenary Fantasies: Abelard's Castration and Confession," *Becoming Male,* 107–28; Yves Ferroul, "Abelard's Blissful Castration," *Becoming Male,* 129–49; Claire Nouvet, "La castration d'Abelard: Impasse et substitution," *Poetique* 83 (1990): 259–80; and Jacqueline Murray, "Mystical Castration: Some Reflections of Peter Abelard, Hugh of Lincoln and Sexual Control," in *Conflicted Identities and Multiple Masculinities: Men in the Medieval West,* ed. Jacqueline Murray (New York: Garland, 1999), 80–84.

7. This term may not be as anachronistic as it first appears, although it does raise the same specter of essentialism that bedeviled Boswell. Nevertheless, Wolfgang Lederer has observed that, while penis envy does not exist in history or myth, " 'castration anxiety,' on the other hand, is a very real thing" (*The Fear of Women* [New York: Grune and Stratton, 1968], 215–17). This essay also tries to emulate Boswell's boldness by focusing on the same broad time frame and by using a similarly eclectic array of sources.

8. For an introduction and overview of castration and eunuchism, especially in late antiquity and the early Middle Ages, see Mathew Kuefler, "Castration and Eunuchism in the Middle Ages," in *Handbook of Medieval Sexuality,* ed. Vern L. Bullough and James A. Brundage (New York: Garland, 1996), 279–306. For eunuchs in the Byzantine East, see Shaun F. Tougher, "Byzantine Eunuchs: An Overview, with Special Reference to their Creation and Origin," in *Women, Men and Eunuchs: Gender in Byzantium,* ed. Liz James (London: Routledge, 1997), 168–84; and Kathryn M. Ringrose, "Living in the Shadows: Eunuchs and Gender in Byzantium," in *Third Sex, Third Gender: Beyond Sexual Dimorphism in Culture and History,* ed. Gilbert Herdt (New York: Zone Books, 1994), 85–109. On eunuchs in antiquity, see Arthur Darby Nock, "Eunuchs in Ancient Religion," *Archiv für Religionswissenschaft* 23 (1925): 25–33; rpt. *Essays on Religion and the Ancient World,* ed. Zeph Stewart (Cambridge, Mass. : Harvard University Press, 1972), 1:7–15, and Walter Stevenson, "The Rise of Eunuchs in Greco-Roman Antiquity," *Journal of the History of Sexuality* 5 (1995): 495–511. For a useful comparative discussion, see Jennifer W. Jay, "Another Side of Chinese Eunuch History: Castration, Marriage, Adoption, and Burial," *Canadian Journal of History* 28 (1993): 460–78.

9. Augustine, *Confessions,* trans. Vernon J. Bourke, Fathers of the Church, 21 (New York: Fathers of the Church, 1953), 2.2.3, p. 35.

10. Jerome, Letter 22, *Ad Eustochium,* in *Corpus Scriptorum Ecclesiasticorum Latinorum* (1866–), 54. The English translation is from *The Letters of Saint Jerome,* trans. Charles Christopher Mierow, *Ancient Christian Writers,* 33 (Westminster, Md.: Newman Press, 1963), 150.

11. Eusebius, while seeming to admire Origen, also concluded that his self-mutilation was a sign of immaturity (*The History of the Church from Christ to Constantine,* trans. G. A. Williamson [Harmondsworth: Penguin, 1965; rpt. 1981], 8.5, pp. 247–48). For a discussion of Origen, see Peter Brown, *The Body and Society: Men, Women, and Sexual Renunciation in Early Christianity* (New York: Columbia University Press, 1988), 161–69. See also the *vita* of Leontius, *Acta Sanctorum* (*AASS*), 4 July. 4. Justin Martyr gave faint praise to a young man who sought castration to avoid sexual temptation. The incident is discussed in James A.

Brundage, *Law, Sex, and Christian Society* (Chicago: University of Chicago Press, 1987), 65.

12. Although it might be argued that the object of desire for the holy man who struggled with his flesh could have been male as much as female, the surviving saints lives or miracle stories explicitly discuss their sexual desire for women. For an overview of some aspects of this phenomenon see Murray, "Mystical Castration."

13. *Li Livres de jostice et de plet,* ed. Louis Nicolas Rapetti (Paris: F. Didot, 1850), 279–80.

14. Matthaei Parisiensis, *Chronica Majora,* ed. Henry Richards Luard (London: Longman, 1880), 5:34. The translation is from Matthew Paris, *English History,* trans. J. A. Giles (London: Henry G. Bohn, 1853), 2:277.

15. Bracton, *On the Laws and Customs of England,* trans. Samuel E. Thorne, 2 vols. (Cambridge, Mass.: Belknap Press, 1968), 2:408.

16. Heath Dillard, *Daughters of the Reconquest: Women in Castilian Town Society, 1100–1300* (Cambridge: Cambridge University Press, 1984), 204.

17. Bracton, 414–15.

18. The Welsh sources in particular link the two forms of mutilation as clearly rending a rival helpless either to avenge himself or to beget heirs who could seek revenge on behalf of the victim. See *Brut y Tywysogyon or The Chronicle of the Princes: Red Book of Hergest Version,* ed. Thomas Jones (Cardiff: University of Wales Press, 1955), 113, 131, 163.

19. I am grateful to Steve Bednarski for bringing this case to my attention and making available to me his transcription of the manuscript.

20. In the twelfth century, the Council of Nablus (1120) recommended that a Christian man who had sexual relations with a Muslim woman should be castrated, as should a Muslim man who raped a Christian woman. James A. Brundage, "Prostitution, Miscegenation and Sexual Purity in the First Crusade," in *Crusade and Settlement,* ed. Peter W. Edbury (Cardiff: University College Cardiff Press, 1985), 207. For an illuminating examination of the anxiety that surrounded sexual activity—or the fear of sexual activity—across religious borders, see David Nirenberg, "Conversion, Sex, and Segregation: Jews and Christians in Medieval Spain," *American Historical Review* 107, no. 4 (Oct. 2002): 1065–93.

21. William of Malmesbury, *The* Vita Wulfstani *of William of Malmesbury,* ed. Reginald R. Darlington, Camden Society 40 (London, 1928), 168–75.

22. *Benedictii abbatis Petriburgensis de vita et miraculis s. Thomae Cantuariensis,* ed. Dr. Giles (Caxton Society, 1850; rpt. New York: Burt Franklin, 1967), 184–93. The same miracle is reported in less detail by William of Canterbury. See *Materials for the History of Thomas Becket,* ed. J. C. Robertson, Rolls Series, vol. 67 (London,1875; rpt. Kraus, 1965), 1:156–58.

23. Paul of Aegina, *The Seven Books of Paulus Aegineta,* trans. Francis Adams (London: Sydenham Society, 1846), 6.68, vol. 2:379.

24. I am grateful to Alastair Summerlee and Jill McCutcheon who patiently answered my many questions about the surgical aspects of castration.

25. This miracle is not included in the printed editions of the *vita* of Gerald of Aurillac (Odo of Cluny, *Vita s. Geraldi Comitis Aurillac,* PL 133, 1.9, cols. 648–49; a more recent edition, with facing translation, is found in *St Odo of Cluny: Being the Life of St Odo of Cluny by John of Salerno and the Life of St Gerald of Aurillac by St Odo,* ed. and trans. G. Sitwell [London:

Sheed and Ward, 1958].) I am grateful to Mathew Kuefler, who is currently preparing a critical edition of the *vita* and miracles, for drawing this case to my attention. He kindly gave me access to his yet unpublished transcription and translation of the addendum to the *vita* of Gerald.

26. Marculph's *vita*, chap. 3, Miracles, c. 19 in *Acta Sanctorum* (*AASS*), 1 May.

27. *Self and Society in Medieval France: The Memoirs of Abbot Guibert of Nogent,* ed. John F. Benton (New York: Harper and Row, 1970; rpt. 1984), 3.11, p. 185.

28. William of Malmesbury, *Vita Wulfstani,* 171.

29. Jean Froissart, *Chronicles,* trans. Geoffrey Brereton (Harmondsworth: Penguin, 1968), 44. This is discussed in Boswell, *CSTH,* 298–301.

30. John Gillingham has argued that the death and mutilation of de Montfort at Evesham marks the end of a period during which the ideals of chivalry had meant that victors did not murder, maim, or execute vanquished enemies of noble rank. "Killing and Mutilating Political Enemies in the British Isles from the late Twelfth to the Early Fourteenth Century: A Comparative Study," in *Britain and Ireland 900–1300,* ed. B. Smith (Cambridge: Cambridge University Press, 1999).

31. For example, Robert of Gloucester used the term *privé membres,* while a London manuscript reports that Simon's amputated testicles (*testiculi*) were put in his nose. Both references are cited by James Orchard Halliwell in his edition of *The Chronicle of William de Rishanger of the Barons' Wars: The Miracles of Simon de Montfort* (London: Camden Society, 1840), xxxi–xxxii.

32. *Annales Londonienses,* in *Chronicles of the Reigns of Edward I and Edward II,* ed. William Stubbs (Rolls Series, 1882; rept. Kraus, 1965), 1:69.

33. *The Chronicle of Walter of Guisborough,* ed. Harry Rothwell, Camden 3d ser., vol. 89 (London: Camden Society, 1957), 201–2.

34. Caesarius of Heisterbach, *Dialogus miraculorum,* ed. Joseph Strange (Cologne: J. M. Heberle, 1856) 4.97, 1:265–66. The only English translation omits the detail of the dog and softens the horror conveyed in the original Latin. *The Dialogue on Miracles,* trans. H. von. E. Scott and C. C. Swinton Bland (London: George Routledge, 1929), 1:302–3.

35. See Caroline Walker Bynum, "Material Continuity, Personal Survival and the Resurrection of the Body: A Scholastic Discussion in Its Medieval Contexts," in *Fragmentation and Redemption: Essays on Gender and the Human Body in Medieval Religion* (New York: Zone Books, 1992), 240–44.

36. There appears to be a transcultural aspect to this fear. The last surviving Chinese imperial eunuch, who died in the 1996, expressed this belief. When, as a child, he had been castrated, his testicles were preserved in a jar which he kept with him throughout his life. To his regret, these were destroyed by Red Guards during the Cultural Revolution. For the eunuch, this meant his testicles would not be reunited with his body in the afterlife. *The New York Times,* 20 December 1996, accessed 24 June 2004 on the Internet at http://acc6.its.brooklyn.cuny.edu/ phalsall/texts/eunuchs2.html.

37. The best overview of the incident remains Giles Constable, "Aelred of Rievaulx and the Nun of Watton: An episode in the Early History of the Gilbertine Order," in *Medieval Women,* ed. Derek Baker (Oxford: Basil Blackwell, 1978), 205–26. The incident, however, attracted the attention of Lina Eckenstein, who included a discussion in her *Woman Under*

Monasticism (Cambridge: Cambridge University Press, 1890), as did Sharon K. Elkins in *Holy Women of Twelfth-Century England* (Chapel Hill: University of North Carolina Press, 1988). These studies focus on the behavior of the nun and what the story can reveal about attitudes towards women and sexual temptation in double monasteries. For a discussion of stories about the sexual transgressions of nuns, see Ruth Mazo Karras, "The Virgin and the Pregnant Abbess: Miracles and Gender in the Middle Ages," *Medieval Perspectives* 3, no. 2 (1988): 112–32.

38. Jo Ann McNamara, trans., "The Nun of Watton," *Magistra* 1, no. 12 (1995): 122–37, at 131.

39. Ibid., 132.

40. Ibid.

41. Ibid.

42. Jacqueline Murray, " 'The Law of Sin That is in My Members': The Problem of Male Embodiment," in *Gender and Holiness.*, ed. Samantha J. E. Riches and Sarah Salih (London: Routledge, 2002), 9–22.

43. Caroline Bynum has provided a useful caution to historians to avoid assuming that medieval people understood the genitals as erotic or necessarily associated with sexual activity. Caroline Walker Bynum, "The Body of Christ in the Late Middle Ages: A Reply to Leo Steinberg," in *Fragmentation and Redemption,* 85–88.

44. The enduring nature of this view of the penis is reflected in the title of a recent popular book: David M. Friedman, *A Mind of Its Own: A Cultural History of the Penis* (New York: The Free Press, 2001).

45. John Benton has suggested that Guibert's discussion of Thomas of Marle, for example, may have been a fabrication and the product of his own troubled imagination (*Self and Society in Medieval France,* 24).

46. Numerous variations of this story are found across Europe, in a variety of vernacular languages. For examples see Stith Thompson, *Motif-Index of Folk-Literature,* rev. ed. (Bloomington: Indiana University Press, 1955), 5:232, 408, 465.

47. Benton, *Self and Society in Medieval France,* 219.

48. Ibid., 27.

49. Ibid., 218.

50. Bynum, "Reply to Leo Steinberg," *Fragmentation and Redemption,* 117.

51. *Malleus Maleficarum, maleficas et earum haeresim framae conterens* (Lugduni: Bourgeat, 1669; rpt. Brussels: Culture et civilisation, 1969), 1.9. There is an English translation available: *The Malleus Maleficarum of Heinrich Kramer and James Sprenger,* trans. Montague Summers (London: Rodker, 1928; rpt. New York: Dover, 1971). For an overview of the intellectual and cultural background of the *Malleus,* see Edward Peters, *The Magician, the Witch and the Law* (Philadelphia: University of Pennsylvania Press, 1978). On the importance and influence of the *Malleus,* see Elaine Camerlynck, "Féminité et sorcellerie chez théoriciens de la démonolgie à la fin du Moyen Age: Etude du *Malleus Maleficarum,*" *Renaissance and Reformation* 19 (1983): 13–25, and Sydney Anglo, "Evident Authority and Authoritative Evidence: The *Malleus Maleficarum,*" in *The Damned Art: Essays in the Literature of Witchcraft,* ed. S. Anglo (London: Routledge and Kegan Paul, 1977), 1–31. For a challenging discussion of the complexities posed by the *Malleus Maleficarum,* from the

perspective of cultural studies, see Kathleen Biddick, "Becoming Ethnographic: Reading Inquisitorial Authority in *The Hammer of Witches,*" in *Figures of Speech: The Body in Medieval Art, History, and Literature,* ed. Allen J. Frantzen and David A. Robertson, Essays in Medieval Studies 11 (Chicago: Illinois Medieval Association, 1995), 21–38.

52. *Malleus Maleficarum,* 1.9. Much the same discussion occurs in 2.1.7.

53. Ibid., 1.9.

54. It is important to note that Freud, too, linked castration anxiety to psychogenic impotence and misogyny. *Freud: Dictionary of Psychoanalysis,* ed. Nandor Fodor and Frank Gaynor (Greenwich, Conn.: Fawcett. 1966), p. 22 s.v. Castration Anxiety.

CHAPTER 14

Knighthood, Compulsory Heterosexuality, and Sodomy

Ruth Mazo Karras

Both scholarly and popular conceptions of the ideology of knighthood in the central and late Middle Ages are deeply intertwined with notions of heterosexual romantic love. Part of being a knight, in narrative convention if not in real life, was acquiring the love of elite women.[1] But the heterosexual relations into which knights enter, in chivalric literature and in historical account, are highly ritualized. Love is a game at which a good knight must succeed, but sexual desire, even if consummated, does not always imply emotional intimacy. Nor does participating in such a game define a knight's "orientation" or make him a "heterosexual." One might speak of the game of love as a type of "compulsory heterosexuality," in the sense that society demands certain behaviors from individuals that do not correspond to the individual's desires; in this case, the behavior is required in order to live up to the chivalric ideal.[2] "Heterosexual" is a highly anachronistic term here, however; nor did participating in the love of ladies make a knight not "homosexual." Engagement in one sort of relationship did not exclude others.

Recent scholarship has argued that the bond between knight and lady is not the only important one in chivalric literature (and life). The homosocial or homoerotic bonds between Amicus and Amelius, Lancelot and Gareth, even Troilus and Pandarus, sometimes compete with heterosocial and heteroerotic commitments, sometimes complement them (a wife for reproduction, a fellow knight for companionship).[3] These bonds could sometimes lead to the suspicion of sodomy. Mathew Kuefler and Richard Zeikowitz argue, for different historical contexts and genres of evidence, that fears or accusations of sodomy were politically motivated, though they disagree on whether such concerns led to a problematization of male intimacy.[4]

Aristocrats (including knights), like the higher clergy, because they held political power, were vulnerable to politically motivated accusations or suspicions of sodomy. However, in some ways, knights would have been less vulnerable than clerics. Both would have had ample opportunities to form intimate friendships with other men, leading in some cases to sexual activity. However, sodomy was not a question of sexual orientation or preference as much as it was a matter of gender inversion.

Sodomy, of course, was an "utterly confused category" in the Middle Ages, a generalized term for disorder and unnatural activity, but when it denoted a specific sexual act it was generally anal penetration.[5] A man could penetrate a woman anally, and this was unacceptable to a church that made reproductive potential the only positive value for sexual activity, but this behavior was still not condemned as harshly as anal penetration of one man by another. To be penetrated was to be feminine; therefore a woman who was penetrated in the wrong place might violate her reproductive nature but not her femininity. A man who was penetrated, however, was feminized.

To be feminized, of course, was unacceptable for a knight. But knights had other ways of proving their manhood that might provide a counterbalance to sexual suspicion. Knightly masculinity was expressed primarily through the successful use of violence, and demonstrated prowess in battle might go a long way toward immunizing a man against accusations of femininity. In addition, as long as he played the game of heterosexual love, establishing himself as the active partner/penetrator, a man did not have to restrict himself to it exclusively. Thus bonds knights formed with each other on or off the battlefield might be safer because a knight had a presumption of masculinity that a cleric did not.

Not all knights, however, could participate in the system of compulsory heterosexuality. Beginning in the twelfth century, the "New Knighthood" so highly praised by Bernard of Clairvaux combined the prowess expected from aristocratic warriors with the asceticism of monastic vows. The military orders were founded with the goal of defending pilgrimage routes to the Holy Places, including the crusader states through which these routes ran; their task brought together religious and secular ambitions, as did the Crusades themselves for many secular knights. The Templars, the first order to take up expressly military activities, were most likely officially established in 1120. The Hospitallers dated back to the late eleventh century, when they were concerned with caring for pilgrims, and became a formal order in 1113, although they did not take on military responsibilities until the 1130s. Other orders followed: the Orders of Calatrava, Santiago, and Alcántara in Spain in the 1150s through 1170s, the Teutonic Knights in the Holy Land in 1198, the Sword-Brothers in Livonia in 1202, and the Order of Dobrzyń in Prussia in 1222. While they may have been relatively few in number compared to those who took temporary crusade vows, the members of the military orders, especially the Templars, caught medieval imaginations as they have caught modern ones as well.[6] The Templars, Hospitallers (Order of St. John of Jerusalem), and Teutonic Knights, the great transnational military orders, received papal support and remained relatively independent of local bishops and secular authorities. Although they were not universally admired, the fact that they were criticized for their ambition is a reflection of the power and prestige they amassed. Secular knights may have had the same goals—military prowess and defense of the faith—but the military orders were centered upon them and (in their conception at any rate) embodied what they saw as the best of both knighthood and monasticism: a virtuous life and the active support of religion.

The military orders took their vows of celibacy seriously. We have no way of knowing whether the members violated those vows any more or less frequently than the members of other religious orders; but of all the suspicions and accusations leveled against the military orders, in literature or in legal proceedings, sexual accusations, involving either women or men, were relatively uncommon until the prosecutions of the Templars under Philip the Fair.[7] The Templars' rule went into more detail than that of the Teutonic Knights about the dangers of sexual involvement with men, although the two treat involvement with women in a similar manner. The Rule of the Templars, in its 1165 version, held:

> The company of women is a dangerous thing, for by it the old devil has led many from the straight path to Paradise. Henceforth, let not ladies be admitted as sisters into the house of the Temple. . . . We believe it to be a dangerous thing for any religious to look upon the face of woman. For this reason none of you may presume to kiss a woman, be it widow, young girl, mother, sister, aunt or any other; and henceforth the Knighthood of Jesus Christ should avoid at all costs the embraces of women.[8]

An additional, later passage states that a brother who "enters an evil place, or a house of iniquity, with a sinful woman, alone or in bad company" was to lose his habit and be put in irons.[9] However, the rule also mentions, in a section again added later, that a brother may be expelled from the house if he "is tainted with the filthy, stinking sin of sodomy, which is so filthy and so stinking and so repugnant that it should not be named." The other offenses that rank with this are the killing of a Christian man or woman, simony, cowardice, heresy, and the like. A group of *exempla* or case studies, which date from 1257–67, reiterate and amplify the offenses that warrant expulsion. Only one *exemplum* is given about male-male sex, here described as "if a brother does anything against nature": "At Château Pélerin there were brothers who practiced wicked sin and caressed each other in their chambers at night; so that those who knew of the deed and others who had suffered greatly by it, told this thing to the Master and to a group of the worthy men of the house." Imprisoned, one of the three men escaped "to the Saracens," one died while attempting to escape, and one remained in irons. With only one *exemplum* this section is shorter than many, but the passage on brothers punished with loss of the habit for having sex with women includes no *exempla*.[10]

The rule of the Teutonic Order treats offenses with women and with men similarly to the prescriptions of the Templar Rule, from which it borrows (although on these particular topics the borrowings are not exact): "They shall avoid conversations in suspect places and times with women and especially with young women and especially detest their kisses, which are signs of secular love and lasciviousness, so that they should not even kiss their own mothers and sisters." If a house of the order had women servants, "a dwelling should be prepared for such women outside the habitation of the brethren, for the chastity of members of the order, even if it is preserved, cannot remain long safely or without scandal."[11] Evidently no such scandal attached to relations with men. However, in setting out offenses according to seriousness, the Rule makes it a third-level offense "if a brother sins with a woman" and a fourth level offense "if a brother commits the unmentionable sin of intercourse with men." The sanction for the latter, as for cowardice and paganism, was expulsion from the order, although a later hand in one German MS of the rule adds a penalty of perpetual imprisonment for the unmentionable sin.[12]

Although as vowed celibates they could not participate in the compulsory heterosexuality of service to the lady, at least in the Teutonic Order knights could substitute service to the Virgin Mary. The order was officially established as the Brothers of the Hospital of St. Mary of the Germans in Jerusalem, and its lands in Prussia were known as the patrimony of the Virgin. Much of the devotional literature produced within the order is directed toward Marian piety (Sts. Barbara, Elizabeth, Maurice, and George were also prominent). This literature included a life of Mary by Philip the Carthusian, written specifically for the Teutonic Order; *Der Sünden Widerstreit* ("The Defense Against Sin"), which argues that chivalrous knights are pleasing to the Virgin; a *Passional* in which she appears as a helper in everyday life; and the work of Tilo von Kulm who presents Christ and his mother in a mystic marriage redolent of chivalric *Minnedienst*.[13] When Western European aristocrats in the late fourteenth and fifteenth centuries traveled to Prussia to take part in the Lithuanian "crusades," they found the Teutonic Knights holding tournaments (although this was prohibited by their rule); the lady these jousts honored was the Virgin.[14]

The Templars, like the Teutonic Knights, certainly had ample opportunity to demonstrate their masculinity through military prowess. However, this masculinity could itself be problematic for a celibate group. Knights may have had a presumption of masculinity that clerics did not, but with it came the obligation to maintain that masculinity. Monks, for example, could be seen as in a sense de-gendered, and therefore chastity was not conceptually problematic for them (however problematic it might be, on an individual psychological level, for them to maintain).[15] Knights, however, as definitely masculine, could be expected to have masculine desires, the desire to penetrate others with one sword or another. If they were not fulfilling that desire with women, they might be doing so with men. Again, to penetrate another man did not make the penetrator feminine, but it did make him implicit in the feminizing of another man, and sodomy accusations could be brought against both partners.

And sodomy accusations were indeed brought against the Templars. Philip IV of France had all the Templars in France arrested in October 1307. In November the pope required the rulers of other countries to do the same. While the pope established a commission to investigate the order, Philip went ahead and burned fifty-four members of the order in 1310. In 1312 the pope suppressed the order and some of its leaders were imprisoned or executed. Sodomy was not the primary charge; blasphemy (including spitting on the cross and denying Christ) and idolatry were the most important. There has been a huge amount of scholarly discussion about the accusations. Some of it has concerned their truth—particularly that of the sodomy and sorcery accusations, which are taken seriously even by scholars who do not think the blasphemy accusation has any basis in reality. Some of it has concerned the political motivations for it—the French crown's financial situation, its concern about the Templars as an alternative center of power, the need for a scapegoat for the failure of the Crusades, the failure of the order to take on new tasks (or its choice to stick to its original mandate). More recently it has concerned the discourse of the accusations themselves: given the political motivations for the accusations, why were these particular charges selected, and what do they tell us about the way people in the Middle Ages understood sodomy (and idolatry, blasphemy, and the other counts)?[16]

The sodomy accusations against the Templars did not assert merely that members of the order committed sodomy with each other, or even that the order tolerated such behavior. Had they been restricted to such allegations, they would not be at all implausible. A wide variety of historical circumstances can give rise to "situational homosexuality," men engaging in sex with other men because they constitute the available partners. Religious orders in particular may have developed a self-selecting membership, as men chose to join who preferred the company, sexual and otherwise, of other men. Or, it could be that sexual desire between men was no more common in an order like the Templars than it was in society generally, but the atmosphere of intimacy in which men of the order lived allowed for the expression and gratification of that desire more than did other circumstances.

Quite a number of Templars testified that they were told it was permissible for brothers to have sex with one another, although they themselves had not done so.[17] It is possible that they were in fact told this, and that the order's unofficial policy (or at least the practice in some houses) was to look the other way. However, given that it was elicited under torture, it would be unwise to assume that it was true. As Anne Gilmour-Bryson points out, "although the Paris trial heard ninety-four Templars state that they had been told homosexual relations were licit, even obligatory in many cases, only two persons gave any direct evidence of its existence."[18] The testimony of one accused Templar, Raymond of Narbonne, that he was told that "it was worse sin to lie with women than with men, and that therefore, if nature should move him to lust, he would approach other brothers," may be plausible.[19] It was not, of course, official order policy, but brothers might well be concerned that members having sex with women might lead to public scandal, whereas members engaging in sex with each other could be kept quiet.

The sodomy accusations, however, alleged more than the occasional or even frequent and permitted practice of male-male intercourse. They alleged that such practices were mandatory: John of Cugy, for example, testified that at his initiation the presiding official commanded him in regard to sodomy that "wherever he would go, he would do the will of the brothers, and that he would have sex with the brothers safely and not deny himself to them . . . but he never did it, because he was never asked."[20] Nevertheless most of the testimony about sodomy speaks not to ritualized practices at initiation but to more private relationships among brothers. The most comprehensive recent analysis of the accusations is that of Anne Gilmour-Bryson, who points out that Templars confessed to these practices only within the jurisdiction of the French crown and in Italy, both places where torture was used.[21] Elsewhere, the same accusations were made, but there were no confessions. The confessions, then, cannot be taken as evidence of practice, leaving scholars to question the prima facie plausibility of the accusations. The sodomy accusation must be seen in the context of the accusations of blasphemy and heresy (specifically, the renunciation of Christ) and idolatry—the worship of a large idol in the shape of a head, or even a demonic cat. Some scholars chose to believe that the Templars had picked up these practices during their years in the Holy Land and had become, in essence, heretics. Contemporary scholarly consensus, however, regards this aspect of the Templar myth in a much more skeptical fashion, and concurs that, while there may have been individual Templars who sodomized (or blasphemed), it was not likely to have been part of the order's procedures.

Before turning from the Templars to the Teutonic Knights, it is worth considering the cultural significance of these accusations, which is none the less for their being dubious or false. Boswell argued in *CSTH* that the thirteenth century saw the turn to persecution of sodomites, and R. I. Moore elaborated on this argument, claiming that it was part of governmental claims to control the social order, due to a fear that difference was not only different but subversive.[22] Zeikowitz argues that the false accusations indicate sodomy was both a real and a plausible concern in the early fourteenth century.[23] But fanciful accusations coupled with claims of idolatry suggest that things by this time were a bit different: that instead of, or alongside, real concern with sodomy (which did continue in the fourteenth century, for example in the case of Edward II and in accusations by the Lollards against the clergy, as well as a scattering of cases from around Europe) it had also become a bogeyman, like Communism in the U.S. in the 1950s, to be used as a convenient accusation against political opponents.[24]

Like the Templars, the Teutonic Knights ran afoul of established political authorities. Their position was unlike that of any other military order in that they were not only an international order but also rulers of Prussia. Although their initial establishment in Prussia in 1229 came at the invitation of Duke Conrad of Mazovia, a member of the Piast dynasty, they had insisted that both he and the Emperor Frederick II, as well as the pope, guarantee their independence of action. By 1295 they had become established as rulers of a territorial state, bordering on Poland and generally with friendly or neutral relations with that country. After the fall of Acre in 1291 Prussia became the main focus of the Teutonic Order (although its headquarters remained at Venice until 1309, when they were moved to Marienburg [Malbork]).

In 1308 the Teutonic Knights seized Pomerelia, including the port of Gdansk (Danzig), already an important trade center, which had been within the Polish sphere of influence. This was difficult to justify on crusading grounds; most of the order's other conquests had been fighting against pagans, or at least recent converts whose Christianity could well be doubted, but Pomerelia was firmly Christian and not allied with the Lithuanians, the order's main pagan adversaries at the time. Pomerelia was caught between the Margrave of Brandenburg and the Polish crown; one faction called on the Teutonic knights for assistance against Brandenburg. They were only too glad to provide it, and in the process ended up seizing Pomerelia for themselves, paying the Margrave to acquire what they considered formal legal possession.[25] German and Polish historians in the twentieth century tended to have different views of the situation, diverging both on the question of whether Pomerelia really "belonged" to Poland and also on the degree of ferocity of the order's conquest.[26]

In 1311 a papal representative arrived in Livonia to hear witnesses in a conflict between the order and the bishop of Riga. All parties involved would have been aware of the ongoing prosecution of the Templars. Included among the accusations against the Teutonic Knights were atrocities committed at Gdansk/Danzig, including the massacre of ten thousand Christians, including infants in the womb. The order and all its members were excommunicated, but the excommunication was lifted after the Grand Master traveled to Avignon and met with the pope. The Polish king then brought another complaint before the pope, specifically dealing with Pomerelia. In 1321 and again in 1339 the order was commanded to return Pomerelia as well as other lands to the Polish crown. It did not, however, obey the command.

The fairness of the decision has been questioned on several grounds, including the pope's financial interests (territory belonging to the Polish crown paid Peter's Pence to Rome, that belonging to the Teutonic Knights did not). Of interest to us here, however, are the kinds of arguments used by the Poles to make their case against the order. This would seem to be a key moment at which an accusation of sodomy could enter. The Templar affair had repercussions across Europe. The Templars themselves had houses in Poland. The advisors of the Polish king (Władislaw Łokietek, at the time of the trial in 1320–21; Kasimierz III, at the time of the 1339 proceedings) would certainly have been aware of the blasphemy, idolatry, and sodomy accusations. The sodomy accusation, in particular, might have been even more plausible against the Teutonic Knights than it was against the Templars. The Templars were not mobilized for military action at the time of the accusations; some of their houses were located in towns where they could have had access to female prostitutes or other women, thus removing one of the bases for "situational" sodomy. They were not permitted to leave the house without permission and could lose the habit for doing so, but it is possible that such rules were not always enforced. The Teutonic Knights in Prussia, however, remained on a military footing and lived mainly in fortresses; servants or peasant women would have been available to them but one might surmise that their more isolated life might result in more sexual relations between members of the order.

The Polish crown did not hesitate to make serious accusations against the Teutonic Knights. Witnesses in the 1321 proceeding included the bishop of Wladislavia (Włocławek), who claimed that "when the lord king, at that time duke, was in possession of that land, the preceptors and commanders and other crusaders of the Teutonic House, invading the town of Gdansk under arms, occupied it by violence, making a great massacre of the knights and Christian people there." Another witness, Lestko, duke of Cujavia, was more specific: "they savagely killed fifty knights, besides townsmen [*villanos*] whose number I do not know, some in churches . . . not respecting sex or age." Count Peter Drogoslawicz of Poznań said that they "made an abominable massacre, and killed the nobles of that land, knights and their wives and children." Other witnesses said that victims were "dragged from the altars of the churches," that so many were killed that "the very dogs lapped up the human blood," that the knights "cruelly put them to the sword in a pagan manner [*more gentilico*]." [27] The testimony was stylized and formulaic (many of the twenty-five witnesses used the same words); the point is that the repeated formulae involved the illegal seizure of land and the killing of civilians, not religious or sexual transgressions.

When sexual transgressions were involved, as in 1339, when the Poles complained about additional territorial incursions, these involved the rape of women. The accusations included "the dishonoring [*stupracionem*] of virgins and honest women," as well as the burning of towns and seizure of livestock and goods. [28] One witness testified that "he saw in Uneyow virgins and other women weeping and wailing about them, because they had disfigured and violated them, and he saw the church of Uneyow and the whole town burned by the said Knights." Another said that, while he himself had only heard about the rapes by hearsay, "his wife had a maid who was violated by them, and a certain other woman was killed by them at the home of a friend of his, because she would not give her consent to them." [29]

What was it about the circumstances that made these accusations the tool of choice rather than the same charges that had been brought against the Templars? One answer, or partial answer, may be that they chose to bring accusations that were true, or that they believed to be true, or that had some kernel of truth to them, rather than trumped-up charges. If the Teutonic Knights' behavior was such as to give the Poles plenty to criticize, there was no need for them to borrow trouble. Instead of accusing the order of renouncing Christianity as the Templars had supposedly done, they could accuse them of mistreating Christians and indeed, as they did over the next hundred years, of hampering the spread of Christianity by their mistreatment of conquered pagan people (as suggested by an anonymous Carthusian writing in the fifteenth century).[30] The accusations were not symbolic as in the case of the Templars, but real; I am not asserting here that they were true in an absolute sense, but that they were plausible and possibly sincere in a way the accusations against the Templars were not.

The nature of the authorities bringing the accusations also explains in part the differences in those accusations. Philip the Fair brought charges in his own courts against knights living in a land he ruled; the Avignon papacy had to acquiesce in those charges. The Polish crown, on the other hand, had no jurisdiction over the Teutonic Knights and had to bring charges that would convince the papal legates, rather than presenting them with a *fait accompli*. The Poles could hardly expect that the curia would wish to suppress the only remaining successful military order.[31]

Nevertheless it would still have been possible for the Poles to introduce accusations of sodomy and blasphemy, not with the goal of suppressing the order but merely to discredit it so as to obtain the return of the lands it had seized. The availability of plausible accusations against the Teutonic Knights does not explain why it was deemed unnecessary to introduce more symbolic ones as well. The blasphemy, idolatry, and sodomy accusations against the Templars were all ways of connecting them with the evil Other. Why were the Teutonic Knights not vulnerable to such claims? At least with regard to the sodomy accusation, the answer has to do with medieval understandings of masculinity.

The Teutonic Knights, like the Templars, rejected the compulsory heterosexuality of knighthood. However, they demonstrated their masculinity on a continuing basis in other ways, through their continued military activities. Those military activities, in the view of the Poles and others, were prolonged beyond necessity, executed too harshly against pagans, directed against Christians when the pagans were sufficiently subdued. But excess of military activity was by no means unmasculine. Thus, because it could transfer its headquarters to Marienburg in Prussia where it already had a crusade underway, the Teutonic Order did not cease effective military activity after defeat in the Holy Land. After the failure of their efforts in the Levant, culminating in the fall of Acre in 1291, the Templars too undertook other military projects, in Spain and in the Baltic, but not on as large a scale. They attempted to put together a navy and to raise funds for more activity in the Holy Land, but major military initiatives were in abeyance, pending funding.

The kinds of accusations that could be brought against an active army—especially one sitting on the border of the accuser—were quite different from those that could be brought against a defeated army engaged in fundraising, and this helps explain the lack of sodomy charges. It might perhaps be thinkable that the Teutonic Knights raped boys or men as well as women among the numerous war captives they took in Prussia (although the sources do not say this). However, if they were sodomizing each other as the Templars were accused of doing, it would mean that they were playing the passive or feminine role, less plausible for the currently militarily active. The masculinity demonstrated through active military pursuits acted as a sort of prophylactic against accusations of effeminacy. They were in effect exempted from "compulsory heterosexuality"—the fact that they did not play the game of love need not, in their case, result in charges of sodomy.

Foundational work in a field, even if it remains influential or even definitive a quarter-century later, always requires revision and modification. In *CSTH*, Boswell employed the category of "gay" without distinguishing between the active and passive partner. Had he lived to see the flowering of research on medieval gender and sexualities during the 1990s, I believe he would have come to acknowledge the importance of that difference. Gender played a much greater role in the understanding of medieval homosexual behavior than Boswell discussed, and masculinity established through military success precluded the accusation of femininity implicit in charges of sodomy within the order.

. *Notes*

I am grateful to Ann Gilmour-Bryson, Michael Lower, and Klaus Van Eickels for their comments.

1. See discussion, with extensive references to previous literature, in Ruth Mazo Karras, *From Boys to Men: Formations of Masculinity in Late Medieval Europe* (Philadelphia: University of Pennsylvania Press, 2003), 47–57. For the central Middle Ages, see Constance Brittain Bouchard, *Strong of Body, Brave and Noble: Chivalry and Society in Medieval France* (Ithaca: Cornell University Press, 1998), 129–44.

2. The term comes from Adrienne Rich, "Compulsory Heterosexuality and Lesbian Existence," *Signs* 5 (1980): 631–60.

3. Mathew Kuefler, "Male Friendship and the Suspicion of Sodomy in Twelfth-Century France," in *Gender and Difference in the Middle Ages,* ed. Sharon Farmer and Carol Braun Pasternack (Minneapolis: University of Minnesota Press, 2003), 145–81; Richard E. Zeikowitz, *Homoeroticism and Chivalry: Discourses of Male Same-Sex Desire in the Fourteenth Century* (New York: Palgrave Macmillan, 2003).

4. Zeikowitz (149) argues that the existence of a "normative homoeroticism" in the fourteenth century did not mean that all intimate male friendships were suspected of sodomy; rather, it created a culture vulnerable to a discourse of sodomy; Kuefler (172) suggests that fear of intimacy between men led to a change in fundamental understandings of masculinity in the twelfth century.

5. Michel Foucault, *The History of Sexuality,* vol. 1, *An Introduction,* trans. Robert Hurley (New York: Vintage, 1990), 101; Karma Lochrie, *Covert Operations: The Medieval Uses of Secrecy* (Philadelphia: University of Pennsylvania Press, 1999), 179–99; Mark Jordan, *The Invention of Sodomy in Christian Theology* (Chicago: University of Chicago Press, 1997), esp. 1–9.

6. Many of the standard works on the Templars have a chapter on their *Nachleben:* see Malcolm Barber, *The New Knighthood: A History of the Order of the Temple* (Cambridge: Cambridge University Press, 1994), 314–34; Helen Nicholson, *The Knights Templar: A New History* (Stroud, Gloucestershire: Sutton, 2001), 238–46. Peter Partner, *The Murdered Magicians: The Templars and their Myth* (Oxford: Oxford University Press, 1981), 89–180, develops the discussion of the Templar myth more fully.

7. Helen Nicholson, *Templars, Hospitallers, and Teutonic Knights: Images of the Military Orders, 1128–1291* (Leicester: Leicester University Press, 1993), 131–33.

8. *The Rule of the Templars: The French Text of the Rule of the Order of the Knights Templar,* trans. J. M. Upton-Ward (Woodbridge, Suffolk: Boydell Press, 1992), 70–71, p. 36.

9. *Rule of the Templars,* 236, p. 74.

10. Rule of the Templars, 418, p. 112; 572–73, p, 148; 594, p. 154.

11. Max Perlbach, ed., *Die Statuten des Deutschen Ordens nach den ältesten Handschriften* (Halle a.S.: Max Niemeyer, 1890), Regel 28, pp. 49–50, and 31, pp. 52–53.

12. Perlbach, *Die Statuten,* Gesetze 38, pp. 838–84, and 39, pp. 85–87; Klaus Militzer, *Von Akkon zur Marienberg: Verfassung, Erwaltung und Sozialstruktur des Deutschen Ordens 1190–1309,* Quellen und Studien zur Geschichte des Deutschen Ordens, 56 (Marburg: N.G. Elwert Verlag, 1999), 92–93. I translate here from the earliest text, in Middle High German, and the Middle Dutch version is similar; the Old French and Latin translations say in the first instance "If he falls into a sin of the flesh" and in the second "If someone commits the detestable vice of sodomy." Presumably the more serious status of sodomy implies that the "sin of the flesh" is not sodomitical, but it is interesting that they omit the qualification that it is with a woman; this could mean that the translator(s) simply assumed it would be with a woman, or that they wished to be more inclusive.

13. Karl Helm and Walther Ziesemer, *Die Literatur des Deutschen Ritterordens,* Giessener Beiträge zur deutschen Philologie, 94 (Giessen: Wihelm Schmitz Verlag, 1951); Mary Ellen

Goenner, *Mary-Verse of the Teutonic Knights,* Catholic University of America Studies in German, 19 (Washington, D.C.: Catholic University of America Press, 1943), esp. 35, 75, 82–139.

14. Werner Paravicini, *Die Preussenreisen des Europäischen Adels* (Sigmaringen: J. Thorbecke Verlag, 1989), 1:303.

15. R. N. Swanson, "Angels Incarnate: Clergy and Masculinity from Gregorian Reform to Reformation," in *Masculinity in Medieval Europe,* ed. D. M. Hadley (London: Longman, 1999), 160–77, discusses the clergy as a third gender, although he does not suggest that masculinity was therefore not problematic for them.

16. For a recent summary see Malcolm Barber, "The Trial of the Templars Revisited," in *The Military Orders,* vol. 2, *Welfare and Warfare,* ed. Helen Nicholson (Aldershot: Ashgate, 1998), 329–42.

17. Anne Gilmour-Bryson, "Sodomy and the Knights Templar," *Journal of the History of Sexuality* 7 (1996), 170–75.

18. Gilmour-Bryson, "Sodomy," 177.

19. Konrad Schottmüller, *Der Untergang des Templerordens* (Berlin: Mittler und Sohn, 1887), 2:29.

20. Schottmüller, *Der Untergang,* 2:41. Further examples cited in Gilmour-Bryson, "Sodomy and the Knights Templar," 168–81.

21. Gilmour-Bryson, "Sodomy and the Knights Templar," 153–54.

22. John Boswell, *Christianity, Social Tolerance, and Homosexuality: Gay People in Western Europe from the Beginning of the Christian Era to the Fourteenth Century* (Chicago: University of Chicago Press, 1980), 269–302; R. I. Moore, *The Formation of a Persecuting Society: Power and Deviance in Western Europe, 950–1250* (Oxford: Blackwell, 1987), 91–94 on sodomites and *passim* for the argument about the protection of the social order from subversion.

23. Zeikowitz, *Homoeroticism and Chivalry,* 107–11.

24. On Edward II see Zeikowitz, *Homoeroticism and Chivalry,* 111–18; on Lollards, Carolyn Dinshaw, *Getting Medieval: Sexualities and Communities, Pre- and Postmodern* (Durham: Duke University Press, 1999), 55–99; on both, Ruth Mazo Karras, "The Lechery that Dare Not Speak its Name: Sodomy and the Vices in Medieval England," in *In the Garden of Evil: The Vices and Culture in the Middle Ages,* ed. Richard Newhauser (Toronto: PIMS Press, 2005).

25. The narrative here comes largely from Hartmut Boockman, *Der Deutsche Orden: Zwölf Kapitel aus seiner Geschichte* (Munich: C. H. Beck, 1982), 138–50. The primary sources are found in *Scriptores Rerum Prussicarum,* ed. T. Hirsch, M. Toeppen and E. Strehlke, 5 vols. (Leipzig, 1861–74).

26. See Michael Burleigh, *Germany Turns Eastward: A Study of Ostforschung in the Third Reich* (Cambridge: Cambridge University press, 1988) for a chilling account of the political ramifications of the question; see esp. 207 for a 1939 attempt to prove that the Kashubians and other groups were not Poles.

27. *Lites ac res gestae inter Polonos Ordinemque Cruciferorum,* 2d ed., vol. 1, ed. Z. Celichowski (Poznań: Bibliotek Kórnickéj, 1890), 19, 21, 25, 28, 29, 32.

28. *Lites ac res gestae,* 97.

29. *Lites ac res gestae,* 180, 204; also 185, 189, 208, 214, 223, 229, 245, 257, 276, 308, 310, 326, 328, 330, 331, 334, 346, (some with specific details, some just testifying in a general way to the truth of the rape accusations).

30. "Die Ermahnung des Carthäusers," ed. Theodor Hirsch, *Scriptores Rerum Prussicarum* 4:448–65, esp. 461. The date of this work is given as 1428 in the text of a chronicle that incorporates it, though some scholars suggest it was written in the 1440s.

31. I am grateful to Michael Lower for pointing this out.

CHAPTER 15

The Body of Gerardesca of Pisa Reclothed and Resexed

Penelope D. Johnson

The extraordinary work and teaching of John E. Boswell contributed to the new ways in which scholars now think about gender in the Middle Ages. *Christianity, Social Tolerance, and Homosexuality* is a massive scholarly achievement, one not without flaws, but a work which has quickly become a study to which other scholars must respond and will continue to do so for years to come. Not only was the work important to the beginnings of queer history but also to the gay rights movement. A further benefit of John Boswell's publications and teaching was to serve as an important impetus in the development of the entire field of gender studies. In my case, studying with Boswell deepened my desire to ask questions about women's experience in the Middle Ages, and particularly to explore the slippery intersections and overlappings of gender. The *vita* of Gerardesca of Pisa, a thirteenth-century holy woman who had been married, exposes how a religious woman's problematic sexual past could be transformed through visionary experience.

Medieval holy women have become familiar to us in the landscape of medieval spirituality in recent scholarship.[1] Positive and negative interpretations of their behavior abound; various methodologies, typologies, and theoretical models have been applied to make sense of their behavior.[2] In most cases we know their lives through the filter of a male pen, most commonly that of the woman's confessor; the ways in which this transmission affects the story are being weighed by scholars along with the goals of the *vitae*—such as advocacy for canonization—to assess female *vitae*.[3] In this examination of a female visionary's recorded spiritual experiences, my intention is not to ask who wrote the life or specifically whose voice is represented; rather, I am assuming that whoever the author may be, the *vita* is a text that contains thirteenth-century concerns shared by at least some contemporary lay and clerical people who sought to live holy lives. Reading the text in this way one is struck by the importance of dressing the body and how reclothing seems to shift or disguise gender in significant ways. Taking Boswell's advice to heart for this article, I am looking for the social assumptions that underlie Gerardesca's visions.

Gerardesca of Pisa was born probably in the first decade of the thirteenth century in Pisa. Although as a little girl she experienced a religious vocation, her wishes were ignored by her mother, and she was married. "Being unworldly she immersed herself—although it was against her will—in all the dangers and pleasures [*voluptatibus*] of marriage."[4] After a while, she felt remorse and shame that she was not pleasing God in her married life and turned to physical mortifications, like intensive praying, fasting, and performing six hundred genuflections at a time to remedy her fallen state. Although the young wife could not fulfill her desire for the religious life by wearing the outward trappings of a religious profession, she bore the habit in her mind.[5] When the couple seemed unable to conceive a child, Gerardesca's mother began fervent prayers for them to have a son. God appeared to the mother as she slept and told her that St. John the Evangelist would be as a son to Gerardesca, a promise that brought great joy both to the mother and to her daughter when she was told of this extraordinary favor. Gerardesca continued to implore her husband that they abandon marriage, eventually succeeding in talking him into jointly entering the religious life, he to become a monk at the monastery of San Savino, she to become a tertiary, living in a cell just outside the monastery's walls.[6] This was a painful decision for her husband, who since puberty had enjoyed sexual activity.[7]

Gerardesca's next reclothing of her body came when she actually put on the monastic habit, an act with sublime implications for the saintly woman who deeply regretted the loss of her virginity and had been envisioning herself decked out in the habit for so long. Gerardesca "who while in the world never appeared happy, never appeared joyous, after receiving the habit of holy religion, found happiness . . . so that her face and eyes . . . sparkled with boundless eagerness."[8] Dressing in the monastic habit of self-denial, penitence, and chastity might be expected to accompany a muting of personal affect. But this was hardly the case for Gerardesca, who was transformed from a state of depression and self-loathing into one of radiant joyfulness.

The written record we have of Gerardesca's religious life is somewhat atypical in that although the holy woman performs some extraordinary spiritual feats, the emphasis is on her visionary experience rather than her miracles, and very little is recounted of her life and acts. Accounts of the visions occupy the bulk of the text, numbering forty-six in the work that survives.[9]

The author is not named, nor is the author's relationship to Gerardesca ever specified, although Elizabeth Petroff suggests that the author may be the monk who is extremely important for the holy woman and for whom she often seeks spiritual favors.[10] We do not know the name, the order, or the relationship to the saint of this man, who is referred to simply as *religiosus devotus,* but it is clear that Gerardesca wanted every spiritual benefit—as well as some worldly ones—for her monastic friend. The visions also reveal that this monk was not always as good a monk as he should have been. Eight visions include him, half of which suggest some of Gerardesca's worries about him. In two the holy woman receives assurances that no sin will at the end of his life block the monk from entering heaven: in one a dove whispers in her ear that the monk will be free of sin and in the other St. John the Evangelist reassures her that the monk will gain eternal salvation.[11] Why Gerardesca needed visionary reassurance becomes evident in two other visions in which the holy woman receives directives from the Virgin Mary to pass on to her friend the monk:

> For this reason you may say to that said monk that he should wholly take care to obey his prelate, whom he does not fear to challenge, for obedience pleases God no less than the host which brings salvation.[12]

The other four visions that involve this monk elevate him into the most exalted ranks in paradise. On Christmas Eve, the Feast of the Nativity, Gerardesca has a glorious vision in which she sees saints and angels, Christ, and St. John the Evangelist ascending to the heavenly Jerusalem to meet the Virgin descending to receive gloves and a ring from her Son and to be clothed by St. John in a wondrous circular mantle. At the very moment when Gerardesca is rapt in this vision, her friend the monk is thinking about the glory that she is experiencing. The Virgin Mary then calls to Jesus and St. John to go and fetch the monk, who thereby becomes a participant in Gerardesca's vision. First he is standing by the Virgin Mary's side and holding onto her cloak, and then he is invited under its nurturing folds.[13] The vision comes to a close with the Virgin recommending the monk first to St. John and then to Christ.[14] Two of the other celebratory visions elevate the monk to the episcopacy, in one when he is given an episcopal mantle (*pluviale*) by the Virgin Mary, carried to her hands by St. John the Baptist and St. John the Evangelist, and the other in which the monk celebrates mass as a bishop alongside Christ, who is singing the eucharistic service.[15] Gerardesca not only wants her special monastic friend to behave himself but also thereby to gain clerical advancement and finally a heavenly resting place. The assurance of his advancement in holiness and ultimate salvation is signified by clothing that either incorporates the monk into the Virgin's robes or dresses him in ecclesiastical garb.

Once Gerardesca took the habit she was theoretically liberated from her husband's control, but she still had to deal with men in her life: indeed, her husband was not far away, since he was professed in the same house to which she was attached; she had received the habit from the abbot of San Savino, who was her close relative;[16] she had a confessor in her life, although we don't know his name; also, as we have seen, she maintained a close friendship with one particular monk; and finally she was beset by a group of friars from San Savino, who made life difficult for her and chose not to respect her.[17] All these relationships complicated the already difficult life of an enclosed tertiary—a life that she was attempting to lead attached to a male religious house. Yet, there was one man in Gerardesca's life who was uncomplicated and affirming: St. John the Evangelist. When Gerardesca's mother had her dream, she understood that St. John assumed the care of her daughter just as he had accepted the care of the Virgin Mary at the foot of the cross. This sharing by Gerardesca and the Virgin of the same holy supporter aided the saint in her transformation from "former wife" to religious woman. St. John appears in more than two-fifths of the visions. In one memorable long vision that takes Gerardesca into the heavenly Jerusalem, the preeminence of St. John the Evangelist is specifically noted as is his privileged relationship with Jesus: St. John alone may celebrate mass in heaven; only he touched the Virgin Mother at her Assumption; he alone orders the celestial kingdom.[18] For Gerardesca to have St. John the Evangelist as her son and protector is validation for the holy self she is struggling to affirm.

Added to the challenges inherent in her profession and in her physical location attached to San Savino were whatever personal conflicts she experienced; one such may have been that despite the traditional rhetoric in the *vita* emphasizing the holy woman's desire to be shed of her husband and their sexual life, Gerardesca may have found leaving her husband and their shared physical life wrenching. One vision that stands out from the rest offers clues and suggests that the holy woman needed to undergo a transformation.[19]

This vision, the twenty-sixth in the *vita,* is the only one in which Gerardesca suffers physical assault, the only time that Mary Magdalen appears among all the saints that people her visions, the only vision in which townsfolk feature almost as prominently as do the saints, and the only vision in which the holy woman repeatedly expresses fear and doubt. There is little that is generic about this vision, and much that suggests it springs from the saint's personal context and life experience. In other words, this vision may offer clues not only to how the religious life was *supposed* to be lived but also to real difficulties that had to be overcome in pursuit of holiness.

When Gerardesca is at prayer one night she experiences temptation.[20] A demon who is a lookalike of her husband, even wearing clothes resembling what he wore before his entry into the religious life, comes to whisper erotic suggestions to her. Gerardesca is terrified and feels that she is in great danger (*tanto periculo*). Would her former husband's sexual invitations feel like such a threat if she were without erotic desires? The holy woman answers the demon, saying that if he were indeed her husband she would kill him herself and consign him to the devil, which sounds like pretty strong stuff if she were uninterested in his blandishments. But the dangers of the flesh can be averted by physical penance, and just as she did to punish herself for the pleasures of marriage, now the demon does to her, scourging her brutally until blood spurts from her mouth and nose from the beating. The saint responds by thanking God for sending this trial to test her like gold between the hammer and anvil, a metaphor with sexual overtones, repeating the possibility that her vow of chastity is being tested.[21] But the demon is not done with her yet; he transports her to a suburb of Pisa, near the church of St. John Gaetano on the Arno River. Here he casts Gerardesca into a little boat, intending to drown her (*volens submergere ipsam*) by striking the boat and sloshing great amounts of water into the small craft. The terrified woman keeps crying out, but the demon continues his unceasing efforts to hurt her.

The saint feels herself tiring, and fears that she may not be able to resist any longer (*resistere non valeret*), and begins to call for the help of God, the Virgin Mary, and particularly St. John the Evangelist. The Virgin and St. John appear with a host of angels to help her, and the Queen of Heaven commands the angels to subdue the demon. The angelic army thrashes the demon soundly, throws him in the air, and flings him in the river. Then they pluck him out again to scourge him on the bank of the river, all to the accompaniment of horrible shrieking by a band of demons, which has assembled to bewail the pain of one of its own. The Virgin and St. John then conduct the saint into the nearby church and leave her there alone.

The reader might well expect the trials of the holy woman to be over now and for her to experience ineffable comfort from the ministrations of her divine rescuers. But, rather than feeling nurtured and safe, Gerardesca is consumed by anxiety that people may find her there alone; she worries "what will they say" (quid dicent). She does not know what to do, and then decides the safest move would be to go to the house of a kinsman and tell him everything that has transpired. But immediately, the next fear that comes to her mind is that he may not believe her (quid si non credet?). The poor woman is approaching her relative's house when she hears the bells for the morning office and changes her mind, deciding instead to go on home. Having made this decision, she crosses the street to head homeward when she sees the watchmen who are guarding the city's grain supply. Once again, fear of negative public opinion washes over her, and she feels helpless, wondering what she would say to the men if they approached her (Si hi venerint ad me, quid dicam? Ignoro quid faciam—Domine, succurre mihi). She walks onward towards the old bridge, when she sees a crowd of men (multitudinem hominum) and is again terrified. But two of the group coming towards her are dressed in women's clothes (in habitu mulierum). Instead of proving a threatening presence, these men/women identify themselves as neighbors and beg her to intercede with the Virgin—who is waiting in the church of St. Martin—to save them from further suffering with which they are afflicted. The ominous male crowd is doubly transformed; first it morphs into former neighbors who shift into nonthreatening female guise, and then the group becomes needy souls in purgatorial places, coming to Gerardesca for help rather than approaching to denounce her for being out alone in the city before dawn like a woman of ill repute. As the holy woman crosses over the Arno she looks back and sees the entire neighborhood sparkling and shining.

Gerardesca's next source of deep anxiety is how to come into the Virgin Mary's presence in her disheveled state: how dare she approach the Mother of God in her torn clothes? But the saint gathers her forces and continues bravely on her way. When Gerardesca finally stands at the feet of the Virgin, Mary deals gently with the bedraggled holy woman and asks Mary Magdalen to shelter Gerardesca under her cloak. After this healing welcome the holy woman goes joyfully with the two Marys, Jesus, St. John the Evangelist, and a great company of angels. As they are processing on their way, they pass by people who cry out to Gerardesca for her help. The Magdalen asks Gerardesca if she has anything she wants to say, and Gerardesca replies that she would like the Virgin Mother to accept the prayers of certain souls and free them from suffering purgatorial pains. In response, Mary Magdalen calls St. John to her and relates what the holy woman has asked. Just at that moment there appears the crowning moment of the vision: the Virgin walking along with the Christ

Child holding on to her belt in the way little children hang affectionately on their mothers' skirts. Mother and Son have a sweet exchange about the souls suffering in purgatorial places, which culminates in the Virgin reminding her hesitant Son that she is not called "Mater misericordiae" for nothing, and will never slam shut the door to her mercies. Christ, thereby encouraged to be empathetic, sends his angels to fling open the portals to Paradise for the saved and to consign the rest to a place of punishment.

The vision closes with the holy woman back home, surrounded by the Virgin, Christ, the Magdalen, and St. John the Evangelist. The Magdalen strips Gerardesca of her ruined garments to view the bruises left from the demon's assault, and the Virgin offers new clothing in conjunction with the kiss of peace, saying: "Because you did not desire to touch the demon with your mouth, I will sweetly kiss your mouth."[22]

This extraordinary vision shares many qualities of dreams with its jumbled events, out-of-context characters, transformations without causality, and strong feelings, which do not always seem appropriate to the setting. The overriding emotion felt by the holy woman is fear; she is frightened of the demon's sexual invitation, of public opinion, of her kinsman's reaction, of a vague, generalized male threatening presence, and of appearing slatternly before the Virgin Mary. "What people think" is a real issue, as it must have been in the Pisa of her day. When the demon appears in her former husband's guise, she—a previously married and sexually active woman—listens to his blandishments; this lapse, and perhaps her deeply regretted lost virginal status, demand corporal chastisement. In the vision the thrashing that is meted out is administered not by her own hand but by that of the demonic former husband lookalike.

For a pious medieval person, punishment was appropriate for impure thoughts. The tradition began with the desert fathers and was reinforced by early saints' *vitae* in which saintly sexual arousal was dealt with by various harsh self-inflicted torments. This tradition remained strong in thirteenth-century Tuscany. Blessed Aldobrandesca of Siena, a close saintly Tuscan contemporary of Gerardesca, became a tertiary of the Umiliati after she was left widowed and childless.[23] Her hagiographer reports in the *vita* that Aldobrandesca experienced demonic temptation, which often caused her when sleeping to remember the physical pleasures of married sex. Her solution to dealing with erotic dreams and memories was to rise from her bed, get down on her knees, and beat herself bloody with a chain. Only physical self-punishment could restore Aldobrandesca to spiritual health after her soul was soiled with impure thoughts.

The *vita* of Gerardesca needs to attest that visionary punishment is equal to the self-inflicted wounds of other female saints like Aldobrandesca. Thus, to ensure that the reader accepts the transformative reality of Gerardesca's visionary pain, the marks of her suffering are seen by the eyes of Christ, his Mother, and their two attendant saints, the Magdalen and St. John, proving the bodily reality of Gerardesca's payment for a former married life and her present resistance to sexual temptation. Eroticism is punished on the one hand by the harsh beating but is subverted on the other by inversion: it is a woman, a saint, who strips off her clothes rather than an eager male lover; it is the Queen of Heaven who gives a kiss rather than a demon/husband. All is made right and her shame and fear annulled by divine forgiveness.

Twice the damaged body of the saint is reclothed, and hence resexed. First, Gerardesca frets over the appropriateness of coming before the virgin Mother of God, when she herself is no longer intact, but is wearing torn clothing (*cum sim undique vestibus lacerata*). The empathetic Virgin Mother then chooses Mary Magdalen, the saint who above all personifies the fallen woman redeemed by divine love, and asks the Magdalen to take Gerardesca under her cloak and cover her.[24] Although this should have lain to rest the holy woman's fears, it fails to restore her fully, so that in the final scene of the vision, the torn clothing is entirely stripped away by the Magdalen, and it is the Virgin Mother herself who not only reclothes the saint but kisses her. The Virgin makes clear that her kiss is a reward for resisting kissing the demon/husband. In both cases Gerardesca's new garments restore her bodily integrity.

The dream/vision allows Gerardesca to articulate women's fear of male violence and sexual predation, a fear not without basis in the daily realities of women's experience.[25] The dangers of male attack are warded off by holy helpers who respond to her prayers and by ways in which clothing is manipulated.

The visionary dream sequence is, in fact, marked throughout by clothing. The demon wears an outfit like one sported by her husband before he entered the religious life. Two importunate souls suffering purgatorial pains seem to be men but wear female clothing. Gerardesca worries about her tattered clothes and is first covered and then stripped by the Magdalen to be finally reclothed by the Virgin Mary. The emphasis on wearing appropriate garments fits into the medieval concern that outward clothing should reveal the inner person. Thus, certain colors, fabrics, and furs were limited to particular classes in increasingly intricate sumptuary laws during the later Middle Ages.[26] In addition, clothing, jewelry, and badges were used to designate those whom society wanted to mark as outsiders, like prostitutes and Jews.[27] Professed individuals undertook wearing designated colors and simple materials to indicate the order to which they belonged, and religious garb could carry with it such immediate identification that during the harassment of Beguines in the Low Countries from 1319 to 1328, Beguines "cast off their gray-brown habits and dressed in ordinary, secular clothes" to avoid persecution.[28]

The emphasis on clothing, dressing, and undressing underscores Gerardesca's body as text and the battle for control of that body/text; she chooses the religious life, talks an unwilling husband into compliance, and gains the ultimate proof of her success when they both receive "the habit of holy religion" (*sacrae religionis habitum*).[29] The abandonment of the habit by the visionary's demon/husband may reflect both Gerardesca's fear that he is lukewarm in his profession and also be a projection of her own doubts and struggles. The unnamed former husband seems more sexually neutral when he wears the habit but is revealed as a sexual threat when dressed in secular clothes.

The group of friars who made life difficult for her was balanced by "her" particular monk to whom she was devoted. However, the holy woman lacked a community of supportive religious women from whom to draw sustenance. It was men—an ex-husband turned monastic, male clerical attackers, a devoted monk, and a saintly evangelist—who were important players in her life. Her dream/vision deals with her fears and feelings engendered by her life in which a number of men living in close proximity in the monastic precincts were the main players, both positive and negative, in her life drama. Thus, the crowds of men may stand in for the friars who oppose her and the demon/husband may represent the husband she left and/or the monk who is her special and particular friend and supporter. Either a relationship with a former spouse or with a close male, monastic friend carried with it dangers in the form of gossip about and jealousy of an intimate interchange with the holy woman. We read Gerardesca's deep-seated fear of shame and whispered slanders—that people may talk—running throughout her vision/dream.

Gerardesca needs power within her community, a power she may be struggling to exercise in San Savino's precincts where her enemies control the institutional resources (perhaps symbolized by the grain supplies). But she can counter their position with her significantly greater power to respond to the pleas of neighbors seeking intercession for their sins if she can overcome her own fears. The resolution of her fears and the challenges she faces comes unexpectedly with the strange cross-dressing incident. The two men, who as they approach are seen to wear women's garb, are folk from Gerardesca's world, her neighbors who have died and now, languishing under purgatorial pain, seek her as intercessor. She yearns to help them from their misery, but how can she serve as an intermediary to Christ and procure their salvation if she is subject to petty criticisms, gossip, and slanders? How can she, a woman whose lost virginity makes her suspect, deal with petitioners? How can she overcome the threats of her male confreres in religion? The answer comes in costume. As the men approach they are wearing women's clothes, subverting the threat they first posed into a nonthreatening, gender-bending composite: the man-woman, the woman-man.[30] The layered dangers of her own sexuality and the challenge of clerical power in San Savino are neutralized by reformatting the dangers she faces under the disguise of women's garb. Now Gerardesca can use her true holiness as a means of accessing forgiveness, bypassing priestly control of penance and absolution by going directly to the Virgin Mother.

Gerardesca must wrest her body away from its own sexual urges, protect it from the slanders and ill will of others eager to bad-mouth her behavior, and cover it in a seemly manner with the habit. She must be ready to go naked under the gaze of the saints to prove her worthiness—worthiness made manifest by the cuts and bruises on her body. The text must be laid open for the reader to know its value and its meaning. When the text is proofed/proved, then it is ready for presentation to the world, whose hostile public opinion is turned aside by her Christ-like body as text.

The saintly woman must live with the loss of her virginity, which covers her with shame; her clothing is torn and tattered. She yearns to be immaculate, intact, whole. To gain spiritual comfort and consolation she must endure suffering, be stripped naked, and reclothed in the eyes of Christ and the saints. It is Mary Magdalen, the fallen woman redeemed by Christ's love, who first hides Gerardesca's damaged body and then, at the dramatic conclusion of the dream/vision, strips away all the tatters and shame, the regrets for lost virginity and sexual pleasures, and frees the visionary to receive the new clothes of Christian renewal and rebirth. It is two women saints, the Virgin and the Magdalen, who create a community of supportive women to help the holy woman overcome the male obstacles that crowds of threatening men represent in her life. Gerardesca has written her body as a new text; at the end of the dream/vision her body is reclothed in holy garments handed to her by the Virgin Mary.

Gerardesca is not a saint given to obsessive self-punishment; we do not know what background, personal qualities, and context allowed her to pursue holiness without needing an *obligato* of severe fasting, flagellation, and extreme austerities. When doubts and fears about a former marriage, a present male friend, and challenges from a group of hostile friars become overwhelming, her dream/vision purges her sins with demonic tortures, authenticated by the gaze of the Virgin and her saints, and then clothes her in a holier habit than she had ever previously worn, one straight from the hands of the Mother of God; thus freed from the disabilities of her female body, its sexual past and its threatened future, Gerardesca is resexed as a *sancta*, a holy spirit within a transformed female body.

• *Notes*

A related earlier paper on Gerardesca of Pisa was presented at *A Workshop of the Program in Medieval Studies, Rutgers University: Religion and Torture,* 20 April 1996.

    1. The richness of studies is such that I can only suggest the major historiographical currents. On sanctity see André Vauchez, *La sainteté en Occident aux derniers siècles du Moyen Age* (Rome: Ecole française de Rome, 1981), translated as *Sainthood in the Later Middle Ages* (Cambridge: Cambridge University Press, 1997); Donald Weinstein and Rudolph M. Bell, *Saints and Society: The Two Worlds of Western Christendom, 1000–1700* (Chicago: University of Chicago Press, 1982); Michael Goodich, *Vita Perfecta: The Ideal of Sainthood in the Thirteenth Century* (Stuttgart: A. Hiersemann, 1982*);* Stephen Wilson, *Studies in Religious Sociology, Folklore and History* (Cambridge: Cambridge University Press, 1983); Thomas J. Heffernan, *Sacred Biography: Saints and their Biographers in the Middle Ages* (Oxford: Oxford University Press, 1988). For important issues about holy women in the Middle Ages, see Michael Goodich, "The Contours of Female Piety in Later Medieval Hagiography," *Church History* 50 (1981): 20–31; *Medieval Women's Visionary Literature,* ed. Elizabeth Petroff (New York: Oxford University Press, 1986); Caroline Walker Bynum, " 'And Woman His Humanity': Female Imagery in the Religious Writing of the Later Middle Ages," in *Gender and Religion: On the Complexity of Symbols,* ed. Caroline Bynum et al. (Boston: Beacon Press, 1986), and *Holy Feast and Holy Fast* (Berkeley and Los Angeles: University of California Press, 1987), and *Fragmentation and Redemption* (New York: Zone Books, 1992); *Maps of Flesh and Light: The Religious Experience of Medieval Women Mystics,* ed. Ulrike Wiethaus (Syracuse, N.Y.: Syracuse University Press, 1993). For saintly Italian women see: Elizabeth Petroff, *Consolation of the Blessed* (New York: Alta Gaia Society, 1979), which contains an English translation of Gerardesca's *vita,* 121–50; Claudio Leonardi and Giovanni Pozzi, *Scrittrici mistiche italiani* (Genoa: Marietti, 1988); Benvenuti Papi, "La santità al femminite: funzioni e rappresentazioni tra medioevo ed età moderna," *Les functions des saints dans le monde occidental (IIIe–XIIIe siècle)* (Rome: L'Ecole française de Rome, 1991); Elizabeth Petroff, *Body and Soul: Essays on Medieval Women and Mysticism* (New York: Oxford University Press, 1994); Diana Webb, *Patrons and Defenders: The Saint in the Italian City States* (New York: Tauris Academic Studies, 1996); Joanna Cannon and André Vauchez, *Margherita of Cortona and the Lorenzetti: Sienese Art and the Cult of a Holy Woman in Medieval Tuscany* (University Park, Penn.: Pennsylvania State University Press, 1999).

    2. The food practices of holy women in the Middle Ages have been, for example, interpreted as evidence of their manipulation of social and spiritual symbols and as evidence

of eating disorders. See, Bynum, *Holy Feast and Holy Fast,* and Rudolph M. Bell, *Holy Anorexia* (Chicago: University of Chicago Press, 1985).

3. See *Gendered Voices: Medieval Saints and Their Interpreters,* ed. Catherine M. Mooney (Philadelphia: University of Pennsylvania Press, 1999) for discussion of reading women's *vitae* through the male lens of the hagiographer. Jane Burns points out that the depiction of women in a socially negative light carries a different meaning when voiced by a man rather than a woman. E. Jane Burns, *Bodytalk: When Women Speak in Old French Literature* (Philadelphia: University of Pennsylvania Press, 1993), xv. A different aspect of male authorship for women readers is dealt with by Anne Clark Bartlett, *Male Authors, Female Readers: Representations and Subjectivity in Middle English Devotional Literature* (Ithaca and London: Cornell University Press, 1995).

4. *Acta Sanctorum* (hereafter, *AASS*), 29 May, chap. 1, par. 1.

5. *AASS,* 29 May, chap. 1, par. 2: "semper portabat in mente quae non adhuc gerebat habitu."

6. See Dyan Elliott, *Spiritual Marriage: Sexual Abstinence in Medieval Wedlock* (Princeton, N.J.: Princeton University Press, 1993) for discussion of a more extreme solution for the married woman who sought to live a holy life without having to pay the marital debt. In Italy it was most common for religious women to seek reclusion; see Vauchez, *Sainthood in the Later Middle Ages,* 195.

7. *AASS,* 29 May, chap. 1, par. 4 "prona sit ab adolescentia sua in malum."

8. *AASS,* 29 May, chap. 1, par. 5. "Illa, dum in seculo mansit, numquam hilaris, numquam laeta videbatur: postquam autem habitum sanctae religionis accepit, sumens de religione laetitiam tanta coepit alacritate perfrui, tantoque gaudio exultare, quod facies ejus et oculi, velut numquam visuri moestitiam, infinibili alacritate splendebant."

9. The text is not complete, some damage having occurred to small sections as well as to the conclusion, which is missing. Petroff, *The Consolation of the Blessed,* 201.

10. Petroff, *The Consolation of the Blessed,* v and 201.

11. *AASS,* 29 May, chap. 7, par. 66, and chap. 5, par. 43.

12. *AASS,* 29 May, chap. 2, par. 20. Also see chap. 3, par. 32 in which the Virgin repeats her exhortation that the monk be obedient to his abbot.

13. The wonderful imagery here, *AASS,* 29 May, chap. 5, par. 22 (which is repeated later in another vision in chap. 5, par. 51) may take its inspiration from the devotional statues of the Virgin as the *Madonna della Misericordia* that open to reveal the souls of the saved clustered in a sheltered space within the mantle of the saint. See discussion in Henk van Os et al., *The Art of Devotion in the Late Middle Ages in Europe, 1300–1500* (Princeton, N.J.: Princeton University Press, 1994), 171.

14. *AASS,* 29 May, chap. 5, par. 44.

15. *AASS,* 29 May, chap. 1, par. 8, and chap. 6, par. 57.

16. *AASS,* 29 May, chap. 1, par. 4 "abbas vir vitae venerabilis, eiusdem sanctae in gradu consanguinitatis propinquus."

17. *AASS,* 29 May, chap. 2, par. 22 and chap. 6, par. 56: "Similiter etiam cum quadam die summo diluculo cogitaret de quibusdam fratribus monasterii S. Savini, qui ei jugiter petram scandali apponebant; haec vel his similia intra claustra sui pectoris exorsa est dicere. Quare mihi tribulationem atque injuriam inferunt? Sane nullam eis molestiam infero:

omnibus servio: et ipsi, cum multi in me ex religiosis fidem habeant, me nullo modo reverentur."

18. *AASS*, 29 May, chap. 4, par. 35–38. St. John who "potentiam tunc ordinandi totam caelestem curiam in honore Dominae nostrae."

19. Ritamary Bradley, "In the Jaws of the Bear: Journeys of Transformation by Women Mystics," in *On Pilgrimage: The Best of Ten Years of Vox Benedictina*, ed. Margot King (Winnipeg, Manitoba: Peregrina, 1994), 550: "The mystical life is a growth process of transformation."

20. The *vita* does not specify the exact form of the experience, so it is difficult to describe it as either a vision or as a dream; it shares qualities of both. *AASS*, 29 May, chap. 5, par. 49–52.

21. John Marshall responded to King Stephen's threat to kill his son William Marshall by saying that John had "the anvils and hammers with which to forge still better sons." Sidney Painter, *William the Marshal: Knight-Errant, Baron, and Regent of England*, Medieval Academy reprints for Teaching (Toronto: University of Toronto Press, 1982), 14.

22. *AASS*, 29 May, chap. 5, par. 52: "Quia noluisti ore tuo tangere daemonem, os tuum dulciter osculor."

23. *AASS*, 26 April. Edited by Petroff, *Consolation of the Blessed*, 166–78.

24. See Katherine Ludwig Jansen, *The Making of the Magdalen: Preaching and Popular Devotion in the Later Middle Ages* (Princeton, N.J.: Princeton University Press, 2000) for a rich discussion of the meanings of this saint for medieval people.

25. See Jocelyn Wogan-Browne, "Saints' Lives and the Female Reader," *Forum for Modern Language Studies* 27 (1991): 314–32, for a good articulation of the real threats lying behind vernacular female saints' *vitae* from twelfth- and thirteenth-century English sources.

26. See, for example, such legislation discussed by Barbara A. Hanawalt, *'Of Good and Ill Repute': Gender and Social Control in Medieval England* (New York: Oxford University Press, 1998), 27 and 54.

27. See Leah Lydia Otis, *Prostitution in Medieval Society: The History of an Urban Institution in Languedoc* (Chicago: University of Chicago Press, 1985) and Ruth Mazo Karras, *Common Women: Prostitution and Sexuality in Medieval England* (New York: Oxford University Press, 1996) for discussions of the colors, clothes, and badges legislated for prostitutes. See Diane Owen Hughes, "Earrings for Circumcision: Distinction and Purification in the Italian Renaissance City," in *Persons in Groups: Social Behavior as Identity Formation in Medieval and Renaissance Europe*, ed. Richard C. Trexler (Binghamton, N.Y.: State University of New York at Binghamton, 1985), 155–82 and in *Past and Present* 112 (1986): 3–59 for sumptuary legislation aimed at both prostitutes and Jews. See Robert Chazan, *Medieval Jewry in Northern France: A Political and Social History* (Baltimore: Johns Hopkins University Press, 1973) for badges required for Jews in France.

28. Walter Simons, *Cities of Ladies: Beguine Communities in the Medieval Low Countries, 1200–1565* (Philadelphia: University of Pennsylvania Press, 2001), 134.

29. *AASS*, 29 May, chap. 1, par. 4.

30. Vern L. Bullough and Bonnie Bullough, *Cross Dressing, Sex, and Gender* (Philadelphia: University of Pennsylvania Press, 1993), 60, argue that when men cross dress, they lose status, seem less male and hence less threatening. Georges Duby notes that

clothing had a primary purpose "to underscore the difference between the sexes" (*A History of Private Life: Revelations of the Medieval World*, ed. Georges Duby and trans. Arthur Goldhammer [Cambridge, Mass.: Harvard University Press, 1988], 526). When men appear in women's clothes, the audience for the *vita* would be immediately aware that gender shifting was occurring.

CHAPTER 16

Francis of Assisi as Mother, Father, and Androgynous Figure

Catherine M. Mooney

Francis of Assisi (1182–1226) stands out among male saints for the ease and frequency with which he speaks of himself and other men as mothers. This essay explores female imagery, particularly that associated with mothering, in thirteenth-century sources by and about Francis of Assisi.[1] These include Francis's own writings, Thomas of Celano's first official *vita* of Francis, and Clare of Assisi's vision of Francis reported in the testimony gathered for the process of her canonization. Although my concern is to understand specifically female imagery with regard to Francis and his early followers, I examine as well other images and subjects that relate to gender, such as masculine imagery or the representation of actual women. Only by exploring the nexus of these related images can we appreciate the import of mothering images as they are applied to Francis and his followers. My method is to proceed text by text, careful not to assume that the same image repeated in differing contexts conveys the same meaning. In this way, I will show the multivalent and often shifting meanings attached to female imagery in these early texts.

In important ways, John Boswell was a catalyst behind this essay. His study *Christianity, Social Tolerance, and Homosexuality* educated a generation of medievalists interested in Christian history to read religious texts for evidence that could build a history of homosexuality.[2] Up until 1980, when his book was published, most religious historians who paid any attention at all to the subject did so by repeating some of the well-known prohibitions regarding homosexuality, citing scripture, the penitentials, and church conciliar legislation. It is not too much to say that Boswell launched a scholarly revolution by reading these and other religious texts for *positive* attitudes about eroticism, sexuality, and homosexuality, arguing newly that the Christian tradition and even the church were not always and simply homophobic. Although some of the conclusions he drew in that book about specific individuals, texts, or factors contributing toward tolerance and intolerance of homosexual behavior have been vigorously challenged, the book stands twenty-five years later as the single most important scholarly impetus behind an entire new field of studies. Two criticisms that have been raised about *CSTH* were that it did not sufficiently address the topics of women, for whom Boswell found a paucity of sources (*CSTH*, xvii), and gender. In conversations with him in the 1980s, he encouraged me to look at both of these issues in my own work on medieval saints. He was particularly interested in the plentiful evidence I had found regarding gendered imagery in texts by and about Francis of Assisi, an individual he had not discussed in *CSTH*, but that he thought constituted a rich resource for the study of gendered notions. Often accused of "essentialism," Boswell understood that gendered imagery shifted in meaning over time and was not necessarily a reliable barometer for judging an individual's or society's attitudes toward actual men and women.

Francis's Writings: Mothers to Each Other

I turn first to Francis's own writings, which I discuss in roughly chronological order, bearing in mind the conjectural nature of the dating of several of the texts.

Letter to the Faithful

In this exhortation addressed to male and female penitents,[3] Francis declares that the Spirit of the Lord dwells within all men and women who do the Father's works, and he relates them to our Lord Jesus Christ in a three-fold manner as "spouses, brothers and sisters, and mothers."[4] Francis elaborates the meaning of each of these terms:

> We are spouses when the faithful soul is joined by the Holy Spirit to our Lord
> Jesus Christ. We are brothers and sisters to him when we do the will of the
> Father who is in heaven. We are mothers when we carry him in our heart

and body through a divine love and a pure and sincere conscience; we give birth to him through a holy activity that ought to shine as an example before others.[5]

Mothers are anyone, male or female, who carry the Lord in their heart and body and give birth to him through exemplary deeds. It is worth noting that body and hearts are, in effect, receptacles—or wombs—for Christ, images that will recur later in Thomas of Celano's portrait of Francis.

Rule for Hermitages

The early friars were known for their practice of withdrawing to hermitages to pray in solitude. In a brief prescriptive text, Francis recommends that three or, at most, four brothers should so withdraw. He continues: "Let two of these be the mothers, and let them have two sons or, at least, one. The two who are the mothers should observe the life of Martha, and the two sons should observe the life of Mary."[6] There is nothing new in Francis's application of the roles of Martha and Mary to men. Since early Christianity, writers had drawn upon the two sisters to illustrate points about action and contemplation, and had recognized that life, even monastic life, involved some combination of both: each monk or nun was both Martha and Mary, even if each might identify primarily with Mary.[7] Francis's prescription that the brothers be mothers and sons (or "children"), on the other hand, is more striking.[8] Some modern translators even enclose the terms "mothers" and "sons" in quotation marks, which are in no way suggested by the manuscript tradition.[9] The added punctuation relays a soupçon of anxiety on the translators' part and unnecessarily distances the brothers from the roles that Francis assigns them when he says that they are to be [sint] mothers and children.

Francis goes on to discuss the daily office the brothers in the hermitage should recite. Speaking specifically of the sons, he says that after Terce "they may end the silence, and they may speak and go to their mothers. And, when they wish, they can beg alms from them like poor little ones because of the love of the Lord God."[10] Francis also insists that the brothers' solitude be jealously guarded: "The brothers who are mothers should take pains to keep far away from everyone and . . . protect their sons from everyone so that no one can speak with them. And the sons may not speak with anyone except their mothers, and the minister and his custodian when they wish to visit."[11]

What are the essential characteristics of these hermit mothers? First, they are "actives": theirs is the "life of Martha," doing deeds, in contrast to the sons who observe the "life of Mary." Although few religious writers would ever directly contest that Mary had chosen the "better part," Francis is among a growing cadre of religious writers who significantly elevate Martha's role by representing her service activities in increasingly positive terms.[12] The other characteristics of the mothers fall under this rubric of activity. Second, they are material providers: when their "little ones" come begging, the mothers give them "alms." This refers not to money, which Francis forbade his brothers from accepting,[13] but to material necessities such as clothing and, especially, because it was so regularly necessary, food. Thomas of Celano's *Second Life* of Francis, in fact, recounts that Francis himself would emerge from his solitary cell to rejoin his brothers only when he needed food.[14] A third characteristic regards the mothers' duty to guard solitude. Although motherly responsibilities may make strict observance impossible for themselves, they are to protect their sons absolutely, policing a boundary so that no one (except the occasional visiting superiors) can speak to them. Francis concludes his text with a final point: the mothers and the sons are to exchange roles.[15] Thus, despite the asymmetry intrinsic to the mother-son relationship, Francis makes mutuality, more than hierarchy, the defining mark of the hermit friars.

In sum, mothers in this text are actives who serve by providing materially for and protecting the solitude of their brothers.

Rule of 1221

The first extant rule by Francis derives its name from the date of the Pentecost chapter meeting at which the final version was completed.[16] Although Francis is likely not the sole author of this text, most scholars agree that it is a more accurate reflection of his personal style and thinking than a rule composed two years later that superseded this rule. Described in its prologue as "the life of the gospel," Francis characteristically wove copious gospel and other scriptural verses throughout the text.[17]

In the section Francis devotes to the subject of begging alms, he encourages the friars to act as mothers toward each other. "Let each confidently make his need known to the other, so that the other might find and serve him what he needs. And let each one love and nourish his brother, just as a mother loves and nourishes her child, according to the means with which God graces him."[18] Francis highlights two interrelated features of motherhood in this passage, one affective or spiritual and the other material. Affectively, each friar should love the other as a mother loves her child. Francis does not elaborate the point here, but it is notable that he does *not* say that the friars should love each other as mothers and children love each other, with the one primarily in the giving position and the other receiving and loving in return as child. Rather, he urges every friar to love as does a mother, regardless of how he may be looked upon and loved by another.

Echoing Francis's *Rule for Hermitages,* mothers are additionally material providers. When Francis says that one friar makes his need (*necessitatem*) known and the other finds and serves (*inveniat et ministret*) him what he needs, he is referring primarily, perhaps solely to material needs and not, as some commentators have suggested, spiritual or affective needs. The context makes this clear: the comment occurs within the section on begging alms; the most common necessity the brothers sought was food; the importance of material food and feeding is evoked in Francis's recommendation that a friar should nourish or "nurse" (*nutriat*) his brother just as a mother nourishes or "nurses" (*nutrit*) her child, and is explicitly underlined in the passage's succeeding verses: "Let the one who does not eat not judge the one who does. Whenever a need arises, all the brothers, wherever they may be, are permitted to consume whatever food people can eat, as the Lord says of David who ate the loaves of offering that only the priest could lawfully eat."[19]

The mother Francis describes in his first rule, then, is one who loves her needy brother as her own child, who nourishes him with food, and otherwise provides materially for him.

Rule of 1223

The other extant rule of Francis is known as the *Rule of 1223,* referring to the year it was approved by Pope Honorius III.[20] There is widespread agreement that Francis was pressed to rewrite his earlier rule or, more likely, to authorize a version of his rule rewritten by others. This later rule, which supersedes the earlier rule, is only about one third as long. It leaves out most of the scriptural quotations that Francis liberally interspersed throughout his earlier rule, relaxes many of the earlier rule's prescriptions, is more tightly organized, and surely reflects the contribution of canonists interested in sharpening the rule's legal expressions to make it acceptable to the Roman Curia. This later rule still includes some first-person references to Francis and no doubt had to meet with his approval before being submitted to the papacy, but there is a sense in which his authorship of this text is at a further remove than his authorship of the *Letter to the Faithful,* the *Rule for Hermitages,* and the *Rule of 1221.*

Among the many passages that have been reworked from the earlier rule is the text that likened the brothers to loving, providing, and nourishing mothers. For the sake of comparison, both texts follow:

Rule of 1221: Let each confidently make his need known to the other, so that the other might find and serve him what he needs. And let each one love and nourish his brother, just as a mother loves and nourishes her child, according to the means with which God graces him.[21]

Rule of 1223: Let each confidently make his need known to the other, because if a mother nourishes and loves her child according to the flesh, how much more diligently ought someone to love and nourish his brother according to the spirit?[22]

In the later rule, the brothers are again associated with mothers in that they give nourishment and love, but rather than being urged to be like (*sicut*) earthly mothers, they are distinguished from mothers by being compared favorably to them (*si mater . . . quanto diligentius debet*). This is so because, first, a mother's love is carnal, "according to the flesh," and thus below the superior spiritual love of a brother. Second, perhaps the mother-child relationship alluded to in the text, with its implications of hierarchy, is rejected in favor of the horizontally ordered relationship of brother-brother. Francis had safeguarded the horizontality of the brothers' relationships in the earlier rule simply by advocating that they all assume the role of mother vis-à-vis the others, but the later rule drops his recommendation that the brothers be like mothers. Third, but less likely since there is no corroborating evidence elsewhere in Francis's writings, is the possibility that a male-male relationship is being privileged over a female-child relationship. However these questions are resolved, it is clear that the collaboratively authored later rule weakens the association Francis established between the friars and mothers in his other texts.

Letter to Brother Leo

Francis wrote three brief texts to his close friend and devoted follower Brother Leo: a parchment that has Francis's "Praises of God" on one side and a blessing for Brother Leo on the other,[23] and a letter.[24] Many scholars believe that the handwriting in the surviving manuscripts belongs to Francis himself. The Italianisms and errors in each text correspond to what we know about Francis's level of learning. And although he probably preferred dictation to writing in his own hand, it is entirely credible that he would take the extra trouble to pen personal texts to a beloved friend. Given the complex and contested manuscript history of so many of the texts attributed to Francis, we should perhaps privilege these manuscripts since they are likely to be accurate reflections of his words. In the letter, Francis says he speaks as a mother to Leo. I present the brief letter it in its entirety:

> To brother Leo, health and peace from your brother Francis. I am speaking this way to you, my son, as a mother, because I briefly set forth and advise in this message all that we said on the road. And if later you need to come to me for counsel, I counsel you thus: In whatever way it seems best to you [singular] to please the Lord God and follow his footstep and poverty, may you [plural] do it with the blessing of the Lord God and under my obedience. And if for the sake of your soul or for some other consolation you need and want to come to me, Leo, come.[25]

There is a cryptic quality to this letter. Apparently Leo had been asking Francis for advice on the road about how he and other brothers should follow the Lord's poverty and "footprint," a typical Franciscan image, albeit usually appearing as "footprints." Leo must have been in some doubt. Francis says he speaks to Leo as a mother in setting down the essence of their conversation, which boils down to encouraging Leo to follow his own lights about how to be a good friar. Francis uses his text to anticipate and preempt any future need the hesitant Leo might have for further counsel. Francis, in essence, writes, "If in the future you need my advice, here it is already: I advise you to trust your own instincts about how best to please the Lord in following him and living poorly." They have already had this conversation on the road, but now Francis reinforces his encouraging words by putting them into writing, providing Leo with a tangible reminder to stave off troubling doubts. But Francis apparently realizes that even this might not suffice to reassure his friend, and he adds: if you still need and want to come to me, Leo, I will make myself available.

Francis represents himself as a mother in this text because his is a mother's inexhaustible care for her child: he guides, encourages, reassures, and makes himself available to do it all over again should this or another need arise.

The Question of Gender Hierarchies in Francis's Writings

One last point lends important context to Francis's description of himself and his brothers as mothers. He never refers to himself or any of the friars as "fathers." Citing Matthew in his earlier rule, he admonishes the brothers: "You are all brothers. Do not call anyone on earth father, indeed, one alone, who is in heaven, is your Father."[26] It is well known, of course, that Francis rejected his own earthly father. He warns the brothers not to use the traditional religious title "prior" that indicated the preeminence of one religious over another, preferring instead the title "minister" which means "servant." He spoke of all the friars as "useless servants" and insisted they be known as "lesser brothers."[27] Such titles are, of course, expressions of his life's commitment to choose what is lesser rather than greater, humble rather than exalted, poor rather than rich. Mothers, according to Francis, are not, like fathers, hierarchically positioned above the brothers. They are not authority figures at all.[28]

One might ask, then, whether Francis and his brothers are mothers simply as one more expression of this same movement away from what is greater and toward the lesser. If this constituted the guiding principle behind Francis's identification with mothers, however, one would expect him to expand his gendered imagery by playing upon other related hierarchical pairs. He and his friars would not only be mothers instead of fathers, but also be women instead of men. In this scenario, Francis might counsel the friars to be humble, obedient, and gentle like women, instead of proud, authoritarian, and forceful like men. Such gendered associations, however reflective of the actual social behavior of men and women, were well-worn tropes in medieval texts. Employing gender hierarchies, moreover, would complement Francis's penchant for symbolic reversals.

Francis is not, however, playing principally upon gender hierarchies when he calls himself and others mothers. In fact, such an interpretation conflicts with the rich, multifaceted, and very positive associations Francis attaches to mothers. Mothering is a beloved role to Francis because it is specifically about active, loving service. In the five texts discussed above, Francis elaborates a complex portrait of mothers: a mother is anyone who carries the Lord in heart and body and who gives birth to the Lord through exemplary deeds. In the hermitage, a mother protects her son's solitary contemplation and provides for her "poor little one's" material needs. Outside the hermitage as well, each friar relates to his needy brother as a mother relates to her own child, nourishing him with food, providing other material necessities, and loving him (or, according to the revised *Rule of 1223,* nourishing and loving him even better than an earthly mother). Finally, Francis as mother guides, encourages, reassures, and makes herself ever available to tend to her needy child Leo.

Women in Francis's Writings

The multifaceted and positive portrait of mothering that Francis paints prompts a question: Does Francis's ready appropriation for himself and his friars of the positive connotations of mothering suggest a more positive valuation of women in general? His frequent references to the Virgin Mary, an exceptional woman, are hardly reliable indicators of his attitudes toward most earthly women, so I pass over these in silence. His *Letter to the Faithful,* as noted, is an exhortation directed explicitly to both male and female penitents, without distinction. Illuminating evidence can also be gleaned from both the earlier and later rules.

Predictably, both rules address the topic of contact between the friars and women. A stock feature of medieval religious rules, sermons, treatises, and saints' *vitae* is the danger women pose to men who elect to be celibate, an assumption Francis shares. In the earlier rule, he counsels the brothers regarding appropriate and inappropriate contact with the other sex:

> All the brothers, wherever they are or go, should guard themselves from the evil regard and company of women. No one should counsel them or travel with them if he is alone, or eat at table out of the same dish with them. Priests who speak with them, giving them penance and other spiritual advice, should do so with propriety. Absolutely no woman should be received under obedience by any friar, rather, once she has been given spiritual counsel, she is to do her penance wherever she wishes.[29]

Francis's earlier rule also stands apart, however, from many medieval religious texts because Francis places the blame for unchastity not on women, as temptresses and vehicles of the devil, but on the friars themselves:

> We should all keep close watch over ourselves and keep all our members clean for the Lord says: Whoever looks at a woman, lusting after her, has already committed adultery with her in his heart. And the Apostle: Indeed, do you not know that your members are the temple of the Holy Spirit? Therefore, whoever violates the temple of God, God will destroy.
>
> If any brother, instigated by the devil, commits fornication, he should be stripped of his habit and sent away for his shameful iniquity, be entirely put aside, and absolutely expelled from our order.[30]

The later rule is considerably terser.[31] Blame is no longer laid explicitly at the feet of the brothers, but, in keeping with Francis's earlier rule, neither does it single out women as the cause of sexual indiscretions. Although there is too little information in Francis's own writings to argue that Francis positively valued women, he certainly did not denigrate them as sexual temptresses.

Thomas of Celano's *First Life* of Francis

I turn now to Thomas of Celano's use of female imagery applied to Francis and others in the first of two major *vitae* he wrote about Francis, often called simply the *First Life*.[32] Pope Gregory IX, a long-time supporter of Francis and his brothers, commissioned Thomas to write this *vita* in 1228, just two years after Francis's death, at the time of his canonization. Although Celano was possibly received into the order by Francis himself and he notes in his prologue that his *vita* draws on things he "heard from [Francis's] own mouth," it is unlikely that Celano had significant personal contact with him. He relied as well on what he "learned from trustworthy and esteemed witnesses," who would still have been plentiful at that time. Celano presented his finished *vita* to the pope in early 1229.[33]

Francis, the Man

In searching Celano's text for gendered imagery of whatever type that could contextualize the specifically female imagery applied to Francis, one is first struck by how very male Francis is in the *First Life,* a representation of Francis that, minimally, is not corroborated in his own writings and that, at times, actually contradicts his self-portrayal.

Early in his text, Celano notes that when Francis was in the throes of his conversion, acquaintances who perceived his changed personality asked him if he was thinking about getting married, to which Francis replied enigmatically that he was planning to marry a bride far surpassing others in beauty and wisdom. Celano glosses this simple heterosexual imagery by explaining that Francis's bride was true religion.[34] Later in the *vita,* in a different context, Celano remarks that Francis carefully protected Lady Holy Poverty,[35] a faintly heterosexual image casting Francis as a sort of chivalrous knight longing for and serving an idealized lady.[36]

Francis's command in his earlier rule to call only God in heaven "Father" was one of a number of his admonitions that would not be completely observed after his death. Opposed to establishing hierarchies among the brothers during his life, the humble "minister" and "servant" of all soared in stature after death and was commonly addressed as "father." Composing his *vita* just after Francis's canonization, Celano reverently refers to Francis with an array of titles such as "blessed Francis," "saint Francis," "the holy man of God" and, frequently throughout the *vita,* as "father Francis," "the holy father," and "blessed father Francis." Often Celano seems to use these titles interchangeably, literary considerations probably prompting him to vary his language from one passage to the next.

Certain types of activities, however, appear to move Celano, consciously or unconsciously, to include a nearby reference to Francis as "father." It is probably intentional that Celano first refers to Francis as "father" only after he had liberated himself from his earthly father and was taking up the gospel command to be poor and preach penance.[37] Other activities that tend to be coupled relatively more frequently with the title "father" are activities traditionally associated with men and masculinity, such as when Francis attracts followers or otherwise appears as a leader. For example, Celano calls Francis "father" for the second time when he reports how Francis gained one of his first followers, Bernard of Quintavalle, who used to receive the "blessed father" frequently as a guest.[38] Francis "was both father and leader" to the brothers.[39] Celano speaks of Francis's "brotherly advice," on the one hand, and his "fatherly command," on the other.[40] He calls him "most holy father" when he recounts an episode in which Francis "refused to flatter kings or princes," "because apostolic authority flourished within him."[41] When Francis teaches, he is also somewhat more likely to be called "father": "Casting aside worldly cares, many people gained self-knowledge in the life and teaching of the most blessed father Francis."[42] This association between Francis as father and Francis as teacher or leader is a tendency, not a rule in the *First Life;* Celano also relates similar episodes without positioning Francis as father.

More notably, this manly Francis appears when he rebukes, corrects, and punishes, which he does frequently throughout the *vita,* often being called "father" or being described in military language as well. This strict disciplinarian side of Francis is often absent in popular portrayals of the saint. If the brothers were negligent or ungrateful, they would "humbly beg and earnestly accept correction and punishment from the holy father."[43] As "father of the poor," Francis "harshly rebuked" a brother who impugned the honesty of a poor man begging alms.[44] In another passage in which Francis disciplined sinners, his manly bearing was underlined by the use of an implicitly male military metaphor. Francis was "Christ's strongest soldier" *(fortissimus miles)* and

> he acted confidently in all things since apostolic authority had been granted to him, never fawning or using seductive flatteries. It was not his custom to touch lightly on people's faults, but to give them jabs. He did not coddle the life of sinners, but struck it with harsh rebuke, since he first convinced himself by action and later convinced others by words. He forthrightly spoke

the truth, fearing no one's criticism, so that even the most educated men, powerful by virtue of their fame and achievement, marveled at his words and shook with fear in his presence.[45]

Military imagery is common throughout Celano's *vita*. Francis had himself been a soldier as a young man. He hoped to win worldly glory from combat, until he realized that his real battles would be against the devil.[46] When Francis confronts the demon, he is a man of power, strength, and aggression. For example, this "glorious father," "well trained in the battle camps of God, provoked by the enemy, planned to stir up new battles."[47] Celano called the men and women who followed Francis "a triple militia."[48] Military imagery is frequently invoked to describe Francis's combats with the devil. "The strongest soldier" "engaged in hand to hand combat with the devil" and asserted that his evil weapons were powerless against him.[49]

Francis is strikingly male, in fact, when he battles demons. For example, whereas Francis is called "father" in only ten of the forty-four miracle episodes that do not involve demons,[50] he is referred to as "father" in five of the six miracle episodes that do involve demons.[51] All cures, of course, highlight Francis's power, but driving out demons suggests personal combat between Francis and the demon, which two of the episodes graphically describe.[52] Further, in the only two nonmiracle episodes where Francis combats demons threatening himself, he is also called "father."[53] Elsewhere, Celano will play upon military metaphors in ways that sometimes reverse their meaning or suggest paradoxes, a point I will touch on below.

Francis as sower and planter is perhaps the most unambiguous metaphor underlining his masculinity. For example, Celano tells us that Francis "planted" (*plantavit*) Clare of Assisi's order known as "the order of the Poor Ladies" in the church of San Damiano. Clare, he says, was his "first plant" (*prima planta*); she and the other ladies were his daughters.[54] Francis sowed his own order of friars as well. Celano writes: "Furrowing the earth with the plow of the word, [Francis] sowed the seed of life [and] brought forth blessed fruit. For straightway many good and suitable men, clerics and laymen, fled the world and manfully crushed the devil," and followed Francis.[55] Francis is unmistakably here and elsewhere a phallic symbol. He plows the earth, which is itself a common female image, and is the vehicle through which God's word, the seed, is planted in that earth, bearing fruit in the form of sons and followers. Such an interpretation is corroborated in yet another passage employing the metaphor of Francis as sower of the seed of God's word, where again the fruit that he brings forth are the men who choose to follow him.[56]

Another passage recounts that Francis made his entire body into a tongue, scattering and filling the earth with the seeds of God's word wherever he went.[57]

Celano bolsters this image of Francis as masculine progenitor when he later recounts that Francis "first planted the order of Lesser Brothers" at Saint Mary of the Portiuncula.[58] This was a small church very dear to Francis, in part, "because he burned with devotion toward the Mother of all good."[59] It is richly significant that Francis, the sower, the vehicle for the seed of God's word, plants his order in a church dedicated to Mary, a woman and mother *par excellence.* That this place is a womb, redolent with feminine associations, is confirmed toward the end of Celano's account. There, the dying Francis enjoins his brothers never to abandon the Portiuncula. He knew, explains Celano, that Saint Mary of the Portiuncula was a place "full with a very fertile grace" (*gratia uberiore repletum*), a phrase evocative, of course, of the gospel passage where Mary receives God's word into her womb. It is worth noting the etymological association between *uberiore,* which I have rendered as "very fruitful," and *uber,* meaning "a breast that gives suck" or "teat." There, in the Portiuncula, says Francis, "when we were [only a] few, the Most High increased our numbers."[60]

Mother Francis: The Androgynous Francis

Celano adds complexity and nuance to his portrayal of this manly Francis by highlighting as well the saint's motherly features, presenting the reader, in effect, with an androgynous Francis. This accords quite well with Celano's penchant for weaving paradoxes throughout Francis's life. Francis is, for example, "the richest poor man."[61] He is a soldier who makes peace.[62] He is also a man with womanly qualities. Francis is a womb; he becomes impregnated and gives birth; he behaves like a mother.

Thus, while Francis sometimes figures as a phallic symbol insofar as he is the conduit for the seed of God's word, he is at other times represented as a womb. Alternating between these images, Francis is both masculine and feminine. In one passage, for example, his "word is a burning flame that penetrates the inmost regions of the heart, and fills the souls of all with wonder."[63] The hearts and souls penetrated by Francis's ardent word are womblike images, the former especially recalling Francis's own comment: "We are mothers when we carry him in our heart."[64] As the recipient of God's word, however, Francis himself is like a womb, a point Celano underlines by describing Francis in similar terms. Francis too "burned inwardly with a divine flame," "a flame conceived in [his] soul."[65] Francis is "that most precious vessel in which the heavenly treasure was hidden."[66] In these passages, the accent is on the female Francis as receptacle of the word that, ultimately, in imitation of the Blessed Virgin, he will birth into the world. Even more explicit testimony to this effect comes to us indirectly. In 1219, while Francis was still alive, Odo of Cheriton related in a sermon that Francis "said he was a woman whom the Lord impregnated with his word, who gave birth to spiritual children."[67]

Francis's love of animals is celebrated in many texts about the saint. In Celano's *First Life,* it is coupled with the motherly roles of loving protector and liberator. Once,

> a brother brought Francis a live young hare that had been trapped in a snare. When he saw it, the blessed man, moved with tenderness, said, "Brother Hare, come here to me. Why did you let yourself get caught like that?" As soon as the brother who was holding him let him go, he ran willingly to the saint and rested in his bosom as the safest place. After he had rested there a little while, the holy father, stroking him caressingly with motherly affection, let him go so that he might return free to the woods. As often as he was put on the ground, he would hurry back to the saint's bosom, who at last ordered the brothers to carry [the hare] home to the nearby forest. Something similar happened with a rabbit, a very wild animal, when [Francis] was on an island in the Lake of Perugia.[68]

Francis loved lambs particularly, Celano notes, for their association with the humble and spotless lamb, Christ.[69] On one occasion Francis encountered two small lambs on their way to market, bound and slung over a man's shoulder. "When blessed Francis heard the bleating lambs, he was inwardly shaken and, drawing near, touched them, showing compassionate affection just as a mother does over a crying child. He asked the man, 'Why are you tormenting my lambs, binding and hanging them in this way?'" When he learned the man needed the money, Francis purchased the lambs' freedom and paid the man to care for and protect them.[70]

Motherliness in these passages is associated with two activities, loving care and protection of the vulnerable, behavior often attributed to mothers, and the somewhat more surprising activity of liberating captives. This more unusual notion resonates with passages elsewhere in the *vita* that ally Francis's father with destruction and captivity and his mother with protection and liberation. When Francis's father heard the rumors and ridicule circulating about his son's magnanimous gifts of money—his father's money—to the poor, he immediately arose, not to liberate [Francis], but rather to destroy him. With no restraint, he pounced [on him] like a wolf on a sheep and, scowling at him with a wild and savage expression, shamelessly and disgracefully seized him and dragged him to his own home. And thus, without any mercy, he shut him up in a dark place for a number of days, and, thinking to bend Francis's spirit to his will, he went at him first with words and then beat and bound him.[71]

Celano starkly contrasts Francis's father with his mother, who entirely disapproved of her husband's behavior. She spoke to her son tenderly and, once aware that Francis was determined to continue his course, "was moved in her maternal interior regarding him and, after breaking his fetters, let him go free."[72] Celano employs similar Latin phrasing to describe Francis's reaction to the bound lambs being carried to market whom he frees, *commota sunt viscera eius,* and his mother's reaction to her son, pounced upon like a sheep and then bound, *commota sunt materna viscera.* I render *viscera* in each case by noting its sense of interiority: Francis "was inwardly shaken," and his mother "was moved in her maternal interior," but *viscera* also carries a more graphic physical sense; it is a term that also, notably, sometimes denotes "fruit of the womb," "offspring," or "child," evocative associations certainly relevant to these passages.

Androgynous Others: Mother Church and Motherly Men

In the minds of many of his contemporaries, Francis of Assisi dramatically transformed and, in the process, saved the medieval church from a host of ills besetting it. He stands out among other medieval saints not only for the sheer grandeur of what is attributed to him, but also because his achievement is tied as much to his person, the mere power of his presence, as to his activities. An almost supernatural and transformative aura surrounds him, converting those who come into contact with him. Francis saves the church by correcting and tempering its less salutary features. Into a church that contemporary caricatures critiqued as avid for status, wealth, and power, Francis introduces the opposite virtues of humility, poverty, and concern for the weak. He refashions this church by incorporating into it both poles of an array of categories, melding the apparently dichotomous into a harmonious whole. For example, he embraces poverty and recommends that his followers be poor, but he also forbids them from criticizing wealthy prelates. Simple and relatively unschooled himself, Francis counseled unlearned friars not to pursue learning, yet he admired theologians and welcomed them into the order. Into the increasingly clericalized church of the Gregorian reform, Francis incorporated an order of lay friars and lay penitents. Similarly, Francis renewed the church, according to Celano, by introducing into it feminine qualities, transforming an eminently male institution into a more androgynous institution. Francis accomplishes this both materially and figuratively.

Concretely, Celano declares that Francis renewed this "Church of Christ in both sexes" by introducing into it the friars, the Poor Ladies, and organized groups of lay penitents.[73] At one level, this is a simple statement of fact. Francis founded not only his own male order of Lesser Brothers, but also, with his famous female follower Clare of Assisi, the Poor Ladies, as Clare's order was first known. He also welcomed the many penitents, both male and female, who flocked to him for guidance and who would eventually become known, after his death, as the Third Order. Crowds of both men and women hurried to behold and hear Francis.[74] Celano declares that he offered a pattern and example for both sexes.[75] While it is true that women do not play a prominent role in Celano's *First Life,* it is also the case that Francis's interactions with women are portrayed positively.[76] Paralleling the saint's own writings, Celano's Francis betrays not a hint of misogyny.

Francis's first work after abandoning his biological father's house and rejecting his paternity was to rebuild the church of San Damiano, an act with both material and figurative significance. San Damiano was a small church that had fallen into disrepair, like many other churches in the Umbrian countryside. As God's house, as a locus for the exercise of priestly sacramental power, and as a building traditionally supervised by the clergy, San Damiano was in a certain sense a male house. Francis first physically repaired the church and then spiritually repaired it, as it were, when he filled it with women, converting it into a monastery for Clare and the Poor Ladies. Celano immediately describes the Poor Ladies highlighting virtues stereotypically associated with women: they are loving, humble, chastely virginal, oblivious of earthly considerations, poor, silent, and patient.[77] In Celano's account, this newly female San Damiano is also a concrete material symbol for Francis's grander task, that of rebuilding the house of God that is the universal church. The hierarchy of this thirteenth-century church was sharply criticized in many quarters for its abusive exercise of power and for its greed, the very traits Celano attributes to Francis's own biological father as well.[78] Mirroring his repair of San Damiano, Francis brings into this universal church the opposite virtues of humility and poverty. Into this very male and fatherly church, Francis introduces conventionally feminine features. This will be borne out especially in Celano's portrayal of Bishop Hugolino, discussed below.

Men in close relationships with Francis are also described in feminine language. Bernard of Quintavalle, inspired by Francis's life and conduct, "conceived reverence and gave birth to the spirit of salvation."[79] When Francis's health took a grave turn for the worse, he chose his friend Brother Elias to be his mother, to care for him materially by making him take his medicine, and to be father of the brothers, to be in authority over them.[80]

More significant are the feminine qualities ascribed to the prelates Pope Innocent III and, especially, Bishop Hugolino, who would later become Pope Gregory IX. There are, in fact, no explicitly gendered references within the single passage concerning Innocent III, but a contemporary reading that considers the possible phallic and feminine significance of the imagery is at least worth considering, especially given its syntony with Celano's use of gendered imagery elsewhere in the text. Pope Innocent, arguably the most powerful of all medieval popes, appears in a dream that symbolizes Francis's successful bid to persuade Innocent to receive Francis's humble order into a church that had been marginalizing and even persecuting similar groups of men and women:

> One night when Francis had gone to sleep, he seemed to be walking along a road next to which was standing a tree of great height. That tree was beautiful and strong, thick and exceedingly high. It happened that while he was approaching it and standing under it, marveling at its beauty and height, the saint suddenly grew to such a height [himself] that he was touching the tip of the tree and, seizing it with his hand, he was easily bending it to the earth. And truly that is how it happened when lord Innocent, a very lofty and exalted tree in the world, so obligingly bent himself to [Francis's] will and request.[81]

One could read this passage about Francis's own transformation from lowly, earthbound man to a tall figure able to bend the beautiful, strong, thick, and tall Innocent as an instance of paired phallic symbols and perhaps argue for a covert homoerotic reading of this passage. However, the fact that Francis begins on the earth, a common symbol for women, and softens Innocent, drawing him back to earth rather than making him taller yet, seems to insinuate a feminine quality into the text. Francis here evinces both female and male characteristics, which together work to transform the powerful Pope Innocent into a more androgynous figure himself, as the saint gently moves the towering figure into a position of humble malleability and receptivity.

Celano is explicit, however, in his attribution of masculine and feminine roles to Bishop Hugolino, who was Francis's friend, admirer and, since 1220, the official ecclesiastical protector of the friars. Hugolino's prominent role throughout the *vita* is due also to the fact that it was he, after becoming Pope Gregory IX in 1227, who commissioned Celano to compose the *First Life* upon Francis's canonization in 1228. Celano frequently describes Hugolino, whom he often calls "father," undertaking manly activities. Hugolino is the "father set over [Francis's] family."[82] He slays with a sword all those seeking to destroy the friars,[83] and is, for the brothers, an arrow, ready when needed.[84] Like Francis, Hugolino also is described as a sower, having planted Francis's order everywhere.[85]

But Bishop Hugolino is additionally a mother to Francis, who clung to the bishop, says Celano "as a son does to a father and as an only child to its mother, sleeping and resting safe in the bosom of his kindness."[86] When Hugolino, now Pope Gregory IX, heard about the many miracles taking place at the saint's tomb after Francis's death in 1226,

> he rejoiced and exulted, danced and was gladdened because in his times he was seeing the Church of God being renewed with new mysteries that were however ancient wonders, and this in his son whom he carried in his sacred womb, cherished in his lap, nursed with the word, and nurtured with the food of salvation.[87]

In Hugolino and his relationship with Francis and the friars one observes the tempering effect of Francis's life and person, often expressed through reversals. A "great pontiff," Hugolino received Francis with humility.[88] Although the bishop was shepherd in fact, he reserved the title of "shepherd" for Francis.[89] So infectious was Francis's life and conduct that the lord bishop and "father" of the friars, "conformed himself to the ways of the friars," being "simple with the simple, humble with the humble, poor with the poor" and "a brother among brothers, least among the lesser."[90] "Father" in authority over his obedient son Francis and the friars, it was frequently Francis who would be father to Hugolino, strengthening him with fatherly blessings.[91] Celano underlines the mutuality and intimacy of their relationship when he says Hugolino's "soul was joined to the soul" of Francis, echoing the biblical verse regarding Jonathan and David, whose love elsewhere is described as surpassing even that between a man and a woman.[92]

Proponents of the poverty movement, including Celano, represented Francis—and his example of poverty, humility, and concern for the weak—as the new grace renovating a church made old by its opulence, arrogance, and rapacity. Francis, who was both father and mother, incorporated contrasting yet complementary values into the church, thereby tempering the extremes of which its detractors and even some of its friends accused it. That the most prominent prelate in the *First Life,* Bishop Hugolino, *papa* and father of the universal church by the time Celano composed his *vita,* is also represented as mother—kind and safe haven, loving nurturer, and wet nurse to Francis—highlights the extent to which Francis's feminine features, his androgyny, were reshaping the church at even its highest levels.

The Stigmata and Androgyny

An episode many interpreters count among the most intensely revelatory of Francis's identity and significance, his reception of the stigmata, also underlines the saint's essentially androgynous character. Celano clearly intended his account of Francis's stigmata to be read at multiple levels, as a literal event open to theological interpretations.[93] Although reading the text with attention to gendered connotations has, to the best of my knowledge, never been attempted, it too yields surprisingly rich results. In a style common to other medieval religious texts, Celano freely intermingles in his account of the stigmata images that are but a slight remove away from the language of explicit sexual encounter. The erotic undertones of conjoined bodies, piercings, bleeding, and intimate union lend a power to this text that many twenty-first century readers might too easily dismiss, embarrassed or incredulous about the prospect of sexual symbolism in religious writing. Although medieval people valued virginity and sexual renunciation more than later Western societies, they were also freer and franker in their use of sexual imagery to express profound religious experience, as numerous devotional texts and accounts of ecstatic union attest.

Two years before his death, while staying in a hermitage in La Verna, Francis saw in a vision a man with six wings like a seraph, affixed to a cross, standing over him. He was beautiful beyond comprehension and looked kindly upon Francis, who, however, reacted with fright upon seeing the bitter suffering of the passion. Anxious about the vision's meaning, he understood only later, when "the marks of the nails began to appear on his hands and feet" just like those he had seen on "the crucified man," that the vision had to do with his own suffering and passion:[94]

> His hands and feet seemed to be pierced through the middle by nails, with the heads of the nails appearing on the inner part of the hands and the upper part of the feet, and their points coming through on the opposite sides. Those

marks were round on the inside of the hands, but oblong on the outside, and small pieces of flesh appeared like the top of the nails bent and driven back, protruding from the remaining flesh. The marks of the nails were stamped on the feet and raised from the flesh in the same way. The right side was as if pierced through with a lance, producing a scar, which frequently dripped blood so that his tunic and undergarments were often sprinkled with sacred blood.[95]

Francis can be seen as both female and male in this episode. On the one hand, he is penetrated, wounded, and bleeds. On the other, and distinct from popular accounts of stigmata that give prominence to the wounds, Celano conspicuously focuses on the nails. These not only pierce the saint, creating the wounds—they also remain in his flesh, indeed, are fashioned from his flesh. No mere passive recipient of stigmata, sent from the crucified man who stands externally over him, Francis incarnates both womb and phallus. When "the marks of the nails began to appear on his hands and feet, just as a little before he had seen them on the crucified man standing over him,"[96] we realize that Francis himself is affixed to that cross *with* the crucified man, as Celano himself makes clear in another passage where he identifies the seraph with Christ.[97] Intimacy is too understated a term to describe the relationship between Francis and the crucified man: they become one like two lovers but, in contrast to lovers, their union perdures in a physical identification, laying the groundwork for later Franciscan claims that Francis was an *alter Christus*.[98]

The veiled eroticism and homoaffectivity that suffuse this episode extend through subsequent passages that recount how Francis sought to hide his secret, the intimate special marks that adorned him like "pearls and precious gems."[99] His friend Elias somehow saw the wound in Francis's side and his friend Rufino discovered it when his hand slipped while rubbing the saint's breast.[100] The people were amazed to see not "the punctures made by the nails in his hands and feet, but the very nails themselves formed out of his flesh . . . and his right side reddened with blood."[101] His brothers rushed to the body, weeping, kissing his hands, feet, and side, the wound in his side recalling to them the wound in Christ's side that had poured forth water and blood for our reconciliation.[102] When Celano then describes the stigmata as a "sacrament," it is not only because the marks are an outward sign of Francis's union with Christ, as scholars have noted, but also because the blood of his side wound is being likened to Jesus' blood which believers receive in the sacrament of the Eucharist.[103] The likeness of Jesus' and Francis's bloody wounds provides an important interpretive key for understanding Clare of Asissi's vision, which evokes the female Francis of the stigmata.

The Process for Clare of Assisi's Canonization: Francis Nursing His Disciple

The process for Clare's canonization began in November, just a few months after her death in August 1253. Preserved only in a fifteenth-century Italian translation, the process includes the testimony of five residents of Assisi and fifteen sisters from Clare's monastery of San Damiano.[104] Sister Filippa, who had known Clare since childhood and then lived with her for almost thirty-eight years in San Damiano, recounts the following vision as part of her testimony:

> Lady Clare also reported that once, in a vision, it seemed to her that she was carrying a vessel of hot water to Saint Francis, with a small towel for drying hands, and she was going up a high ladder, but she walked so lightly that it was as if she was walking on level ground. Once she had reached Saint Francis, the saint drew a bosom from his breast and said to the virgin Clare, "Come, take, and suck." And when she had sucked, the saint urged her to suck again; and when she did, what she was sucking from it was so sweet and delectable that she could in no way explain it. When she had finished sucking, the nipple or mouth of the breast from which the milk came remained between blessed Clare's lips, and taking what remained there in [her] mouth with [her] hands, it seemed to her that it was gold so clear and lucid that everything was seen in it as if in a mirror.[105]

Three other sisters who gave witness testify that they also knew about this vision, although the scribe records their confirmations in brief phrases, without indicating whether or not they, like Filippa, provided details about the vision.[106] Neither the scribe nor the sisters express any sense of embarrassment or need to explain the vision.

The vision's rich symbolic imagery is illuminated by examining similar imagery in other medieval texts and by situating it specifically within the historical context of Clare and the Poor Ladies. Clare would, no doubt, have been familiar with Francis's description of himself as a mother through her personal contact with him, through hearing others speak of him, and per- haps also through reading Celano's or others' accounts of Francis. Her vision suggests one way in which she used such imagery to understand Francis's relationship to her and, probably by extension, the Poor Ladies.

An obvious theme in the vision regards Clare's asymmetrical relationship with Francis. She serves Francis when she brings to him water and a towel for drying his hands. Francis stands above her and Clare must rise to reach him. Francis directs her actions and Clare obeys. As a child, or as an adult in the role of a child—the vision does not specify—Clare depends upon Francis for nourishment. Francis is the generous giver, while Clare is the grateful recipient.

The episode of Francis's stigmata further illuminates Francis as female in this vision. Medieval people frequently thought of the wound in Christ's side, to which Francis's wound was likened, as a breast, the source of life-giving blood. The metaphor made sense theologically because it was through Jesus' bloody death that believers gained life and, further, his blood (and body) fed them in the Eucharist. It made sense scientifically since medieval medical theory assumed that breast milk was produced from blood. Christ's body was thought of as female also because it was physical, and women were associated particularly with physicality.[107] When Clare sucks Francis's breast, she is in a sense recognizing his association with Christ, confirming in another way Celano's claim that Francis's stigmata was a sacrament.

Clare does not, however, merely relate to Francis as his servant, child, and dependent. By physically and spiritually imbibing his milk, she is graphically reaffirming her spiritual lineage with him. This had become crucial for her and her sisters especially after Francis's death because of a growing division among the friars regarding their responsibilities toward the Poor Ladies. Although some Franciscans welcomed their spiritual association with the Ladies, the general trajectory of all the mendicant orders was to limit and control their contact with and responsibilities for women. This is evident already in Celano's ambiguous treatment of Clare and her sisters in his *Second Life,* finished in 1247, some twenty years after his *First Life* and six years before Clare's death and the process for her canonization. This later *vita* acknowledges, on the one hand, Francis's promise of perpetual help for the Ladies and his estimation that they were led by the same spirit as his friars.[108] On the other hand, Celano also distances Francis from the Ladies, both through emphasizing how seldom Francis visited them, and through including cautionary and even misogynistic remarks attributed to Francis about the dangers of women, including holy women.[109] Celano never even mentions Clare once by name in this later *vita.*[110] Yet, as enclosed nuns, Clare and her sisters relied on the friars not only for spiritual sustenance but also for begging food and other necessities. Clare had for many years been fighting to maintain the Poor Ladies' "privilege of poverty" which allowed them, in contrast to other enclosed nuns, to live only from alms, receiving no income from lands or other assets. A number of Francis's earliest followers apparently saw her persistent struggle to remain living in radical poverty as true to Francis of Assisi's own vision, in contrast to the laxer brothers so often mentioned in Celano's *Second Life.*[111]

In the face of these challenges, Clare's vision—and the way it draws on Francis's maternal imagery—strengthens her position. Mother Francis invites her, twice, to drink directly from his breast. In line with twelfth-century uses of this image, this probably represented the instruction she received directly from Francis,[112] but more than that, it affirmed a visceral connection with him that could not be broken. Holding his nipple, revealingly called the "mouth" of his breast, in her mouth is more intimate than a kiss. She sucks his blood-milk and, in a sense, becomes Francis as his fluid becomes part of her own body. This is confirmed when she takes what remained in her mouth into her hands and sees that it is gold so clear that she can see everything as if it were a mirror. In a letter to Agnes of Prague, Clare speaks of seeing Christ in a mirror,[113] much as she now saw Christ in Francis. Gazing upon that mirror, she would also, of course, see her very self. In her *Testament,* Clare confidently associated the Poor Ladies themselves with a mirror, telling them that the Lord had made them an example and mirror for others.[114] Thus, through the image of the mirror, Clare manages to join Christ, Francis, herself, and her sisters into an intimate association.

◆ ◆ ◆

The thirteenth-century texts considered in this essay show the shifting meanings attached to female and especially mothering imagery applied to Francis of Assisi and other men. The polysemous nature of gendered imagery in these texts precludes simple summary. Another sort of conclusion, however, leaves to one side much of the imagery with its overlapping meanings and highlights instead two salient changes across these texts that suggest a Franciscan world in transition. First, there is the contrast between Francis's Francis, who favors female imagery for himself, eschews hierarchy, and refuses to be called father, and Celano's Francis who is not only female, but especially male. This Francis, a father in charge who regularly rebukes, disciplines, and punishes his friars, suggests a body of men intent on rooting out abuses, making rules, and settling dissensions among themselves. Second, there is the Francis of Clare's vision, conjured in powerful response to those who would undermine her status as follower of Francis and thereby marginalize the Poor Ladies. Considered in these stark terms, one wonders whether the transformation of Francis and his first followers into an established and powerful institution has not contributed toward a reassertion of the patriarchal status quo that Francis had initially challenged with his own creative use and appropriation of female imagery.

- *Notes*

1. I would like to thank Francine Cardman and Mary Rose D'Angelo for their helpful suggestions.

2. John E. Boswell, *Christianity, Social Tolerance, and Homosexuality: Gay People in Western Europe from the Beginning of the Christian Era to the Fourteenth Century* (Chicago: University of Chicago Press, 1980).

3. The *Letter to the Faithful* appears in two versions: "Epistola ad fideles (Recensio prior)" and "Epistola ad fideles (Recensio posterior)," in *Fontes franciscani* (hereafter *FF*), ed. Enrico Menestò et al. (Assisi: Edizioni Porziuncula, 1995), 71–76 and 77–86, respectively. The allegedly later "posterior" version is about twice the length of the "prior" version, which it includes virtually verbatim. For a judicious overview of debates regarding the relationship between the two texts and their intended audience, see Théophile Desbonnets, "Aspect historique et critique des écrits de François," in Francis of Assisi, *Écrits*, ed. Kajetan Esser, trans. Théophile Desbonnets et al. (Paris: Cerf, 1981; repr. with add. and corr., 2003), 33–34. Stanislao da Campagnola, *FF*, 20, suggests the "Recensio prior" was composed before 1221 and the "Recensio posterior" around 1225 or 1226, dates still open to debate.

For readers wishing to consult English translations of these and other texts by and about Francis cited in this essay, see *St. Francis of Assisi: Writings and Early Biographies: English Omnibus of Sources for the Life of St. Francis*, ed. Marion A. Habig, 4th rev. ed. (Chicago: Franciscan Herald Press, 1983) or *Francis of Assisi: Early Documents*, ed. Regis J. Armstrong, J. A. Wayne Hellmann, and William J. Short, 3 vols. (New York: New City Press, 1998–2001) (hereafter *Early Documents*).

4. "Recensio prior," 1.7, p. 73: " . . . et sunt sponsi, fratres et matres Domini nostri Jesu Christi"; "Recensio posterior," 50, p. 83. I render *fratres* as "brothers and sisters" rather than the more traditional "brothers" because the text is clearly addressed to both men and women, as attested in "Recensio prior," 1.5, p. 73; 2.1, p. 74; "Recensio posterior," 48, p. 83. All translations in this essay are my own.

5. "Recensio prior," 1.8–10, pp. 73–74: "Sponsi sumus, quando Spiritu Sancto coniungitur fidelis anima Domino nostro Jesu Christo. Fratres ei sumus, quando facimus voluntatem patris qui in caelis est. Matres, quando portamus eum in corde et corpore nostro per divinum amorem et puram et sinceram conscientiam; parturimus eum per sanctam operationem, quae lucere debet aliis in exemplum." Cf. "Recensio posterior," 51–53, p. 83.

6. *Rule for Hermitages*: "Regula pro eremitoriis," in *FF*, 213–16. Desbonnets, "Aspect historique," in *Écrits*, 28–29, indicates the text was composed in 1217 or thereafter; Da Campagnola, in his "Introduzione" to Francis's writings in *FF*, 21, suggests 1217/18–1221. "Regula pro eremitoriis," 1, p. 215: " . . . duo ex ipsis sint matres et habeant duos filios vel unum ad minus. Isti duo qui sunt matres, teneant vitam Marthae et duo filii teneant vitam Mariae."

7. Giles Constable, "The Interpretation of Mary and Martha," in *Three Studies in Medieval and Religious and Social Thought* (Cambridge: Cambridge University Press, 1995).

8. While *filios* can be rendered as either "children" or, given the particular individuals Francis is describing, "sons," it is worth bearing in mind the different valence of each term.

9. E.g., *Saint François d'Assise: Documents, écrits et premières biographies,* ed. Théophile Desbonnets and Damien Vorreux (Paris: Éditions Franciscaines, 1968), 99; *Early Documents,* vol. 1, *The Saint,* ed. Armstrong et al., 61.

10. "Regula pro eremitoriis," 4–5, p. 215: " . . . absolvant silentium; et possint loqui et ire ad matres suas. Et, quando placuerit, possint petere ab eis eleemosynam sicut parvuli pauperes propter amorem Domini Dei."

11. "Regula pro eremitoriis," 8–9, pp. 215–16: "Isti fratres, qui sunt matres, studeant manere remote ab omni persona; et per obedientiam sui ministri custodiant filios suos ab omni persona, ut nemo possit loqui cum eis. Et isti filii non loquantur cum aliqua persona nisi cum matribus suis et cum ministro et custode suo, quando placuerit eos visitare cum benedictione Domini Dei."

12. Constable, "The Interpretation of Mary and Martha," 40–44, 90–92.

13. "Regula non bullata," chap. 2, 5–7, in *FF,* 186; "Regula bullata," chap. 4, in *FF,* 175; chap. 5, 4, in *FF,* 175–76.

14. *Second Life:* "Vita secunda sancti Francisci," 45.1, in *FF,* 486. Celano finished his *Second Life* in 1247.

15. "Regula pro eremitoriis," 10, p. 216. See "Vita secunda," 178, pp. 599–601, for a concrete example of the brothers exchanging roles on a weekly basis.

16. *Rule of 1221:* "Regula non bullata," in *FF,* 183–212. It is also known in English as *The First Rule* or *The Earlier Rule.* Its Latin title, "Regula non bullata," means "the rule not confirmed with a bull," indicating that the rule never received papal approbation.

17. "Regula non bullata," Prologus, 2, p. 185. Jordan of Giano, writing perhaps in the early 1260s, reported that Brother Caesar of Speyer helped Francis compose the rule: *Chronica fratris Jordani,* ed. H. Boehmer (Paris: Librarie Fischbacher, 1908), 15; English trans., E. Gurney Salter, *The Coming of the Friars Minor to England and to Germany* (New York: Dutton, 1926; Whitefish, Mont.: Kessinger, 2003).

18. "Regula non bullata," chap. 9, 10–11, p. 194: "Et secure manifestet unus alteri necessitatem suam, ut sibi necessaria inveniat et ministret. Et quilibet diligat et nutriat fratrem suum, sicut mater diligit et nutrit filium suum, in quibus ei Deus gratiam largietur."

19. "Regula non bullata," chap. 9, 12–13, pp. 194–95: "Et qui non manducat, manducantem non iudicet. Et quandocumque necessitas supervenerit, liceat universis fratribus, ubicumque fuerint, uti omnibus cibis, quos possunt homines manducare, sicut Dominus dicit de David, qui comedit panes propositionis, quos non licebat manducare nisi sacerdotibus."

20. *Rule of 1223:* "Regula bullata," in *FF,* 169–81. It is also known in English as *The Second Rule* or *The Later Rule.* Its Latin title, "Regula bullata," refers to the fact that it received formal papal approval in the bull, *Solet annuere,* issued by Honorius III, 29 November 1223.

21. For the Latin, see n. 18.

22. "Regula bullata," chap. 6, 9, p. 177: "Et secure manifestet unus alteri necessitatem suam, quia, si mater nutrit et diligit filium suum carnalem, quanto diligentius debet quis diligere et nutrire fratrem suum spiritualem?"

23. "Chartula fratri Leoni data," in *FF,* 43–51. Da Campagnola, in his "Introduzione" to Francis's writings in *FF,* 20, dates the manuscript to September 1224. Duane Lapsanski, who

says the parchment cannot be securely dated, discusses it and provides photocopies: "The Autographs on the 'Chartula' of St. Francis of Assisi," *Archivum Franciscanum Historicum 67* (1974): 18–37, see 19. See Celano, "Vita secunda," 49, on Francis's composition of both texts.

24. *Letter to Brother Leo:* "Epistola ad Fratrem Leonem," in *FF*, 87–92. Da Campagnola, in his "Introduzione" to Francis's writings in *FF*, 21, dates the letter to the final years before Francis's death in 1226. On the manuscript, see Attilio Bartoli Langeli, "Gli scritti da Francesco: L'autografia di un 'illitteratus,' " in *Frate Francesco d'Assisi: Atti del XXI Convegno internazionale, Assisi, 14–16 ottobre 1993* (Spoleto: Centro Italiano di Studi sull'Alto Medioevo, 1994), 101–59.

25. "Epistola ad Fratrem Leonem," 89: "Frater Leo, frater Francisco tuo salutem et pacem. Ita dico tibi, fili mei, sicut mater: quia omnia verba, quae diximus in via, breviter in hoc verba [!] dispono et consilio, et si dopo [tibi?] oportet propter consilium venire ad me, quia ita consilio tibi: In quocumque modo melius videtur tibi placere Domino Deo et sequi vestigiam [!] et paupertatem suam, faciatis cum beneditione Domini Dei et mea obedientia. Et, si tibi est necessarium animam tuam propter aliam consolationem tuam, et vis, Leo venire ad me, veni." Francis's ungrammatical Latin allows for some variations of translation, but these do not affect the substance of my argument.

26. "Regula non bullata," chap. 22, 33–34, p. 207; Matt. 23:9–10. See also another version of an early rule, "Fragmenta alterius regulae non bullatae," 20, in *FF*, 125.

27. "Regula non bullata," chap. 6, 3, p. 191 (prior, lesser brothers); chap. 4, 2, p. 188, and chap. 4, 6, p. 189 (minister, servant); chap. 11, 3, p. 196, and chap. 23, 7, p. 210 (useless servants).

28. Francis's use of maternal imagery to soften or negate his own position as an authority figure recalls Bernard of Clairvaux's and other twelfth-century Cistercians' similar use of maternal imagery, as discussed by Caroline Walker Bynum, "Jesus and Abbot as Mother: Some Themes in Twelfth-Century Cistercian Writing," in *Jesus as Mother: Studies in the Spirituality of the High Middle Ages* (Berkeley and Los Angeles: University of California Press, 1982).

29. "Regula non bullata," chap. 12, 1–4, pp. 196–97: "Omnes fratres, ubicumque sunt vel vadunt, caveant sibi a malo visu et frequentia mulierum. Et nullus cum eis consilietur aut per viam vadat solus aut ad mensam in una paropside comedat. Sacerdotes honeste loquantur cum eis dando poenitentiam vel aliud spirituale consilium. Et nulla penitus mulier ab aliquo fratre recipiatur ad obedientiam, sed dato sibi consilio spirituali, ubi voluerit agat poenitentiam." See also "Fragmenta alterius regulae non bullatae," 31–32, p. 126.

30. "Regula non bullata," chaps. 12.5–13.1, p. 197: "Et multum omnes nos custodiamus et omnia membra nostra munda teneamus, quia dicit Dominus: Qui viderit mulierem ad concupiscendam eam, iam moechatus est eam in corde suo. Et apostolus: An ignoratis, quia membra vestra templum sunt Spiritus Sancti?; itaque qui templum Dei violaverit, disperdet illum Deus.

Si quis fratrum diabolo instigante fornicaretur, habitu exuatur, quem pro sua turpi iniquitate amisit, et ex toto deponat et a nostra religione penitus repellatur."

31. "Regula bullata," chap. 11, 2–4, p. 180: "I strictly command all the brothers not to have suspicious contacts or conversations with women. They are not to enter monasteries of nuns unless they have been granted special license by the Apostolic See. They are not to become godfathers of men or women, so that scandal may not arise among the brothers or about them on account of this." ["Praecipio firmiter fratribus universis, ne habeant suspecta consortia vel consilia mulierum, et ne igrediantur monasteria monacharum praeter illos, quibus a sede apostolica concessa est licentia specialis; nec fiant compatres virorum vel mulierum nec hac occasione inter fratres vel de fratribus scandalum oriatur."]

32. *First Life:* "Vita prima sancti Francisci," in *FF,* 273–424.

33. "Vita prima," Prologus, 1.1, p. 275.

34. "Vita prima," 7, p. 283.

35. "Vita prima," 51.4, p. 325.

36. In Celano's *Second Life,* composed almost twenty years later, he will conflate and transform these images.

37. "Vita prima," 22.4, p. 297.

38. "Vita Prima," 24.3, pp. 298–99; see also 24.6, p. 299; 37.3–4, pp. 311–12.

39. "Vita prima," 110.4, p. 388: "pater et dux." See also 35.4, p. 309.

40. "Vita Prima," 45.3, p. 319: "fraterno consilio seu paterno imperio."

41. "Vita Prima," 43.2–6, pp. 317–18.

42. "Vita prima," 37.3, pp. 311–12; see also 26.1, p. 300; 30.7–8, p. 304; 41.6, p. 316; 45.6, p. 320; 58.1–11, pp. 332–34; 80.1, p. 355; 118.1–2, p. 397.

43. "Vita prima," 30.5, p. 304.

44. "Vita prima," 76.7–8, pp. 351–52; v. 8.: "durissime increpavit."

45. "Vita prima," 36.1–3, pp. 310–11; vv. 2–3: "Erat in omnibus fiducialius agens ex auctoritate apostolica sibi concessa, nullis utens adulationibus, nullis seductoriis blandimentis. Nesciebat aliquorum culpas palpare sed pungere, nec vitam fovere peccantium sed aspera increpatione percutere, quoniam sibi primo suaserat opere quod verbis aliis suadebat; et non timens reprehensorem, veritatem fidentissime loquebatur, ita ut etiam litteratissimi viri, gloria et dignitate pollentes, eius mirarentur sermones et timore utili eius praesentia terrerentur."

46. "Vita prima," 4–5, pp. 280–81.

47. "Vita prima," 103.1, p. 380; and see 103.2–3, p. 380.

48. "Vita prima," 37.6, p. 312. This is a possible reference to clergy, religious, and laity, or to Francis's followers the Lesser Brothers, the Poor Ladies, and lay penitents.

49. "Vita prima," 72.1–2, p. 347: "Manu ad manum cum diabolo confligebat"; "fortissimus miles" (alternatively "the bravest soldier"). For other examples of military imagery, see 9.1, p. 284; 11.1, p. 287; 39.3, p. 313.

50. "Vita prima," 128, pp. 407–8; 131, 132, 133, 134 (two examples), 135, pp. 408–11; 145, p. 418 (an episode involving a friar, that is, a "son" of Francis); 149.1–3, pp. 421–22; 150.4–5, pp. 422–23. For the thirty-four other miracle episodes not involving demons, see 63.4–13, pp. 338–39; 64 (generic references to many cures), 65, 66, 67 (two examples), pp. 339–42; 127.2–4 , p. 407; 129, 130, p. 408; 136 (six examples), p. 412; 139, 140 (four examples), 141 (five examples), 142 (two examples), 143, 144, pp. 414–18; 146 (two examples), 147, pp. 419–21; 149.4–6, p. 422; 150.1–3, p. 422.

51. "Vita prima," 68 (where "perhaps" a demon is the cause of a friar's illness), 69, 70, pp. 343–46; 137, pp. 412–13; 138.3, p. 413 (a generic reference to cures of many people tortured by demons). For the one cure in which Francis drove out a demon and is not referred to as "father," see 138.1–2, p. 413, although this cure immediately precedes one of the five instances listed above in which he is addressed as "father."

52. "Vita prima," 69, 70, pp. 343–46. Francis is still living at the time of these cures. The episodes lacking explicit combat language include just one cure during his life, 68, p. 343, with the remaining three taking place after his death, 137, 138, 139, pp. 412–14.

53. "Vita prima," 22.6, p. 297; 72.1–2, pp. 347–48.

54. "Vita prima," 116.4 and 6, pp. 395–96. Clare calls both herself and the Poor Ladies Francis's "little plant" ("plantuncula"; "plantulam"); "Testament," in *Escritos de Santa Clara y documentos complementarios,* ed. Ignacio Omaechevarría, 2d ed. (Madrid: Biblioteca de Autores Cristianos, 1982), 343, 345; see also her "Rule," 1.3, p. 268, and "Blessing," p. 452. For readers wishing to consult English translations of texts by and about Clare cited in this essay, see *Clare of Assisi: Early Documents,* ed. and trans., Regis J. Armstrong (Saint Bonaventure, New York: Franciscan Institute Publications, 1993)

55. "Vita prima," 56.1–2, p. 330: "terram deambulat, eamque verbi vomere scindens, seminat semen vitae, fructum proferens benedictum. Statim namque quamplures boni et idonei viri, clerici et laici, fugientes mundum et diabolum viriliter elidentes."

56. "Vita prima," 62.1–3, p. 337.

57. "Vita prima," 97.3–4, p. 373. See 65.2, p. 340, for another reference to Francis scattering the seed of life: "spargeret semen vitae."

58. "Vita prima," 88.3, p. 364: " . . . ordinem fratrum Minorum ipse primo plantavit."

59. "Vita prima," 21.3, p. 296: " . . . quia devotione fervebat erga totius bonitatis Matrem."

60. "Vita prima," 106.2–7, p. 383; v. 5: "Hic cum pauci essemus nos augmentavit Altissimus."

61. "Vita prima," 76.3, p. 351.

62. "Vita prima," 36.1, p. 310.

63. "Vita prima," 23.2, p. 298: "Erat verbum eius velut ignis ardens, penetrans intima cordis, et omnium mentes admiratione replebat."

64. "Epistola ad fideles (Recensio prior)," 1.8–10, pp. 73–74; and see "Recensio posterior," 51–53, p. 83.

65. "Vita prima," 6.11, p. 282: "Ardebat intus igne divino et conceptum ardorem mentis celare de foris non valebat."

66. "Vita prima," 98.1, p. 374: "illud pretiosissimum vasculum in quo caelestis thesaurus erat absconditus"; and see 43.4, pp. 317–18.

67. "S. Francisci parabola in sermonibus Odonis de Ceritonia," *Archivum Franciscanum Historicum* 22 (1929): 585: " . . . dixit se esse mulierem quam Dominus verbo suo impregnavit, qui filios spirituales genuit." On Odo, see A. C. Friend, "Master Odo of Cheriton," *Speculum* 23 (1948): 641–58.

68. "Vita prima," 60.1–5, pp. 335–36: " . . . lepusculus unus captus laqueo, a fratre quodam vivus apportatus est ei. Quem videns vir beatissimus, pietate commotus ait: 'Frater lepuscule, veni ad me. Quare sic te decipi permisisti?' Statimque a fratre dimissus qui eum

tenebat, ad sanctum confugit et velut in tutissimo loco, nullo cogente, in eius sinu quievit. Cumque aliquantulum quievisset ibidem, pater sanctus eum materno affectu demulcens, dimisit eum, ut liber ad nemus rediret. Qui cum saepe in terra positus, ad sancti sinum recurreret, iussit eum tandem ad silvam, quae propinqua erat, a fratribus deportari. Simile quiddam contigit de quodam cuniculo, quod animal valde indomesticum est, cum esset in insula laci Perusii."

69. "Vita prima," 77.2–8, pp. 352–53; 86.4, p. 361; 87.4–6, pp. 362–63.

70. "Vita prima," 79.1–10, pp. 354–55; vv. 2–3: "Cumque agnos balantes beatus Franciscus audisset, commota sunt viscera eius, et appropinquans tetigit eos, quasi mater super plorantem filium, affectum compassionis ostendens. Et ait ad virum: 'Quare fratres meos agnos sic ligatos et suspensos excrucias?' "

71. "Vita prima," 12.2–4, pp. 287–88: " . . . continuo surgit, non ad liberandum eum, sed potius ad perdendum; nullaque moderatione servata, tamquam lupus ad ovem advolat et torvo ac truci vultu illum respiciens, iniecta manu, inverecunde ac inhoneste satis ad propriam domum pertraxit eum. Sicque omni miseratione subtracta, per plures dies eum in tenebroso loco reclusit, et putans animum eius flectere ad sui consensum, primo verbis deinde verberibus et vinculis agit."

72. "Vita prima," 13.1–2, pp. 288–89; v. 2: " . . . commota sunt materna viscera super eum, et confractis vinculis, liberum eum abire permisit."

73. "Vita prima," 37.5–6, p. 312; v. 6: " . . . in utroque sexu Christi renovatur Ecclesia. . . ."

74. "Vita prima," 36.4–5, p. 311; see also 23.6–8, p. 298; 62.4–5, pp. 337–38; 85.1–7, pp. 360–61; 124.8, p. 403.

75. "Vita prima," 90.2, p. 366.

76. In addition to his contacts with the Poor Ladies and women he encountered while preaching, Francis healed both women and men. Of the fifty references to Francis's miracle-working powers, thirty-two concern boys and men (64–66, pp. 339–42; 68, p. 343; 128–31, pp. 407–9; 133–50, pp. 409–23), and sixteen concern girls and women (63–64, pp. 338–40; 67, p. 342; 69–70, pp. 343–46; 127, p. 407; 132, p. 409; 134, p. 410; 136, p. 412; 138, p. 413; 141–42, pp. 415–16; 150, p. 422), with two references to unspecified numbers of men and women (64, 4, p. 340; 138, 3, p. 413).

77. "Vita prima," 18–20, pp. 293–95.

78. "Vita prima," 12–14, pp. 287–90. On the evolving portrayals of Francis's father in the early *vitae,* see Richard C. Trexler, *Naked Before the Father: The Renunciation of Francis of Assisi* (New York: P. Lang, 1989).

79. "Vita prima," 24.3, p. 299: " . . . concepit timorem et salutis spiritum parturivit."

80. "Vita prima," 98.7–8, p. 375.

81. "Vita prima," 33.10–13, p. 307: "Nam cum nocte quadam se sopori dedisset, visum est sibi per quamdam viam ambulare, iuxta quam arbor magnae proceritatis stabat. Arbor illa pulchra et fortis, grossa et alta nimis. Factum est autem dum appropinquaret ad eam, et sub ea stans eius pulchritudinem et altitudinem miraretur, subito ipse sanctus ad tantam devenit altitudinem, ut cacumen arboris tangeret, eamque manu capiens facillime inclinaret ad terras. Et revera sic actum est, cum dominus Innocentius, arbor in mundo excelsior et sublimior, eius petitioni et voluntati se tam benignissime inclinavit."

82. "Vita prima," 73.7, p. 349: " . . . erat pater super eius familiam constitutus."

83. "Vita prima," 74.4–7, p. 349.

84. "Vita prima," 99.8, p. 376.

85. "Vita prima," 99.6, p. 376.

86. "Vita prima," 74.1, p. 349: "Adhaeserat ei namque sanctus Franciscus, tamquam filius patri et unicus matri suae, securus in sinu clementiae suae dormiens et quiescens."

87. "Vita prima," 121.4, p. 401: "Gaudet et exsultat, tripudiat et laetatur, cum temporibus suis novis mysteriis sed antiquis mirabilibus Ecclesiam Dei videat innovari, et hoc in filio suo, quem sacro portavit in utero, fovit in gremio, lactavit verbo et educavit cibo salutis." When Gregory reached Assisi to visit the saint's tomb, he struck his breast, wept, and bowed his head with abundant or, more literally, "a very fertile" (*uberiore*) devotion; "Vita prima," 123.6, p. 402.

88. "Vita prima," 75.1–2, p. 350.

89. "Vita prima," 74.2, p. 349.

90. "Vita prima," 99.4–5, p. 376: "Conformabat se dominus ille moribus fratrum, et in desiderio sanctitatis cum simplicibus erat simplex, cum humilibus erat humilis, cum pauperibus erat pauper. Erat frater inter fratres, inter minores minimus."

91. "Vita prima," 100.2b–9, esp. 8–9, pp. 377–78.

92. 1 Sam 18:1; 2 Sam 1:26. Celano elaborates the parallel when he says that Hugolino extended his protection over Francis, echoing Jonathan's protection of David when he gave the latter his robe, armor, sword, etc.; 1 Sam 18:1–4. Francis is called "another David" elsewhere in the *vita*: 5.9, p. 281.

93. The "Vita prima" might be the first written account of the stigmata, since the letter purportedly written by Brother Elias upon Francis's death announcing the stigmata has no manuscript history. It first appeared in 1620 and shows signs of having been composed well after Celano's *First Life;* Felice Accrocca, "Un apocrifo la 'Lettera enciclica di frate Elia sul transito di S. Francesco'?" *Collectanea Franciscana* 65 (1995): 473–509, English trans. in *Greyfriars Review* 13 (1999). On Elias, see Dieter Berg, "Elias von Cortona: Studien zu Leben und Werk des zweiten Generalministers im Franziskanerorden," *Wissenschaft und Weisheit* 41 (1978): 102–26; Giulia Barone, "Frate Elia," *Bullettino dell'Istituto Storico Italiano per il Medioevo e Archivio Muratoriano* 85 (1974–75): 89–144, Eng. trans. in *Greyfriars Review* 13 (1999). On Francis's stigmata, see André Vauchez, "Les stigmates de saint François et leurs détracteurs dans les derniers siècles du moyen âge," *Mélanges d'archéologie et d'histoire* 80 (1968): 595–625; Ottaviano Schmucki, *The Stigmata of St. Francis of Assisi: A Critical Investigation in the Light of Thirteenth-Century Sources,* trans. Canisius F. Connors (St. Bonaventure, N.Y.: Franciscan Institute, 1991); Chiara Frugoni, *Francesco e l'invenzione delle stimmate: Una storia per parole e immagini fino a Bonaventura e Giotto* (Turin: G. Einaudi, 1993).

94. "Vita prima," 94.1–7, pp. 369–70; v. 7: " . . . coeperunt in manibus eius et pedibus apparere signa clavorum, quemadmodum paulo ante virum supra se viderat crucifixum."

95. "Vita prima," 95.1–4, pp. 370–71: "Manus et pedes eius in ipso medio clavis confixae videbantur, clavorum capitibus in interiore parte manuum et superiore pedum apparentibus, et eorum acuminibus exsistentibus ex adverso. Erant enim signa illa rotunda interius in manibus, exterius autem oblonga, et caruncula quaedam apparebat quasi summitas clavorum retorta et repercussa, quae carnem reliquam excedebat. Sic et in

pedibus impressa erant signa clavorum et a carne reliqua elevata. Dextrum quoque latus quasi lancea transfixum, cicatrice obducta, erat, quod saepe sanguinem emittebat, ita ut tunica eius cum femoralibus multoties respergeretur sanguine sacro."

96. For the Latin, see n. 94.

97. "Vita prima," 90.7, p. 366.

98. Note also that Celano uses the term "lover" in a passage on the stigmata in the "Vita secunda"; 135.2, p. 564: "Primo in tempore, quo verus Christi amor in eamdem imaginem transformarat amantem" ("From the very first, when true love for Christ transformed the lover into the very image of Christ").

99. "Vita prima," 95.10, p. 372: "margaritis tamquam pretiosissimis gemmis." On hiding the stigmata, see 95.5–96.2, pp. 371–72.

100. "Vita prima," 95.5–8, p. 371.

101. "Vita prima," 113.1, p. 391: ". . . cernere mirabile erat in medio manuum et pedum ipsius non clavorum quidem puncturas sed ipsos clavos ex eius carne compositos, ferri retenta nigredine, ac dextrum latus sanguine rubricatum."

102. "Vita prima," 113.3–4, p. 391. Celano again emphasizes the blood of Christ, and by implication that of Francis, at 114.2, p. 392. For the association between the wound in Christ's side and a vagina or breast in the late Middle Ages, see Flora Lewis, "The Wound in Christ's Side and the Instruments of the Passion: Gendered Experience and Response," in *Women and the Book: Assessing the Visual Image*, ed. Lesley Smith and Jane H. M. Taylor (Toronto: University of Toronto Press, 1997), figs. 89–90, and pp. 215–16.

103. "Vita prima," 114.1–2, p. 392; v. 2: "sacramentum."

104. On the process, see Zeffirino Lazzeri, "Il processo di canonizzazione di S. Chiara d'Assisi," *Archivum Franciscanum Historicum* 13 (1920): 403–38 (on the manuscript, see 408–12, 437–38); Marco Bartoli, "Il processo di canonizzazione come fonte per la ricostruzione del profilo storico di Chiara d'Assisi," in *Dialoghi con Chiara di Assisi,* ed. Luigi Giacometti (Assisi: Edizioni Porziuncola, 1995).

105. Recorded testimony of Sister Filippa, in "Il processo di canonizzazione di Santa Chiara d'Assisi," 3.29, in *FF,* p. 2473: "Referiva anco epsa madonna Chiara, che una volta in visione li pareva che epsa portava ad sancto Francesco uno vaso de acqua calda, con uno sciucchatoio da sciucchare le mane, et salliva per una scala alta, ma andava cusì legieramente, quasi come andasse per piana terra. Et essendo pervenuta ad sancto Francesco, epso sancto trasse del suo seno una mammilla et disse ad essa vergine Chiara: 'Viene, receve et sugge': Et avendo lei succhato, epso sancto la admoniva che suggesse un'altra volta; et epsa suggendo, quello che de lì suggeva, era tanto dolce et delectevole, che per nesuno modo lo poteria explicare. Et havendo succhato, quella rotondità overo boccha de la poppa dondo escie lo lacte remase intra li labri de epsa beata Chiara; et pigliando epsa con le mane quello che li era remaso nella boccha, li pareva che fusse oro così chiaro et lucido, che ce se vedeva tucta, come quasi in uno specchio." When Clare might have had this vision is unknown; Marco Bartoli, "Analisi storica e interpretazione psicoanalitica di una visione di sancta Chiara d'Assisi," *Archivum Franciscanum Historicum* 73 (1980): 449–72, Eng. trans. in *Greyfriars Review* 6 (1992), conjectures that the vision occurred after Francis's death in 1226 and probably toward the end of Clare's life in 1253; see this essay for another interpretation of Clare's vision, more speculative than mine. For readers wishing to consult

English translations of texts by and about Clare cited in this essay, see *Clare of Assisi: Early Documents,* cited in n. 54.

106. "Il processo," in *FF:* Sister Amata, 4.16, p. 2478; Sister Cecilia, 6.13, pp. 2481–82; Sister Balvina, daughter of Messer Martino of Coccorano, 7.10, p. 2484.

107. See Caroline Walker Bynum, *Holy Feast and Holy Fast: The Religious Significance of Food to Medieval Women* (Berkeley: University of California Press, 1987) 94, 269–73, 278, on the relationship between blood and milk, Christ's crucified body as female, and the association of his wounds with women's breasts; for specific examples of medieval men and women drinking from Christ's wound-breast, see 105, 116, 118, 132–33, 142, 166, 172–73, 247, 282, 317 n. 56, 355 n. 103, 375 n. 122; and for iconography on this theme, see figs. 12, 25–29; on women's physicality, see 260–69, and also Bynum, " ' . . . And Woman His Humanity': Female Imagery in the Religious Writing of the Later Middle Ages," in *Fragmentation and Redemption: Essays on Gender and the Human Body in Medieval Religion* (New York: Zone Books, 1991).

108. "Vita secunda," 204.4–6, p. 621.

109. On Francis's infrequent visits, see "Vita secunda," 204, p. 621; 205, p. 621; see also 206, p. 622; but cf. 106.5–6, p. 540. In contrast, in the "Vita prima," Celano had cited the lament of the Poor Ladies at Francis's death that they would be deprived of his *usual* visits; see 117.2, p. 396. On Francis's cautions, see "Vita secunda," 112–14, pp. 545–48; and also 115–16, pp. 548–50.

110. In a passage that must allude to Clare and to another woman whom Francis admired, Jacopa de Settesoli, Celano leaves both women anonymous; "Vita secunda," 112.10–11, p. 546.

111. Internal disagreements regarding the practice of poverty, ecclesiastical privileges, and studies beleaguered the brothers and constitute a *leitmotif* running throughout the work and affect the presentation of Francis; see, for example, "Vita secunda," 53, p. 493; 64, pp. 501–3; 69–70, pp. 507–9; 80–81, pp. 517–18; 156–57, pp. 582–83; 188, pp. 607–8; 195, pp. 613–14; 221, 8–10, p. 638.

112. Bynum, *Holy Feast, Holy Fast,* 101.

113. "Carta IV," in *Escritos,* 395–98.

114. "Testamento," 3, in *Escritos,* 341–42. On this multivalent image, see also Regis J. Armstrong, "Clare of Assisi: The Mirror Mystic," *The Cord* 35 (1985): 195–202.

Jeffrey A. Bowman is associate professor of history and the John B. McCoy–Bank One Distinguished Teaching Professor at Kenyon College. He is the author of *Shifting Landmarks: Property, Proof, and Dispute in Catalonia around the Year 1000.*

Carolyn Dinshaw is professor of English at New York University, where she founded and directed the Center for the Study of Gender and Sexuality from 1999 to 2005. She is the author of *Getting Medieval: Sexualities and Communities, Pre- and Post-Modern* and *Chaucer's Sexual Poetics.* She is cofounder and co-editor (1993–2005) of *GLQ: A Journal for Lesbian and Gay Studies.*

Ralph Hexter, former executive dean of Letters and Science and professor of classics and comparative literature at the University of California, Berkeley, is now president of Hampshire College. He is the author of *Ovid and Medieval Schooling: Medieval School Commentaries on Ovid's Ars Amatoria, Epistulae ex Ponto and Epistulae Heroidae.*

Mark D. Jordan is the Asa Griggs Candler Professor of Religion at Emory University. He is the author of *The Invention of Sodomy in Christian Theology, The Silence of Sodom: Homosexuality in Modern Catholicism, The Ethics of Sex,* and *Blessing Same-Sex Unions: The Perils of Queer Romance and the Confusions of Christian Marriage.*

Penelope D. Johnson is professor emerita of history at New York University. She is the author of *Equal in Monastic Profession: Religious*

Women in Medieval France and *Prayer, Patronage, and Power: The Abbey of La Trinité, Vendôme, 1032–1187.*

Ruth Mazo Karras is professor of history at the University of Minnesota, Twin Cities. She is the author of *Common Women: Prostitution in Medieval England, From Boys to Men: Formations of Masculinity in Late Medieval Europe,* and *Sexuality in Medieval Europe: Doing Unto Others.* She is also general editor of the Middle Ages series at the University of Pennsylvania Press.

Mathew Kuefler is associate professor of history at San Diego State University. He is editor of the Journal of the History of Sexuality and the author of *The Manly Eunuch: Masculinity, Gender Ambiguity, and Christian Ideology in Late Antiquity,* and the forthcoming *The History of Sexuality Sourcebook.*

Dale B. Martin is the Woolsey Professor of Religious Studies at Yale University. He is the author of *The Corinthian Body* and *Inventing Superstition: From the Hippocratics to the Christians* and the editor (with Patricia Cox Miller) of *The Cultural Turn in Late Ancient Studies: Gender, Asceticism, and Historiography.*

Mark Masterson is lecturer of Classics at Victoria University of Wellington, New Zealand. He has published on Vitruvius and Statius and is at present completing a manuscript on masculinity in the fourth-century CE Roman Empire.

E. Ann Matter is professor of religious studies at the University of Pennsylvania. She is the author of *The Voice of My Beloved: The Song of Songs in Western Medieval Christianity* and *Creative Women in Medieval and Early Modern Italy: A Religious and Artistic Renaissance,* edited with John Coakley.

Catherine M. Mooney is associate professor of church history at the Weston Jesuit School of Theology in Cambridge, Massachusetts. She is the author of *Philippine Duchesne: A Woman with the Poor* and editor of *Gendered Voices: Medieval Saints and Their Interpreters.*

Jacqueline Murray is dean of arts and professor of history at the University of Guelph, and adjunct professor at the Center for Medieval Studies at the University of Toronto. She is the author of *Love, Marriage, and the Family in the Middle Ages, Conflicted Identities and Multiple Masculinities: Men in the Medieval West,* and the editor (with Konrad Eisenbichler) of *Desire and Discipline: Sex and Sexuality in the Premodern West*.

Bruce O'Brien is professor of history at Mary Washington College. He is the author of *God's Peace and King's Peace: The Laws of Edward the Confessor*.

Amy Richlin is professor of classics at the University of California at Los Angeles. She is the author of *The Garden of Priapus: Sexuality and Aggression in Roman Humor* and editor (with Nancy Sorkin Rabinowitz) of *Feminist Theory and the Classics*.

Bernard Schlager is consultant for national programming at the Center for Lesbian and Gay Studies in Religion and Ministry at Pacific School of Religion where he also serves as adjunct faculty in cultural and historical studies of religion. He is co-editing the forthcoming *Encyclopedia of Homosexuality, Religion, and American Culture*.